The Korean Financial Crisis of 1997

The Korean Financial Crisis of 1997

ONSET, TURNAROUND, AND THEREAFTER

Kyu-Sung LEE

1818 H Street NW
Washington DC 20433
Telephone: 202-473-1000
Internet: www.worldbank.org

1 2 3 4 14 13 12 11

ISBN: 978-0-8213-8239-4
eISBN: 978-0-8213-8550-0
DOI: 10.1596/978-0-8213-8239-4

Library of Congress Cataloging-in-Publication Data

Yi, Kyu-song, 1939–
The Korean financial crisis of 1997 : onset, turnaround, and thereafter / Kyu-Sung Lee.
p. cm.
Includes bibliographical references and index.
ISBN 978-0-8213-8239-4 — ISBN 978-0-8213-8550-0 (electronic)
1. Financial crises—Korea (South)—History 20th century. 2. Korea (South)—Economic policy—1988– 3. Korea (South) Economic conditions—1988– I. Title.
HB3817.5.Y5 2011
330.95195'044—dc22

2010047700

Cover design: Drew Fasick.

This publication was made possible by the generous support of Citibank Korea Inc. and KORAMCO REITs Management and Trust Company Ltd.

Contents

Preface

It is a distinct pleasure for me to publish this English version of *The Korean Financial Crisis of 1997: Onset, Turnaround, and Thereafter*, which I originally authored in Korean in 2006. This book is an extensive account of the experience of the Republic of Korea during and immediately after the 1997 financial crisis. The book documents the unfolding crisis from 1996, shortly before the crisis erupted, until 1999, when the economy began to rebound from the nadir of the crisis and economic growth turned positive.

My primary motivation for writing this book has been to preserve the facts and the circumstances surrounding a financial crisis that proved to be the most significant development in Korea's modern economic history. The toll the crisis took on Korea has been so severe that many Koreans still regard it as the most devastating debacle to befall Korea since the Korean War (1950–53) more than a half century ago. As the country staggered on the verge of insolvency, the economy went into a free fall, businesses collapsed en masse, countless jobs were lost, and the country as a whole suffered from enormous pain and hardship. For many Koreans who had taken so much pride during the decades of rapid economic growth, the crisis prompted a deep sense of failure, anger, and disgust.

On the upside, the crisis provided a unique opportunity for the extensive restructuring of corporate and financial companies, particularly in terms of financial soundness, corporate governance, and core business structure. It provided a basis for fundamental reforms to revamp and reorient the nation's economy away from heavy-handed government regulations, protectionism, and nepotism and toward genuine democracy, the rule of law, and conformity with global standards. No less important was the vision the government offered in retying the social safety net and drafting a blueprint for Korea's transition to a knowledge-based economy.

In writing this book, I have had the advantage of serving as the Minister of Finance and Economy from March 1998 to May 1999, which enabled me to compile a detailed record of events and analyses during the crisis years. I feel a sense of personal responsibility to document what transpired throughout my tenure at the Ministry of Finance and Economy. At that time, the Korean economy was buffeted by one shock after another. It was a difficult period, when an average of more than 100 companies went bankrupt each day and the number of laid-off workers increased from 500,000 to more than 1.2 million in only a few months. The rapid deterioration of the situation was alarming. So, Korea was obliged to manage the economy—allow me to use early aviation parlance—according to visual flight rules rather than relying on the instrument panel.

This book chronicles how Korea dealt with and overcame the crisis over time. The book is organized into 11 chapters. Chapter 1 outlines the troubling financial market conditions at home and abroad before the crisis. Chapter 2 then delves into the origin of the crisis and offers analyses on the shortcomings of the Korean economy and the instability of the international financial system. In chapter 3, policy measures the government executed in the wake of the onset of the crisis are described and analyzed.

Chapter 4 probes the steps taken to reduce the risk of sovereign insolvency in the face of the cool market reaction to the initial package of crisis response measures announced by the International Monetary Fund in December 1997. Chapter 5 describes the background within which the government established the institutional framework necessary for corporate, financial, and labor market restructuring between December 1997 and April 1998. The government efforts to secure additional foreign currency liquidity through the markets and to devise initiatives to counter the massive unemployment are discussed in detail.

In chapter 6, the situation during May and June 1998 is explored with a focus on the closure of nonviable corporate and financial companies and the efforts to drive down interest rates and revive credit flows. This is followed, in chapter 7, by an analysis of the first phase of financial sector restructuring, which started in the third quarter of 1998, and the measures adopted to shore up potential growth and cope with the pressing problem of unemployment.

Chapters 8 and 9 deal separately with the restructuring of the top five *chaebols* (the large family-controlled and family-run groups that dominate business in Korea), the economic stimulus packages applied during the fourth quarter of 1998, the efforts to restore financial market stability and economic growth, and the initial phase of foreign exchange liberalization measures, which were implemented during the first half of 1999. Chapter 10 then discusses the situation during the second half of 1999, with a particular focus on the collapse of the Daewoo business group, including the steps taken to contain the resulting fallout, as well as measures aimed at expanding the economic recovery. The chapter also examines the strategy the government developed to lay the groundwork for a transition to a knowledge-based economy, the economic hardship the crisis inflicted on low- and middle-income households, and the government's social welfare initiatives.

Chapter 11, the final chapter, offers a diagnosis of the Korean economy, along with an analysis of the policy implications and the responses for the future. I contend in this chapter that, even after the enormous sacrifices of the people and the positive structural reforms, not all the reform efforts have succeeded and that key tasks necessary for a genuine transformation of the economy remain unaccomplished. Thus, for example, labor relations continue to be plagued by conflicts and confrontations despite the earnest efforts to foster a cooperative labor and management culture. Likewise, accounting irregularities persist despite the adoption of the International Accounting Standards and numerous reform drives to ensure business management transparency. In full recognition of these issues, I suggest policy responses so that the Korean economy can leap to a higher level.

This book is necessarily voluminous because it provides a highly detailed account of Korea's financial crisis and recovery. So, permit me to offer a quick summary of the remedies I prescribe through this book to prevent future financial crises and keep the economy firmly on track to steady growth.

First, key economic variables such as interest rates and foreign exchange rates should not be distorted. Of course, these variables zigzag from the course directed by economic fundamentals from time to time, particularly in the short run, in all markets. It is important, however, that they eventually return to a natural, desirable range. If this is to occur, markets must be given room to maneuver, and a little ebb and flow must be allowed.

Second, the economy must adapt to the evolving economic environment. Amid ongoing market globalization, production is becoming increasingly knowledge-intensive, and environmental concerns are leading to a worldwide reexamination of the optimal pace of sustainable economic growth. This may well represent an irreversible historic trend, but it is also, nonetheless, an opportunity that may be exploited. We must be mindful of this possibility and remain proactive, not reactive.

Third, the social safety net must be reinforced and augmented. A transition to a higher level cannot take place in a context of the growing instability of a society. Taking the leap to a higher level and strengthening the social safety net are interdependent. They are two sides of one coin.

Fourth, the intellectual capacity and the sphere of creative activity must be drastically expanded in Korea. This goal takes on added importance in light of the dual dilemma Korea faces because of the country's low birthrate and aging population. At a time when the knowledge competitiveness of Korea is lagging behind that of other countries, the content, structure, and quality of Korea's educational system must improve to foster more creativity and greater adaptability in society. The establishment of a lifelong learning system for the benefit of all citizens is a crucial priority.

Fifth, social governance must be sound. Today, Korea is a diverse, multifaceted society. Diversity can be a source of fresh ideas and strength, but also a source of conflict and discord. If Korea is to renew itself, it must build a good system of governance that promotes mutual cooperation and healthy competition rather than confrontation and ill will.

All this is easier said than done. As Korea faces up to the challenges ahead, it must not lose sight of the direction it wishes to take. The country's leaders must show wisdom and perseverance in this effort. At the same time, the people must free themselves from the unrealistic yet widely accepted myths that permeate society. They must be able to perceive change in the environment and favor a forward-looking vision for a promising future.

I am grateful to Citibank Korea Inc. and KORAMCO REITs Management and Trust Company Ltd. for their gracious financial support for the translation of the original Korean text into English. I wish to express my appreciation also to the Korea Development Institute and the World Bank for their thoughtfulness in making this publication available.

Finally, I have benefited greatly from the acuteness and precision of Robert Zimmerman, who edited my English text, and from Janice Tuten and Patricia Katayama, who oversaw this publication at the World Bank's Office of the Publisher.

Kyu-Sung LEE
Seoul
December 2010

About the Author

Kyu-Sung LEE served as Korea's Minister of Finance from December 1988 to March 1990, and as Minister of Finance and Economy from March 1998 to May 1999, when he was appointed to tackle and overcome the foreign exchange crisis by the then President Kim Dae-Jung. At present, he is the chairman of KORAMCO REITs Management and Trust Company Ltd. and a visiting professor at the Graduate School of Management at Korea Advanced Institute of Science and Technology (KAIST). He has a bachelor's degree in economics from Seoul National University and received an honorary doctorate in economics from Chungnam National University in 1990.

Abbreviations

ADB	Asian Development Bank
AMF	Asian Monetary Fund
BIS	Bank for International Settlements
BOK	Bank of Korea
CCL	contingent credit line
CP	commercial paper
EPCC	Economic Policy Coordination Committee
EU	European Union
FDI	foreign direct investment
FKI	Federation of Korean Industries
FSC	Financial Supervisory Commission
FSF	Financial Stability Forum
FSS	Financial Supervisory Service
G-3	Group of Three: European Union, Japan, United States
G-7	Group of Seven: Canada, France, Germany, Italy, Japan, United Kingdom, United States
G-22	Group of Seven, plus Argentina; Australia; Brazil; China; Hong Kong SAR, China; India; Indonesia; Republic of Korea; Malaysia; Mexico; Poland; Russian Federation; Singapore; South Africa; Thailand
G-33	Group of 22, plus Belgium, Chile, Côte d'Ivoire, Arab Republic of Egypt, Morocco, the Netherlands, Saudi Arabia, Spain, Sweden, Switzerland, Turkey
GDP	gross domestic product
ICT	information and communication technology
IMD	International Institute for Management Development
IMF	International Monetary Fund
IT	information technology
KAMCO	Korea Asset Management Corporation
KCTU	Korean Confederation of Trade Unions
KDB	Korea Development Bank
KDI	Korea Development Institute
KDIC	Korea Deposit Insurance Corporation
KEPCO	Korea Electric Power Corporation

KOSDAQ	Korea Securities Dealers Automated Quotations
KOSPI	Korea Composite Stock Price Index
KTC	Korea Tripartite Commission
LIBOR	London Interbank Offered Rate
LOI	Letter of Intent
LTCM	Long-Term Capital Management (a hedge fund)
M&A	mergers and acquisitions
MOFE	Ministry of Finance and Economy
NPA Fund	Non-Performing Asset Management Fund
OBS	Office of Bank Supervision
OECD	Organisation for Economic Co-operation and Development
P&A	purchase of assets and assumption of liabilities
PPM	parts per million
R&D	research and development
SAR	special administrative region (Hong Kong)
SMEs	small and medium enterprises
W	won (Korean currency unit)
WTO	World Trade Organization

Note: All dollar amounts are U.S. dollars (US$) unless otherwise indicated.

1

The Unfolding of the Korean Financial Crisis

1996: A Year of Uncertainty

Causes for Concern

Key economic indicators on the Republic of Korea in 1996 suggested that the economy was on firm ground. The real growth rate in gross domestic product (GDP) had reached 6.8 percent; consumer prices had risen 4.9 percent; and the unemployment rate had peaked at 2 percent. Other than an unusually large jump in the current account deficit, which neared US$23 billion for the year, the economy seemed to be chugging along and looked robust. Nonetheless, by then, there were many alarming signs of problems ahead.

The first major concern was the cyclical phase of the Korean economy. By the second half of 1995, the economy was in the early stages of a cyclical contraction, and most companies had begun to experience falling sales and profits by early 1996. However, the overwhelming reliance of Korean companies on production plant industries made it exceedingly difficult to cut back or otherwise adjust production. As a result, business inventories continued to grow, and many companies had begun struggling to obtain funding for business operations.[1]

Moreover, the prices of semiconductors, steel, and petrochemicals—all of which were Korea's key strategic exports—were falling rapidly because of global oversupply. The semiconductor industry was hit particularly hard because the price of a 16M D-RAM chip had collapsed from US$50 at the end of 1995 to US$9 by the end of 1996. Korea's terms of trade suffered as well. The unit price of Korean exports plummeted 13.4 percent in 1996, while the unit price of imports fell only 1.2 percent, an alarming drop by any measure. It did not help Korean exporters that the Japanese yen weakened against the U.S. dollar, from ¥94.06 in 1995 to ¥108.78 in 1996, giving significant competitive price advantages to Japanese exporters. The worsening terms of trade in Korea had slowed the pace of the growth in gross national income to 4.8 percent, well below the growth rate in gross domestic product, and this triggered a sharp deficit in the trade balance. Overseas travel spending by Koreans and interest expenses on foreign debt put pressure on the current account deficits.

Second, there was a palpable sense of unease both internally and externally about Korea's embrace of economic liberalization. With the conclusion of the Uruguay Round toward the end of 1993, Korea was all but set to open its markets wider than ever before, particularly the long-protected agricultural and financial service sectors. The pace of financial sector liberalization was about to accelerate even more rapidly when Korea joined the Organisation for Economic Co-operation and Development (OECD) in 1996.

For a relatively small economy such as that of Korea, engaging in economic liberalization by joining the OECD may have made sense especially in the efficient allocation of capital. Unfortunately, in Korea's case, the financial sector liberalization and other major economic reform measures were not accompanied by efforts to establish sound financial supervision and prudential regulations, as well as other institutional arrangements capable of facilitating market liberalization in a safe and sound manner. Many therefore suspected that Korea had embraced full membership in the OECD and all the obligations that came with it too hastily and without adequately priming the economy or the people for the wrenching changes that lay ahead. The question was whether Korea was up to the arduous task of opening its economy successfully after it had joined the OECD. The answer was unclear at best.

Third, there was apprehension over the structural weaknesses in the economy. In many crucial areas, the Korean economy had been suffering from unsustainably high costs (high interest rates, high wages, high land prices, and high logistics costs), as well as from low efficiency, as evidenced by falling corporate profits and stagnant international competitiveness. More than other features, the high-cost, low-efficiency characteristics of the economy mirrored the many structural weaknesses within.

Table 1.1 illustrates the high-cost characteristics of the Korean economy. The low efficiency was partly caused by the cyclical contraction phase the economy was experiencing. Nonetheless, the fact that nearly all business enterprises suffered from inefficiency suggests that something other than a mere cyclical factor was at work. As shown in table 1.2, the ratio of ordinary incomes to the sales of manufacturing companies had decreased precipitously, from 3.6 percent in 1995 to 1.0 percent in 1996. Likewise, the capital ratio had dropped from 25.9 to 24.0 percent. Among large companies subject to independent outside auditing, the interest coverage ratio had dropped disturbingly from 1.5 in 1995 to 1.2 in

Table 1.1 Interest Rates, Wages, Land Prices, and Logistics Costs, by Economy

Indicator	*Korea, Rep.*	*United States*	*Japan*	*Taiwan, China*
Real interest rate, end of 1995, %	8.1	3.0	1.2	5.4
Annual growth in wages, 1987–94 average, %	16.2[a]	2.7	3.0	10.3
Land prices in industrial complexes, 1995 average, US$ per square meter	226.8	5.1	195.6	48.4[b]
Ratio of logistics costs to sales, 1994 average, %	14.3	7.7	8.8	—

Source: MOFE 1996.
Note: Numbers are rounded. — = not available.
a. 1987–95.
b. Pontian Industrial Complex, Malaysia.

1996. Amid the signs of growing weakness, Doosan and several other large companies embarked on what was then considered bold business restructuring. But most companies simply adopted a wait-and-see attitude. Inevitably, a heightened sense of unease began to settle in about the possibility that businesses might start to fail in droves.

The Government Response

In early 1996, the government set its sights on maintaining the momentum of economic growth for the next two or three years, while controlling inflation and addressing the underlying structural weaknesses. It began to implement a series of measures aimed at stabilizing interest rates, wages, and land prices, as well as reducing the cost of delivering goods from manufacturers to consumers.

On September 3, 1996, the Ministry of Finance and Economy (MOFE) announced the September 3 Measures, which called for macroeconomic stability, but imposed restraint on the use of excessively contractionary policies that might cool the economy and damage small and medium companies.[2] The government stressed that it would strive to contain inflationary pressures by taking specifically targeted steps and encouraging savings. It pledged to invigorate the languid business climate through deregulation aimed at reducing the cost of doing business and through

Table 1.2 Trends in Key Financial Indicators, Manufacturing, 1985–98
percent

Year	*Capital ratio*	*Ratio of ordinary incomes to sales*	*Growth rate in sales*	*Growth rate in per capita value added*
1985	22.3	2.5	9.8	9.3
1986	22.2	3.6	16.8	13.4
1987	22.7	3.6	22.6	17.7
1988	25.3	4.1	15.8	21.1
1989	28.2	2.5	7.0	19.4
1990	25.9	2.3	18.8	18.7
1991	24.5	1.8	17.4	15.2
1992	23.8	1.5	10.3	12.5
1993	25.3	1.7	9.9	14.0
1994	24.8	2.7	18.2	18.1
1995	25.9	3.6	20.4	19.2
1996	24.0	1.0	10.3	1.1
1997	20.2	–0.3	11.0	4.7
1998	24.8	–1.8	0.7	11.7

Source: Bank of Korea (BOK various years), *Financial Statement Analysis.*
Note: Numbers are rounded to the nearest 10th.

more predictable, less abrupt economic policies. The government emphasized its support for exporters to help turn around the rising current account deficit.[3]

More important, the government proposed a major labor reform bill to the National Assembly, the legislative branch in Korea. The need for a more flexible labor market was both obvious and urgent, but the political parties failed to come to a quick agreement. After much bickering and delay, the reform bill was enacted in a year-end legislative session at the National Assembly amid acrimony and without the vote of the opposition political parties. The one-sided passage of the reform bill soured the political mood and created a volatile backdrop that quickly provoked the labor unions to counter with debilitating strikes the next month, in 1997. With a lame-duck president in his last year in office and unable or unwilling to wield much power, the government stumbled badly in the face of the labor unrest.

In many ways, the foreboding that loomed over the economy in 1996 was a reflection of the long-overlooked malaise—structural and otherwise—that had been brought into sharp relief by the faltering economy. In the face of sweeping market liberalization, the government found its options limited. Worse still, as social and political discord intensified, the government was increasingly impotent and ineffective in carrying out policies designed to patch up the widening holes in the economy. However, in reality, the economy had by then become so convoluted and intractable that it was impossible even to agree on where to begin (MOFE 1996). The economy was unquestionably in for a turbulent ride.

The Hanbo Bankruptcy and the Degradation in External Creditworthiness, January–March 1997

Labor Strikes and the Hanbo Bankruptcy

Early in 1997, the economy was rocked by a series of damaging developments. For nearly the entire month of January, labor unions staged massive strikes that, according to the Ministry of Labor, cost W 2.85 trillion in lost production, which easily surpasses the W 1.8 trillion in strike-related production losses in the whole of 1996 (MOFE 1997a).

On January 23, the Hanbo Group, the 14th largest business group in Korea at the time, was declared bankrupt. Persistent rumors of trouble at the group had been circulating since July 1996. When the Office of Bank Supervision at the Bank of Korea (BOK), the central bank, evaluated the business group in February 1997, the group's assets were estimated at W 5 trillion and its liabilities at W 6.6 trillion. The bankruptcy dealt a severe blow not only to the banks that had been lending to Hanbo, but also to the struggling economy. It came as a shock to foreign investors.

When a warning by a senior presidential aide of the possible failure of a commercial bank was reported by the press, the shock multiplied. Until then, large corporate or bank failures had generally been taken care of by the government, and foreign investors had not suffered any losses because of implicit and explicit government guarantees. Soon after the news of the Hanbo failure hit the market, several Korean bank branches operating in Japan were denied access to credit by Japanese banks. The news prompted the governor of the BOK to pledge publicly that the BOK would guarantee all debt liabilities of Korean bank branches operating overseas.

Outside Korea, doubts began to spread not only about the financial soundness and the general health of Hanbo creditors and the corporate companies with which Hanbo dealt, but also about the health of Korean banks and corporate companies in general. In early February, many widely circulated foreign news media, including the *New York Times* and the *International Herald Tribune*, started to raise the possibility of a financial crisis in Korea. On February 20, Moody's announced that the long-term credit ratings of Chohung Bank, Korea Exchange Bank, and

Korea First Bank—three commercial lenders with large credit exposures in Hanbo—would be downgraded by one notch. The destabilizing effect of the troubles at Hanbo reverberated throughout the financial system, and credit began to dry up for many small and medium companies as lenders became increasingly nervous about corporate credit risks. The bankruptcy of Sammi Group, another well-known large business group, on March 19 added to the worries of financial companies at home and abroad.

On January 24, one day after the Hanbo bankruptcy, the government announced measures to deal with the bankruptcy and its aftershocks. The measures consisted mainly of credit support for Hanbo suppliers so as to prevent a cascade of bankruptcies, as well as steps to deal with Hanbo's major construction projects that were under way in which many conflicting business interests were involved. On February 10, the government followed up with specific support measures for small and medium companies. Key among these were a provision of W 700 billion for the purchase of commercial paper and bills issued by small and medium companies and an outlay of W 1.4 trillion to stabilize businesses and prevent bankruptcy. The government pledged to appropriate funds for various credit guarantees and to provide support for companies in trouble. These steps partially succeeded in soothing the fears of financial companies, and the general credit situation had improved by March.

Developments in Financial Markets

The yield on benchmark three-year corporate bonds, which averaged 11.87 percent in 1996, climbed to 12.15 percent in January and to 12.17 percent in February the following year amid fears of impending corporate failures and liquidity shortages. Then, in March, the yield jumped sharply to 12.69 percent. The overnight call rate for financial companies averaged 11.36 and 11.46 percent, respectively, for the first two months of 1997 (compared with 12.35 percent for 1996), and then reached 12.91 percent in March. The ratio of dishonored bills picked up, from 0.14 percent in 1996 to 0.23 percent in the first quarter of 1997.

The Korea composite stock price index (KOSPI), the benchmark stock index, ended 1996 at 690.6 and started 1997 without any clear direction or momentum. It fell to 669.6 in January, rose to 698.1 in February, fell to 656.7 in March, and bounced back to 694.3 in April. Amid much volatility in the market, stock sell-offs by foreign investors were apparent; the net sell-off totaled W 87.1 billion in February, W 215.4 billion in March, and W 134.1 billion in April.

As a result of the spiraling current account deficit and the sluggish inflow of foreign capital, the supply-demand situation in the foreign exchange market was deteriorating, and foreign exchange reserves started to drain away. After topping US$23.0 billion in 1996, the current account posted another deficit of US$7.4 billion in the first quarter of 1997.

Foreign capital inflows totaled US$5.3 billion in the first quarter of 1996, but, a year later, topped US$4.0 billion in the first three months of 1997. After the Hanbo default, many Korean commercial banks and merchant banks started having difficulty securing fresh credit, as well as rollovers on existing short-term loans from foreign lenders (table 1.3).

March is the month during which most Japanese banks call back their loans for the close of the accounting year. For Korean banks, many of which rely heavily on Japanese banks for loans and other credit, March is thus a time to scramble. Ominously, Japanese banks called back US$4.7 billion in loans from 12 Korean banks during the first three months of 1997. Amid the nervousness and the tightening credit from outside, some banks began to face a severe shortage in foreign currency credits and were obliged to resort to US$1 billion in emergency loans from the BOK in February. During the same month, the BOK was forced to extend US$3.2 billion in the form of deposits to overseas Korean bank branches that faced funding difficulties. These deposits reached US$1 billion in March, bringing the total to US$8.0 billion by the end of the month, up from the US$3.8 billion in January.

Because of the appreciating U.S. dollar and the unfavorable foreign exchange supply and demand conditions, the Korean won tumbled. This fueled the expectation in the market that it would fall still more. Leads and lags in foreign exchange transactions—whereby the demand for dollars accelerates, while the dollar supply slows in anticipation of an increase in exchange rates—were taking hold. One example was the increase in

Table 1.3 Trends in Short-Term Borrowing, Commercial Banks, First Half of 1997

Indicator	*Bank*	*Jan.*	*Feb.*	*Mar.*	*Apr.*	*May*	*June*
Roll-over ratio, %	Big 7 commercial banks, average	115	94	109	95	101	106
	Korea First Bank	100	66	64	65	72	82
	Seoul Bank	96	70	75	83	87	80
Spread of three-month bonds, basis points	Big 7 commercial banks, average	25	36	40	46	49	58
	Korea First Bank	31	39	47	57	51	74
	Seoul Bank	35	44	55	60	59	85

Source: Foreign Exchange Regulations and External Debt Division, Ministry of Finance and Economy.

Note: The Big 7 are the seven largest commercial banks: Korea Development Bank (KDB), Export-Import Bank of Korea, Korea Long-Term Credit Bank, Kookmin Bank, Housing & Commercial Bank, and Industrial Bank of Korea. The numbers regarding roll-over ratio in the table are rounded to the nearest integer.

resident foreign currency deposits, which grew steadily from US$1.47 billion at the end of December 1996 to US$2.99 billion at the end of January 1997 and US$4.39 billion at the end of March 1997.

Concerned about the direction of the weakening won, the monetary authorities pumped US$12.35 billion—US$8.51 billion in spot transactions and US$3.84 billion in forward contracts—into foreign exchange markets during the first quarter of 1997 (BAI 1998). In the meantime, the central bank's foreign exchange reserves had fallen by US$4.1 billion since the beginning of 1997, to US$29.2 billion at the end of March. The won/dollar exchange rate continued to rise despite the stabilization efforts of the monetary authorities, jumping from W 844.2 at the end of 1996 to W 897.1 by the end of March 1997, a 5.9 percent depreciation in a mere three months.

If one symptom of a financial crisis is a situation in which the market expectation about the behavior of a country's currency is reversed (for whatever reason) so that the currency comes under speculative attack, while the monetary authorities believe that the market expectation is wrong and intervene in foreign exchange markets to counter the speculative attack, then Korea was certainly displaying this symptom of crisis by March 1997. However, because this turn of events had not yet reached a crisis point or triggered a moratorium, what transpired in early 1997 may be more aptly characterized as a faint tremor, that is, a precursor of the shocks that were to occur later in the year.

A Momentary Lull in Financial Markets, April–June 1997

Developments in Financial Markets

By April, the turmoil caused by the bankruptcy of the Hanbo and Sammi business groups and the debilitating nationwide labor strikes had somewhat dissipated. Market interest rates returned to more normal levels and, from May to June, showed signs of stabilizing. In May, the overnight call rate, which had spiraled upward since the beginning of the year, dropped to 12.41 percent. The yield on benchmark three-year corporate bonds turned around in the second quarter and steadied at 12.22 percent. In June, both the call rate and corporate bond yield dropped further, to 11.17 percent and 11.65 percent, respectively.

Stocks rallied. The KOSPI jumped by 37.6 points, to 694.3 in April and then to 713.1 in May and 765.2 in June. The stock purchases of foreign investors fell by W 134.1 billion in April, a noticeable improvement over the W 215.4 billion drop in March. Then, in May, the net stock purchases of foreign investors increased to W 1.9 trillion. This was followed by another month of net stock purchases totaling W 633.2 billion in June.

But the economy remained generally sluggish even as interest rates stabilized, the stock market rallied, and exports increased modestly. Most companies therefore continued to struggle in a tough business environment, and corporate bankruptcies did not cease. In April, Jinro, a large distiller, faced insolvency. In May, the Samlib General Food, Dainong, and Han Shin groups had similar difficulties. Then, in late June, the Kia Group, under strain because of a cash shortage, announced business restructuring and turnaround plans. Amid the mounting pressures on the economy, Standard and Poor's downgraded by one notch the short- and long-term credit ratings of Korea First Bank, the main creditor bank of Hanbo, on April 18. On June 27, Moody's followed suit by downgrading Korea's sovereign credit rating from stable to negative.

The availability of credit for corporate companies continued to diminish as commercial banks and merchant banks called back loans at maturity and tightened the release of new credit. Merchant banks, in particular, sharply cut back on their purchases of bills from corporate companies (loans) after finding few buyers for them (deposits) and running into financing difficulties. The nationwide ratio of dishonored bills averaged 0.23 percent, about the same as the ratio during the first quarter.

Meanwhile, the current account deficit reached US$7.4 billion for the first three months of the year, but, in the second quarter, it fell to US$2.7 billion. The trigger for the drop in the deficit was a rebound in exports during the second quarter and a noticeable reduction in imports as the economy continued to slow. Exports grew in part because more firms were looking to overseas sales as a way to make up for the slump in domestic demand. But the expectations of a weakening of the dollar played a role. The yen was soon gaining against the dollar; the yen/dollar exchange rate fell from ¥127.09 per dollar at the end of April to ¥114.65 at the end of June.

Net capital inflows grew from US$4.04 billion in the first quarter to US$6.57 billion in the second quarter. The conditions for overseas borrowing by commercial banks improved as well. The spread in interest rates widened somewhat, but the rollover on short-term loans was above 100 percent (see table 1.3). Thus, as a result of increases in net capital inflows and improved borrowing conditions overseas, the won/dollar exchange rate actually fell, from W 897.1 per dollar at the end of March to W 892.1 at the end of April. It then dropped to W 891.8 in May and to W 888.1 in June. Total foreign exchange reserves rose from US$29.15 billion at the end of March to US$33.32 billion by the end of June.

The Government Response

Battered by the aftershocks from the bankruptcy of Hanbo and Sammi, the government prodded financial companies to come up with an agreement to provide a grace period—a suspended default—to companies about to default on their debt. The Korea Federation of Banks, an association of banks, followed through with an agreement on April 1. After some fine-tuning on April 18, the suspended default period was first applied to Jinro on April 21. It was also used to save Dainong Group from defaulting on its debt payment due on May 28. Essentially, the goal of the grace period was to restrain lenders from rushing to claim their loans and give cash-strapped companies a cooling-off period of about three months to help them find new financing or alternatives and thus avoid bankruptcy.

On April 24, the government announced a new package of measures designed to facilitate the effective resolution of the distressed assets held by financial companies and support the turnaround of companies in financial difficulty. One key element in the package was a significantly expanded role for the Korea Asset Management Corporation (KAMCO), which the government envisioned could take over the distressed assets of banks and other financial companies and facilitate the asset disposition—for example, land and subsidiary business units—of companies facing a temporary financial squeeze as they executed business restructuring. Included in the package was a plan for financial companies to inject W 100 billion into KAMCO as fresh capital and create a W 1.5 trillion asset resolution fund, the Non-Performing Asset Management Fund, or NPA Fund. The fund would be formed through newly issued debt securities, borrowing, and the contributions of financial companies. The government announced that it would propose a special law in support of these plans.

In recognition of the fact that financial markets were weighed down by rampant rumors of more large corporate failures in the works, the government issued its assessment of financial market trends and announced the additional measures it planned to implement to bring calm to the markets. These measures included the removal of the cap on the brokerage amounts for call transactions, the repeal of the mandatory purchase of central bank–issued monetary stabilization bonds for financial companies, and steps to stimulate markets in trading repurchase agreements and bills. On May 15, the government significantly relaxed restrictions on debt issues and capital increases in an effort to help companies raise capital more easily through debt and equity markets.

To encourage foreign capital inflows, the government decided to accelerate the timetable previously set for the opening of capital markets. On April 10, the ceiling on beneficiary certificates available solely to foreigners and offered by investment trust companies was raised. Two days later, on April 12, foreign exchange management regulations were significantly relaxed to encourage inflows of foreign capital. This was followed by an easing in stock acquisitions for foreign investors (May 2), fresh plans for an accelerated and wider opening of bond markets (May 19), and the adoption of measures for the securitization of assets denominated in foreign currencies and held by domestic financial companies (June 12).

There was a clear recognition within government policy circles that a major structural reform was urgently needed in the financial sector to ensure sustained financial market stability and future growth. It was understood that there needed to be a bold break from old customs, conventions, and business-as-usual attitudes that had long stifled desirable changes and innovations. In short, it was recognized that a serious, far-reaching reform was required at the most basic level. This was the goal behind the announcement by President Kim Young-Sam on January 7, 1997 of the proposal to create the Financial Reform Committee.

The committee was officially launched on January 22. It consisted of 31 experts and representatives from the business community, the financial service industry, and academia. With the aim of revitalizing the financial system, the committee began to work on a short-term reform agenda. In its first report, released on April 14, the committee stressed the need to repeal Korea's myriad, outdated development-era laws and regulations and to strengthen the role of the markets. A second report followed on June 4 that detailed a mid- to long-term reform agenda.

The government decided to put into effect quickly the recommendations contained in the committee's first report that did not require passage by the legislature. The measures to be pursued included permitting financial service firms to offer a wider range of products and services, allowing companies greater managerial freedom, removing restrictions on the interest rates associated with certain deposits and the fees for services in securities, and deregulating certain international financial transactions. For steps requiring the approval of the legislature, the government presented several new laws and amendments to the National Assembly. By August, these had been enacted during a special legislative session.

In the committee's second report, several major recommendations were made in regard to the central bank, the structure of financial oversight, restructuring and consolidation in the financial service industry, and improvements in the efficiency of financial markets. However, when the second report was released, it was received with both alarm and outrage by the BOK. The central bank was particularly incensed by the proposals that the head of the Monetary Board should serve concurrently as governor of the BOK and that the Office of Bank Supervision should become independent of the BOK and be integrated with other supervisory authorities to create Korea's first integrated financial supervisory authority.[4] The BOK contended that this initiative would severely undermine its authority and independence. Public opinion was divided, and most political leaders, mindful of the upcoming presidential election, shied away from taking a firm stance. Amid debate and rising tensions, the government forged ahead and submitted 13 reform bills to the National Assembly on August 23.

On June 20, the government announced 21 national priority tasks that it described as necessary preparations for the 21st century. The principal rationale was that, as globalization and market integration accelerated, Korea faced the risk of being left behind if it did not engage in serious reform and restructuring. In essence, the diagnosis was that the weaknesses and shortcomings of the economy could be traced to Korea's general failure to reform and adapt to the new reality. The range of the priority tasks was wide, from rethinking the role of the government to promoting information technology.

A Looming Crisis in Financial Markets, July–September 1997

The Emerging Crisis in Thailand

After the relative calm of the second quarter of 1997, financial markets were gripped by renewed concerns in July amid reports of an unfolding financial crisis in Thailand and the suspended default agreed to by Kia Group creditors.

Thailand's troubles with external debt and currency depreciation could not be good news for Korea. Because of sluggish exports, Thailand's current account deficit rose to a peak of 8 percent of GDP in 1996. Far worse, after the collapse of local real estate markets following years of booms, speculation, and excess supply, local lenders were beginning to experience a tidal wave of defaults on the bad loans on their books. Confidence in Thailand's ability to honor its external debt plummeted. In September 1996, Moody's downgraded Thailand's short-term sovereign ratings.

Trading of the Thai baht picked up significantly following the creation of the Bangkok International Banking Facilities in 1993. The baht was, de facto, pegged to the U.S. dollar as if it were in a fixed exchange system. Though the exchange rate system of Thailand was a multicurrency basket system, the share of the dollar in the basket of currencies was as much as 80 percent.

In November 1996, the baht came under pressure because of the outflow of foreign capital and dollar purchases by Thai companies. In February and May 1997, it came under massive speculative attack by hedge funds. In a move to defend the baht, the Thai central bank used up more than US$10 billion on May 14. On May 13 and 14, it intervened in foreign exchange markets in concert with the central banks of Hong Kong SAR, China; Malaysia; and Singapore. On May 15, it went a step further by banning Thai financial companies from lending baht to foreign financial companies except for legitimate business transactions. This was followed by an increase in the overnight interest rate in offshore credit markets to a staggering 1,000 percent.

Initially, the efforts of the Thai central bank appeared to pay off. However, the speculative selling off of baht continued more or less unabated.

As a result, the Thai central bank's usable foreign exchange reserves, net of future obligations (from forward contracts), fell from between US$6 billion and US$7 billion in early June to between US$4 billion and US$5 billion by June 20–26. By the end of the month, the reserves were depleted to US$2.8 billion. Amid signs that the situation was spiraling out of control, Thailand finally decided, on July 2, to convert its exchange rate system to a managed floating rate system. The exchange rate against the dollar was then suddenly raised from B 24.35 to B 29.00 and, by the end of July, to B 32.00.

The contagion of the baht crisis quickly spread to Thailand's neighbors, many of which already had fairly substantial current account deficits. On July 11, both Indonesia and the Philippines widened their daily exchange rate floating band margins from 8 to 12 percent. On July 14, Malaysia all but gave up its effort to defend the falling ringgit, and Prime Minister Mahathir Mohamad began to attack hedge funds as evil speculators. By early August, the Indonesian rupiah, the Malaysian ringgit, and the Philippine peso had depreciated by 16.7, 14.0, and 12.3 percent, respectively. Even the Singapore dollar began to show signs of weakening.

According to information gathered by the BOK, developments in the flow of international investment capital at the time can be described as follows. First, global equity funds reduced their exposure in Japan (from 18.9 percent in January to 16.6 percent in October) and in other Asian equity markets (from 10.5 to 7.1 percent) beginning especially in June and shifted their money to southeastern European markets (from 14.2 to 16.5 percent), while simultaneously increasing their cash holdings (from 3.6 to 8.2 percent) as a precaution against investor redemption demand and as part of regional portfolio adjustments. Second, similar to equity investors, global bond funds shifted their investments away from Asia. They reduced their investments in the region (from 5.3 percent in January to 1.9 percent in October) and increased their exposure in Canada (from 5.3 to 10.3 percent) and Japan (from 9.7 to 11.8 percent). Their cash holdings jumped from 3.3 to 6.8 percent. The unfolding of the currency crisis in Southeast Asia in July, coupled with the massive stock sell-off in Hong Kong SAR, China on October 23, dealt a heavy blow in terms of global investor sentiment. As investors fled to safe havens in the United States and elsewhere, treasury yields in most developed markets dropped sharply (table 1.4).

The crisis in Southeast Asia prompted Japan to propose the establishment of the Asian Monetary Fund (AMF), closely modeled on the International Monetary Fund (IMF), with about US$100 billion in financing, to deal with the region's crisis and supplement the work of the IMF, though it would act independently if this were warranted. The creation of the AMF was discussed on September 21 at a meeting of the finance ministers of 11 Southeast Asian countries and the head of the IMF during the IMF and World Bank Group Annual Meetings of the Boards of Governors, which was held in Hong Kong SAR, China. But the proposal did not achieve con-

Table 1.4 Trends in Yields on Treasury Bonds in Major Countries
percent

		1997					
Country	*1996*	*June*	*Sept.*	*Oct. 22*	*Oct. 23*	*Oct. 24*	*Oct. 27*
United States	6.43	6.51	6.12	6.14	6.02	5.99	5.81
Japan	2.76	2.60	2.12	1.93	1.91	1.90	1.86
Germany	5.78	5.70	5.52	5.75	5.69	5.65	5.68

Source: International Department, Bank of Korea.
Note: The table refers to 10-year treasury bonds.

sensus because of the lukewarm response of China and the opposition of the IMF and the United States. Nonetheless, the region's finance ministers did agree, at a subsequent meeting on November 18–19, to adopt the Manila Framework, a new regional monitoring system in lieu of the AMF.

The Suspended Kia Default and the Bad Loans of Financial Institutions

On July 15, the Kia Group, the eighth largest business group in Korea at the time, was granted a suspended default by its creditors. Korea First Bank, Kia's main creditor bank, decided to include 18 Kia-affiliated companies in the suspended default and allow the companies a grace period until September 29. Kia had faced pressure since the spring of 1997 because of persistent rumors of cash flow troubles. From April to June, Kia's creditor institutions called back loans totaling about W 500 billion to W 600 billion. On May 23, Korea First Bank sought to alleviate Kia's short-term funding problem through an injection of W 63.8 billion to the company. However, this proved insufficient to offset the efforts by merchant banks and other nonbank lenders to collect on their loans. Only when the moment came to decide whether Kia should be declared bankrupt did the creditors agree to a suspended default.

Unlike other *chaebols* (the large family-controlled and family-run groups that dominate business in Korea), Kia was owned by minority shareholders and run by a cadre of professional managers headed by chairman Kim Seon-Hong. The labor union at Kia had been able to exert significant influence on management, and, because of the widely diluted share structure and the ownership by small investors, Kia was often heralded as a people's company.

The most direct reason for Kia's near bankruptcy was the excessive borrowing by Kia Special Steel for investment and the heavy losses incurred by Kisan Construction. But there were other reasons. For example, the hands of Kia management were tied by the aggressive demands of the company's labor union. Declining revenues from the sale of automobiles and steel because of a slowdown in the economy played a part. In fact, it was said that Kia was suffering from three consecutive years of net losses.

As the troubles at Kia mounted, the losses by creditor banks, particularly Korea First Bank and Seoul Bank, spiraled upward.[5] For Korea First Bank, the main creditor of Hanbo and Kia, the magnitude of nonperforming loans was striking: W 4.52 trillion, or about 16.7 percent of all the outstanding loans on the books as of the end of September 1997. The bank's Bank for International Settlements capital ratio fell precipitously. Likewise, Seoul Bank suffered from W 3.46 trillion in nonperforming loans, about 15.1 percent of the total as of the end of September. Table 1.5 summarizes the size of nonperforming loans held by commercial banks at the time.

The balance sheets of merchant banks were littered with troubled loans, amounting to W 5.49 trillion (including loans to companies that had been granted suspended default at the end of September), or 135.6 percent of total capital. Among 14 merchant banks, many of which engaged in short-term financing, the ratio exceeded 200 percent, indicating the complete erosion of capital.[6] As the situation turned from bad to worse, financial markets began to wobble badly. On July 26 and August 6, respectively, Moody's and Standard and Poor's each placed five commercial banks under review for possible downward adjustments and downgraded Korea's sovereign rating from stable to negative.

Developments in Financial Markets

Following the July 15 announcement of the suspended Kia default, both the overnight call rate and benchmark corporate bond yields moved upward, averaging 11.41 and 11.86 percent, respectively, for the month. In August, they jumped to 12.39 and 12.11 percent, respectively, amid worries about the financial crisis unfolding in Southeast Asia and about the soundness of the balance sheets of domestic financial companies and the ability of these companies to maintain their credit access to foreign

Table 1.5 Nonperforming Loans of Commercial Banks, End of Period, 1997

Indicator	*March*	*June*	*September*	*December*
Nonperforming loans, W, billions[a]	16,377.1	16,866.7	21,461.0	22,063.4
Nonperforming loan ratio, %	5.4	5.5	6.8	6.4

Source: Financial Supervisory Service.

a. Loans classified as either substandard or doubtful or the estimated loss assets.

lenders. By September, the rates had risen to 13.17 and 12.36 percent, respectively, as the funding situation deteriorated among the merchant banks and the news of the Kia application for court-mediated debt composition hit the markets.

For businesses, obtaining credit remained exceedingly difficult as commercial banks and merchant banks sought to limit their credit exposure amid the rising number of corporate bankruptcies. With the loss of confidence among depositors, Korea First Bank, Seoul Bank, and the merchant banks began to have trouble attracting new deposits. In August, securities firms were allowed to trade commercial paper, which enabled them to recover some of the liquidity that had dried up among the merchant banks. The ratio of dishonored bills issued by companies averaged 0.25 percent during the third quarter of 1997.

The stock market moved downward. The KOSPI declined by 12.9 points, to 752.3, from June to July and continued to fall, to 740.5 in August and to 676.5 in September. Net stock purchases by foreign investors totaled W 231.9 billion in July, sharply down from the W 633.2 billion in June. In August and September, net stock selling by foreign investors totaled W 87.2 billion and W 290.5 billion, respectively.

The overall balance of payments situation turned unfavorable in the third quarter after some improvement during the second quarter. The current account deficit posted a shortfall of US$2.01 billion, slightly less than the shortfall in the second quarter. The balance of goods traded was in the negative, at only US$30 million as a result of a surge in semiconductor exports and a drop in imports, particularly capital goods and raw materials. The net flow of foreign capital dropped to a meager US$620 million in the third quarter as the inflow of foreign stock investment, which had been on the rise since May, reversed in August and foreign lenders called back large sums of short-term loans from domestic financial companies.

From July to November, roll-over ratios generally fell, and the interest rate spread (the risk premium) rose on short-term borrowing by domestic banks (table 1.6). On August 12, some commercial banks had to resort to US$700 million in loans from the BOK because of foreign currency funding difficulties. Long-term borrowing conditions worsened for domestic banks as well.[7]

Overseas borrowing conditions deteriorated further in June, and merchant banks began increasingly to rely on domestic commercial banks for foreign currency. When the foreign currency funding of commercial banks began to dry up as well, the merchant banks resorted to extreme short-term borrowing. The situation was becoming particularly adverse for the regional merchant banks, and, by late July, they were buying dollars with their own funds. When it became apparent that merchant banks would not be able to complete foreign currency transactions on their own, the BOK decided, on August 18, to lend US$500 million in emergency funding from its foreign exchange reserves. The funding crisis gripping merchant banks

Table 1.6 Trends in Short-Term Borrowing by Commercial Banks, July–November 1997

Indicator	*Bank*	*July*	*Aug.*	*Sept.*	*Oct.*	*Nov.*
Roll-over ratio, %	Average of Big 7 commercial banks	89	79	83	87	59
	Korea First Bank	63	69	68	67	58
	Seoul Bank	73	64	57	68	50
Spread, three-month bonds, basis points	Average of Big 7 commercial banks	55	67	80	84	124
	Korea First Bank	71	78	100	89	153
	Seoul Bank	71	107	122	110	153

Source: Foreign Exchange Regulations and External Debt Division, Ministry of Finance and Economy.

Note: The numbers regarding roll-over ratio in the table are rounded to the nearest integer.

was largely a result of a mismatch between the short-term borrowing and the long-term lending of the banks. By the end of September, merchant banks were covering 62.2 percent of their foreign currency borrowings with short-term credit, while allocating 84.3 percent of their foreign currency borrowings to long-term investment.

In the meantime, the won was losing ground against the U.S. dollar. In July, the won weakened amid an appreciating dollar and the troubles at Kia to W 892, a 0.4 percent drop since the end of June. In August, with rising demand for dollars from importers and the mounting difficulties faced by domestic financial companies in securing credit from foreign lenders, the won slid by 1.1 percent, to W 902 per dollar. The depreciation of the won continued in September, raising the exchange rate to W 914.8 by the end of the month, which resulted in a 7.7 percent drop in the value of the won over the previous year.

Throughout the second quarter, the monetary authorities purchased US$7.76 billion in the spot and forward markets under favorable foreign exchange market conditions. But, in the third quarter, when dollar demand and supply conditions took a turn for the worse in the wake of the troubles at Kia, the authorities were all but forced to pump more foreign currencies into the markets. Thus, during the quarter, a total of US$8.03 billion—US$4.51 billion in the spot market and US$3.52 billion in the forward market—was sold in foreign exchange markets. The effect of these interventions was clear: from the end of June to the end of September, total foreign exchange reserves dropped from US$33.32 billion to US$30.43 billion.

As the crisis mood of the markets deepened, the phenomenon of leads and lags intensified. For example, resident foreign currency deposits, which had fallen as low as US$1.97 billion by the end of June, had jumped to US$3.74 billion by the end of September. It was widely suspected by this time that banks authorized to deal in foreign exchange transactions were so short on foreign currencies that they were refusing negotiations on long-term export bills, though goods had already cleared customs.

The Government Response

With financial markets in turmoil, the MOFE announced, on August 25, measures aimed at restoring calm in financial markets and boosting investor confidence. The government believed that Korea's economic fundamentals and its ability to service external debt were sound, but that the distress caused by the insolvency of a few large companies precipitated by the evolving economic realities was putting a heavy strain on financial markets and the economy as a whole. Given the significant downside risks to the financial system arising from the uncertainties about the viability of some of the financial companies, measures were needed that would boost market stability.

The government's response consisted of three parts: support for financial market stability, the restoration of the confidence of foreign investors, and support for Korea First Bank and the merchant banks. To foster financial market stability, the BOK planned to provide liquidity support to the commercial banks and merchant banks that were under strain because of mounting bad assets, along with a transfer of W 500 billion from available government funds to these banks in the form of deposits. In addition, the BOK allowed merchant banks to trade repurchase agreements, and the government considered injecting capital into troubled commercial banks in the form of equity investments.

Moreover, as a step to help distressed financial companies clean up the bad assets on their balance sheets, the government proposed expanding the NPA Fund under the supervision of KAMCO to the tune of W 3.5 trillion. To facilitate the disposition of the real estate held by corporate and financial companies, the government proposed to implement special surtax exemptions and allow the state-run Korea Land Corporation to acquire land up to a total value of W 500 billion. The basic understanding was that the financial companies receiving government support should complete the turnaround within three years (but within an absolute maximum of five years). If companies failed to make satisfactory progress, the government was to call back the credit assistance and demand extensive business restructuring.

To improve the confidence of foreign investors, the government strongly intimated that it would back all the external liabilities of domestic financial companies (and their overseas branches) in the event of imminent default or insolvency. Since the shortage of foreign currency liquidity among financial companies weighed heavily on foreign lenders, the government set its sights on expanding foreign borrowing through the state-run banks, repealing restrictions on trade-related foreign currency transactions, removing caps on the stock acquisitions of foreign investors, opening up the bond markets, and securitizing assets denominated in foreign currencies. The government considered that it had to step up an investor relations campaign targeted at overseas investors and lenders and emphasize the fundamental soundness of the Korean economy and the government's unwavering commitment to economy-wide reform and restructuring. One key event planned during this time was a special presentation on the Korean economy during the IMF and World Bank Group Annual Meetings of the Boards of Governors in Hong Kong SAR, China on September 20.

For the gravely strained Korea First Bank, the government envisioned new credit facilities through the BOK and a capital injection in the bank through a new issue of treasury bonds. It planned to support the bank's efforts to dispose of or otherwise clean up its nonperforming loan holdings through KAMCO. Other steps, such as the timely supply of foreign currency credit through the BOK to cover short-term liquidity shortages and a government pledge to back the liabilities of the Korea First Bank, were outlined.

For the distressed merchant banks, the government let it be known that it was ready to provide credit support through the BOK and to guarantee repayment to foreign lenders if the merchant banks defaulted on the obligations associated with their borrowing.

Dealing with the Kia Failure

The government and creditor banks decided to tackle the Kia failure along two different tracks. One was to lend a helping hand to the many small and medium Kia suppliers that depended heavily on Kia for business and to Kia itself so that the company could resume normal operations. The government therefore leaned on financial companies to accept bills from Kia suppliers so as to help them avoid cash flow problems. Other measures embraced by the government included deferred tax collection and an expansion to more businesses in the coverage of the credit guarantees provided through the state-run Credit Guarantee Fund. To help Kia resume normal operations, the government requested that companies such as POSCO, a steel producer, supply necessary raw materials without disruption. An emergency line of credit was made available to Kia based only on assurances of the company's own efforts.

The other track was focused on eliminating the reasons for the Kia failure. At a meeting on August 4, the heads of the financial creditor companies reached an agreement to extend the suspended default until September 29 and to demand that the company replace its management and downsize its workforce. The government publicly expressed its support for the creditor agreement. However, Kia rejected the demands of the creditors as unworkable, and the situation quickly took yet another turn for the worse with no end in sight.

The pressure of labor unions and civic groups aggravated the situation. The Federation of Korean Trade Unions and the Korean Confederation of Trade Unions, the two major national labor groups, joined hands with more than 60 civic groups to launch a national campaign to save Kia. They staunchly opposed the sale of the company. Soon, the political parties jumped into the fray and clouded matters even more. It was obvious that, with the presidential election looming, the political parties were seeking to gain political leverage from the Kia crisis rather than promoting a rational economic and business discourse that could actually help resolve the problems.

After the two months of the suspended Kia default had elapsed, the creditors and the company, on September 17, came to the agreement that (1) the debt payments of Kia Motors would be deferred, and the company would push for a turnaround under the management of the creditors; (2) Asia Motors would be sold to Daewoo Motor; (3) Kia Special Steel would be jointly managed by Daewoo, Hyundai, and Kia; (4) the incumbent management would step down; and (5) the company's labor union would support the agreement through a written document. However, on September 22, Kia management refused to resign or submit a letter from the labor union accepting the demands of the creditors. Instead, the company's management took the matter to court and applied for a composition for the four principal companies in the Kia Group: Asia Motors, Kia Inter-Trade, Kia Motors, and Kia Special Steel.

In response, the creditors terminated the suspended default on September 29 as planned and demanded that Kia withdraw the composition application to the court and, instead, apply for court receivership. Kia management refused to do this and decided to apply for court receivership only for Kia Special Steel.

On October 22, the government, which had maintained that the matter should be resolved between the company and the creditors, announced that the state-run Korea Development Bank (KDB) would lead the effort to initiate court receivership on behalf of and jointly with the creditor financial companies on the premise that the bank would swap its Kia loans for an equity share. On October 24, 10 creditor banks jointly filed for court receivership for Asia Motors and Kia Motors. (The court approved the request on April 15, 1998.) Kim Seon-Hong, Kia's chairman, who had tried vehemently to fend off the creditors, finally resigned from his post after the court receivership request was filed, exactly 107 days after Kia had been rescued from bankruptcy by the creditors.

Onset of the Financial Crisis and the Request for an IMF Rescue, October–November 1997

The Southeast Asian Contagion and the Cascade of Corporate Bankruptcies

Taiwan, China decided to cease defending its currency on October 17, and the currency slid 3.6 percent against the U.S. dollar the next day. On October 23, the stock market in Hong Kong SAR, China crashed to the tune of 10.4 percent. This was followed by a broad sell-off in the U.S. stock markets on October 27. There was no mistaking what was happening: the financial crisis that had started in Southeast Asia was spreading, and it was heading north. Speculation was rampant by then that Korea was next.

In October, the market was rocked by rumors of the imminent bankruptcy of Haitai, NewCore, Ssangbangwool, and other large Korean companies. The rumors proved more or less accurate when Ssangbangwool defaulted on its debts on October 15. Then, on October 29, Taeil Metal Co. was granted a suspended default. The cascade of large corporate bankruptcies continued in November. On the first day of the month, Haitai was declared bankrupt. Three days later, it was NewCore's turn. On December 15, Halla Group and Coryo Securities were declared bankrupt. The chain of bankruptcies heightened the fears of an imminent collapse of large financial companies, a prospect that still seemed otherworldly despite all the signs.

The market was dealt more blows when Standard and Poor's downgraded the short- and long-term credit ratings of three large commercial banks—Hanil, Korea Exchange, and Shinhan—on October 2 and then, on October 24, downgraded Korea's long-term sovereign rating from AA– to A+ and its short-term sovereign rating from A1+ to A1. The downgrading did not end there. On November 25, Standard and Poor's lowered Korea's long-term sovereign rating to A– and the short-term rating to A2. Moody's followed suit by lowering Korea's short-term sovereign rating from P1 to P2 on October 28. It then proceeded to downgrade the ratings of four commercial banks—Commercial Bank of Korea, Korea Exchange, Korea First, and Seoul Bank—on October 31. Moody's then aggressively pulled Korea's long-term sovereign rating two notches down, from A1 to A3, and its short-term rating further down, to P3, on November 28. Likewise, Fitch, another major credit-rating provider, lowered Korea's sovereign rating from AA– to A+ on November 18 then to a single A on November 26.

Foreign news coverage of Korea's predicament was turning increasingly negative. The *Financial Times*, on October 23, and the *Economist*, on October 25, each reported that the government announcement of the court receivership of Kia on the premise that the state-run KDB was swapping its loans for an equity share was yet another example of the government's policy of throwing lifelines to nonviable companies and represented one more setback to business restructuring in Korea. On November 3, immediately after the bankruptcy of Haitai, the *Wall Street Journal Asia* alluded to the heightened risk of a financial crisis in Korea as a result of the massive losses incurred by Korean corporate and financial companies. The tone of the *International Herald Tribune* was similar on November 6. Both papers noted that, despite the repeated interventions by the BOK, the won had continued to depreciate. Then, on November 5, *Bloomberg News* reported that Korea's external debt amounted to US$110 billion, of which US$80 billion was due by the end of the year. The paper said that Korea's foreign exchange reserves totaled about US$15 billion and that Korea was thus headed for a severe financial crisis. The worrisome foreign coverage of Korea's situation was not lost on the foreign investors and financial institutions that dealt with Korean businesses. The outlook for Korea was only getting gloomier.

Developments in Financial Markets

Worries mounted on financial markets in October and November. The overnight call rate climbed to 12.5 percent in early October and to the 13 percent range on November 11. The rate continued to rise and reached the 14 percent range on November 24 and peaked at 15.39 percent two days later, on November 26. The call rate averaged 13.56 percent in October and 14.0 percent in November. The return on benchmark three-year corporate bonds was held at 12.42 percent until October 25 and rose modestly to 12.6 percent on November 10. It had increased to the 13 percent range by November 18 and picked up sharply to 18.55 percent on November 26. The more serious problem was that businesses were unable to raise funds even at these extremely high rates.

The monthly average KOSPI lost 92.4 points in October, declining to a record low of 470.8. The market rebounded to 555.74 on November 5 on the back of a higher stock investment cap for foreign investors. But the weight of the rapidly deteriorating market situation proved too much for investors, and the index slid back to 485.43 on November 22, before the government had reached out to the IMF for help. On November 29, the index found a new bottom at 407.86. The monthly average lost 89.9 points in November. Net stock sales by foreign investors amounted to W 950.3 billion in October and W 566.8 billion in November.

Bank lending was fairly steady in October (table 1.7). But lending by merchant banks continued to shrink. In a move to inject liquidity into

Table 1.7 Trends in Loans by Financial Companies, 1995–97
won, billions

			1997				
Company	*1995*	*1996*	*Annual*	*Oct.*	*Nov.*	*Dec.*	*Q4*
Banks	16,627.4	24,706.5	23,216.8	3,932.1	1,203.7	–8,388.0	–3,252.2
	(12.2)	(16.2)	(13.1)	(15.8)	(17.3)	(13.1)	—
Discounted bills[a]	3,355.0	2,621.5	36.6	324.7	1,384.5	–2,204.9	–495.7
Overdraft checking accounts	–1,905.7	–618.7	177.4	68.0	–584.3	–3,508.9	–4,025.2
Loans for operations	10,757.6	20,493.2	18,525.0	2,980.6	–65.7	–2,037.6	877.3
Merchant banks	16,445.1	23,511.6	–12,977.5	–1,492.5	–1,213.3	–13,549.2	–16,255.0
	(35.9)	(37.8)	(–15.1)	(11.4)	(5.8)	(–13.0)	
Securities companies, discounted bills	—	—	15,114.3	1,312.1	2,927.8	7,189.3	11,429.2
Trust accounts of banks	7,177.7	10,573.5	7,223.1	1,820.3	1,415.8	2,080.8	5,316.9
	(18.6)	(23.1)	(12.8)	(16.0)	(14.9)	(15.5)	
Development banks[b]	5,238.0	7,608.2	16,517.9	1,422.6	5,056.0	4,708.5	11,187.1
	(15.3)	(19.3)	(35.1)	(15.9)	(26.1)	(35.1)	
Life insurers	3,028.5	7,049.9	5,882.1	1,289.1	781.3	855.5	2,925.9
	(10.6)	(22.2)	(15.2)	(13.7)	(14.9)	(15.2)	

Source: Financial Policy Division, Ministry of Finance and Economy.

Note: Numbers in parentheses denote the growth rate from the end of the same period in the previous year. — = not available.

a. Including trade bills.

b. KDB and Export-Import Bank of Korea.

the market, the BOK allowed securities firms to trade repurchase agreements on October 2. Two weeks later, on October 16, the BOK extended a special credit totaling W 1 trillion to 16 merchant banks. Net debt and equity issues fell in October relative to the previous month (table 1.8).

During November, bank lending through account overdrafts started to drop mainly because banks started to call back loans to merchant banks. Lending by merchant banks continued to fall. New stock issues fell, although net debt issues increased somewhat from the previous month. However, corporate bond markets all but froze: no bidders were in sight. The dishonored bill ratio averaged 0.43 percent in October and 0.38 percent in November. By then, however, a long line of imminent bankruptcies of large companies was in the works, and a crushing credit crunch raised its head.

The situation in the foreign exchange market was holding somewhat steady until volatility returned to markets in Hong Kong SAR, China and in Taiwan, China in mid-October. With a spate of downgrading by the credit-rating providers and a torrent of pessimistic news coverage by the foreign press, the pressure was felt widely in foreign exchange markets.

The current account was in the negative, at US$490 million in October, down from US$510 million in September. The capital account was positive, at US$920 million, mainly because of fresh overseas debt issues and long-term borrowing. Foreign investors took US$760 million out of the stock market, and merchant banks had to repay US$1.1 billion for their short-term loans from foreign lenders. Nonetheless, the state-run banks, the Korea Electric Power Corporation, and several private sector companies with top-notch creditworthiness managed to issue US$1.47 billion worth of bonds in foreign markets and secure another US$1.9 billion in long-term loans from overseas lenders.

The conditions for overseas borrowing did not look particularly dismal in October relative to September. The roll-over ratio for the seven largest commercial banks (the Big 7) averaged 86.5 percent in October, slightly up from the 82.8 percent in September (see table 1.6). But the spread was somewhat wider than the 80 basis points in September. Mid- to long-term borrowing continued more or less, but the interest rates on these loans were on the rise (see table 1.10 elsewhere below).

By late October, the conditions for borrowing had worsened precipitously not only for long-term loans, but also for short-term loans. The situation was particularly forbidding in markets in Hong Kong SAR, China and in markets in Tokyo, the two key sources of credit for Korea. Soon, new borrowing by financial companies all but seized up, and interest rates skyrocketed. On October 30, several merchant banks nearly failed to carry out their payment obligations and managed to avoid default only because of lending provided through the foreign exchange reserves of the BOK and support from Shinhan Bank.

Table 1.8 Trends in Securities Issues in Capital Markets, 1995–97
won, billions

			1997				
Security	*1995*	*1996*	*Annual*	*Oct.*	*Nov.*	*Dec.*	*Q4*
A. Stock	6,164.0	5,042.9	3,155.6	275.5	208.4	140.6	624.5
B. Net corporate bond issues	13,358.1	15,040.0	13,774.9	297.8	1,205.7	4,144.4	5,647.9
Issues	23,581.2	29,902.5	34,322.1	2,071.7	2,783.1	7,410.8	12,265.6
Redemption	10,223.1	14,862.5	20,547.2	1,773.9	1,577.4	3,266.4	6,617.7
Total, A + B	19,522.1	20,082.9	16,930.5	573.3	1,414.1	4,285.0	6,272.4

Source: Financial Policy Division, Ministry of Finance and Economy.

The won/dollar exchange rate hovered around W 914 per U.S. dollar until October 21. But, the next day, it jumped to W 922.7 and then to W 927.9 on October 27. For the last five days of the month, the exchange rate continued to rise and topped W 965.1 on October 31, resulting in a drop in the value of the won by 5.2 percent since the end of September and by 12.5 percent since the beginning of the year.

Because there was no new foreign borrowing and because of the rapidly depreciating won, the foreign exchange market came to a halt even as financial and large corporate companies scrambled to secure dollars. Some turned to the overnight call market and other short-term credit markets for fresh credit with which to buy dollars. Call rates therefore jumped sharply, and the won lost more ground against the dollar.

Throughout October, the monetary authorities intervened to stabilize the exchange rate by selling US$2.09 billion in the spot market and US$3.19 billion in the forward market. During the first 15 days of the month, US$670 million was sold on the forward market, and, during the second half of the month, US$2.09 billion went to the spot market and US$2.52 billion to the forward market.

Foreign exchange reserves totaled US$30.51 billion at the end of October, up US$80 million from the US$30.43 billion at the end of September. The increase occurred despite the massive dollar-selling intervention because the BOK called back foreign currency deposits that it had placed under the management of commercial banks. However, excluding foreign exchange reserves such as foreign currency deposits in the overseas branches of domestic commercial banks (about US$8.01 billion), usable foreign reserve holdings amounted to a meager US$22.3 billion.

The won continued to slide and lose value against the dollar. Meanwhile, the BOK and the MOFE took divergent positions on dealing with the situation. For the MOFE, the best approach involved defending the won so as to restore market confidence. This contrasted with the stance of the BOK, which saw much more benefit from letting the won move freely as the markets saw fit, while preventing any rapid depletion in foreign exchange reserves.

On October 28, the foreign exchange management authorities reversed their policy and decided to refrain from intervening in the markets until the morning of October 30. The effect of this nonintervention unaccompanied by a widening or total removal of the daily floating band margin was immediately felt on the markets. From October 28 to October 30, the won hit the daily floating ceiling and depreciated 2.25 percent a day; with no bids for the won, currency trading sometimes stopped altogether.

President Kim Young-Sam and his key economic ministers held a meeting on October 27 and concluded that, notwithstanding the turmoil in financial markets, Korea's economic fundamentals were more than sufficiently strong to absorb the shock from the Southeast Asian crisis, and Korea would thereby avoid a full-blown financial crisis of its own.

On October 29, the government announced a package of measures to calm the market. First, it decided to open up domestic bond markets even more and to allow foreign investors unlimited access, beginning January 1, 1998, for the purchase of unsecured long-term bonds issued by large companies. Second, the government raised the ceiling on overseas cash borrowing for facility investment and encouraged financial companies to become more involved in the overseas sales to foreign investors of assets denominated in foreign currencies. The essential goal of these measures was to improve the foreign currency liquidity of domestic corporate and financial firms.

To reduce the volatility of the won and bring down short- and long-term interest rates to more sustainable levels, the government let it be known that it would take steps to prevent a rapid depreciation of the won. Other measures aimed at stimulating stock markets, improving the safety and soundness of the financial system, and accelerating corporate restructuring were included in the package. However, none of these measures succeeded in restoring calm to the markets or among investors. Indeed, foreign exchange markets were in panic mode by early November.

In November, the current account became a surplus of US$860 million for the first time in 1997. However, the net capital flow was in the negative, at US$4.46 billion. Specifically, foreign investors withdrew US$980 million (net) from stock markets despite the decision, on November 3, to raise the ceiling on the stock investments of foreigners. Foreign investors took US$580 million (net) out of Korean bond markets. Long-term borrowing from overseas lenders increased by US$560 million, but repayments on short-term overseas loans totaled US$5 billion.

The conditions for short-term borrowing by banks from overseas lenders deteriorated sharply in November as well. For the Big 7, the roll-over ratio fell drastically, to 58.8 percent from 86.5 percent in October (see table 1.6). The spread widened significantly, to 124 basis points from 84 basis points in October.

Table 1.9 Overnight Borrowing by Commercial Banks, End of Period, 1997

Indicator	*Jan.*	*Mar.*	*June*	*July*	*Sept.*	*Oct.*	*Nov. 16*
Average overnight interest rate, basis points	—	22	86	74	103	136	144
Average overnight borrowing per bank, US$, millions	50	110	360	360	360	390	350

Source: BOK 1997a.
Note: The table refers to the Big 7 commercial banks. — = not available.

Cut off from financing from abroad and facing a severely dropping roll-over ratio, domestic financial companies turned to the overnight markets to secure foreign exchange. As a result, the overnight interest rate shot up (table 1.9). The situation was becoming similarly serious for the state-run banks and companies and for top-notch private sector companies. Both the ¥40 billion Samurai bond that was to be offered by the KDB and the US$400 million Euro bond that was to be offered by the Export-Import Bank of Korea were scrapped because of the lack of investors. The spread on mid- to long-term global bonds jumped noticeably (table 1.10).

In late October, as panic continued to grip the market, the commercial banks with relatively robust credit ratings, such as Hanil, Korea Exchange, and Shinhan, experienced a large drop in available short-term lines of credit. Table 1.11 shows the lines of credit available to banks at the time. While the large commercial banks were encountering increasing difficulty in gaining foreign currency liquidity, the situation among the smaller merchant banks became even more ominous. By that time, financial companies could only turn to the BOK for their day-to-day foreign currency needs. Table 1.12 shows the extent to which the BOK was involved in supporting the day-to-day foreign currency liquidity of commercial and merchant banks.

The need for support for the overseas branches of domestic banks became inevitable. During the first half of November, the BOK gave out US$840 million to make up the shortfalls of overseas branches and ended up depositing US$8.1 billion in these branches during the second half of the month. By the end of November, the total amount deposited at overseas branches out of BOK foreign exchange reserves had increased drastically, to over US$16.9 billion.

During this time, the leads and lags in foreign currency transactions intensified. The government leaned heavily on large corporate and financial companies to postpone dollar purchases and accelerate dollar selling, but to no avail. Large companies set aside export earnings without converting them to the local currency. The result was a steep increase in foreign currency deposits (table 1.13). The balance of payments table for the month of November showed unusually large numbers of errors and omissions, to the tune of US$2.35 billion, an indication of the worsening leads and lags in foreign exchange settlements.

The won/dollar exchange rate was somewhat steady at W 960 per U.S. dollar until November 5, but took a jump to W 975 the following day. On November 10, it shot up past the W 1,000 mark, but came back to W 988 from November 11 to November 14. Then, for four consecutive days beginning on November 17, the won hit the daily floating ceiling and hovered near W 1,000 per dollar.

On November 20, in an acknowledgment of the market reality, the government expanded the daily floating band margin to ±10.0 percent from ±2.25 percent. The same day, the won hit the ceiling at W 1,139,

Table 1.10 Trends in Spreads on Global Bonds, 1997
basis points

Bank	*July 14*	*July 16*	*Sept. 19*	*Sept. 23*	*Oct. 23*	*Oct. 27*	*Oct. 29*	*Oct. 31*	*Nov. 6*
KDB									
10 year	80	82	120	121	165	300	300	285	340
7 year[a]	n.a.	n.a.	112	114	155	290	290	280	335
4 year[a]	n.a.	n.a.	95	95	140	270	270	260	330
Korea Electric Power Corporation, 10 year	97	80	114	114	n.a.	n.a.	n.a.	290	340
POSCO, 10 year	90	93	135	137	190	330	330	350	380

Source: BOK 1997a.
Note: n.a. = not applicable.
a. On September 17, a global bond of US$1.5 billion (7-year: T + 115 basis points; 4-year: T + 98 basis points) was issued.

Table 1.11 Lines of Credit by Banks, 1997
US$, billions

Period	*Chohung*	*Commercial Bank of Korea*	*Korea First*	*Hanil*	*Seoul*	*Korea Exchange*	*Shinhan*	*Total*
February–March[a]	1.06	1.63	2.56	1.08	1.50	0.36	0.90	9.09
July 16–September 30[b]	1.07	1.30	1.35	1.58	0.55	0.83	0.39	7.07
October	0.22	0.11	0.13	0.53	0.11	0.41	0.41	1.92

Source: BOK 1997a.

a. Hanbo Group declared bankruptcy on January 23.

b. Kia Group was granted a suspended default on July 15.

Table 1.12 Day-to-Day Foreign Currency Provision, November 1997
US$, millions

Date	*Day-to-day foreign currency needs*	*Total*	*Provision*
3	Kyongnam 54, Coryo 46.2, Youngnam 25.6	125.8	Foreign currency reserves (overnight)
4	Kyongnam 33, Coryo 21.5, Daehan 15, Samyang 37.5	107.0	Foreign currency reserves (overnight)
6	Kyongnam 25, Hangil 27, Kyungil 4.5	56.5	Foreign currency reserves (overnight)
10	Korea First 80, Seoul 80	160.0	Foreign currency reserves (overnight)
13	Seoul 120	120.0	Foreign currency reserves (overnight)
14	Korea First 360, Seoul 210, Chohung 120, Hanil 130, Samsam 15, Hangil 13, Kyungil 17.6	862.6	Foreign currency reserves (overnight)
17	Korea First 448, Seoul 212, Chohung 206, Hanil 250, Commercial Bank of Korea 285, Samyang 29.5, Kyongnam 18.6, Coryo 51	1,500.1	Foreign currency reserves (overnight)
18	Korea First 400, Seoul 316, Chohung 257, Commercial Bank of Korea 170, Samyang 30.6, Kyongnam 20.5, Coryo 20.1, Shinsegae 10.5	1,224.7	Foreign currency reserves (overnight) Industrial Bank of Korea New York branch (10.5)
19	Korea First 586, Seoul 326, Chohung 556, Hanil 370, Commercial Bank of Korea 460, Korea Exchange 40, Samyang 43.1, Kyongnam 50.4, Coryo 17	2,448.5	Foreign currency reserves (overnight)
20	Korea First 673, Seoul 426, Chohung 456, Commercial Bank of Korea 495, Hanil 392, Samyang 57.3, Kyongnam 62.4, Samsam 27	2,588.7	Foreign currency reserves (overnight)
21	Korea First 676, Seoul 540, Chohung 439, Commercial Bank of Korea 670, Hanil 320, Samyang 14.3, Kyongnam 69.8, Coryo 74	2,793.1	Foreign currency reserves (overnight)

Source: Foreign Exchange Management Division, Ministry of Finance and Economy.

Table 1.13 Trends in Foreign Currency Deposits by Residents, End of Period, 1997
US$, billions

		1997				
Indicator	*1996*	*Mar.*	*June*	*Sept.*	*Oct.*	*Nov.*
Resident foreign currency deposits	1.47	4.39	1.97	3.74	4.68	5.30

Source: Foreign Exchange Regulations and External Debt Division, Ministry of Finance and Economy.

but, from November 21 to 27, it stuck fairly close to the W 1,100 mark. Then, on November 28, the exchange rate took a sharp climb, finishing the month at W 1,163.8, up 17.1 percent from the end of October and 27.5 percent since the beginning of the year.

In response to the volatile exchange rate, which appeared out of control, the foreign exchange management authorities intervened and sold U.S. dollars to hold the line at W 1,000 per dollar. During the first half of November, the authorities sold over US$4.0 billion on the spot market and US$200 million on the forward market. Despite the repeated interventions, the pace of dollar buying continued to pick up. Then, for four days beginning November 17, foreign currency trading was suspended. For all practical purposes, the government was no longer able to defend the won. The dollar sales in the second half of November—US$1.64 billion on the spot market and US$700 million on the forward market—were, in fact, undertaken to settle overseas transactions that companies could not carry out on their own rather than to limit the uncontrolled slide of the won.

Foreign exchange reserves rapidly fell in November. Usable reserves, which had stood at US$22.30 billion at the end of October, fell to US$21.51 on November 3, to US$20.96 billion on November 5, to US$20.38 billion on November 8, to US$16.33 billion on November 17, to US$13.19 billion on November 20, and to US$7.26 billion at the end of the month. The reserves were then so depleted that they were insufficient to settle even one month's worth of imports. Korea now faced an imminent default. The situation was grave.

The Government Response and Seeking Help from the IMF

By early November, it was becoming increasingly clear that the situation was too serious and matters too urgent for the government to handle alone. At a meeting on November 13, the minister of finance and economy, the governor of the BOK, and the senior secretary to the president for economic affairs debated whether help should be sought from the IMF.

This was followed by an unreported visit to Korea by Michel Camdessus, the managing director of the IMF, to discuss IMF help for Korea.

On November 18, the financial reform legislation that the government had eagerly awaited failed to pass the National Assembly. The government had pushed hard for the passage of the legislation amid the growing crisis and over the resistance of the BOK. But, with a presidential election around the corner, politics prevailed. The National Assembly did manage to pass a bill that allowed the government to provide a repayment guarantee on W 2 trillion in debt issued for the NPA Fund.

On November 19, the minister of finance and economy and the senior secretary to the president for economic affairs were replaced. On the day of his appointment, the new finance minister announced comprehensive measures aimed at financial market stability and restructuring. First, the NPA Fund was to be expanded from W 3.5 trillion to W 10 trillion, and KAMCO was to buy distressed assets from commercial banks and merchant banks at the maximum recoverable amount.

Second, the merchant banks, all suffering from acute foreign currency shortages, were to push for mergers and takeovers with other financial companies by the end of the year and resolve their foreign currency cash flow problems through asset securitization. Those failing to carry out the new mandate were to be barred from new foreign currency transactions beginning in January 1998.

Third, new guidelines and support measures for mergers and restructuring in the financial service industry were to be finalized by the end of November. Restructuring was to be carried out on a voluntary basis in the form of mergers and outright sales to new buyers. Due diligence on assets and liabilities was to be carried out by the end of January 1998 for merchant banks, by the end of March 1998 for commercial banks, and by the end of June 1998 for other entities. All these institutions were to be rated into three groups, each with a different set of assigned measures.

Fourth, full protection was to be given to bank deposits, and full disclosure was to be required on the magnitude of foreign exchange reserves, short- and long-term external debt, bad assets, and other relevant information so as to facilitate financial sector restructuring. The deposit insurance program took shape in detail on November 25. Through this program, depositors were to be given full protection on the principal and interest from November 19, 1997 to the end of 2000. As a step toward the replenishment of the deposit insurance fund, the deposit insurance premium charged to financial companies was to be raised by 50 percent.

Last, the daily floating band margin for the won was to be widened from ±2.25 to ±10 percent. Bond markets were to be opened up to foreign investors by mid-December 1997. For example, foreign investors were to be given unrestricted access to the markets for bonds with a maturity of three years or longer (secured and unsecured) and to the markets for convertible bonds. The cap on currency swap transactions and cash borrowing by foreign bank branches in Korea was to be raised as well.

Measures to promote the participation of institutional investors in the stock market were announced on November 26. The ceiling on development trusts (a type of money-in-trust) was to be raised to W 2 trillion so as to encourage banks to expand their equity investments from trust accounts. The interest paid on equity-type investment trusts with a fixed return was to be deregulated. In addition, a spot fund of W 2 trillion was to be created by investment trust companies. Investment trust companies were to be allowed to trade repurchase agreements with the BOK.

The government sent an assistant minister of finance and economy to the Japanese finance ministry in a bid to secure emergency funding for the BOK from the Japanese central bank. On November 28, the minister of finance and economy went to Japan to secure that country's support. The mission, however, did not succeed.

These events were the backdrop of the government's decision to seek the support of the IMF. On November 21, the government officially asked the IMF for standby credit. In response, the IMF sent its mission to Korea and, on December 3, 1997, after a series of negotiations, came to an agreement with the government on emergency funding.

Notes

1. It was said that much of the economic growth in 1996 was, in fact, driven by inventory growth; according to some estimates, the economy would have achieved about 3 percent growth without the inventory run-ups during 1996.

2. In 2008, the MOFE and the Ministry of Planning and Budget were merged into the Ministry of Strategy and Finance, while the authority of the MOFE on financial policies was transferred to the Financial Services Commission.

3. At a meeting of economic ministers chaired by President Kim Young-Sam on October 9, 1996, a plan to raise Korea's economic competitiveness by at least 10 percent was put forth and adopted.

4. The Monetary Board had been responsible for the formulation of monetary and credit policies and oversight of the Office of Bank Supervision before the establishment of the Financial Supervisory Commission in April 1998. The Financial Supervisory Service was established in January 1999 as Korea's first integrated supervisory authority responsible for oversight of banking, securities, insurance, and nonbank financial companies.

5. By the time Kia applied for court receivership, the group's borrowing from financial companies had reached W 9.7 trillion.

6. The 14 merchant banks were Cheongsol, Daegu, Daehan, Hansol, Hanwha, Jeil, Kyongnam, Kyungil, Nara, Samsam, Shinhan, Shinsegae, Ssangyong, and Ulsan.

7. It was thus a great relief to the state-run Korea Development Bank (KDB) when it managed to secure US$1.5 billion through a long-term overseas borrowing on September 17.

2

Origin of the Crisis

Divergent Views of the Crisis

Root Causes

The financial crisis in the Republic of Korea has been extensively studied and scrutinized by policy makers, academics, and market analysts in and outside Korea. While most analysts approach the subject with either an analytical framework or policy prescriptions in mind, some probe practical, legal, and criminal accountability issues as well. For example, in early 1998, the Board of Audit and Inspection, the government audit agency, conducted a special audit of the government's management of foreign exchange reserves and its financial market oversight. Similarly, there were a number of criminal cases during the postcrisis years. For nearly a month in early 1999, a special committee of the National Assembly, the legislative branch in Korea, sought an account of the crisis and the government's conduct.

While analysts of the crisis vary in their descriptions and explanations, many trace the root cause of the crisis to deeply embedded, but long-neglected, structural weaknesses in the economy. These range from crony capitalism and structural vulnerabilities in the corporate and financial sectors to the large current account deficits. Mismanagement of external liabilities is also cited. Others attribute the cause of the crisis to uncontrollable outside shocks. External elements often cited include the contagion arising from the crisis that erupted in Thailand in the summer of 1997, the sudden reversal of the flow of foreign capital because of the herd behavior of overseas lenders, sharp price drops for semiconductors and other major Korean export items, and the depreciation of the Japanese yen.

In chapter 1 of this book, the backdrop and the events leading up to the crisis are presented to provide the context within which the crisis unfolded in Korea. However, this is insufficient for a full analysis of the crisis. For a more thorough examination, we must go beyond the events and take a more comprehensive look at the local and international context. In this chapter, the root causes of the Korean financial crisis are traced through an analysis of the crisis in relation to the macroeconomy, structural flaws, capital liberalization, the international financial architecture, and the Korean government's pre- and postcrisis management of risk.

Precrisis Responses and Postcrisis Analysis

In analyzing the crisis, we must bear in mind an important point: the responses before the crisis hit and during the crisis did not have the benefit of hindsight. Many have pointed to the inevitability of the crisis. But the likelihood of a full-blown financial crisis was considered remote before the crisis erupted and was not taken seriously at the time. There are several reasons for this. First, in a highly fluid environment, actions must rely on imperfect information. The full and accurate assessment of a situation is all but impossible in such circumstances. This dilemma is confounded by the constraints decision makers face in collecting accurate information at the proper time. Even under the best conditions, the production of an optimal policy prescription is always a challenge, and the link between a policy action and the effect of the action is often not obvious, which complicates an already murky situation.

Second, the range of policy options available to policy makers is usually quite limited. Policy constraints take on added urgency whenever many conflicting priorities and interests are in play. This may mean that policy effectiveness is no longer the sole consideration or the main criterion for policy makers. Compromises usually have to be made, and the interests of parties with a stake in the outcome must be taken into account and accommodated as much as possible. The result is often that policy choices are narrowed, and decisions take more time. In small open economies such as Korea, policy options can become additionally restricted because of the necessity to heed prevailing global standards and the sentiment of markets, as well as the expectations of investors in the larger economies who shape the debate and set the priorities for others. In other words, the crisis response is not a painting on a clean canvas; rather, the canvas is already crowded.

Third, policy choices are often swayed by the beliefs and analytical tools of the decision makers; for example, it matters whether decision makers subscribe to the perceptions and prescriptions espoused by the rational expectations school or to those espoused by the neo-Keynesian school.

It is easy to contrast what happened with what should have happened if one has the benefit of 20–20 hindsight. This is not to say that ex post analysis merits less weight than ex ante analysis. Quite the contrary, not repeating the same mistake in the future requires that we engage in thorough ex post analyses so that the correct lessons are drawn from our past experiences.

The Macroeconomy and the Financial Crisis

The Link between Macroeconomic Fundamentals and the Financial Crisis

As the economy staggered toward crisis, President Kim Young-Sam and his economic ministers held a meeting on October 27, 1997. The meeting produced the assessment that, notwithstanding the deepening distress in financial markets, the soundness of Korea's economic fundamentals would protect the economy from the crisis that had engulfed Southeast Asian economies in the summer of that year. The International Monetary Fund (IMF) had made a similar point on October 15 at its annual consultation meeting, arguing that there were clear downside risks, but that Korea's macroeconomy was firmly grounded, and the current account deficit was improving. While acknowledging Korea's external funding difficulties, the IMF noted that it expected appropriate steps to be taken by the government. It also stressed that its main concern was the efficiency and soundness of Korea's financial system, in particular, the clean-up of distressed bank assets. Thus, both the IMF and the Korean government shared the view that, because of its strong macroeconomic fundamentals, Korea would be spared from the crisis that was spreading across Southeast Asia.

So, it pays to ask: why was it being argued that a sound macroeconomy would keep a financial crisis at bay? First, in terms of the relationship between economic growth and financial crisis, the likelihood of a crisis is small if growth is at least strong enough to service external debt. Theoretically, external debt does not grow if the economic growth rate exceeds the interest rate on the external debt. Otherwise, the ability to service foreign debt diminishes, and the size of the debt rises.

The question then is whether an economy can continue to borrow from external sources and achieve growth at a rate higher than the interest rate on the debt. This is not really a proper question because it assumes that one must engage in a Ponzi scheme in finance, whereby borrowed money is continually used to pay off interest and principal. If a country is to maintain the ability to service its foreign debt, it must be able to hold a balanced or favorable long-term position on its current account.

The difference between private savings and investment usually shows up as the sum of the government budget balance and the trade balances. The existence of a current account deficit would therefore mean that investment is in excess of savings or that there is a government deficit. It is paramount that significant savings and productive investment, along with a sound government budget balance, be maintained to ensure the healthy, long-term ability to service debt.

This is why domestic savings, a current account balance, and a government budget balance are used as key measures of the strength and the direction of a country's currency. The typical pattern observed in a crisis country is a prolonged economic slump accompanied by a large budget deficit and current account deficit leading to spiraling external debt that undermines the country's debt servicing ability and leaves the country vulnerable to a debilitating crisis.

A Look at Korea's Precrisis Macroeconomy

Key macroeconomic indicators for Korea from 1993 to 1996 are shown in table 2.1. During the period, the economy forged ahead with high growth and fairly good employment rates. Inflation was under control, and the government budget balance was showing a surplus, albeit a small one.

Even in October 1997, when Southeast Asia was struggling under a massive financial crisis and large Korean companies and financial institutions were being squeezed under the weight of out-of-control bankruptcies and rising nonperforming loans, the IMF projected the growth of the Korean economy at around 6 percent for 1997 and 1998 and inflation at

Table 2.1 Macroeconomic Indicators, 1993–96
percent

Indicator	*1993*	*1994*	*1995*	*1996*
GDP growth rate	5.5	8.3	8.9	6.8
Growth rate of gross national income	5.7	8.4	8.1	4.8
Unemployment rate	2.8	2.4	2.0	2.0
Growth rate of consumer prices	4.8	6.2	4.5	4.9
Current account, US$, millions	989.5	-3,866.9	-8,507.7	-23,004.7
Ratio of current account to GDP	0.3	-1.0	-1.7	-4.4
Ratio of gross savings to GDP	36.2	35.5	35.5	33.8
Ratio of government budget balance to GDP	0.3	0.4	0.3	0.3

Source: Bank of Korea (BOK) 1999a.
Note: GDP = gross domestic product.

or below 4 percent. Indeed, an observer looking at Korea's macroeconomy alone would have similarly concluded that the economy was on track and faring better than many others.

One source of potential trouble was the mounting current account deficit. Other than four consecutive years of fairly substantial current account surpluses beginning in 1986 and the US$989 million surplus in 1993, the economy showed persistent current account deficits. In 1996, the deficit reached US$23 billion, one of the largest deficits ever. This was viewed by many as excessively high for a small, open economy such as Korea, even though it was still below 5 percent of gross domestic product (GDP).

The current account deficit came to US$7.4 billion in the first quarter of 1997, but it showed significant improvement in the following quarter. In October 1997, the IMF forecast a deficit of US$14 billion for 1997 and US$11.5 billion for 1998.

Despite the current account deficits, including the large jump in 1996, Korea managed to keep the deficit under 5 percent of GDP. It was generally assumed at the time that a current account deficit below the 5 percent threshold would be manageable and would not pose any particular risk to the economy. The consensus forecast was that the deficit would reach around 2.9 percent of GDP in 1997 and 2.3 percent in 1998. Thus, the spike in 1996 was viewed as an aberration, and the deficit was expected to return soon to a more normal level. All in all, Korea's current account deficit was considered within the normal range, and the macroeconomy was not thought to be in danger.

Nonetheless, there were other signs that all was not well with the economy. First, despite the relatively high GDP growth, the economy was headed for a contraction beginning in the second half of 1995. A sharp rise in inventory was one piece of the evidence for this. In 1996, the growth of real gross national income, a key measure of economic well-being, was 4.8 percent, well below the 6.8 percent real GDP growth for the year. Moreover, the nominal GDP growth rate of 6.25 percent trailed the 6.29 percent interest rate on external borrowing.[1] These broad indicators undercut the prognosis that the macroeconomy was sound.

Another point of contention aside from the huge level of the current account deficit was the persistent overvaluation of the Korean won. Some analysts pointed to evidence for such an overvaluation from 1995 to 1996 (table 2.2). It was argued that, if Korea's high wage growth was taken into account, the real exchange rate would be overvalued even more. The disparate depreciation of the won and the Japanese yen relative to the U.S. dollar in 1995 and 1996 was taken as another sign of the overvalued won. While the Japanese yen fell 13.9 percent against the dollar during the period, the won depreciated only 6.6 percent.

The overvaluation of the won may have contributed to the financial crisis through two channels. One was by widening the trade deficit by encouraging imports and discouraging exports. It has been pointed out

Table 2.2 Trends in the Real Exchange Rate, 1993–97
index, 1993 = 100

Indicator	*1993*	*1994*	*1995*	*1996*	*1997*
¥/W	100	104.3	94.7	87.9	92.6
US$/W	100	95.0	91.3	98.3	101.3

Source: Cho 1998.

that the large deficit in 1996 stemmed from the overvalued won, along with reduced export earnings because of the oversupply of some of Korea's major export goods. Another channel was the speculative attacks that fueled exchange rate volatility. Many blamed the attacks on the Thai baht, which was widely seen as overvalued and which was considered one of the culprits in the crisis in Thailand (see chapter 1). To be sure, speculative attacks on an overvalued won were not the root cause of the crisis. Because Korea had controls in place at the time that barred the short selling of the won for purposes other than legitimate business transactions in the forward market, it was difficult for speculators to attack the won freely.

So, taken as a whole, the macroeconomy was clearly showing signs of vulnerability before the crisis erupted. The question is whether the macroeconomic vulnerability was sufficiently serious to bring the economy to the brink of a major financial crisis. The macroeconomy did not raise any particular alarm (see above). Indeed, the macroeconomic outlook was quite favorable. Forecasts showed the GDP growth rate in the 6 percent range for 1997 and 1998, inflation within 4 percent, and the current account deficit below US$10 billion. The macroeconomic concerns could not be easily dismissed, but few believed they were serious enough to raise the prospect of a financial crisis around the corner. Rather, it was structural problems such as the high wages and the low level of efficiency in the microeconomy that had the market worried.

External Liabilities and the Crisis

The accumulation of a large external debt burden over a prolonged period can have an adverse effect on a country's debt servicing ability. The magnitude of Korea's external debt therefore merits close scrutiny. Korea's external debt statistics were compiled using World Bank standards, whereby external debt is essentially defined as the balance of the unpaid debt among domestic borrowers such as the public sector, the private sector, and the financial sector. However, when the crisis broke out, foreign lenders questioned Korea's external debt figures, arguing that the large liabilities of the overseas branches of domestic banks must be included in the total debt. Following consultations with the IMF, the government decided to include in the gross external debt statistics the borrowing by the overseas branches, as well as other offshore borrowing by domestic financial companies. The government referred to the new figures as gross external liabilities. Table 2.3 sums up changes in Korea's external debt situation around the time of the crisis.

The gross external liabilities figures would have placed Korea among the moderately indebted borrower group or the borrower without debt servicing problem group under the World Bank criteria (table 2.4). The World Bank classifies countries that borrow from overseas lenders into heavily indebted countries, moderately indebted countries, and countries without debt servicing problems using four basic criteria.[2]

However, a close examination of the external debt figures shows that the pace of Korea's gross external liabilities and net external debt (in U.S. dollars) from 1994 to 1996 easily exceeded Korea's nominal GDP growth rate. Moreover, in 1996, the nominal GDP growth rate fell slightly short of the interest rates charged by foreign lenders. These observations, taken together, make clear that Korea's debt servicing ability was deteriorating well before the onset of the crisis. In this regard, it might be argued that red

Table 2.3 External Debt, 1992–97
US$, billions

Indicator	*1992*	*1993*	*1994*	*1995*	*1996*	*1997*
External debt[a]	42.8	43.9	66.0	87.1	112.6	128.0
(Long term)	(24.3)	(24.7)	(37.2)	(44.1)	(53.1)	(79.4)
(Short term)	(18.5)	(19.2)	(28.8)	(42.9)	(59.5)	(48.6)
Public sector	5.6	3.8	7.2	6.7	6.1	22.3
Private sector	13.7	15.6	25.2	31.2	40.9	47.1
Financial sector	23.5	24.4	33.7	49.2	65.6	58.7
Gross external liabilities[b]	62.9	67.0	97.4	127.5	163.5	159.2
(Long term)	(26.0)	(26.7)	(43.5)	(55.6)	(70.2)	(95.7)
(Short term)	(37.0)	(40.3)	(53.9)	(71.9)	(93.3)	(63.6)
Public sector	5.6	3.8	7.2	6.7	6.1	22.3
Private sector	13.7	15.6	25.2	31.2	40.9	47.1
Financial sector	43.6	47.5	65.1	89.6	116.5	89.9

Source: Foreign Exchange Regulations and External Debt Division, Ministry of Finance and Economy.

a. Resident liabilities determined according to World Bank standards.

b. External debt (defined by the World Bank), plus borrowing by overseas branches and offshore borrowing by domestic financial companies.

Table 2.4 Indicators of the Ability to Service External Debt, 1991–98

Indicator	*1991*	*1992*	*1993*	*1994*	*1995*	*1996*	*1997*	*1998*
Gross external liabilities,[a] US$, billions	—	62.9	67.0	97.4	127.4	163.4	159.2	148.7
Year-on-year growth rate, %	—	—	(6.52)	(45.37)	(30.80)	(28.26)	(–2.57)	(–6.60)
Current GDP,[b] US$, billions	295.1	314.7	345.7	402.4	489.4	520.0	476.6	321.3
Year-on-year growth rate, %	(16.87)	(6.64)	(9.85)	(16.40)	(21.62)	(6.25)	(–8.35)	(–32.59)
Gross external liabilities/GDP, %	—	19.99	19.38	24.20	26.03	31.42	33.40	46.28
Net external debt,[c] US$, billions	11.9	11.1	7.9	24.5	35.5	53.8	54.1	20.1
Year-on-year growth rate, %	—	(–6.72)	(–28.83)	—	(44.90)	(51.55)	(0.56)	(–62.85)
Proportion relative to GDP	(4.71)	(3.76)	(2.51)	(2.51)	(7.25)	(10.35)	(11.35)	(6.26)
Interest rate on overseas borrowing by the Korea Development Bank,[d] %	—	—	6.51	7.68	7.54	6.29	12.43	11.19
Trade balance/current GDP, %	-2.31	-0.56	0.67	-0.71	-0.91	-2.88	-0.67	12.81
Debt service ratio,[c] %	6.0	6.2	9.1	6.2	5.4	5.8	6.4	12.8
Interest service ratio,[c] %	—	—	2.9	2.2	2.5	2.6	3.0	4.4
Gross external liabilities/exports, %	—	82.08	81.47	101.44	101.87	125.97	116.92	112.38
Growth rate of exports, %	10.54	6.63	7.31	16.75	30.25	3.72	4.97	-2.83

Source: Ham 1999.

Note: — = not available.

a. As of the end of the year.

b. Based on the 1995 New System of National Accounts.

c. Net external debt before 1993, debt service ratio, and interest service ratio are understood according to World Bank definitions.

d. Year-average yields on 10-year bonds to be matured in 2003.

flags should have been raised about Korea's macroeconomic weaknesses and the magnitude of the external debt.

However, it bears repeating: the macroindicators widely used at the time did not point to an imminent crisis in Korea. This suggests that problems with macroeconomic soundness or debt servicing ability may be necessary, but not sufficient conditions for a crisis. Korea's experience clearly demonstrates that a seemingly sound economy is no guarantee against a financial crisis if the creditworthiness of the economy is called into question because of a particular series of events or a sudden external shock. In this sense, a financial crisis may possess the characteristics of a game based on confidence that the actors play within the economy. We note elsewhere above that the loss of confidence stemming from weaknesses in the macroeconomy must be given due weight, but the fragility of microeconomic factors had an even bigger role in the case of Korea. So, what were the microeconomic factors and how did they contribute to Korea's financial crisis?

Korea's Structural Weaknesses and Vulnerabilities

The Slow Pace of Reform

Korea's precrisis economy was under strain because of a high-cost, low-efficiency dilemma (see chapter 1). By 1997, the distress in the corporate and financial sectors was palpable. Starting with the Hanbo Group, a cascade of large corporate bankruptcies shook the economy. During the year, 62 listed companies actually entered bankruptcy, more than a 10-fold increase from the six companies the previous year.

The problems were no less serious in the financial sector. The share of nonperforming bank loans had jumped from 4.1 percent at the end of 1996 to 6.4 percent by the end of 1997. Among merchant banks, the value of nonperforming loans had soared from W 1.3 trillion at the end of 1996 to W 3.9 trillion by the end of October 1997. If the troubled loans of companies under suspended default are included, the value of nonperforming loans on the balance sheets of merchant banks came to approximately W 5.5 trillion.

In the meantime, efforts to amend outdated labor laws and inject greater flexibility into labor markets in an attempt to give fresh vigor to the economy badly faltered as a result of bitter social divisions and political posturing in the National Assembly. About the only initiative the reform efforts mustered was a two-year postponement of the implementation of laws allowing companies freely to lay off workers because of operational difficulties.

Not surprisingly, foreign lenders began to cast doubt on the ability of Korean corporate and financial companies to pay back their debts on time. Foreign companies contemplating direct investments in Korea also hesitated or decided not to invest and cited Korea's rigid labor market. The issue of confidence was coming into play.

It was difficult to dismiss the mounting problems in the corporate and financial sectors as merely a one-time predicament caused by a cyclical downturn. In reality, the problems were manifestations of cracks in the microfoundations supporting the activities of Korean business enterprises and financial companies. They were more structural in nature than cyclical. It was also true that many Korean businesses and financial firms lacked the wherewithal to cushion against hard times. Nor did they practice a sort of corporate governance that measured up to investor expectations of transparency and accountability. The economy continued to be dominated by the *chaebols* (the large family-controlled groups that dominate business in Korea), which seemed to be pursuing extensive growth and diversification. Many mockingly likened the chaebols to an octopus with numerous tentacles. Meanwhile, the technological prowess of Korea was being challenged by emerging countries even as it fell well short of the prowess of the developed countries.

Within Korea, social structures were becoming more pluralistic as the country developed. Conflicts among various interest groups were also becoming more frequent. But, despite the rapid changes, no effective systems had emerged to promote conflict resolution and build consensus on divisive issues so as to encourage harmony at the broad societal level. This was true not only in confrontations between labor and management. There was also extreme regionalism, as well as a bewildering array of interest groups with narrow economic or political agendas. Security concerns about the Democratic People's Republic of Korea were always present in the background. The forces of market liberalization and globalization were rapidly gaining momentum, and the world was shrinking. The rules and expectations of the market were changing, and global standards were being established and embraced. But the Republic of Korea stumbled badly on all these fronts. In a nutshell, the socioeconomic predicament Korea faced was largely a result of the failure to adapt to an evolving reality. The simple fact was that insufficient efforts had been undertaken since the 1970s to reform and revitalize the economy.

The Cracks in Korea's Microeconomic Foundations

Korea embarked on economic development in earnest in the 1960s through growth plans mapped out by the government. At the time, the government-led development strategy was the only realistic option available for catching up with the developed economies because of the limited pool of capital, skilled managers, and entrepreneurs. So, the government set the development priorities, selected the promising companies, and gave them beneficial and wide-ranging tax incentives. Long-term loans were also secured at home and abroad at favorable interest rates.

The strategy of pooling resources and skills with private sector companies proved successful in the early stages of economic development in narrowing the gap with the developed countries. In fact, the development strategy proved so effective that it was often hailed as a model for other developing countries. How successful was Korea? By the end of 1998, Korea's GDP ranked 12th, its exports 10th, and its imports 12th among the countries of the Organisation for Economic Co-operation and Development (OECD). In many respects, Korea's industrial structures also closely resembled those of the developed countries.

In appearance at least, Korea did look like it was rapidly catching up with the world's richest economies. Beneath the surface, however, there were many shortcomings and weaknesses, and many observers at home and abroad seized on these to question Korea's economic development model.

One key weakness was the wobbly financial foundation of Korean corporate and financial companies. Table 2.5 illustrates the relative financial weaknesses of Korean companies. Korean banks managed to hold their Bank for International Settlements capital ratios above the recommended 8 percent level until 1996, the year before the crisis. The amount of nonperforming assets was also shrinking. However, the problem was that Korea used prudential soundness criteria that were more generous—that is, less strict—than those used widely elsewhere. As a result, distresses that should have been identified and addressed remained either hidden or ignored. Too often, the standards used to classify bank assets and set loan-loss provisions were lax or questionable.

One crucial contributing factor behind the rickety financial structure of Korean companies was the long-accepted dependence on debt-financed investment that had originated during the early development era. Unlike the growth of foreign companies, business growth among Korean companies

Table 2.5 International Comparison of Corporate Financial Structures
percent

	Korea, Rep.				*United States*	*Japan*	*Taiwan, China*
Indicator	*1994*	*1996*	*1997*	*1998*	*1997*	*1997*	*1995*
Capital ratio	24.8	24.0	20.2	24.4	39.4	34.9	53.9
Total liabilities/ total assets	44.5	47.7	54.2	50.8	25.5	33.1	26.2
Current ratio	94.6	91.9	91.8	89.8	134.9	129.8	129.4
Fixed ratio	220.2	237.0	261.1	242.5	166.0	133.0	109.7

Source: BOK (various years), *Financial Statement Analysis.*

was associated with the accumulation of debt. So, it is important to analyze the effects of long-accumulated debt on the financial soundness of Korean companies and the overall economy.

It may be argued that debt-financed business growth makes strategic sense in an expanding economy. However, if revenue growth becomes sluggish and companies face a tough business environment, debt-financed growth loses its appeal, and the downside risks become real. Corporate weaknesses quickly spill over to the financial sector and can threaten the entire economy. This is particularly true if large companies with huge debts are mismanaged and encounter difficulties in expanding.

Large business failures had occurred from time to time throughout Korea's economic development era. However, rather than letting these companies clean house through market mechanisms, the government came to the rescue and eliminated the mess through structural adjustments. In the late 1960s, Cheong Wa Dae—the Blue House, or executive office and official residence of the president of Korea—had a unit that coordinated the restructuring of failing companies. In 1972, the government issued the August 3 Measures, which protected all heavily indebted companies. The government-led restructuring of troubled private companies continued in the 1980s through, for example, the restructuring of heavy industries and chemical industries in the early 1980s and the Kukje Group in 1985.

The government usually arranged for financial assistance or the takeover of failing companies. The provision of financial assistance raised the obvious question of favors and privileges for a select few. The takeovers were perceived as government favors for the companies that acquired the troubled entities through the schemes. Meanwhile, the targeted companies likened the takeovers to theft, pointing out that other companies were in trouble, but were left untouched.

Direct government interventions in the management of scarce capital resources were considered crucial to the success of the economic development strategy. Thus, rather than acting as rational profit-seeking commercial business enterprises, financial companies were forced to assume the role of agents of the government in allocating capital wherever the government wished. And, as companies became increasingly dependent on loans, the demand for capital always outpaced the supply.

The primary focus of financial companies was on who should receive their loans. Almost the only criteria was whether the borrower had sufficient collateral to cover the loan in case of default or whether the borrower was a sufficiently large company. There was a widespread belief that large companies would never be allowed to fail because they were important beneficiaries and managers of the government's priority development projects. The same was also the case of financial companies because of the threat their failure would represent to the broader economy. Thus, when such companies ran into trouble, the government made sure to let them carry on their business, often after special financing had been arranged by the Bank of Korea (BOK), the central bank. As a result, there was not a single bank failure in Korea prior to the 1997 financial crisis.

The problem of moral hazard arising from the belief that some companies and banks were simply too big or too important to fail was clear. Banks knew that the government would come to the rescue if they ran into trouble and, accordingly, did not hesitate to give massive loans to large companies even if the risk was high. For their part, large companies believed, rightly, that their survival would not be seriously threatened as long as they ingratiated themselves and maintained cozy, well-greased relationships with those in powerful positions. Thus, they ventured recklessly into high-profit, high-risk initiatives. They took a bet: "heads I win, tails the government loses."

Extensive Growth above All

In such an environment, it made good sense for corporate and financial companies to focus on expanding and growing in size, but not necessarily based on their core competitive strengths. Leveraging their outsized borrowing ability, large companies concentrated on becoming larger and entering new areas of activity. Similarly, financial companies pursued a growth-above-all-else strategy by extending more credit to large companies, opening new branch operations, and trying to attract fresh customer deposits. Moreover, large corporate and financial companies came to rely on short-term financing for long-term facility investments or on long-term loans to establish more dominant positions against their competitors. They even managed to exploit the premium from the interest rate differences between short- and long-term financing in the process. Safeguards against liquidity shortfalls or maturity mismatches were not seriously contemplated.

The pursuit of extensive growth above all else led inevitably to the concentration of economic power among only a few chaebols, a grave structural threat to the economy. In 1997, according to data of Statistics Korea, the Korea National Statistical Office, companies belonging to the top 30 chaebols accounted for 40.0 percent of all the goods shipped to consumer markets and 38.2 percent of the value added in the economy, but only 18.1 percent of the workforce. At the end of April in the same year, according to data of the Korea Fair Trade Commission, the government's competition watchdog, each of the top 30 chaebols owned an average of 27.3 companies in 19.8 distinct lines of business.

One salient characteristic of the chaebols is the commanding monopolistic market power they wield in numerous lines of business. Because of their diversity and their grip on a wide range of industrial sectors, their conglomerate power far exceeds the market power of a monopolistic company active in only one area of business; they therefore have distinct competitive advantages.

However, traditionally, the chaebols have suffered from an utter lack of transparency and accountability (discussed in detail on page 50, *The Unending Cycle*). Their concentration of economic power led to wide-ranging socioeconomic problems such as unsavory ties between businesses and the government and unfair competition with non-chaebol companies. Meanwhile, many of the diversified chaebol businesses struggled with difficulties generated by overinvestment and inefficiency. Petrochemicals, semiconductors, automobiles, and the aerospace industry, among others, are typical examples of industrial sectors in which the chaebols had made excessive, overlapping investments in the years leading up to the financial crisis.

Inevitably, some chaebol-affiliated companies began to show cracks. However, rather than allowing the poorly performing businesses to fail, the chaebols pulled them along with the rest of their affiliated companies through mutual debt guarantees and intratrading in an effort to keep the mounting distress in the shadows. By 1997, this was no longer viable because the entire economy was under siege.

The Lagging Technological Base

Despite the drive for significant growth, the technological base of Korean firms was well below that of companies in the developed countries and was thus evidence of a serious structural weakness in the economy.

In Korea's industrial development, the low-wage workforce in the 1960s made up for an acute shortage of capital and technology and laid the foundation for the development of light industries. In the late 1970s, heavy industries and chemical industries emerged, followed by semiconductors and information technologies in the 1980s. Throughout this period, however, firms continued to rely on imports of key components and capital goods. This was partly a result of the focus of firms on the development of component assembling technologies that would yield quick returns on investment. Korea thereby achieved a globally competitive position in processing technologies. However, in development technologies for core components and capital goods, it continued to depend on the developed countries.

The problem of dependence on the technologies of developed countries was exacerbated by the rapid advances in the economies of China and Southeast Asia. Thus, Korea faced the dilemma of lagging behind developed countries, while being chased closely by emerging countries. In a report titled *Revitalizing the Korean Economy toward the 21st Century*, Booz Allen Hamilton (1997) depicted Korea's technological dilemma with the image of a nut in a nutcracker.

As new waves of technology sweep across the globe, knowledge (information) is increasingly being developed, stored, and transferred in digital format, and many advanced economies are making significant strides in the transition to a truly knowledge-based economy. Indeed, it is estimated that nearly half the GDP of leading OECD countries is already being produced by knowledge-based industries. From computers, aerospace, and electronics to communication and information, the growth in knowledge-based industries has been phenomenal in recent years. For Korea, the challenge has been to catch up with advanced economies and accelerate the transition to such an economy.

Social Conflict and a Lack of Discipline

Social stability is crucial for sustained economic growth because few investments for the future take place if the present is uncertain. Thus, in an extreme example, no meaningful economic activity can occur in times of war. Even in peacetime, bitter conflicts among social groups or competing regions within a country severely diminish the likelihood of normal economic activity. Political wrangling and acrimony produce the same result by making it all but impossible for a government to pursue consistent economic policies. It is, in fact, quite common for a developing country to be faced with stunted investment because of a volatile political environment.

One undeniable risk factor that has always lurked in the background for the Republic of Korea is the Democratic People's Republic of Korea. The unpredictable regime there gives pause not only to the Republic of Korea, but also to foreign investors. Indeed, when Standard and Poor's downgraded Korea's sovereign rating on October 24, 1997, it cited the factor of the Democratic People's Republic of Korea—this time the hostile relations between the former and the latter and the extreme economic hardship of the latter—as one of its justifications.

The inability of the Republic of Korea to resolve emerging small and large social conflicts, as well as deepening divisions and chasms within society beginning in the second half of the 1980s, also weighed heavily on the economy. The most serious conflicts were confrontations between labor and management. In the course of Korea's economic development beginning in the 1960s, all socioeconomic conflicts were harshly suppressed by the government, usually under the pretence of national security or political stability.

Obviously, this is no way to secure long-term socioeconomic order or harmony, because along with economic development came more diverse socioeconomic challenges and forces. For example, according to the Ministry of Labor, the number of professional occupations had jumped from 3,260 in 1969 to 10,451 by 1986. By 1995, the number had risen even higher, to 11,537. Data of Statistics Korea show that approximately 63 percent of the workforce was employed in the agricultural and fishery sectors in the 1960s, but the figure had dropped to 24.9 percent by 1985 and 12.4 percent by 1995. The workforce during these years was increasingly dominated by growth in the share of production workers and office administrators and managers.

As the population became more well educated and information began to flow more easily, society as a whole also became more open and individualistic. This metamorphosis in society meant that it was no longer feasible for the government to instill social harmony by using the bait of economic development. Consensus and harmony had to be backed by the free will of the people.

After the declaration on June 29, 1987 by Roh Tae-Woo, the presidential candidate of the ruling party, that the presidential election would be direct and democratic, Korea entered a new era of freedom after decades of authoritarian military rule. But the democratization process was also accompanied by a tendency toward aggression and disregard for the rule of law. A culture of self-interest had settled in.

This was clearly evident in labor relations. Negotiations counted for little in settling differences between management and the labor unions. Mostly, it was a sheer display of power that ultimately resolved differences and conflicts. In the past, the authoritarian rule of the government had maintained the appearance of order. In the rapidly democratizing Korea, self-interest groups sought an upper hand through blatant aggression.

In the political arena, it was not the competition of ideas or policies that drove political parties or politicians, but bitter regionalism and region-based political parties. Sorely lacking were any democratic structures that might have alleviated the pressure to resort to confrontation each time a conflict arose. The political impasse left little room for mature and rational public discourse, and this inevitably took a heavy toll on the economy.

After the Kim Young-Sam administration came into office, expectations were high that the country had finally moved beyond the extremism of the predemocracy era and might now become a more orderly, well-balanced, and mature democracy.[3] But this was not to be. Public systems of control, restraint, and accountability, after years of neglect, quickly broke down.

The symptoms of the lack of discipline became painfully clear when a major bridge and a large department store in Seoul collapsed, killing hundreds of people because timely countermeasures had not been taken. Then, subway trains derailed because of negligent rail repairs. Likewise, in the private lives of ordinary citizens, it was hard to find many motives for the respect and goodwill needed to encourage social discipline.

The Unending Cycle: Locking Out Nature and the Lack of Global Standards

Outside Korea, the world was changing rapidly. Globalization was accelerating the flow of goods and services across borders. Businesses were building new networks and forming strategic alliances in an effort to improve production and marketing. They were creating cooperative relations even while competing in the global marketplace.

Companies invest where there is well-developed market infrastructure and a pool of abundant skilled workers. Where this appears is not important as long as the investment environment is attractive. The question of domestic or foreign ownership no longer matters as much as it once did. A borderless ownership concept has taken root, whether foreign companies hire local workers or domestic companies invest abroad. So, to outbid others, countries are striving to create a business-friendly climate and attract foreign investors, often through generous tax incentives on dividends and on interest income.

As the pace of capital account liberalization picked up and as the barriers to cross-border capital flows came down, financial markets were rapidly becoming integrated. Pension funds and other institutional investors expanded their investment portfolios to include assets abroad because returns were unavailable at home. Businesses looked beyond home markets for cheaper, more abundant capital. Cross-border financing activities among financial institutions rose sharply.

Globalization helped open new export markets and stimulated the investment from abroad that boosted the productivity of industries at home. Thus, first and foremost, Korea's justification for globalization was its own national interests, not any need to kowtow to outside pressures to open up domestic markets.

Korea pushed hard for globalization, but many Koreans were convinced that foreign investors should be excluded. This narrow attitude toward foreign inflows was so rigid that many foreign companies viewed Korea as one of the most difficult places for business, and domestic companies continued to depend on the government for policy support and protection. It thus came as no surprise that Korea lagged well behind China and Singapore in attracting foreign investment. Long protected by government regulations, domestic corporations and financial companies never developed significant international competitive power because of their weaknesses of high cost and low efficiency.

If Korea was to take advantage of globalization and market integration, it had to adapt to the prevailing global order as quickly as possible. This did not mean all that was right about Korea had to be suppressed. Rather, it meant embracing standards and practices widely accepted elsewhere, while exploiting Korea's own strengths. In the 19th century, Korea had missed an opportunity to reform and modernize in parallel with the world economic powers. It could avoid making the same mistake by taking bold steps to improve its business standards and practices so that they were on a par with the best in the world. Passively dismissing the need for change merely as a reflection of external pressure would not serve Korea's long-term interests.

With globalization has arisen the urgency of standardizing and harmonizing business practices across the world. Cultural barriers and divergent levels of economic development are obstacles to globalization. Among the key benefits of standardization and harmonization are the reduction in the constraints on information flows, enhanced technology acquisition, the elimination of technical hurdles to international trade, and better access to global financial markets. Cross-border differences in industrial standards, quality controls, measurement, and health and sanitation standards act as impediments to the international trade in goods and services.[4]

There was a growing transnational movement to identify global best practices and standards in management systems with the goal of improving transparency and ensuring a level playing field in cross-border competition. Widely accepted standards included the International Accounting Standards (International Accounting Standards Board) and the International Standards on Auditing and the International Audit Practice Statements (International Federation of Accountants). Others included the Core Principles for Effective Banking Supervision (Basel Committee on Banking Supervision), the Objectives and Principles of Securities Regulation and Disclosure Standards to Facilitate Cross-Border Offering and Initial Listings by Multinational Issuers (International Organization of Securities Commissions), and the Principles of Corporate Governance (OECD).

Despite this movement toward global standards, Korea stagnated in several important areas. Standardization in the trade in goods and services was more or less in place. However, in corporate governance with respect to transparency or accountability, Korea fell short of the expected standards. In Korea, corporate governance was directed or ignored arbitrarily by owner-controlled management. This was true even among listed companies, leaving little or no room for minority shareholders or creditors to exercise checks on management.

In a formal sense, corporate accounting in Korea appeared to measure up to global standards. But, in substance and practice, there were too many loopholes and exemptions that deviated from the original intentions behind the standards. In particular, the rules on loan-loss provisioning and securities valuations among financial companies were frequently modified at the whim of regulators. The justification offered for such sporadic prudential control was that banks incurring losses under strict standards would not be able to maintain public confidence. There were also numerous flaws and shortcomings in the auditing of corporate financial reporting, and it was not uncommon for companies suddenly to declare bankruptcy even though they had been audited and given a seal of approval as viable ongoing business concerns. Because there was such little transparency and because poor practices had been generally accepted in the corporate management world for years, the credibility of Korea was already suspect when the series of corporate bankruptcies rocked the country in early 1997.

The Risks of Capital Liberalization

Capital Account Liberalization and the Current Account Balance

Capital liberalization usually refers to the free flow of capital and the more efficient allocation of capital across borders. There is a risk that the flow of capital, if unrestricted, can quickly deviate from the expected course, lead to currency speculation and volatile market conditions, and cause the affected economy to become vulnerable to a crisis. Because of this and other risks that typically accompany capital liberalization, it is imperative that appropriate policies and prudential controls be put in place to prevent disruptions in normal market activities. Under such circumstances, policy makers must recognize the importance of maintaining healthy current account balances in the course of capital liberalization, as well as the importance of the effective management of external debt.

Korea began to open up its equity markets to foreign investors in January 1992 as one of the first major steps toward the liberalization of its capital markets. Capital market liberalization accelerated following the successful conclusion of financial service negotiations during the Uruguay Round and after Korea joined the OECD in 1996. Capital liberalization meant that Korean corporate and financial companies could now easily expand their business networks in overseas markets and borrow from foreign lenders. Expecting the won to remain stable, Korean business and financial firms naturally preferred to borrow from foreign lenders, who offered lower interest rates relative to domestic lenders.

Thus, the movement of capital picked up sharply in the 1990s (table 2.6). The surge in inbound foreign portfolio investment and external borrowing was particularly striking during this period. The result was a surplus in the capital account and a reversal in the current account from a surplus to a deficit. From 1994 to 1996, a sharp increase in the capital account surplus began to exert upward pressure on the won. At the same time, because the capital account surplus was increasing the supply of money, the monetary authorities were obliged to seek new ways to recycle inflows of foreign exchange.[5]

It was soon accepted that the current account deficit could be easily kept under control through the inflow of foreign capital (that is, a capital account surplus). It was even argued by some in policy circles that, in an era of globalization, the international balance of payments no longer meant what it had once meant and that an unfavorable balance of payments position was no longer a serious drag on an economy (Nam 1998). It is usually the case that, in a liberalized capital market, it is much easier to keep a current account deficit under control through capital inflows. Its

Table 2.6 Trends in the Balance of Payments, 1986–98
annual average, US$, billions

Indicator	*1986–89*	*1990–93*	*1994–96*	*1997*	*1998*
Current account	8.66	–3.32	–11.79	–8.17	40.56
Capital account	-5.63	4.58	16.80	1.31	-3.25
Direct investment	0.06	–0.44	–1.92	–1.61	0.62
Foreign direct investment	0.80	0.82	1.64	2.84	5.42
Direct investment abroad	-0.75	–1.26	–3.56	–4.45	–4.80
Portfolio investment	-0.61	4.74	10.97	14.30	-1.88
Foreign portfolio investment	-0.31	4.52	14.40	12.28	-0.29
Stock	0.00	2.42	4.60	2.53	3.86
Bonds	-0.31	2.10	9.81	9.76	-4.15
Portfolio investment abroad	-0.30	0.22	–3.44	2.01	-1.59
Other investment	-4.84	0.66	8.27	-10.77	-2.16
Other foreign investment	-4.04	3.99	19.88	2.80	-8.86
Borrowing	-4.22	2.46	15.47	3.78	-1.51
Trade credits	0.37	1.28	3.85	–2.30	-7.10
Deposits	-0.19	0.25	0.56	1.32	-0.25
Other investment abroad	-0.80	–3.33	–11.62	–13.57	6.69
Lending	-0.18	–1.65	–4.19	–11.87	3.60
Trade credits	-0.15	0.82	–0.65	–3.31	0.92
Deposits	-0.47	–2.50	–6.78	1.61	2.17
Changes in reserves	-3.22	–1.10	–4.36	11.92	-30.98
Errors and omissions	0.20	–0.16	–0.65	–5.07	–6.33

Source: BOK (various years), *Balance of Payments.*

Note: Negative numbers indicate net outflow; otherwise, the numbers show net inflow.

membership in the OECD meant that Korea could now borrow at lower cost because the Bank for International Settlements classified the government debt of OECD member countries as risk-free assets. Nonetheless, even a well-managed current account deficit can lead to problems if the market sentiment reverses and a continued capital account surplus cannot be counted on (see elsewhere below).

In a highly volatile market environment in which interest and exchange rates can change direction quickly and in which investors are sensitive to even a small deviation from what they expected, maintaining a stable capital account surplus is not an easy task. Even with steady capital inflows, problems stemming from persistent current account deficits can multiply if the imported capital is directed toward overinvestment in a few selected industries or if it revolves around unproductive real estate investment and consumption.

Despite the risks arising because of the poorly managed influx of foreign capital, Korean companies aggressively embraced high-growth strategies backed by foreign funding following the capital liberalization in 1993. The economy thus became vulnerable to a sudden capital withdrawal by foreign investors. One important lesson for Korea from the crisis was that capital inflows can prove detrimental to the economy if they are associated with mismanaged current account deficits.

Korea and the Southeast Asian economies that were hit by the 1997 financial crisis all went through essentially the same precrisis experience: accelerated capital liberalization, large capital account surpluses, high rates of economic growth, overvalued currencies, and spiraling current account deficits. Seen from this perspective, it may be argued that the Asian financial crisis was a capital account crisis precipitated by failures to keep current account deficits in check in the midst of the influx of foreign capital in liberalized capital markets (Yoshitomi and Ohno 1999).

Capital Liberalization and External Debt Management

During the Kim Young-Sam administration, Korea's external debt spiked from US$62.9 billion in 1992 to US$163.4 billion in 1996, an increase of more than US$100 billion (see table 2.4). Only US$6.1 billion of the total was accounted for by public sector debt; the rest was mostly private sector debt.

With the surge in private sector debt, an alarming number of business and financial companies became exposed to currency risk. Worse, most of the external debt was based on floating interest rates. Thus, the danger was not limited to the currency risk; there was also an interest risk. Despite these risks, financial companies were, more or less, focused on borrowing cheaply from abroad and lending to borrowers at home at higher rates—the carry trade—without adequately covering their currency and interest rate positions.

Still worse, most financial companies were using their short-term borrowing for longer-term lending. For example, in 1996, short-term overseas borrowing by commercial banks and merchant banks totaled US$92.8 billion and US$12.0 billion, respectively, but short-term lending amounted to US$72.1 billion and US$800 million, respectively. The maturity mismatch thus heightened the likelihood of liquidity problems. It bears repeating: for the financial companies, exploiting the term premiums seemed to matter more than the liquidity risk.

Domestic financial companies were also using their borrowing from overseas to invest in overseas debt securities, particularly in bonds that had been issued in the Russian Federation and in Southeast Asian countries and that offered high yields at high risks. The practice of using short-term borrowing to invest in high-risk, high-yield securities picked up noticeably in the 1990s after Korean domestic financial companies had set up business operations in Hong Kong SAR, China. Thus, default risk was yet another serious risk that the domestic financial companies seemed willing to run.

Amid the rapidly deteriorating external debt situation, foreign lenders began to call back their loans in droves in late October 1997. Domestic commercial banks repaid approximately US$33 billion in external debt in 1997, but, in reality, they had no means of repaying in full. It is difficult to fathom now why Korean corporate and financial companies so recklessly mismanaged their external debt.

One obvious problem was that Korea's capital liberalization took place in the absence of any meaningful financial sector reforms. If a capital liberalization is to be effective at encouraging more efficient resource allocation and stability in the macroeconomy, financial companies must be well managed and strong because of the crucial role they play in directing capital flows. Not only do they have to possess significant business and risk management skills, but they also must possess a sound cushion of capital. They must conduct their business operations prudently and rationally in pursuit of profit; that is, they must act as if market discipline is being enforced. In Korea, the expectation that the government would come to the rescue of financial companies and never let them fail represented a moral hazard: financial companies were not acting with market discipline.

Another factor in understanding the recklessness of the external borrowing by Korean businesses and financial companies is represented by the deficiencies in the broad institutional arrangements in Korea. Effective prudential supervision should have been carried out and backed by a clearly established legal framework, that is, the watchdog function should have been upgraded. A system to identify and monitor weak points and risk factors and warn of problems on the horizon should have been created.

In retrospect, it is clear that Korea urgently needed to reinforce and augment the prudential supervision of financial institutions. In June 1997, there were some restrictions on foreign currency lending and leasing. But the restrictions—for example, that mid- and long-term foreign currency borrowing relative to foreign currency lending should be greater than 50 percent—either were too loose to deter any risky behavior or were simply ignored by financial companies and the supervisory authority. Prudential requirements on foreign exchange liquidity were not adopted until June 1997 amid the rapidly deteriorating liquidity situation in financial markets. Thus, the criticism that Korea rushed to remove capital controls, while paying little attention to the associated risks, is well founded.

One might nonetheless argue that an economy cannot afford to spend too much time preparing for capital liberalization, particularly given the rapid pace of globalization. To a significant degree, the capital markets in Korea had to be opened up because of the economic realities. Few would doubt that this might have been a unique opportunity to boost the economy. So, Korea should have laid a proper groundwork through sound prudential controls, along with a robust legal and regulatory framework that would have addressed the downsides of capital liberalization.

What was amiss in Korea's capital market opening was the absence of any specific preparations and implementation plans for the sequential liberalization of foreign direct investment (FDI), foreign investment in domestic securities markets, and external borrowing. The sequence was crucial because these steps would shape the external debt structure of Korea and determine how vulnerable the economy was going to be if it came under pressure.

In the Korean case, the proportion of external borrowing and foreign portfolio investment was much higher than the proportion of FDI. Indeed, the government offered numerous tax and other incentives to attract FDI. However, the government's efforts were met with a lukewarm response by foreign investors, many of whom were suspicious of the bitter labor relations in Korea. Moreover, domestic companies preferred growth financed by foreign debt rather than growth through joint ventures with foreign companies. The general industrial policy at the time also favored the protection of domestic companies rather than active efforts to attract foreign businesses so as to promote competition at home. The range of the initiatives that foreign companies could undertake in Korea was therefore quite restricted.

Excessive short-term external debt and a high share of foreign investment in domestic securities markets are two factors that can lead to an unstable external debt structure. This is so because both characteristics are usually associated with hot money. Instead of supporting more stable long-term borrowing, however, Korea aggressively removed capital controls on trade financing and short-term borrowing by financial companies as it liberalized the capital markets. The result was a shaky external debt structure. In fact, the government imposed annual quotas on mid- to long-term foreign borrowing by individual domestic financial companies, but did not impose any quotas on short-term borrowing. Only in March 1997 did the government lift the restrictions on mid- and long-term borrowing because of the pressure of the Hanbo default and the rapidly deteriorating overseas borrowing conditions.

From time to time, financial companies face temporary difficulties repaying external debt. In such situations, foreign exchange reserves can be utilized if there are ample reserves and the fundamental debt servicing ability of the financial companies is not in doubt. Foreign lenders also take into account whether the government is willing to act as the lender of last resort and tap into its reserves to repay external debt. The size of the reserves is thus a crucial factor. If investors sense that the reserves are inadequate relative to the magnitude of the short-term external debt, they may overreact or even panic.

Relative to the short-term debt, Korea's foreign exchange reserves were at low levels. The short-term external debt (measured using World Bank criteria) was 2.06 times greater than the foreign exchange reserves at the end of June 1997 (table 2.7). Even relative to the crisis countries in Southeast Asia, Korea's reserves were low and its short-term debt was high.

According to official government policy, the reserves had to be sufficient to cover potential risks arising because of the Democratic People's Republic of Korea. The reality, however, was that the reserves could not even readily offset the short-term external debt. One key contributing factor in this shortage in foreign exchange reserves was the fact that the BOK deposited a substantial portion of the reserves in domestic commercial banks, which, in turn, used them for lending to domestic companies. The reserves available to repay external debt were only barely adequate to cover imports for two and a half months, the level recommended by the IMF.

Capital Liberalization and Currency Overvaluation

Because the exchange rate is an important variable affecting all major trade and capital accounts in an open economy, the maintenance of an exchange rate that adequately reflects market realities is crucial in keeping crisis at bay in times of economic difficulty. Beginning in March 1990, Korea adopted the market average exchange rate system to reflect market movements. However, the won failed to track market valuation adequately and became overvalued, a distortion that proved consequential in the 1997 financial crisis (see elsewhere above). Why did the won not adequately reflect the market valuation of the currency? What was wrong with Korea's exchange rate system?

There are several answers. First, the government's exchange rate policy was significantly influenced by the government's desire to maintain price stability. Korea's heavy dependence on imported raw materials, as well as its weak currency, could always become a cause of inflation. A natural bias therefore existed in favor of a strong won as a way to tame inflation at home. But a strong won tended to lead to a current account deficit. In

Table 2.7 Ratio of Short-Term External Debt to Foreign Reserves, Crisis Countries
percent

Date	*Indonesia*	*Korea, Rep.*	*Malaysia*	*Philippines*	*Thailand*	*Argentina*	*Brazil*	*Chile*	*Mexico*
June 1990	2.21	1.06	0.22	3.18	0.59	2.09	2.63	0.89	2.24
June 1994	1.73	1.61	0.25	0.41	0.99	1.33	0.70	0.51	1.72
June 1997	1.70	2.06	0.61	0.85	1.45	1.21	0.79	0.45	1.19

Source: Federal Reserve Bank of Atlanta 1999.

retrospect, the government's decision in 1996 not to adjust the won to markets, but to focus instead on controlling inflation and on a campaign to increase competitiveness by 10 percent was not wise. Price stability and export competitiveness should not have been pursued through an overvalued currency; rather, they should have been pursued in parallel with steps to adjust the currency to market prices.

Second, during 1995–96, as the pace of capital liberalization picked up, there was a surge in capital inflows. The Korean economy has relatively small foreign exchange markets, and the sudden increase in capital from abroad represented pressure for the appreciation of the currency. The government's response was to redirect the inbound foreign capital back overseas and direct the central bank to intervene in the markets and buy foreign currencies. However, such an intervention inevitably leads to increases in the monetary base. So, the BOK implemented sterilization measures to offset the capital inflows. Data analysis during the 1990s indicated that approximately 70 percent of the capital originating from abroad was sterilized. In the short run, sterilization can be effective in countering the growth of the monetary base, but it also exerted upward pressure on interest rates at home, which was a fresh incentive for domestic firms and financial institutions to borrow from foreign lenders at lower rates. This meant that the pressure on the won to appreciate was maintained.

The impossible trinity hypothesis or trilemma—the simultaneous existence of a fixed exchange rate, the free movement of capital, and an independent monetary policy—may be instructive in the case here. It is said that achieving even two of the three is a challenge in most countries. In short, under a fully liberalized capital market, it is exceedingly difficult to maintain an exchange rate that holds the current account in balance, while exercising an independent monetary policy that encourages price stability and employment. The challenge is to strive for balance in the combination of foreign exchange rate policy, monetary policy, and fiscal policy.

The International Financial Architecture and the Financial Crisis

The Crisis-Prone International Financial Architecture

It has been assumed up to this point that the international financial architecture provides a neutral backdrop for the analysis of the origins of Korea's financial crisis. What if the assumption is false, and the shortcomings and flaws of the international financial architecture rendered Korea highly susceptible to financial crisis?

One should recall that the 1997 Asian financial crisis began in Thailand and spread to Korea through Malaysia; Indonesia; the Philippines; Singapore; Taiwan, China; and Hong Kong SAR, China. The contagion affected Hong Kong SAR, China; Singapore; and Taiwan, China less than the rest of the Asian economies. However, it also sparked sharp swings in the exchange rates of these economies. While the crisis economies shared many similarities, they also differed in many notable ways. Nonetheless, the crisis spread indiscriminately throughout the region.

It has been observed that the frequency and the severity of financial crises picked up appreciably beginning in the 1980s when major financial reforms and capital liberalization were undertaken worldwide. The foreign debt crisis triggered in 1982 by the declaration by Mexico that it was imposing a moratorium on its foreign debt was so severe in South America that the 1980s were dubbed the lost decade in the region. In 1992, speculative attacks by hedge funds on the British pound confounded the monetary authorities of the United Kingdom and led to a sharp depreciation of the pound. The effect was felt in Italy and Spain, and the lira and the peseta both took a nosedive. Finland also experienced a significant currency depreciation, a severe economic contraction, and a financial crisis. This was followed by distress in the European Monetary System in 1993, a renewed crisis in Mexico in 1994, the Asian financial crisis in 1997, and the crisis in Brazil and Russia in 1998.

The seeming ease with which a financial crisis can spread from one country to another and the increased frequency and severity of such crises in recent years certainly raise questions about the international financial architecture. An apt analogy may be the cause-effect relationship between car accidents and road conditions; that is, it may well be the case that one or two accidents at the same sharp curve on the same road can be attributed either to the lack of skills of the driver or to problems with the vehicle involved, but, if similar accidents occur repeatedly at the same location, then one might blame the road conditions (Stiglitz 1999).

The international financial architecture in the late 1990s had been influenced by a series of market upheavals since the early 1970s. The collapse of the fixed exchange rate system under the Bretton Woods regime in the early 1970s heralded the arrival of flexible exchange rates. Capital market liberalization subsequently accelerated worldwide in the 1980s. Financial market reform and deregulation, which had begun gradually in the 1970s, also swept across markets in the 1980s.

Such worldwide market-oriented financial innovation generated a fundamental transformation in the understanding of the financial scenery. Whereas the fixed exchange rate system did not leave much room to maneuver among monetary authorities, the new flexible rate system, which tied the current account and the capital account to the exchange rate, enabled monetary authorities to shift their focus to price stability and employment. Previously, authorities had regularly sought to control interest rates, direct capital to areas in which it was deemed most desirable, and exercise moral suasion over financial institutions. In the new era, it was the market that governed interest rates and credit allocations. The market also required that the supervision of financial institutions should be more transparent than ever before. Whereas financial service firms had previously operated within tightly drawn boundaries across business activities, and competition and innovation had been heavily regulated, the dominating forces were now deregulation, innovation, and competition in the marketplace.

The Instability of the International Financial System: Boom and Bust

The push for economic growth fueled by imprudent overseas borrowing has been cited as one of the main contributing factors in Korea's financial crisis (see elsewhere above). However, if there is reckless borrowing, is there not also reckless lending? What prompted foreign lenders to lend so much to Korean borrowers?

Among many responses to these questions, two stand out. First, there was an unmistakable perception among foreign investors that the Korean economy, along with other East Asian economies, was on the rise and would yield higher returns than most economies elsewhere. It may be fair to say that foreign lenders were blinded by the spectacular economic growth of many Asian economies and uniformly expected the region's robust growth to continue well into the foreseeable future. Korea was one of the most shining targets for this optimism. Starting in the 1960s, the Korean economy had been expanding rapidly, and it had quickly become a paragon of economic progress among developing countries. Korea exited from the oil shocks of the 1970s relatively unscathed. It had hosted the Olympic Games in the summer of 1988. It had reached a per capita income of US$10,000 in 1995, and, in 1996, it had joined the OECD, an exclusive club of developed countries.

Second, foreign investors implicitly assumed that Asian governments would ultimately come to the rescue and repay the debt of their domestic borrowers in the event of default. As a result, lending to Asian borrowers appeared to be associated with little or no risk. Indeed, in Korea, the government had never allowed a major domestic company or financial institution to default on a foreign liability. Thus, facing the prospect of high returns at little or no risk of default, foreign lenders rushed to satisfy borrowers in the East Asian countries. Korea was no exception, and the flow of foreign money surged sharply from 1994 to 1996.

For the five Asian economies engulfed in the 1997 financial crisis, the net inflow of private capital skyrocketed from US$40.5 billion in 1994 to US$79.0 billion in 1995 and US$103.2 billion in 1996 (table 2.8). By any measure, this pace was clearly not sustainable. The borrowing terms were also quite favorable. In the case of Korea, the spread on the 10-year bond issued by the government-run Korea Development Bank did not go higher than 60 basis points until January 1997.

Table 2.8 Balance of Payments, Republic of Korea and Five Asian Countries
US$, billions

Indicator	*1994* Asia 5	*1994* Korea, Rep.	*1995* Asia 5	*1995* Korea, Rep.	*1996* Asia 5	*1996* Korea, Rep.	*1997* Asia 5	*1997* Korea, Rep.	*1998* Asia 5[a]	*1998* Korea, Rep.
Current account	–24.6	–3.9	–41.0	–8.5	–54.6	–23.0	–26.3	–8.2	58.5	40.6
Capital account	47.4	10.3	81.5	16.8	100.6	23.3	28.8	1.3	–0.5	–3.3
Private sector	40.5	10.7	79.0	17.5	103.2	23.9	–1.1	–14.3	–28.3	–12.8
Direct/indirect investment	12.2	4.5	15.9	9.8	19.7	12.8	3.6	12.7	8.5	–1.3
Direct investment	4.7	–1.7	4.9	–1.8	5.8	–2.3	6.8	–1.6	6.4	0.6
Indirect investment	7.6	6.1	11.0	11.6	13.9	15.2	–3.2	14.3	2.1	–1.9
Other investment	28.2	6.3	63.1	7.7	83.5	11.1	–4.7	–27.0	–36.8	–11.5
Banks	24.0	—	53.2	—	65.3	—	–25.6	—	–35.0	—
Other	4.2	—	9.9	—	18.2	—	21.0	—	–1.7	—
Public sector	7.0	–0.5	2.5	–0.7	–2.6	–0.6	29.9	15.7	27.8	9.6
International financial institutions	–0.4	—	–0.3	—	–2.0	—	22.1	—	21.6	—
Monetary authorities and government	7.4	—	2.9	—	–0.6	—	7.9	—	6.1	—
Errors and omissions	–17.5	–1.8	–26.5	–1.2	–26.8	1.1	–35.0	–5.1	–16.9	–6.3
Changes in reserve assets	–5.4	–4.7	–14.0	–7.0	–19.3	–1.4	32.5	11.9	–41.1	–31.0

Sources: For the five Asian countries: IIF 1998, 1999. For the Republic of Korea: Bank of Korea.
Note: The five Asian countries are Indonesia, the Republic of Korea, Malaysia, the Philippines, and Thailand. — = not available.
a. Estimates of the Institute of International Finance.

The unprecedented pace of economic growth in Korea and other Asian economies was more than sufficient to stir up ebullient optimism in international financial markets. The expectations ran even higher and reached a fever pitch when the growth of the Asian economies was hailed by the widely followed credit-rating providers and investment banks: a classic case of herd behavior. What ensued was market euphoria and an expanding pool of credit eager to find new borrowers. Predictably, there was also speculation. The unchecked optimism soon mutated into a self-fulfilling prophecy. The more astute observers might have referred to it as a mania.

However, beginning in 1997, the large inflow of private capital driven by unrestrained investment fever began to dry up, and then it came to an abrupt end. For the five crisis economies of Asia, there was a net outflow of US$1.1 billion in 1997. The same year, Korea experienced a net capital outflow totaling US$14.3 billion. Borrowing terms also sharply deteriorated; by the end of October 1997, the spread on a 10-year bond issued by the Korea Development Bank had soared to 285 basis points.

The sharp reversal from a net capital inflow to a net outflow may be traced to the short-term nature of the capital inflows. At a more basic level, however, the reversal may be ascribed to the pessimism that rapidly materialized in the economic outlook on the affected economies among foreign lenders and investors. The heated investment rush quickly dissipated as the doubts mounted. Suddenly, the emerging markets had become pariahs among foreign investors.

Several developments led to this reversal in foreign investor sentiment. In a 1994 paper, "The Myth of Asia's Miracle," Paul Krugman (1994), the widely respected U.S. economist, argued that Asia's high growth was propelled merely by increases in labor and capital factors, that is, simple input-driven growth, not advances in technology or productivity gains. This analysis challenged the prevailing wisdom of the lasting power of Asian economic growth and prompted a fresh assessment of the region's fundamental strength and growth outlook. Krugman's idea soon took hold, and skepticism of the conventional view spread among foreign lenders and investors.

The skepticism deepened when the current account deficits of these emerging markets grew significantly in 1996. The distress in the corporate and financial sectors was palpable. In Korea, a chain of large corporate bankruptcies in 1997 rattled the market. Because of the growth in short-term external debt, many began to cast doubt on the country's debt-repaying ability. Pessimism began to build, the pace of capital withdrawal picked up, and the boom was becoming a bust.

Speculators saw opportunities to exploit the shifting market sentiment. Thailand came under attack from hedge funds as the likelihood of a crisis increased (see above). The bet was that the Thai baht would inevitably fall. The baht wobbled badly under the concerted attacks and soon collapsed as speculators had predicted. To profit more from the fall of the baht, speculators spread fear in the markets and urged other investors to jump on the bandwagon. The outcome was almost preordained.

The Contagion

Widespread currency depreciation ensued soon after Thailand moved to a managed floating exchange rate system, on July 2, 1997 (see chapter 1). The currency in Taiwan, China fell in October, and the stock market in Hong Kong SAR, China crashed. The won was suffering from heavy blows by the end of the month. It was clear that the Thai contagion was spreading. What is the path or mechanism through which such a crisis spreads from one economy to another?

A crisis usually initially spills over to countries that trade and invest heavily in the crisis country. Thus, a country that exports significantly to a crisis country is likely to see a sharp drop in exports. A country with significant investment in a crisis country is also likely to experience a precipitous drop in investment yields. One path for a contagion is therefore through exposure in trade and investment. A contagion can also spread to countries with a large loan exposure or substantial portfolio investment in the crisis country. This is what happened in markets in the United States when the Dow Jones Industrial Average plummeted 554 points on October 27, 1997 following a more than 10 percent drop in the markets in Hong Kong SAR, China. Given the sizable portfolio investment in the market in Hong Kong SAR, China by U.S. investors, this reaction was not surprising. Countries in which macroeconomic conditions are similar to those in a crisis country are also vulnerable. When Thailand faced slowing export growth amid a rising current account deficit, Indonesia became vulnerable because of its macroeconomic similarities to Thailand. Meanwhile, foreign investors gave little or no consideration to the differences or the uniqueness of features among the economies in the region, but approached the risks inherent in the emerging markets from the same perspective and tended to view the Asian markets as a homogeneous mass.

By these criteria, Korea was unusually vulnerable to a contagion from Southeast Asia. It had invested and traded heavily in the countries in the region. Its portfolio investment in the region was sizable. In terms of macroeconomic similarities, Korea, like the Southeast Asian countries, had to contend with persistent current account deficits. Korea was also an emerging economy.

Thus, the case can be made that the crisis in Southeast Asia was a major trigger for the crisis in Korea. How much of a decisive role did the Southeast Asian crisis play in triggering the Korean financial crisis in 1997? Although it is difficult to quantify, the effect was clearly felt in Korea. Until the onset of the crisis in Thailand, foreign lenders and investors had not been particularly alarmed about the underlying risks in Korea. The Thai crisis was a wake-up call.

Exchange Rates for Key Currencies and Interest Rate Volatility

Accelerating globalization increased the likelihood of contagion in times of economic crisis. The ease and speed with which the effect of one country's economic policies might spread to another have also increased. Moreover, because of the disproportionately large size of the economies of the European Union, Japan, and the United States (the G-3), the economic policies of these countries can sometimes have a huge impact on the rest of the world. Korea is a case in point: the Korean economy expanded or contracted repeatedly in parallel with the strength or weakness of the Japanese yen and interest rates in international credit markets. Thus, when the yen was strong and interest rates were low, the Korean economy exhibited substantial growth and current account surpluses. The opposite was true when the yen was weak and interest rates were high. Part of the underlying problem was the volatility in the exchange rates and interest rates of the G-3.

The yen/dollar exchange rate fell sharply, from ¥114.88 per U.S. dollar in March 1993 to ¥84.63 in June 1995 (figure 2.1). By December 1996, however, the yen had bounced back to ¥115.70 and then, by March the following year, to ¥123.79. The mark/dollar exchange rate also exhibited similar volatility, falling from DM 1.61 per U.S. dollar in March 1993 to DM 1.37 two years later, then to DM 1.52 in September 1996. It then soared to DM 1.68 in March 1997. The volatility of the G-3 currencies over a span of several years is apparent. But the same volatility is observed even over a relatively short period. For example, the yen/dollar exchange

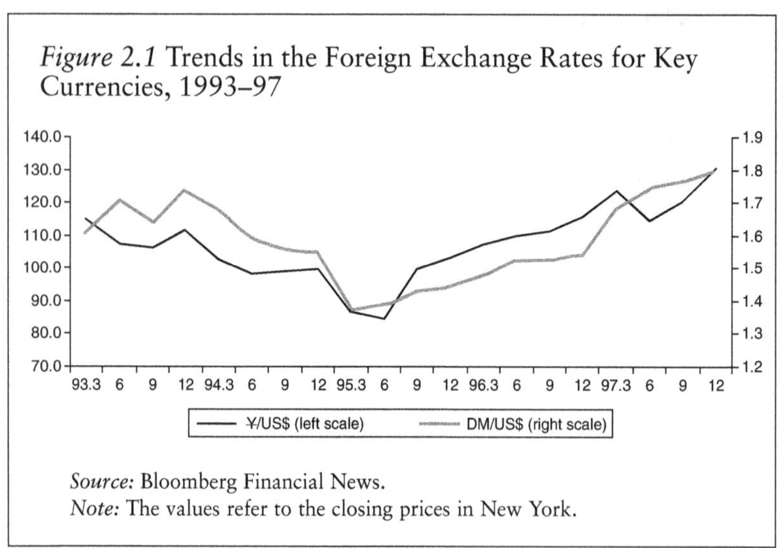

Figure 2.1 Trends in the Foreign Exchange Rates for Key Currencies, 1993–97

Source: Bloomberg Financial News.
Note: The values refer to the closing prices in New York.

rate during January 1998 peaked at ¥133.63 on the 6th and bottomed at ¥125.03 on the 28th. In October the same year, the yen peaked at ¥135.75 on the 1st and bottomed at ¥114.35 on the 19th.

The interest rates of the G-3 displayed similar patterns. The U.S. discount rate climbed from 3.50 percent at the end of 1991 to 5.25 percent at the end of 1995. It then dropped to 4.50 percent at the end of 1998. The Japanese discount rate, which had reached as high as 4.5 percent by the end of 1991, had fallen precipitously, to 0.5 percent, by the end of 1995. After that, the Japanese discount rate effectively remained at 0 percent. In the case of Germany, the discount rate fell from 8 percent at the end of 1991 to 3 percent at the end of 1995 and to 2.5 percent at the end of 1998. For long-term (10-year) treasury yields, the average German, Japanese, and U.S. rates in 1991 hovered around 8.50, 6.34, and 8.16 percent, respectively. By 1998, they had fallen to 4.60, 1.54, and 5.69 percent, respectively. Clearly, there was much volatility and variance in the interest rates in the G-3.

In the trilemma (the impossibility of simultaneously achieving a stable exchange rate, the free movement of capital, and an independent monetary policy), the approach of the G-3 has been, more or less, to pursue independent monetary policies and the free movement of capital, while allowing the market to set the exchange rate.

The benign-neglect policies of the world's leading countries even in times of volatile exchange rate movement have sometimes put the emerging countries in difficulty. This is because sharp swings in key currencies can have enormous impacts on emerging economies. For instance, a Korean exporter who sold goods worth DM 20,000 would have received US$14,000 in mid-1995, but only US$11,300 in mid-1997 because of the relative strength of the dollar. Raising the price of export goods to make up for losses because of the fluctuations in the key currencies was difficult and rare. More than 80 percent of the trade with Germany was conducted using the dollar, and many Korean companies suffered trade losses in 1997.

The fluctuations in the key currencies also have a direct impact on financial markets. If export revenues decline because of swings in exchange rates, exporters face difficulties servicing their debt, and foreign creditors may then begin to lose confidence, thus subjecting the economy to potential disruption.

The effect of the monetary policies of the G-3 on the emerging markets is also noteworthy. On the one hand, the G-3 carry out independent monetary policies in pursuit of price stability, and it is true that this independence of the G-3 has contributed significantly to global price stability. On the other hand, interest rate volatility in the G-3—especially the high interest rate differentials among the three—can cause capital destined for emerging markets to be diverted to other developed economies. The low interest rate differentials that prevailed in the developed economies in the early 1990s were one of the reasons for the capital flows to the emerging markets.

Crisis Prevention and Remedies

Many have voiced grave concern about the pitfalls and shortcomings of the principle of the unfettered free movement of capital on which international financial markets operate. The renowned economist Charles P. Kindleberger (1984) emphasized that manias and crashes have been regularly occurring features of the free and open global financial system. He hypothesized that, over the last 400 years, there has been a financial crisis in Europe roughly every 10 years. In today's highly integrated markets, nearly every country is affected by the frequent disruptions in financial markets worldwide.

Well-functioning crisis-prevention organizations and systems capable of effectively dealing with disruptions are therefore essential if the benefits of liberalized global capital markets are to be fully realized. In particular, considerate measures for the participation of the private sector in crisis control and resolution and to strengthen the crisis management function of international financial institutions such as the IMF are keenly needed to preempt potential market distress. It is often the multinational private financial companies and institutional investors who deluge emerging markets with capital, but then stop this flow at the first sign of potential trouble, thereby sowing the seeds of disruption. But, when the disruption appears, it is the IMF and other international financial institutions that are forced to come to the rescue.

Such bailouts only heighten the risk of moral hazard and leave wide open the possibility of future crisis. The time has therefore come for private investors to bail in and be rewarded or punished for their investment decisions. The avenues for private sector participation in crisis-prevention endeavors may include contingent lines of credit and options to extend loan maturities. Unambiguous principles and procedures for postcrisis debt rescheduling by debtors and creditors must also be established.

In the reform of international financial institutions, standards in information disclosure and transparency must be enhanced. In highly competitive financial markets, information asymmetry can lead to unwarranted risky behavior. So, it is essential that information—whether information on economic policy or financial statistics—flow freely and be readily available to markets. Unfortunately, this has proven easier said than done. Principles and standards governing bank supervision, accounting and audit, corporate governance, and bankruptcy vary across countries. Thus, it is often difficult to make sense of the information available. The IMF and other international financial institutions can make a difference in this area through more aggressive campaigns to promote transparency and to monitor information disclosures. Efforts to harmonize laws and regulations across countries must be stepped up.

As promptly as possible, the IMF should adopt a system of contingent credit lines to act as a crisis-prevention tool. In today's financial market environment, capital flows are often unstable, and a disruption can easily spread across borders and regions. Additional support measures are therefore urgently needed. A guarantee facility specifically aimed at helping countries return expeditiously to international markets after financial chaos or a panic should be supported by the World Bank and other regional development institutions. In the long run, new measures must be implemented to enhance the ability of the IMF to act as the international lender of last resort. In times of crises, the IMF should act not only as a supplier of liquidity to offset deficiencies in the circulation of currencies, but also as the facilitator of a turnaround so as to help maintain calm and order in financial markets.

It is difficult to attribute the Asian financial crisis only to the internal failures of the affected economies. The risky behavior of international investors, as well as the international financial architecture that accommodated this behavior, must be scrutinized. Lawrence H. Summers, the former U.S. secretary of the treasury, once likened the difference between past financial environments and the more recent ones to the difference between the age of automobiles and the age of jetliners. Current emerging economies must accelerate financial restructuring and reform so that they are prepared for the age of jetliners. The role of the international financial community is to minimize the risk of jet travel and act in concert to enhance the stability of the international financial architecture.

Lax Crisis Management in Korea

Wishful Thinking to Ease the Reality

In July 1997, when Thailand had nearly depleted its foreign exchange reserves and switched to a floating exchange rate system, the Ministry of Finance and Economy (MOFE) prepared a confidential report titled "Is There Any Difference between the Baht and Kia?" (MOFE 1997b). The report contained an analysis by UBS, the Swiss bank, that included the information that its banking pressure index pointed to the significant likelihood that a crisis would occur in Korea's financial sector. It also noted that foreign financial companies had already determined that there was mounting financial distress in Korea and raised the possibility that the distress in the financial sector, aggravated by the Kia crisis, could be potentially devastating and evolve into a full-blown currency crisis.

In international financial markets, investors were losing their confidence in Korea. The government began to take measures to counter the crisis. These included a further opening of equity markets, stepped-up efforts to attract foreign capital, and restructuring in the business and financial sectors. The government also focused on longer-term policy objectives in the financial sector and attempted to clarify the general policy directions for the future. It considered the measures to be appropriate. However, the attempt to contain the threat of a crisis was neither well coordinated nor effectively executed. For example, the government failed to carry out its plan to clean up nonperforming assets in the banking sector by transferring them to the Korea Asset Management Corporation. It also failed to draft meaningful financial sector reform legislation and forcefully act to address the problems created by the large corporate bankruptcies. As a result, the government was widely accused of being obsessed with selling its "Vision for the 21st Century" to the public rather than demonstrating any serious resolve to deal with the looming crisis. Because the market was in near panic, the effective implementation of policies aimed at restoring confidence was critical.

To be fair, predicting with any degree of confidence how markets will react is always a challenge, but this is particularly so during a panic because, if a massive bubble builds up in the economy, a great deal of expertise and foresight is required to keep it from bursting. Too often, this is one reason why markets experience repeated boom-bust cycles. In the case of Korea, neither government policy makers nor countless market experts in and outside Korea took the threat seriously of the possible outbreak of a debilitating financial crisis.

Nonetheless, the government should have responded more aggressively to the mounting concerns among investors and in international financial markets. It may well have been a case of wishful thinking on the part of the government. Perhaps it expected its economic fundamentals to be secure against the kinds of devastating crisis that had engulfed Thailand and other Southeast Asian economies. The reality was that even a slight hint of trouble was sufficient to trigger a serious market downturn. But somehow this was not the perception that prevailed at the time. Yet, as Professor Lester Thurow of the Massachusetts Institute of Technology aptly noted, African gazelles run at the slightest whistle of the grass they feed on as if they sense the presence of a lion in the vicinity.

An Unconvincing Show of Resolve to Restore Market Confidence

The government did attempt to tackle the structural weaknesses deeply embedded in the economy and shore up deteriorating market confidence. On August 25, 1997, it announced a package of measures designed to calm the market and reassure investors. The package included government backing for the foreign creditors of domestic financial companies and a pledge to use all the means necessary to ensure that the debts of domestic financial companies in trouble would be paid in full.

But the August 25 measures were received with skepticism in the market. It was felt that they were not sufficiently substantive or concrete. They were not viewed as the strong show of the resolve to fix problems that the government intended. During the Korean Forum at the IMF and World Bank Group Annual Meetings of the Boards of Governors in Hong Kong SAR, China in September 1997, the government's willingness to back

Korean financial companies was explained. The announcement failed to assure the markets. It merely raised suspicions in the foreign media that the government was intent on resorting to yet more ill-conceived bailout plans.

The government should have come up with specific steps and a convincing implementation plan. It should have met with the individual foreign creditors and candidly offered assurances that the distress at home would be dealt with and that settling the liabilities of domestic financial companies would be a priority. But the task of assuring foreign creditors was left to mid-level government bureaucrats stationed overseas. Senior policy makers should have made clear to the markets that the steps the government would take were not merely bailouts of failing financial institutions, but carefully and realistically drafted plans to stave off a looming crisis. In parallel with the effort to restore market confidence, the government should have set about reforming and restructuring the financial and corporate sectors. The government announcement of the guarantee on the debts of domestic financial companies failed to gain the confidence of the market at the right time.

Conflict among the Authorities

The BOK and the MOFE were the two governmental bodies that were charged with containing any looming financial crisis. But the liberalized financial landscape was as foreign to the BOK and the MOFE as it was to other government ministries. Because the BOK and the MOFE lacked experience in managing an escalating crisis, they should have consulted with each other and worked hand-in-hand to deal with the crisis. Instead, they clashed. There was a standoff between the BOK and the MOFE over proposed amendments to the Bank of Korea Act that contained provisions affecting some operations of the BOK (see chapter 1). Employees of the BOK staged heated protests before the National Assembly, while MOFE staff were busy trying to get the amendments approved by the National Assembly. By July 1997, Korea's financial markets were spiraling downward, but the BOK and the MOFE, the two most important institutions, staffed with the best and brightest of Korea, were locked in a tough war until mid-November, shortly before the full-blown crisis erupted. To the dismay of the markets, the two also differed sharply on exchange rate policy and favored opposing remedies at a time when the foreign exchange market was in near paralysis.

Notes

1. Nominal GDP is computed using 1996 constant U.S. dollars; see table 2.4.

2. The criteria used to classify a borrower into the moderately indebted group are as follows: (1) The total external debt is below 30 to 50 percent of nominal GDP. (2) The total external debt is below 165 to 275 percent of the value of the

exports of goods and services. (3) The debt service ratio (interest and principal repayment of external debt/exports of goods and services) is below 18 to 30 percent. (4) The interest service ratio (interest payment of external debt/exports of goods and services) is below 12 to 20 percent.

3. Kim Young-Sam was elected the 14th President of Korea on December 18, 1992. He took office on February 25, 1993 for a single five-year term.

4. Both the World Trade Organization and the International Organization for Standardization promote standardization on these and other issues as a way to facilitate international trade.

5. In response, the BOK engaged in swap agreements with domestic firms on overseas investment funds so as to remove the currency risks and encourage overseas investment.

3

Overview of Korea's Postcrisis Responses

Crisis Recovery and Policy Challenges

An Opportunity for Fundamental Reform and Revival

The financial crisis in the Republic of Korea erupted in late 1997 with a crippling shortage of foreign exchange liquidity. It quickly spread throughout the economy and raised the specter of a bankrupt country in complete paralysis. Exchange rates and interest rates skyrocketed to stratospheric levels, and the long-accepted belief that financial companies never fail in Korea was suddenly shattered when merchant banks and securities firms started to fail and close their doors in droves. A debilitating credit crunch also gripped markets, making it exceedingly tough even for the healthiest companies to obtain credit. Associated with projections of massive, widespread unemployment, but woefully inadequate social welfare and safety nets, the crisis threatened the lives of hundreds of thousands of ordinary citizens. Many Koreans started calling the crisis the worst disaster since the Korean War in the early 1950s.

Prior to the crisis, most ordinary Koreans had been led to believe that it was only a matter of time before their country joined the ranks of the world's richest, most advanced nations. This was a well-founded belief because Korea had broken through the US$10,000 per capita income mark in 1995 and had joined the Organisation for Economic Co-operation and Development—the club of rich nations—in 1996. So, understandably, people felt betrayed, cheated, and humiliated. Indeed, most Koreans had a rude awakening as they helplessly watched their seemingly invincible economic juggernaut collapse and then kneel before the International Monetary Fund (IMF) for a lifeline.

Following the conclusion of the standby arrangement with the IMF on December 3, 1997, all the major local newspapers lamented that it was a day of national humiliation. The sense of despair and wounded pride only deepened with the disclosure of the terms of the agreement that Korea was forced to sign with the IMF.[1] Many Koreans likened the agreement to a theft of their economic sovereignty. As the shock and the bitterness spread, however, a consensus began to emerge that the crisis should be viewed as an opportunity to fix all that was wrong with Korea Inc. and revitalize the economy. Some comfort was taken from the fact that even developed countries such as the United Kingdom had once had to reach out to the IMF for exactly the same assistance that Korea was now requesting. The emerging consensus was that the prescriptions the IMF recommended in exchange for the standby credit should be met not only to clean up the financial sector, but also to break from the past and chart a new course for the future.[2]

Korea faced four broad challenges in the effort to rebound from the crisis and chart a new path for the country: (1) containing the crisis and cushioning its impact, (2) taking the right lessons from the crisis and putting together crisis-prevention measures, (3) faithfully carrying out postcrisis economic revitalization programs, and (4) organizing the institutional arrangements necessary for the effective implementation of the three other tasks. Because these challenges were closely related to each other, it was evident from the outset that they had to be carried out simultaneously. However, none of the tasks was going to be easy; they had never been attempted before. Meticulous preparations and unwavering resolve were needed for success (Lee 1998).

Containing the Crisis and Cushioning the Impact

To meet the first challenge, containing the crisis and cushioning its impact, the government had to secure as much foreign exchange liquidity as possible because even the substantial line of credit from the IMF fell short of the requirements if a sovereign default were to be avoided. The lesson of the Latin American economies that had lost the decade of the 1980s because of foreign debt defaults and had then suffered enormous economic hardships was not lost on policy makers. So, the immediate challenge was to boost the foreign currency holdings from abroad.

One overriding objective of the IMF standby arrangement was the stabilization of the Korean won. This was to be accomplished through tight monetary and fiscal policies. As a result, market interest rates soared to levels that were impossible for ordinary businesses to bear. Should the ballooning interest rates persist, even the strongest companies would have gone bankrupt. Creating the market conditions within which interest rates could be brought down was a must.

The restoration of confidence in Korea's economic prospects was critical to securing foreign exchange liquidity. The government therefore had to give the market a candid account of the health of the economy and the measures that had been planned to respond to the crisis. It had to lay out a convincing vision of the country's economic future. The government recognized that strengthening cooperative relations with international financial institutions and major private foreign creditors and their governments and attracting foreign direct investment were crucial to the success of any postcrisis recovery plans. In addition, the government had to carry out the crisis recovery measures it had agreed to with the IMF. There was no mistaking it: more than words were needed; there also had to be action.

The second challenge involved relieving the credit crunch and preventing the collapse of the companies that represented the core industrial strength of the country. Several merchant banks and securities firms had failed at the onset of the crisis, and commercial banks soon began to feel threatened and had to curtail lending sharply as they struggled to comply with the minimum capital requirements recommended by the Bank for International Settlements. The credit crunch was becoming tighter day by day, and even companies with a promising business outlook were pushed to the brink of default because of the liquidity squeeze. The situation among small and medium companies was particularly dire because they usually lacked any meaningful credit relationship with commercial banks. Many were soon forced to default on bank loans.

In normal times, there are upsides to corporate insolvency and business failures. But, in a crisis, there is simply no immediate benefit to the economy if business insolvency and failures occur on a massive scale, especially because of a temporary liquidity shortage. The cost of bringing a failed company back to life can be as high as or much higher than starting from scratch.

At the core, the remedy to the debilitating credit crunch involved restoring market confidence through credible corporate and financial sector reform and restructuring; that is, the credit market was not going to improve until banks secured their capital position beyond the minimum standards set by the Bank for International Settlements and until companies reduced default risk through robust earnings. The most practical approach was to let nonviable companies and financial institutions fail and, where possible, lend a helping hand to the viable ones. Helping small and medium companies establish relationship banking ties with commercial banks as a way to encourage greater credit access was also thought to be necessary to reduce the incidence of defaults. However, restructuring and relationship banking were not going to relieve the situation quickly; they would take time. They therefore had to be supplemented by short-term steps that could produce more immediate results and contain the crisis. Expanding credit guarantees for small and medium companies and for export financing was seen as a crucial early action.

The third challenge was to deal with the soaring job losses and economic hardships that ordinary households faced in the wake of the crisis.

Ominously, early on, it had been estimated that crisis-related job losses would exceed one million. Because of the enormous economic pressure job losses created on households, unemployment had to be addressed urgently. Failure to do so promptly and effectively would stoke public anger and make dealing with the crisis even more arduous. The falling won was already fueling inflation and causing more hardship on many households. But Korea had no meaningful social welfare and safety nets.

It was clear that government actions in economic reform and the establishment of adequate social safety nets would not prove successful without a broad mandate from the people for change. A national consensus was required on the steps to be taken, especially a consensus on the Korea Tripartite Commission, which represented labor, management, and government.

Revising Crisis-Prevention Measures

Because of the complexity and multiple roots of the crisis, the lessons to be drawn from the crisis are varied and difficult to identify. Nonetheless, several lessons stand out.

The first is the overriding importance of macroeconomic fundamentals. An economy must grow within the constraints of stable inflation and a well-disciplined current account. A declining capacity to service foreign debt because of slow growth is certainly not desirable, but neither is a blind focus on growth at the expense of an out-of-control current account deficit that may render the economy unable to cope with mounting foreign debt. High domestic savings, the productive and efficient use of foreign capital, and fiscal soundness all contribute to macroeconomic fundamentals. In an open, liberalized capital market setting, it is difficult to carry out consistently independent monetary policies to achieve the twin goal of price stability and employment, while keeping the exchange rate at a level that allows a balanced current account to be maintained. It is imperative that the economy strike a balance among the exchange rate, interest rates, and government budget allocations.

The second lesson is that underlying economic structures must be sound, and social harmony and stability must be the norm. A strong financial system that allocates capital efficiently, cushions shocks from inside and outside, and keeps markets calm and orderly even in times of disruption and distress should be a top policy priority. In this endeavor, financial companies must strive for soundness and competitiveness and carry on as rational profit-making business enterprises. Government meddling in financial markets should never occur, or it should be kept to an absolute minimum. Well-functioning financial market infrastructure with effective prudential controls and financial oversight is crucial.

In the corporate sector, the crisis made abundantly clear that debt-financed growth cannot endure and that too much debt leaves businesses vulnerable to risks that are beyond their control. The emphasis on the size of business enterprises and the strategy of growth fueled by diversification—often ridiculed as the expansion strategy used by department stores—were mistaken. Korean companies had to focus on their core industrial strengths. Corporate governance also had to improve drastically so as to measure up to global standards. Business transparency, management accountability, and checks and balances all had to be significantly enhanced.

Korea had to maintain social stability and resolve differences without resorting to bitter conflicts and confrontations. It had to reject extremism and find an orderly, workable balance. In other words, Korea had to become a more mature society in which all people could live in harmony. Fairness in the way public and private institutions set the rules and conduct their affairs was imperative. Rules and policies that are perceived as unfair do not bring people together or encourage compromise, and conflicts can then erupt and become entrenched. The omnipresent tension between management and labor in Korea provides an instructive example of what can go wrong if management and labor do not work to build a fair and cooperative framework for the resolution of differences. Transparency, accountability, and the effective rule of law must be strengthened. Good governance that encourages social cohesion and compromise is desperately needed.

The third lesson is that Korea's experiences pointed to the need for reforms in the international financial system that foster stability. For the emerging countries, full capital market liberalization should be preceded by improvements in underdeveloped financial systems in an orderly fashion. Safeguards against sudden shifts or reversals in international capital flows or investor sentiment should be put into place. Earnest efforts to reduce the volatility of the exchange rates with the dollar, the euro, and the yen must be undertaken. As the 1997 Asian financial crisis showed, small open economies are highly vulnerable to disturbances because of sudden, unexpected movements in key currencies. This vulnerability points to the need for greater foreign exchange policy coordination among the European Union, Japan, and the United States.

Foreign lenders must share the burdens and costs of a financial crisis. This is because they are usually the first in line to benefit from bailouts even if they explicitly assume the risk of lending. Deterring such moral hazard must be a key part of crisis prevention.

Minimizing information asymmetry is critical in avoiding disruptions and discouraging herd behavior in international financial markets. The reality is that neither the availability nor the flow of information in international financial markets is at a satisfactory level for gathering economic statistical data or determining the future course of policy. The disparate principles and standards that countries follow in bank supervision, accounting and financial reporting, corporate governance, and bankruptcy, for example, often make it difficult for outsiders to reach informed judgments and sound decisions. The IMF and other international financial institutions can help by supporting more transparency and monitoring. Encouraging cross-border harmony through global best practices can contribute to more seamless information flows and better understanding across markets.

Credit support from the IMF and other international financial institutions must be enhanced. Crisis prevention requires the maintenance of an appropriate level of foreign exchange liquidity that takes into account the magnitude of existing short-term external debt. However, there is a limit to the ability of small emerging economies to raise foreign exchange given the high cost. In the event of the spread of a contagion from a crisis country, the IMF and the World Bank must be able to provide immediate contingent credit lines and credit guarantee facilities. Moreover, IMF quotas must more accurately reflect the economic realities in recipient countries to ensure that standby arrangements meet actual needs. Other actions are also required to expand the role of the IMF as the world's most effective lender of last resort and caretaker during a financial crisis and other severe shocks. Organizational reforms within the IMF in support of this goal should be initiated. The enhanced funding capacity of the IMF and other international financial institutions, together with backup facilities between countries and regional cooperative frameworks, should also be pursued.

The Search for New Engines of Growth

Because of the growing globalization of markets, cybernated transactions in commerce, and knowledge-driven processes in production, the world is involved in a momentous transition. The developed countries have made significant strides in the transition to a knowledge-based economy. Indeed, it has been estimated that more than half of the output of the developed countries already originates in knowledge-based sources. The main engine of growth in these economies has changed from energy and capital to knowledge and technology.

In Korea, future growth that is driven by additional labor input is difficult to envision because of the country's low birthrates and aging population. The limited domestic market also represents a cap on the potential for significant growth. These factors suggest that the future engine of growth in Korea will have to be knowledge based and that the economy will have to compete globally. This is increasingly being seen not as an option, but as a necessity. Globalization means that global markets must be available for Korean products and services, but it also means that domestic markets must be open to the world. So, Korean companies and the Korean people must shed any close-mindedness and embrace globalization.

For a successful transition to a knowledge-based economy, innovation in advanced technologies is essential. Korea's growth has been fueled and supported by borrowed technologies to a significant degree, and this dependency will likely continue for some time. But in allowing this dependency to continue, Korea also risks becoming caught in a low-technology trap whereby it remains dependent on outside technologies. Korea would then likely be unable to narrow the gap with the developed countries, and its technological lead over other emerging countries would shrink. Economic growth would necessarily stagnate.

Korea must therefore chart a new course toward a knowledge-based economy led by innovation and creativity. There are several policy recommendations toward this end (MOFE 1998a). First, genuine educational reform that rewards creative thinking and encourages the full utilization of individual talent and potential should be promoted. Lifetime training and education should also be created and integrated into the educational system to foster a flexible, well-trained workforce. Second, a strong national commitment should be made to supporting the growth of the information and communication industry and expanding information infrastructure such as the information highway. Third, investments in basic science should be boosted, and productive science and technology investments that increase productivity should be encouraged. Research and development led by market demand should be continually supported. Fourth, a comprehensive strategy to promote technology-intensive industries and services should be put in place to cultivate next-generation economic structures. Venture capital, technology start-ups, and other small, highly specialized companies should be encouraged to take the lead in this endeavor. Fifth, within the service sector, the tourism and cultural industries should be cultivated through aggressive policy support so as to become key national industries in the 21st century.

The Establishment of the Institutional Backbone for the New Leap Forward

A reinforced democracy and the market economy: foundations for a new era. For successful broadbased reform to establish a knowledge-based economy, there must first be a collective consensus among the people on the need for change. Effective political leadership that produces results, not merely talk, is a must. A strong institutional and organizational framework that can act as the foundation for sustained reform should be developed. Much can be said about the need for a well-functioning institutional framework that can spur an economic revival (Lee 1996).

One prerequisite for a successful transition to a knowledge-based economy is the propelling force of innovation and creativity. Another is the need to nurture a sound and competitive industrial microfoundation, which, in Korea, has largely been achieved through huge debt-financed investment and a focus on extensive growth. Promoting fairness in the everyday lives of citizens is essential in minimizing social conflict and confrontation. Adapting to global standards is critical in gaining access to global markets. In short, the new framework must be able to promote and support creativity, soundness, fairness, and adaptability in the economic and business realm in line with the *Zeitgeist*, the spirit of the times.

For innovation and creativity, economic freedom in the marketplace is paramount. Technological innovation is often the result of a long series of tests and experiments. New, better products and production processes become possible only after repeated trial and error. To initiate such experiments, private business should have the right to dispose of the necessary human and physical resources freely. Government intervention or interference in business investment decisions too often distorts the allocation of scarce resources and prompts companies to engage in rent seeking. The result is the unproductive use of scarce resources, and this retards technological progress and innovation. It is imperative that innovators be rewarded in the marketplace through competition. The tough, uncompromising enforcement of property rights, patents, and intellectual property rights is crucial. The Western countries have grown rich because of the economic freedom their companies enjoy in the marketplace and the rewards made possible by government enforcement of rules designed to protect innovators (Rosenberg and Birdzell 1986).

For the sound growth of corporate and financial companies, a market environment must be created in which restructuring can take place anywhere any time. This allows competitive companies to move into more productive and more rewarding businesses, while noncompetitive companies are forced to exit from the marketplace without hindering competition or innovation or imposing a heavy cost on the market. The principle of risk and reward must be firmly established and never compromised. In this endeavor, market discipline is essential in preventing moral hazard and ensuring that companies succeed or fail on their own merits.

New mechanisms and institutions are also needed to secure fairness and the rule of law so as to encourage social harmony and cooperation. In particular, Korea must strive to give its citizens equitable opportunities for upward mobility. At the negotiating table, it must prevent abuses of power by those in advantageous positions and offset the anger and obstinacy of those in disadvantageous positions. Korea also must provide transparent and level playing fields and enforce the law without discrimination or bias. To adapt to globalization, it must initiate more efforts to open up the economy, spur foreign trade and investment, and adhere to the best global standards and practices. Concrete steps designed to cushion the impact of liberalization should be taken. Korea cannot afford to be too slow to change, nor can it hurry along at a mindless pace.

The core foundation for all these challenges is an open, dynamic market economy and a vibrant democracy. When the new administration led by President Kim Dae-Jung came into office on February 25, 1998, it billed itself as a people's government. President Kim Dae-Jung also staked Korea's future, rightly, on democracy and the market economy.

Reinforcing the market economy: the social safety net and lifetime learning. We are living at a time of epic change. The globalized and knowledge-based society of today stands out among societies in history. It may well have potentially enormous ramifications for the future. It calls for a loosening of rigid attitudes and mindsets to foster flexible adaption to change.

Because epochal transformations lead to realignments in social values and norms and in industrial structures, they can also threaten the existing order. For example, the highest honors in the old, traditional Korea were reserved for the country and the family, but, in modern Korea, people have come to value individual freedom far more. The changing fortunes of different industries and the alterations in the underlying structure of the country speak volumes about the transformation under way in Korea. Whereas the globally uncompetitive agricultural sector staggers and languishes, manufacturing industries for export are booming. Because of the digital divide, people with the skills to process information and knowledge are gaining an upper hand in the labor market, while people lacking such skills are falling behind.

There is a growing gap between the haves and the have-nots, and the middle class is shrinking to an extent not seen in the past. The income gap between the top and the bottom in society has widened. One consequence has been a loosening in social cohesion and a less stable social environment. Investment and other productive activities cannot thrive in such an unstable environment. Problems cannot be addressed through market mechanisms alone. The gulf among different income groups, for example, cannot be remedied using quick fixes; a solution requires a concerted long-term commitment to social welfare and safety nets. Investment in education and training, which contribute to the productivity of workers, is an obvious remedy. However, such investment usually falls short of the optimal level in the marketplace. So, a full-fledged commitment to investment in lifetime learning and training among workers is needed.

Korea in the 21st Century

What can Korea look forward to if it is able to advance on the path to democracy and embrace a free-market economy?[3] First, it will be a transparent society. The principles of equal opportunity for success, individual risk and reward, and accountability will be firmly established. The rule of law, the level playing field, and fair competition will dictate the outcome and the reward, not kinship or the schools one has attended. Mutual trust and respect will be the norm, and social harmony will be firmly rooted.

Second, it will be a dynamic society with a core of industrial strength and an economy that thrives through knowledge-based creation, diffusion, and application. Its potential and international competitiveness will continue to improve.

Third, it will be an advanced welfare society. The social safety nets that provide basic necessities to all citizens will be expanded. Income distribution will be fair, and the quality of life of the majority will continue to rise.

Fourth, it will be a free, open society. The people will recognize that opening up to the world is not a risk, but an opportunity for wealth and value creation. Global standards will prevail in the way public and private sector enterprises conduct business.

Fifth, there will no longer be confrontation between the Democratic People's Republic of Korea and the Republic of Korea; they will peacefully coexist or will become unified.

The Implementation of Postcrisis Measures

The Prerequisites for Postcrisis Recovery Programs

Sound foundations had to be laid to achieve a successful postcrisis recovery. First, it was clear from the start that any major step to combat the crisis had to be backed by the people if it was to have a realistic chance of success because of the sacrifices it would exact from the people. The downsizing and closing of businesses were inevitable, and massive layoffs were sure to follow. The falling won guaranteed that consumer prices would surge. It was likely that low- and middle-income groups would bear the brunt of the pain the recovery programs were going to inflict.

In early 1998, the government, together with management and labor, formed the Korea Tripartite Commission with the express goal of equitably sharing the pain the recovery programs were going to cause. It was an important step that enabled the government to forge ahead and ensure the backing of the people. The active participation of individual citizens is essential to the successful execution of a recovery program. An early sign of the success in Korea was the enthusiastic reception by the public and the news media worldwide of the gold collection campaign to boost foreign exchange reserves.

The recovery from the crisis called for fresh mindsets. Companies had to abandon the attitude that they could carry on doing business as usual; they had to awaken to the new reality that they must thrive or perish on their own merits. Wage earners had to acknowledge that wage growth cannot exceed productivity growth and that untenable demands would be followed by rising unemployment. Unlike in the past, merely working hard was not going to be sufficient; working smart was more important. For the government, paternalistic policies that improperly meddle in the private sector had to be discontinued in favor of deregulation, market integrity, and macroeconomic soundness. The government had to provide viable social safety nets.

Second, the recovery programs had to garner the backing and cooperation of the international community. Thus, for example, the government had to secure funding from the IMF and gain access to credit from the major foreign lenders so as to stabilize the precipitously depreciating won.

Third, the effective leadership of President Kim Dae-Jung was vital. It was imperative for him to persuade and lead the people to execute faithfully the much-needed reforms and restructuring. He also had to take charge of his administration to ensure the consistent execution of the recovery programs and earn the confidence and trust of foreign lenders and investors. In an auspicious development early on, President Kim let it be known in an interview soon after his election and before taking office that his government would faithfully carry out its pledge to the IMF in exchange for the standby credit. In meetings with Michel Camdessus, the IMF managing director, and Lawrence Summers, the deputy secretary of the U.S. Treasury, President Kim exceeded the demands of the IMF by signaling his resolve to bring about genuine and meaningful reform and restructuring. He engaged in aggressive diplomatic initiatives to gather support from abroad for Korea's recovery efforts.

The Consistent Implementation of Policy Programs

Policy consistency was critical in the recovery period because of the risk of the loss of confidence and credibility through the implementation of inconsistent policies that might derail all government initiatives. Coordination and cooperation among the government economic ministries and agencies and the identification of systemic approaches to problems proved crucial. As president-elect, Kim Dae-Jung had met with President Kim Young-Sam on December 20, 1997, and agreed that a joint presidential committee on economic policies would be formed to ensure policy consistency throughout the transition period. This was followed by the appointment of 12 key senior political leaders and government administrators two days later, on December 22. This joint presidential committee dealt with several major issues, including negotiations with foreign creditors on the rollover of short-term external debt; the capital write-offs and recapitalization at the Korea First Bank and Seoul Bank; the restructuring of merchant banks; the establishment of five basic principles on business restructuring; assistance for small and medium companies, construction companies, and exporters; adjustments to the government budget for 1998; and new initiatives to attract foreign investors.

Soon after coming to office, President Kim created the Economic Policy Coordination Committee (EPCC), on March 5, 1998, for the explicit purpose of overseeing the reforms and ensuring consistent policy execution. The committee was headed by the president and made up of 11 key government economic ministers and advisors. It was to meet weekly, but this was not always possible, and it was usually left to the economic ministers to coordinate priority tasks. On May 29, 1998, a regular meeting of economic ministers was instituted to coordinate the ongoing economic agenda among the various government ministries. In May 1999, the government initiated an organizational reform and created the National Economy Advisory Council to help the president formulate key economic policies, and the EPCC, which had been headed by the president, was turned over to the minister of finance and economy. The relevant law and the enforcement decree for the creation of the National Economy Advisory Council took effect on August 31 and September 30, 1999, respectively.

IMF Prescriptions: A Bittersweet Pill

The policy consultations with the IMF did not focus solely on the rescue package. For monitoring purposes, the IMF conducts annual consultations with its member countries as provided for by article IV of the Agreement of the International Monetary Fund. Upon the conclusion of the annual consultation, the IMF issues a staff report on the article IV consultation that includes a summary analysis of the economy of the member country; the report also covers such issues as the impact of specific government policies on the current and capital accounts, growth, and employment. The Executive Board of the IMF discusses the staff report and determines whether the economic policies of the member country comply with the country's obligations under the Articles of Agreement.

For member countries in economic distress, the IMF can decide to supply a credit support package. However, the IMF must first verify the ability of the recipient country to repay the debt, and, as a part of this process, the recipient country must negotiate with the IMF on the economic programs to be implemented to address the underlying causes of the distress. The demands made on the recipient country by the IMF are known as conditionality. The terms of the IMF loans are usually covered in the Letter of Intent and the standby agreement, and the conditionality describes the policy understanding and the macroeconomic variables to be implemented by the recipient country. The loans are also associated with a set of performance criteria that must be satisfied to avoid the suspension of the IMF assistance. The usual items covered in the performance criteria are macroeconomic variables such as money reserves, net international reserves, and net domestic assets.

The size of the credit support to be provided by the IMF and the policy prescriptions to be followed by the recipient country in return for the IMF support must be determined with an eye to restoring the confidence of international financial markets. In Korea's case, the package that resulted, on December 3, 1997, from the first round of negotiations between the government and the IMF failed to measure up to the expectations of international financial markets, and the government was therefore unable to calm the crisis at this early stage. Not obtaining the support they had anticipated from international markets, the government and the IMF sought backup support from the major developed countries.

It took Korea only one and a half years to recover from the crisis. This period was short relative to the time required in other crisis countries. There was widespread recognition that the policy programs that the government agreed to with the IMF were critical in giving assurances to the market and restoring confidence.

However, the general acknowledgment of the people of the need for the rescue package was also a key factor in enabling the government to move forward. This represented a noteworthy display of collective foresight considering that the Korean people would have to do the heavy lifting and bear the brunt of the pain of the recovery. Indeed, had the people not recognized their ownership of the prescriptions agreed to with the IMF, Korea's recovery would not have been possible.

From 1965 to 1987, Korea had signed 16 standby agreements with the IMF for a total of SDR 2.48 billion. In some ways, the challenge before the government in having to sell tough policies to the people had been greatly alleviated by the fact that the IMF had been viewed, more or less, as an objective third party with no ax to grind.

However, the perception of the IMF this time was quite different from the perception in the past. To be sure, the local press initially took a rather harsh view of the policy prescriptions that resulted from the first round of negotiations with the IMF. Even then, presidential candidate Kim Dae-Jung, certainly a serious contender, expressed the wish for a less painful deal for Korea from the IMF only a few days before the election on December 18, 1997. Part of the reason for the shift in the perception of the IMF was the more aggressive and more extensive policy prescriptions the IMF now demanded (see chapter 4). Nonetheless, in the end, Korea managed to carry out faithfully what it pledged to do. Differences persisted during the early talks between the two parties, but, beginning with the sixth round of negotiations in May 1998, the gap between them had sharply narrowed, giving the government much-needed room to maneuver in setting new economic policies.

Notes

1. Editorial, *JoongAng Daily*, December 5, 1997.
2. Editorial, *Chosun Daily*, November 25, 1997.
3. This subsection owes much to MOFE (1998a), part 1, chapter 4.

4

Initial Responses to the Crisis, December 1997

Actions by the IMF, December 3, 1997

On December 3, 1997, the government of the Republic of Korea sent the International Monetary Fund (IMF) a Letter of Intent (LOI) that outlined the steps the government intended to take to obtain the financial support of the IMF. The following day, the Executive Board of the IMF approved the standby arrangement with Korea. In keeping with past practice, the IMF set up a resident representative office in Seoul in March 1998 and dispatched John Dodsworth to take charge. The diagnosis of the underlying causes of the crisis and the initial responses that the Korean government shared with the IMF can be found in "Korea: Memorandum on the Economic Program," which was attached to the LOI. The diagnosis took on great significance because it set the basic tone and the direction for the follow-up reform and restructuring measures the government promised the IMF it would adopt to deal with the crisis.

Recognition of the Crisis

This subsection contains part I ("Background") of "Korea: Memorandum on the Economic Program," the attachment to the LOI sent by the government of Korea to the IMF on December 3, 1997.[1] *The text of this subsection therefore refers to the situation on that date.*

For the past several decades, prudent macroeconomic policies and continuing structural reforms have propelled Korea along a path of rapid economic development. With per capita GDP [gross domestic product] rising at an annual average rate of nearly 7 percent, the once poor agrarian economy has been transformed into an advanced industrial economy. At the same time, in the process of development, the limitations of Korea's system of detailed government intervention at the micro level have become increasingly apparent. In particular, the legacy of government intervention has left an inefficient financial sector and a highly leveraged corporate sector that lack effective market discipline.

In recent years, the government has implemented structural reforms in a wide range of areas, particularly the financial sector. However, the present financial crisis demonstrates that a more comprehensive and rapid pace of reforms is required to achieve a strong and transparent financial system which operates free of political interference and according to the rules and practices of the advanced industrial countries. Such a financial system is essential for the Korean economy to meet the challenges of globalization and return to a path of rapid sustained growth.

Until the present financial crisis, macroeconomic performance in Korea was broadly favorable. During the first three quarters of 1997, real GDP grew by about 6 percent and consumer price inflation declined slightly to 4 percent, while the external current account deficit is expected to narrow to less than 3 percent of GDP in 1997. Fiscal policy has remained prudent, with the budget for 1997 projected to record a small deficit. The monetary aggregate (MCT) has edged down to the bottom of the target range in line with the inflation objective.[2]

However, since the beginning of the year, an unprecedented number of highly leveraged conglomerates (*chaebols* [the large family-controlled and family-run groups that dominate business in Korea]) have moved into bankruptcy. The high rate of bankruptcies reflected a number of factors, including excessive investment in certain sectors, weakening export prices, and the government's greater willingness to allow troubled chaebols to fail. The bankruptcies spilled over into a sharp increase in nonperforming loans (defined according to international standards) to W 32 trillion (7 percent of GDP) by end-September, about double their level at end-1996.

The present difficulties in the financial sector stem from a lack of market orientation in financial institutions combined with lax prudential supervision. Financial companies have priced risks poorly and have been willing to finance an excessively large portion of investment plans of the corporate sector, resulting in high leveraging. At the same time, the dramatic decline in stock prices has cut the value of banks' equity and further reduced their net worth. These developments have led to successive downgrades of Korean financial institutions by international credit rating agencies and a sharp tightening in the availability of external finance.

Korea's external financing situation deteriorated sharply after October 23, following the decline in the Hong Kong SAR, China stock market and the downgrading of Korea's sovereign risk status by Standard and Poor's. New external financing has virtually dried up and substantial difficulties are being experienced in rolling over the relatively large amount of short-term debt (estimated at US$100 billion). The won depreciated by about 20 percent against the U.S. dollar through November 30; the stock market index fell by some 30 percent to a 10-year low. Gross official reserves declined sharply, with a large amount used to finance the repayment of short-term debt of Korean commercial banks' offshore branches. While the contagion effects of developments in Southeast Asia contributed to the current crisis, the magnitude and speed of the deterioration in the financial situation owed much to the fundamental weaknesses in Korea's financial and corporate sectors.

Response Strategy

In containing the crisis, the government and the IMF set the priority on cobbling together a sufficient rescue package to calm the fears of foreign creditors and a credible policy package to address the underlying economic problems so as to restore market confidence and put the economy back on track.

The policy framework in the economic program was built around the following: (1) a strong macroeconomic framework designed to continue the orderly adjustment in the external current account and to contain inflationary pressures and involving a tighter monetary stance and substantial fiscal adjustment; (2) a comprehensive strategy to restructure and recapitalize the financial sector and make it more transparent, more market oriented, more well supervised, and free of political interference in business decisions; (3) measures to improve corporate governance; (4) the accelerated liberalization of capital account transactions; (5) further trade liberalization; and (6) improvement in the transparency and timely reporting of economic data.

The tight macroeconomic policies would provide the right conditions to support comprehensive structural reforms. Tight fiscal policy was initially intended to provide some modest support for external adjustment and make room for the noninflationary financing of the carrying costs of the needed banking restructuring. Tight monetary policy was aimed mainly at preventing a spiral of depreciation and inflation from emerging. Monetary tightening was thought to be inevitable to stabilize the badly tumbling Korean won, which was sure to stoke inflation and fuel further depreciation of the won, a vicious cycle (Lane et al. 1999).

The Korean government and the IMF, in principle, shared the basic strategy and thrust of the economic program, but disagreement did come up on issues such as the scope and the severity of the economic measures to be implemented. For its part, the government wanted to avoid a drastic drop in growth and a skyrocketing boost in interest rates in 1998. The government also wanted to buy time for the failing merchant banks and commercial banks, as had been its hope when it had announced restructuring measures on November 19, 1997. For accelerated trade and capital liberalization, the preferred position of the government was to pace this at the speed it had agreed to during negotiations at the World

Trade Organization and the Organisation for Economic Co-operation and Development.

However, the IMF had far stronger and more extensive measures in mind. It demanded high interest rates and wanted to impose a cap on the government budget. It also insisted on an immediate shutdown of failing merchant banks and full removal of the barriers to foreign trade and investment. It was during this time that David Lipton, the U.S. under secretary of the treasury for international affairs, visited Korea and held frequent talks with Hubert Neiss, IMF director of Asian affairs, to push for IMF measures. Michel Camdessus, the IMF managing director, also visited Korea as the technical details were being hammered out and demanded sharply enlarged response and liberalization packages. The IMF insisted that, ahead of the presidential elections, the major presidential candidates make a pledge to abide by the terms of the standby arrangement. The government attempted to water down some of the more austere measures being put forth by the IMF, but, in the end, it had no choice but to accept what the IMF asked for. To urge on nervous government officials, Michel Camdessus emphatically argued that the crisis was a blessing in disguise because it would help Korea cure its long-overlooked ills and come out of the crisis wholly revitalized and reinvigorated for a confident, bright future.

The IMF Standby Arrangement

Through a standby arrangement, the IMF pledged US$21 billion (approximately SDR 15.5 billion) over a three-year period, and, in return, Korea was to carry out the economic program to which it had committed with the IMF. In addition to the IMF funding, the Asian Development Bank (ADB) and the World Bank promised to support Korea with up to US$4 billion and US$10 billion, respectively. As a second line of defense, 13 major developed countries pledged US$23.35 billion.[3] The total rescue funding available was therefore US$58.35 billion.

Given the need for an immediate release of a large amount of relief money up front, the IMF agreed to make available 60 percent of its own funding within six months. In a sign of strong commitment to Korea, the IMF Executive Board quickly approved the release of US$5.5 billion on December 4, only one day after the standby arrangement was finalized. A detailed disbursement schedule of the IMF credit is shown in table 4.1.

Korea: Memorandum on the Economic Program

The Performance Criteria

The Korean government committed to the following performance criteria under the first standby arrangement with the IMF. The information is

Table 4.1 Disbursement Schedule of the IMF Credit
SDR, billions

Date		*Disbursement limit*
1997	December 18	4.1
1998	January 8	6.7
	February 15	8.2
	May 15	10.8
	August 15	12.6
1999	February 15	14.05
	May 15	14.23125
	August 15	14.4125
	November 15	14.59375
2000	February 15	14.775
	May 15	14.95625
	August 15	15.1375
	November 15	15.31875

Source: International Finance Division, Ministry of Finance and Economy.

contained in annexes A to D of the LOI sent by the government of Korea to the IMF on December 3, 1997.

1. Monetary sector
   - Outstanding stock (end of month) — Limit (W, billion)
   - Net domestic assets
     - September 1997 — 1,721
     - December 1997 (performance criterion) — 10,950
   - Reserve money
     - September 1997 (actual) — 22,275
     - December 1997 (indicative limit) — 23,270
   - Broad money (M3)
     - September 1997 (estimated) — 688,760
     - December 1997 (indicative limit) — 709,775
2. Net foreign reserves of the Bank of Korea (BOK) — Lower limit (US$, billion)
   - September 1997 — 21.1
   - December 1997 — 11.2
3. Consolidated central government balance 1997 (indicative floor) — Lower limit (W, billion) 2,000

4. Interest rate on foreign exchange injections by the BOK to Korean commercial banks or their overseas branches
   - Through the period to the completion of the second biweekly review, the interest rates charged by the BOK on foreign exchange injections into Korean commercial banks or their overseas branches shall not be below 400 basis points above the London Interbank Offered Rate (LIBOR). This will be a performance criterion.
   - This floor shall be reviewed at the time of the second biweekly review of the program, and a new performance criterion may be set for the period after January 8, 1998.

Summary of the Economic Program

Following is a summary of the economic program to which the government of Korea committed under the IMF standby arrangement. The information is contained in "Korea: Memorandum on the Economic Program," the attachment to the LOI sent by the government of Korea to the IMF on December 3, 1997, and refers to the situation on that date.

Macroeconomic policies

1. *Objectives*
   - The program is intended to narrow the external current account deficit to below 1 percent of GDP in 1998 and 1999, contain inflation at or below 5 percent, and—hoping for an early return of confidence—limit the deceleration in real GDP growth to about 3 percent in 1998, followed by a recovery toward potential in 1999.
2. *Monetary policy and exchange rate policy*
   - To demonstrate to markets the resolve of the authorities in confronting the crisis, monetary policy will be tightened immediately to restore and sustain calm in the markets and contain the impact of the recent won depreciation on inflation.
   - In line with this policy, the large liquidity injection in recent days will be reversed, and money market rates, presently 14–16 percent, will be allowed to rise to a level that stabilizes markets. Money growth during 1998 will be limited to a rate consistent with containing inflation at 5 percent or less.
   - A flexible exchange rate policy will be maintained, with interventions limited to smoothing operations.
3. *Fiscal policy*
   - A tight fiscal policy will be maintained in 1998 to alleviate the burden on monetary policy and to provide for the still uncertain costs of restructuring the financial sector. The 1998 budget of the consolidated central government provided for a small surplus (0.25 percent of GDP). The cyclical slowdown is projected

to worsen the 1998 budget balance of the consolidated central government by about 0.8 percent of GDP. The present estimate of the interest costs of financial sector restructuring is 0.8 percent of GDP. Offsetting measures amounting to about 1.5 percent of GDP will be taken to achieve, at a minimum, budget balance and, preferably, a small surplus.

- This will be achieved by revenue and expenditure measures to be determined shortly. These may include increasing value added tax coverage and removing exemptions, widening the corporate tax base by reducing exemptions and certain tax incentives, widening the income tax base by reducing exemptions and deductions, increasing special consumption taxes and the traffic tax, reducing current expenditures that particularly support the corporate sector, and reducing low priority capital expenditures.

Financial sector restructuring

1. *The following financial sector reform bills submitted to the National Assembly will be passed before the end of the year*
   - A revised Bank of Korea Act that provides for central bank independence with price stability as the main mandate. A bill to consolidate the supervision of all banks, including specialized banks, merchant banks, securities firms, and insurance companies, in an agency with operational and financial autonomy and with all the powers needed to deal effectively with troubled financial institutions. A bill requiring that corporate financial statements be prepared on a consolidated basis and be certified by external auditors.
2. *Restructuring and reform measures*
   - Troubled financial companies will be closed or, if they are deemed viable, restructured or recapitalized. A credible and clearly defined exit strategy will include closures, as well as mergers and acquisitions by domestic and foreign institutions, provided the viability of the new groupings is assured. Clear principles on the sharing of losses among equity holders and creditors will be established.
   - The disposal of nonperforming loans will be accelerated. The present blanket guarantees that will end in three years will be replaced by a limited deposit insurance scheme. A timetable will be established for all banks to meet or exceed Basel standards. Prudential standards will be upgraded to meet Basel core principles. Any support to financial companies will be given on strict conditions.
   - All support to financial companies, other than BOK liquidity credits, will be provided according to preestablished rules and recorded transparently. Accounting standards and disclosure rules will be strengthened to meet international practice. The financial statements of large financial companies will be audited by internationally recognized firms. The manpower in the unit that

supervises merchant banks will be sufficiently increased to make supervision effective and to allow for the proper handling of troubled banks.

- The schedule for permitting foreign entry into the domestic financial sector will be accelerated, including allowing foreigners to establish bank subsidiaries and brokerage houses by mid-1998. The borrowing and lending activities of the overseas branches of Korean banks will be closely monitored to ensure that they are sound. Nonviable branches will be closed.
- BOK's international reserve management will be reviewed with the intention of bringing it closer to international practice. Deposits with overseas branches of domestic banks will not be increased further, but gradually withdrawn as circumstances allow. Financial institutions will be encouraged to improve their risk assessment and pricing procedures and to strengthen loan recovery; actions in these areas will be reviewed as part of prudential supervision.

Other structural measures

1. *Trade liberalization*

   Timetables will be set, in compliance with World Trade Organization commitments, at the time of the first review so as to eliminate trade-related subsidies, restrictive import licensing, and the import diversification program and to streamline and improve the transparency of import certification procedures.
2. *Capital account liberalization*
   - The timetable for capital account liberalization will be accelerated. Foreign investment in the Korean equity market will be further liberalized by increasing the ceiling on aggregate ownership from 26 percent to 50 percent by the end of 1997 and to 55 percent by the end of 1998. Effective immediately, for foreign banks seeking to purchase equity in domestic banks in excess of the 4 percent limit requiring supervisory authority approval, the supervisory authority will allow such purchases provided that the acquisitions contribute to the efficiency and soundness of the banking sector. Legislation will be submitted to the first special session of the National Assembly to harmonize the Korean regime on equity purchases with the practices of the Organisation for Economic Co-operation and Development (with due safeguards against the abuse of dominant positions).
   - The Korean government will allow foreign investors access, without restriction, to domestic money market instruments and the domestic corporate bond markets, further reduce restrictions on foreign direct investment through the simplification of procedures, and eliminate restrictions on foreign borrowing by corporations.

3. *Corporate governance and corporate structure*
    - Before the first program review, a timetable will be set to improve the transparency of corporate balance sheets, including profit and loss accounts, by enforcing accounting standards in line with generally accepted accounting practices, including through independent external audits, full disclosure, and the provision of consolidated statements for business conglomerates.
    - The commercial orientation of bank lending will be fully respected, and the government will not intervene in bank management and lending decisions. Directed lending that remains will be eliminated immediately. While policy lending (agriculture, small businesses, and so on) will be maintained, the interest subsidy will be borne by the budget. No government subsidized support or tax privileges will be provided to bail out individual corporations. The real name system in financial transactions will be maintained, although with some possible revisions.
    - Measures will be worked out and implemented to reduce the high debt-to-equity ratio of corporations, and capital markets will be developed to reduce the share of bank financing by corporations (these will be reviewed as part of the first program review). Measures will be worked out and implemented to change the system of mutual guarantees within chaebols to reduce the risks the system involves.
4. *Labor market reform*
    - The capacity of the new employment insurance system will be strengthened to facilitate the redeployment of labor, in parallel with additional steps to improve labor market flexibility.
5. *Information provision*
    - Data on foreign exchange reserves will be regularly published, including the composition of reserves and the net forward position, with a two-week delay, initially. Data on financial institutions, including nonperforming loans, capital adequacy, and ownership structures and affiliations, will be published twice a year. Data on short-term external debt will be published quarterly.

Actions Prior to the IMF Standby Arrangement

Prior to IMF Executive Board approval of a standby arrangement, it is not unusual for the recipient country to take prior actions—also known as front-loaded adjustments—to satisfy certain preconditions for the IMF financial support. For its part, the Korean government took several key steps ahead of the approval of the IMF rescue package to help restore market confidence. The prior actions were identified in close consultation with the IMF and reported to the IMF in a confidential document, along with the LOI. The prior actions included the following:

- Action is being taken to bring the call rate to 25 percent by Friday, December 5. The rate will be maintained at that level until such time—in consultation with IMF staff—that it can be progressively brought down to a range of 18–20 percent. New injections of foreign exchange by the BOK to Korean commercial banks or their overseas branches carry a penalty rate of 400 basis points above LIBOR. This penalty rate will be periodically reviewed.
- Announce an increase in the traffic tax and the special consumption tax as a fiscal action to ensure that the budgetary position remains sufficiently tight.
- Announce an increase in the ceiling on the aggregate ownership by foreigners of listed Korean shares from 26 to 50 percent by the end of 1997 and to 55 percent by the end of 1998 and an increase in the ceiling on individual foreign ownership from 7 to 50 percent by the end of 1997, excluding hostile takeovers; legislation concerning hostile takeovers will be submitted to the first special session of the National Assembly so as to harmonize Korean legislation on the abuse of dominant positions with the practices of other industrial countries.
- The operation of nine technically insolvent merchant banks has been suspended as of December 2, 1997, with the depositors fully protected. The consolidated deposit insurance corporation, which is to be created after the National Assembly passes the necessary legislation before the end of the year, will issue bonds to provide the funds to meet deposit insurance obligations. The government will guarantee these bonds and bear the interest costs.
- Announce the government plan to propose an amendment of the related laws to the first session of the National Assembly immediately after the elections so as to allow foreign financial institutions to participate in the mergers and acquisitions of domestic financial institutions in a friendly manner and on the principle of equality. For merchant banks, foreign participation is allowed up to 100 percent.

Banking Reforms

In addition to the actions to be taken prior to the standby arrangements, the confidential document also described the government's intention to begin a first round of efforts to clean up the financial sector and contained a list of tough measures on banking reform. The steps included the following.

- With regard to the nine suspended merchant banks, they will each be immediately placed under the control of the Ministry of Finance and Economy (MOFE) and required to submit a rehabilitation plan within 30 days to recapitalize the institution; the plans will be evaluated in consultation with the IMF. If the MOFE fails to approve such a plan, the license of the institution will be revoked. Without approved rehabilitation plans, these banks will not be eligible to participate in the Korea Asset Management Corporation (KAMCO) program of bad asset purchases or receive any financing through the deposit insurance fund. Until the rehabilitation plan has been approved, the control officer appointed by the MOFE will cease lending by the institution to any new borrowers (including interbank lending), permit no increase in the institution's off–balance sheet exposure (that is, an extension of guarantees), and prohibit the purchase of any securities other than those guaranteed by the government. The control officer may continue to allow limited additional lending to existing borrowers on a case-by-case basis. Rehabilitation will be monitored in close consultation with the IMF. If the head of the supervisory authority concludes that rehabilitation has not been successful within three months, the institution will be closed.

- The remaining merchant banks will be required to present a program of recapitalization and downsizing by December 31, 1997 that will allow them to meet at least a 4 percent capital requirement ratio by March 31, 1998, a 6 percent ratio by June 30, 1998, and an 8 percent ratio by June 1999. These ratios will be computed after applying the provisioning requirements set for commercial banks. Failure to obtain supervisory approval of the program or to meet the schedule will lead to suspension of foreign exchange business and can lead to the revocation of licenses.
- The two commercial banks in distress will each be required to submit a plan within two months for approval in consultation with the IMF to meet Basel capital standards within four months after approval of the plan. Until such a plan has been approved by the supervisory authority, these banks will be held under intensive oversight by the supervisory authority. The plan could initially include merger with another financial company or disposal of some or all of banking business so as to restore profitability to an acceptable level and meet the minimum solvency requirements set by the supervisory authority. Rehabilitation will be monitored in close consultation with the IMF. If the head of the supervisory authority concludes that rehabilitation has not been successful within four months, the institution will be closed.
- Other commercial banks will be required to make full provisioning for their impaired assets and for their securities losses by the end of March 1998. They will agree to a timetable with the supervisory authority by June 1998 to achieve current minimum capital standards within a time frame of six months to two years. The program will include a precise implementation schedule. Until such

recapitalization is achieved, they will be prevented from distributing dividends, their senior management remuneration will be frozen, and significant expansions of their operations will be subject to prior approval of the supervisory authority.

- The rehabilitation plans submitted to the supervisory authority by financial companies will specify the sources and amounts of new capital and clear schedules to meet Basel capital adequacy standards and provisioning requirements; provide confirmation of this by the supplier of funds; indicate changes in management and ownership if intended; and present business plans that define the activities on which the institutions will concentrate and those that they will dispose of, set out measures to reduce costs, and describe detailed steps to improve internal governance, risk assessment and pricing, and loan recovery. When and if such a plan is approved by the relevant supervisory authority, the institution will enter into a managerial contract or memorandum of understanding, which will include a schedule for implementation. In case an institution's plan is rejected by the supervisory authority because it is not considered credible or has not been implemented as agreed, the institution will come under the direct control of the supervisory authority until the final disposition of its business.
- All forms of subsidized public assistance to banking institutions will be authorized only after current shareholders and, in case of liquidation, nonguaranteed creditors, in that order, have absorbed existing losses. Any purchase of assets or advances made by KAMCO will be made at the resale price of the assets as estimated by the appraisers. No KAMCO transactions will result in any subsidy.
- In consultation with the IMF, the Korean government will prepare an action program to strengthen financial supervision and regulation in accordance with international best practice standards. To carry out this program, the government will seek technical assistance from the IMF and other international institutions. During economic program reviews, it will consult with the IMF regarding progress in implementing this action program.
- Specialized banks and development institutions will be subject to the same prudential standards that apply to commercial banks, and their financial statements will be subject to external audits under the same rules applicable to other financial companies.

Averting National Insolvency

The Lukewarm Response of the Market

The standby arrangement was organized fairly quickly, and the US$58 billion credit support made available to the government was initially thought to be sufficient to close the immediate financing gap Korea faced. The early consensus was that the policies prescribed by the IMF would soon bring back confidence and put the economy back on track. Unexpectedly, however, the reception by the market was far from enthusiastic.

It was lukewarm at best because a spate of more bad news soon followed the announcement of the rescue package. Indeed, the international credit-rating agencies began to downgrade Korea's sovereign rating. On December 11, Standard and Poor's lowered its long-term rating on Korea from A– to BBB– and its short-term rating from A2 to A3. Then, on December 23, it further downgraded the long-term sovereign rating to B+ and the short-term rating to C. Moody's and Fitch quickly followed suit.

The downgrading effectively reclassified Korean debt securities into junk bonds, which meant that fresh credit from foreign lenders would be all but unavailable, and debt rollover would become even more difficult than it already was. During the month of December, the short-term debt conditions of the Big 7 commercial banks were so dire that the roll-over ratio was below 30 percent, and the interest rate spread jumped to 245 basis points. Table 4.2 shows the roll-over ratios of the short-term external debt of domestic financial companies as of the end of 1997 as estimated by Samsung Economic Research Institute.

With domestic financial companies unable to roll over their short-term external debt and provide much-needed liquidity to the market, the foreign exchange markets all but froze. December is usually a time of high demand for foreign currencies among importers because of the year-end settlement of transactions. So, the supply shortage was particularly acute during this month. Leads and lags in the foreign exchange markets also intensified. When the news broke that IMF financial assistance would not be made immediately available to foreign exchange markets, but would be added to the foreign exchange reserves, which targeted the accumulation of US$11.2 billion by year-end, the foreign exchange markets went into a tailspin.

The won/U.S. dollar exchange rate climbed quickly in a reflection of the market panic. On December 4, the won settled at around W 1,100 against the dollar based on the upbeat sentiment following the conclusion of the standby arrangement. But the next day, it spiraled to W 1,200 and hit the daily cap for the next four days. Foreign currency trading all but ceased (BOK 1997b). On December 16, the government repealed the daily floating cap on the won and let it float. By December 24, the exchange rate for the U.S. dollar had reached W 1,964.8.

Facing an extreme shortage of dollars, domestic financial companies had to turn to the BOK for emergency assistance. The central bank obliged by providing US$1.49 billion to merchant banks and US$12.88 billion to commercial banks in December. It also sold US$1.48 billion to the market in December to assist those with legitimate foreign currency needs. The prospect of the complete depletion of the foreign exchange reserves of the central bank became more tangible, and the most urgent problem

Table 4.2 The Rollover of Short-Term External Debt among Financial Companies
percent

Event, group, and indicator	*1996*	*1997*				
	December	*January*	*April*	*July*	*October*	*December*
Event		Hanbo bankruptcy	Chaebol bankruptcy in droves	Suspended default of Kia	Stock market plummet, Hong Kong SAR, China	Korea crisis
A Group	100	100	100	90	70	50
B Group	100	100	90	70	10	0
C Group	100	90	50	20	10	0
Overseas finance market movement	Good conditions for rollover and new borrowing	C group facing difficulty in overseas financing and requests for BOK foreign exchange support	B group facing difficulty in overseas financing and increase in Korean risk premium	A group facing difficulty in overseas financing, and Korean risk premium jumped up to the level of a junk bond	Rapidly falling roll-over rate, downgrading Korea's sovereign rating; impossible to avoid currency crisis	Impossible for overseas financing and external debt payments

Source: Kim 1998.

Note: A Group: overseas higher credit ratings (Korea Development Bank, Export-Import Bank of Korea, and so on). B Group: overseas medium credit ratings (Korea Long-Term Credit Bank, Shinhan Bank, and so on). C Group: overseas lower credit ratings (merchant banks, Korea First Bank, Seoul Bank, and so on).

was to prevent national insolvency. By December 11, the reserves stood at US$9.6 billion. However, even with the US$5.5 billion in the pipeline from the ADB and the IMF by year's end, it was doubtful whether there would be enough to cover the US$13 billion needed by domestic financial companies and the US$2 billion to US$3 billion needed by others. The outlook was grim.

Second Review and Consultation with the IMF, December 18, 1997

With no break in sight, both the government and the IMF hurried to come up with follow-up measures. One proposal was to accelerate the delivery of the funds and the execution of the economic program to raise market confidence. This decision was important because the amount of the funds to be delivered to Korea in December was quite small despite the substantial size of the total rescue package. Under the circumstances, it made sense to accelerate the funding. Another proposal was to facilitate short-term rollovers by having the government guarantee maturing debt and issue sovereign bonds to overseas investors to raise additional funds.

On December 18, the IMF Executive Board reviewed the progress Korea had made in implementing its economic program and approved the second disbursement of US$3.5 billion under the existing US$21 billion standby credit. It also decided to utilize the newly created Supplemental Reserve Facility of US$13.5 billion that was to be provided to Korea for a year beginning on the date of the delivery of the second round of funds. This was necessary because of the large amount of funds needed by Korea. The size of Korea's rescue package exceeded the customary 300 percent of the IMF quota, reaching 1,939 percent, substantially larger than the amount provided to countries recently hit by financial crises (490 percent for Indonesia, 688 percent for Mexico, and 505 percent for Thailand). The Supplemental Reserve Facility was to be set for one year with the interest rate fixed at the SDR rate, plus 300 basis points. After the first year, the interest rate was to be increased by 50 basis points; it was to be increased by 50 basis points every six months thereafter, but capped at 500 basis points.

The fresh LOI sent on December 18 stated that, even though confidence had been recovering only slowly, the Korean government believed that the situation would improve in the coming months as the program continued to be implemented. It stressed that the major candidates in the upcoming presidential elections had reaffirmed their strong support for the program. It suggested that the IMF attributed the continued loss of confidence at least partly to doubts about Korea's commitment to deliver on its promises, as well as the political uncertainties arising from the presidential elections. The *Wall Street Journal* reported on December 11 that fund managers had replied in the negative when asked whether Korea had hit the bottom and expressed doubt about whether Korea was going to make all the painful changes it had pledged to the IMF (Cho 1997). The newspaper claimed that this was one reason foreign investors were still leaving Korea.

Although such a recognition prevailed abroad, the Korean government had made decisive progress in all areas identified in the "Korea: memorandum" and had surpassed the understandings in several important areas. The government had taken action to implement the fiscal measures needed to achieve the fiscal targets for 1998. It had permitted a substantial increase in market interest rates, to around 25 percent, to demonstrate to the markets its resolve to confront the crisis, and the cabinet had approved the amendment to the presidential decree to raise the ceiling on interest rates to 40 percent to allow for more increases in interest rates as necessary.

The government had also eliminated the 10 percent daily floating band margin in the market average exchange rate system to allow the won to be freely determined by market forces. In the area of the interest rates on foreign exchange injections by the BOK to commercial banks, the penalty rate of LIBOR, plus 400 basis points that had been agreed to under the program had been raised to 700 basis points. To improve the transparency of the data on reserves, BOK deposits with overseas branches of domestic banks had been reduced. The ceilings on foreign purchases of Korean equity had been raised; foreign investment in the bond markets had been further liberalized; greater foreign ownership of banks had been allowed; and the restrictions on overseas borrowing by corporations had been eased. In a sign of its resolve, the government also suspended the business operations of five merchant banks, bringing to 14 the number of merchant banks suspended (of the total of 30 merchant banks in existence).

Third Review and Consultation with the IMF, December 24, 1997

Despite the additional steps the government and the IMF took on December 18 to reassure the markets, market conditions continued to turn for the worse. In a December 24 article, the *Kyunghyang Daily*, a local newspaper, reported that the pledge by President-elect Kim Dae-Jung following his victory in the presidential elections to act forcefully to deliver on the promises Korea had made to the IMF did little to turn the situation around. The article argued that, contrary to the upbeat expectations of improvement following the presidential elections, Korea was under enormous pressure because of the sharp sovereign downgrading, the collapse of the stock markets, and the record-high interest rates and that the country was getting perilously close to insolvency. The gloom was encapsulated in the term 333 Club that had been coined sarcastically to herald the new era introduced by the exchange rate of W 3,000 per U.S. dollar, the 300 of the Korea composite stock price index, and the 30 percent interest rate.

Facing enormous pressure to stem the tide of extremely volatile and adverse developments all around, the government consulted closely with the IMF, Japan, the United States, and others for support. The Joint Presidential Committee on Economic Policies formed by the outgoing Kim Young-Sam administration and advisors of incoming President Kim Dae-Jung coordinated the responses. The government also consulted with David Lipton, the U.S. under secretary of the treasury for international affairs, and Hubert Neiss, the IMF director of Asian affairs, in mapping additional steps on December 24.

The government thus identified several new strategies. First, it promised to accelerate the implementation of the economic program on monetary policies, financial sector reform, capital market opening, trade policies, and the management of the reserves and the exchange rate policy. Second, the government discussed the possibility with foreign lenders of improving the rollovers on the short-term borrowing of domestic financial companies and gaining access to fresh mid-term market borrowing. Third, the government discussed the possibility of additional advanced disbursements of official resources. The government sent an LOI to the IMF on December 24 requesting that the schedule of disbursements under the arrangement be modified so as to deliver US$2 billion of the package on December 30.[4] It also said that US$8 billion of the second line of defense provided by the 13 developed countries would be requested for early January 1998. Foreign lenders in the G-7 countries were also to be asked to extend voluntarily the maturity of their short-term loans to Korea.

The plan was met with a measure of acceptance, and, on December 29, the major international creditor banks agreed to stretch the maturity on Korea's short-term debt temporarily. The IMF Executive Board also agreed, on December 30, to advance the date of the disbursement of US$2 billion, originally set for January 8, 1998, to December 30, 1997. One key point in this endeavor was that Korea agreed to step up the economic reforms and trade and capital market liberalization measures contained in the economic program and accelerate the timetable in return for the early delivery of the rescue package. However, because the steps in trade and capital market liberalization were not immediate confidence-building measures, criticism soon surfaced that the countries supposedly lending a helping hand to Korea were, in fact, looking out for their own interests.

Support of the ADB and the World Bank

The World Bank and the ADB disbursed US$3 billion and US$2 billion on December 23 and 24, 1997, respectively. The government began its negotiations with the World Bank on December 8, concluded the talks on December 21, and received the US$3 billion as an economic reconstruction loan. Under the terms of the agreement, the borrower was the Korean government, and the interest rate was set at LIBOR, plus 1 percent. The service charge was 2 percent of the borrowed amount for the first year, 1 percent in the second year, and 0.5 percent in the third year. The loan was to mature in 10 years, with a five-year grace period. The economic program worked out in return for the loan consisted of a Letter of Development Policy that spelled out the government's restructuring plans and a policy matrix that contained the specific execution measures. The main elements of the policy matrix covered normalization issues concerning the suspended merchant banks, prudential bank supervision, the creation of integrated financial supervision authority, the activities of KAMCO, and the reporting on consolidated financial statements, all of which had already been agreed to in negotiations with the IMF.

Talks with the ADB on a financial sector program loan occurred on December 7–10 and concluded with the approval of the ADB Board of Directors on December 19. Under the terms of the agreement, the borrower was the Korean government, and the loan amount was set at US$4 billion, of which US$2 billion was to be disbursed in December 1997, US$1 billion in January 1998, US$700 million in December 1998, and the remaining US$300 million in December 1999. The interest rate was set at LIBOR, plus 0.4 percent, with interest payments to be made every six months; the principal amount was to be paid in full in seven years. The matters covered in the Letter of Development Policy and the policy matrix ranged from improvements in the asset quality and management of banks and nonbank financial companies and in the efficiency of financial markets in enhancing the transparency of corporate financial reporting and disclosures. The measures did not vary much from those in the IMF programs.

Legislative Efforts in the National Assembly

As it had pledged to the IMF, Korea had to enact reform legislation by the end of 1997. The key measures the National Assembly passed in special legislative sessions during December 22–30, 1997 are summarized as follows.

December 22, 1997

- A consent bill for a government guarantee on the repayment of the principal and interest of the Non-Performing Asset Management Fund bond to be issued in 1997 and 1998; the total amount of the bond was W 17 trillion.
- A consent bill for the issuance of the Foreign Exchange Stabilization Fund bond in 1997 and 1998; the bond, which was denominated in foreign currency, was to be issued for up to US$10 billion.
- A consent bill for a government guarantee on the debt of domestic banks denominated in foreign currency and due in 1997 and 1998.

- A consent bill for government borrowing plans; the plans involved a borrowing of US$4 billion from the ADB and US$10 billion from the World Bank beginning in December 1997.

December 29, 1997

- Amendment of the Traffic Tax Act: the tax rate on gasoline and diesel fuel was to increase from W 345 to W 455 per liter and from W 48 to W 85 per liter, respectively.
- Amendment of the Special Consumption Tax Act: the tax rate on kerosene was to increase from W 25 to W 60 per liter; the tax rate on golf clubs, air conditioners, and fur, among other items, was to increase from 15 or 20 percent to 30 percent.
- Legislation of the Act on Real Name Financial Transactions and Guarantee of Secrecy (in substitution of a presidential emergency decree).
- Amendment of the Bank of Korea Act: banking supervision was to be separated from the BOK and transferred to the newly created Financial Supervisory Commission (FSC) and the Financial Supervisory Service (FSS).
- Legislation of the Act on the Establishment of Financial Supervisory Organizations: the financial oversight functions divided among the Office of Bank Supervision in the BOK, the Securities Supervisory Board, the Insurance Supervisory Board, and the MOFE were to be consolidated and integrated under the newly created FSC and FSS.
- Amendment of the Banking Act: the authority for banking supervision was to be assumed by the FSC; the proportion of nonstanding bank board members was to be raised to encourage the participation of shareholders in management.
- Amendment of the Mutual Savings and Finance Company Act: the FSC and the FSS were to supervise mutual savings and finance companies; the Korea Deposit Insurance Corporation (KDIC) was to take charge of the insurance on the deposits.
- Amendment of the Securities and Exchange Act: the Securities Supervisory Board was to be abolished, and its oversight authorities were to be assumed by the FSC, the FSS, and the Securities and Futures Commission.
- Amendment of the Futures Trading Act: the Futures Trading Commission was to be abolished, and its oversight authority, as well as the authority to investigate unlawful securities trading, was to be assumed by the FSC and the Securities and Futures Commission.
- Amendment of the Act on External Audit of Stock Companies: large business groups designated by the presidential decree must report independently audited consolidated financial statements.
- Amendment of the Merchant Banks Act: the act may establish fit and proper criteria for the board members of merchant banks; the FSC

may order suspension or recommend the dismissal of board members who fail to satisfy the criteria.

- Legislation of the Act on Rearrangement of the Certified Public Accountant Act (and so on) in accordance with the legislation of the Act on Establishment of Financial Supervisory Organizations: the MOFE was to assume the licensing authority for financial companies; the FSC and the FSS were to supervise the business activities of financial companies; 36 acts were amended by this act.
- Amendment of the Depositor Protection Act: the KDIC was to assume the full authority for deposit insurance; financial companies to be covered under the deposit insurance protection program were to be expanded to include securities companies, insurance providers, merchant banks, mutual savings and finance companies, and credit unions.
- Amendment of the Act on the Structural Improvement of the Financial Industry: the authority for mergers and acquisitions and the clean-up of distressed financial companies was to be shared and rearranged among the MOFE, the FSC, and the KDIC.
- Amendment of the Insurance Business Act: the insurance supervision authority, except the issuance or revocation of licenses, was to be transferred from the MOFE to the FSC; the supervision authority of the Insurance Supervision Board was to be assumed by the FSS.
- Amendment of the Trust Business Act: the MOFE was to issue or revoke licenses for trust (asset management) companies; all other oversight and enforcement authorities were to be held under the FSC.
- Amendment of the Credit Unions Act: where the National Credit Union Federation of Korea acted as an agent for the government, public institutions, or financial institutions, it was to be subject to the rules and regulations stipulated in the Banking Act and the Bank of Korea Act.
- Abolition of the Interest Limitation Act: the regulations on permitted interest rates were to be repealed.
- A consent bill for the government guarantee on the repayment of the principal and interest of the Korea deposit insurance fund bond to be issued in 1997 and 1998; the total amount of the bond was W 12 trillion.

Seeking Access to Foreign Currencies

The government sought access to foreign currencies to supplement the IMF funding. On December 15, 1997, the MOFE came up with plans for a foreign bond offering totaling US$10 billion: US$9 billion in foreign issues and US$1 billion in domestic issues, respectively, in January and February 1998. It also sought to have the US$20 billion short-term external debt owed to foreign creditor banks by domestic financial companies rolled over by entering into negotiations with the heads of the Korean branches of foreign banks. However, the negotiations did not yield the desired results because of the limited responsibility of the Korean branches in decisions on such matters.

The U.S. Treasury Department urged prompt rescue actions on Korea to avert a major disaster, but it also emphasized that foreign private creditors must roll over Korea's short-term debt because the money of U.S. taxpayers should be used to assist Korea, not to bail out Korea's foreign private creditors. On December 22, 1997, at the behest of the U.S. Treasury Department and the IMF, the Federal Reserve Bank of New York held a meeting with representatives of Bankers Trust Company, Bank of America, Bank of New York, Chase Manhattan Bank, Citibank, and J. P. Morgan to request rollovers of Korea's maturing debt. However, the meeting ended without result.

On December 24, the situation took a more optimistic turn when the 13 countries that had agreed to provide a second line of defense to Korea decided to persuade creditors in their own countries to extend the maturity of Korea's short-term debt. Following the agreement, the Federal Reserve Bank of New York convened a second meeting of creditor banks. This time, these banks agreed to a rollover. In the United Kingdom, the Bank of England gathered together its own creditor banks and produced temporary rollovers until March 31, 1998. It selected HSBC as the coordinator for the creditor banks. At similar meetings held in Germany on December 29, creditors agreed to a one-month extension of maturing debt. On the same day, the major creditor banks met at J. P. Morgan and confirmed a temporary extension for debt maturing at the end of 1997. The amount to be rolled over was approximately US$15 billion. The extension was until January 15 or March 31, 1998.

The government formed a special task force on December 27 to coordinate the debt settlement efforts. The following day, it retained attorneys Mark Walker and Robert Davis of the law firm Cleary, Gottlieb, Steen & Hamilton as legal counsel. On December 29, J. P. Morgan made a proposal for the rollover of Korea's debt at a meeting of the major creditor banks. The proposal was forwarded to the Korean government on December 30. Under the proposal, the government was to issue sovereign bonds to replace the outstanding debt of Korean banks maturing in 1998 and raise additional funds simultaneously. Yields on the new bond issues were to be determined using a modified Dutch auction. Therefore, the government now entered a phase in which it had to decide on the best strategy for covering maturing debt and raising fresh funds through new sovereign bond issues.

The Capital Account and the Movement of the Won, December 1997

The sharp drop in imports during December helped the current account post a US$3.59 billion surplus. However, the capital account was in deficit by US$6.37 billion largely because of the payment of US$12.07 billion on short-term debt, the withdrawal of US$1.57 billion by foreign bond investors, and a drop of US$2.01 billion in trade-related credit lines. The net capital flow into the stock market was US$320 million for the month. It should be noted that US$16.12 billion came in from the ADB, the IMF, and the World Bank in December alone. Table 4.3 shows the flow of funds from the major international financial institutions as of the end of March 1998.

The value of the loans called back and the credit lines cut by foreign banks with respect to Korean banks totaled US$33.31 billion in 1997, down 56.7 percent since the end of 1996 (table 4.4). Japanese banks led the pack with US$12.53 billion. They were followed by European banks, with US$9.02 billion, and U.S. banks, with US$4.12 billion. On December 1, 1997, usable foreign exchange reserves stood at US$6.69 billion; they jumped to US$11.06 billion on December 5. The reserves then fell to US$6.44 billion on December 15 and US$3.94 billion on December 18. After infusions by the ADB and the World Bank, the reserves bounced back to US$8.76 billion on December 26 and to US$8.87 billion at the end of the year. The won had depreciated 40.3 percent by the year's end from a year earlier and 17.8 percent from the previous month. On December 24,

Table 4.3 Flow of Funds from Major International Financial Institutions, End of March, 1998
US$, billions

Year	*Date*[a]	*IMF*	*World Bank*	*ADB*	*Total*
1997	Dec. 4	5.5	n.a.	n.a.	5.5
	Dec. 18	3.5	n.a.	n.a.	3.5
	Dec. 23	n.a.	3.0	n.a.	3.0
	Dec. 24	n.a.	n.a.	2.0	2.0
	Dec. 30	2.0	n.a.	n.a.	2.0
	Subtotal	11.0	3.0	2.0	16.0
1998	Jan. 5	n.a.	n.a.	1.0	1.0
	Jan. 8	2.0	n.a.	n.a.	2.0
	Feb. 17	2.0	n.a.	n.a.	2.0
	Mar. 27	n.a.	2.0	n.a.	2.0
	Subtotal	4.0	2.0	1.0	7.0
Total		15.0	5.0	3.0	23.0

Source: International Organization Division, Ministry of Finance and Economy.
Note: n.a. = not applicable.
a. Dates of approval by the IMF Executive Board. Dates of disbursement for the ADB and the World Bank.

Table 4.4 Short-Term Overseas Borrowing, by Region, End of Period, 1997
% and US$, billions

Economy	*A. 1996*	*1997*					
		B. June	*October*	*November*	*C. December*	*Change, B–A*	*Change, C–A*
Total[a]	58.70	53.92	49.42	40.13	25.39	–4.78	–33.31
	—	(–8.1)	(–8.3)	(–18.8)	(–36.7)	(–8.1)	(–56.7)
Japan	21.33	16.58	15.74	14.02	8.80	–4.75	–12.53
	—	(–22.3)	(–5.1)	(–10.9)	(–37.2)	(–22.3)	(–58.7)
United States	7.61	7.28	6.00	4.97	3.49	–0.33	–4.12
	—	(–4.3)	(–17.6)	(–17.2)	(–29.8)	(–4.3)	(–54.1)
Europe	18.66	18.03	16.98	13.60	9.61	–0.63	–9.02
	—	(–3.4)	(–5.8)	(–19.9)	(–29.3)	(–3.4)	(–48.3)
Others[b]	11.10	12.03	10.70	7.54	3.49	0.93	–7.61

Source: Foreign Exchange Regulations and External Debt Division, Ministry of Finance and Economy.

Note: Numbers in parentheses denote the growth rate since the end of the previous period. — = not available.

a. Three-month maturity borrowing of the Big 7 commercial banks: Korea Development Bank, Export-Import Bank of Korea, Korea Long-Term Credit Bank, Kookmin Bank, Housing & Commercial Bank, and Industrial Bank of Korea.

b. Banks in Hong Kong SAR, China and banks in other Asian countries.

Table 4.5 Movements in the W/US$ Exchange Rate, by Day, December 1997
won

Rate	1	3	9	10	11	12	17	20	24	26	27	31
W/US$	1,170.0	1,240.6	1,332.5	1,423.6	1,563.5	1,737.6	1,405.9	1,618.1	1,964.8	1,850.1	1,512.9	1,415.2

Source: Economic Analysis Division, Ministry of Finance and Economy.

the exchange rate of the won for the U.S. dollar climbed to W 1,964.8, only to fall back to W 1,415.2 by year's end (table 4.5).

Notes

1. See http://www.imf.org/external/np/loi/120397.HTM.
2. MCT = currency in circulation + demand deposits (subtotal called M1) + time and savings deposits + resident's foreign currency deposits (subtotal called M2) + certificates of deposit + money in trust (excludes certificates of deposit and money in trust of development institutions).
3. Japan (US$10 billion); the United States (US$5 billion); France, Germany, Italy, and the United Kingdom together (US$5 billion); Belgium, the Netherlands, Sweden, and Switzerland together (US$1.25 billion); Australia (US$1 billion); Canada (US$1 billion); and New Zealand (US$100 million).
4. See https://www.imf.org/external/np/loi/122497.htm.

5

Securing Foreign Currency Liquidity and Laying the Groundwork for Reform and Restructuring, December 1997–April 1998

Securing Foreign Currency Liquidity

Maturity Extensions on Short-Term Debt

The major foreign creditor banks decided, at the end of 1997, to give temporary maturity extensions on the short-term external debt of financial companies in the Republic of Korea. The challenge then was to turn the short-term debt into mid- to long-term debt and to avoid a potential default. On January 7, 1998, the Ministry of Finance and Economy (MOFE) took the following positions on efforts to improve foreign exchange liquidity: (1) Rather than seeking maturity extensions and new debt issues simultaneously as proposed by J. P. Morgan, maturity extensions should be achieved prior to any new debt issues. (2) The government would guarantee the principal and interest on the maturity-extended loans. (3) The decision on interest rates should be negotiated.

On January 18, 1998, the government sent a mission led by Kim Yong-Hwan, the head of the Joint Presidential Committee on Economic Policies, to the United States to negotiate the rollover of short-term debt. Chung Duk-Koo, assistant minister of finance and economy, led the team that conducted the negotiations with the foreign creditor banks. The foreign creditor bank group was made up of representatives of 13 banks in seven countries and led by William R. Rhodes, vice-chairman of Citibank.

The negotiations in New York kicked off on January 21 and wrapped up on January 29. Under the agreement that was reached, debt with maturity shorter than one year and set to mature during 1998 was to be guaranteed by the government, but the maturity was to be transformed into one, two, or three years.[1] The interest rate spread was set at the London Interbank Offered Rate (LIBOR), plus 2.25 percentage points for loans due within one year; LIBOR, plus 2.50 percentage points for loans due in two years; and LIBOR, plus 2.75 percentage points for loans due in three years. For loans due in two or three years, early callback was to be allowed after six months.

The government held road shows on maturity extensions in major international financial centers from February 27 to March 8 with some success. Through these meetings, the government was able to persuade foreign creditors to roll over US$21.84 billion of US$22.65 billion in maturing debt (as of March 16) at a roll-over ratio of 96.5 percent. Loans given a one-year maturity extension totaled US$3.767 billion (17.2 percent of the total roll-over amount); loans given a two-year extension, US$9.119 billion (45 percent of the total); and loans given a three-year extension, US$8.253 billion (37.9 percent of the total). A total of 134 creditor banks in 32 countries agreed to the government-led roll-over efforts.

For the domestic financial companies receiving a government debt guarantee, the government decided to impose guarantee fees ranging from 0.2 to 1.5 percent of the guaranteed amount depending on the debtor institution's credit rating or the Bank for International Settlements (BIS) capital ratio. It also required the debtor institutions to set up a debt reduction fund and put aside 0.25 percent of the total foreign debt each month (for a one-year total of 3 percent).

Once the maturity extensions for financial companies had been successfully addressed, attention turned to corporate companies facing possible debt callbacks from foreign creditors. At the time, it was estimated that US$60 billion in corporate debt was due in 1998; of this sum, approximately US$10 billion was actually expected to be repaid, not rolled over, by domestic companies in 1998.

The top five *chaebols*—the large family-controlled and family-run groups that dominate business in Korea—accounted for most of the corporate debt at the time, and rumors were rampant in the markets that certain chaebol companies were on the brink of default. The government decided not to use public funds to bail out these companies or give them debt payment guarantees. The debt problems had to be resolved by the companies themselves.

The Sovereign Bond Offering

The government next decided to proceed quickly with a sovereign bond offering to foreign investors. The reason overseas foreign investors were targeted was not only to improve foreign exchange liquidity, but also to establish a basis for funding in international financial markets for domestic corporate and financial companies in need of fresh foreign currency. Initially, the government set the issuance target at US$3 billion; the amount was to increase after foreign investors had reacted favorably. The maturity was to be set at 5 and 10 years in recognition of the preference of foreign investors for loan terms longer than 10 years. Considering that recent overseas bond offerings generally did not feature call options for issuers, there was some concern about whether the 10-year debt maturity was excessively long. However, the concern gave way to the recognition that the bond offerings had to cater to the preference of foreign investors if they were to be successful.

The yield on the bond offering was difficult to predict because it was the first sovereign bond offering in foreign currencies, and there was thus no good benchmark yield to emulate. However, because Korea's sovereign ratings had dropped below investment grade and because Moody's had downgraded Japan's sovereign debt rating on April 3, 1998, the conditions were certainly not favorable, and the yield was likely to be high.

On March 21, 1998, the government filed registration statements with the U.S. Securities and Exchange Commission for a US$5 billion bond offering. It also launched road shows for investors in 14 cities in seven countries from March 26 to April 3. On April 8, the price and the amount of the bond offering were finalized. The total issuance amount was set at US$4 billion, US$1 billion more than initially planned. US$1 billion was offered at a five-year maturity, and US$3 billion at a 10-year maturity. Investors responded positively to the bond offering, resulting in US$12 billion in investment requests. The spread over U.S. Treasury bonds (with five-year yields at 5.503 percent and 10-year yields at 5.534 percent as of April 8) was 3.45 percentage points for the five-year bonds and 3.55 percentage points for the 10-year bonds. The spreads were more favorable than the US$3 billion to US$6 billion at 3.5 to 3.75 percentage-point spreads that the markets had anticipated.[2]

The bond offering was described as a smash hit in international debt markets, and Korea was generally praised for its ability to return to international debt markets a mere four months after the onset of the financial crisis; it had taken Mexico 13 months to resume a debt offering in international debt markets after its financial crisis. The key ingredient of the success was the confidence foreign investors placed in Korea and its potential to turn around from junk bond to investment grade status in the near future. It must be said that it was also an expression of confidence in Korea's blueprint for economic reform and in President Kim Dae-Jung's leadership in managing and overcoming the crisis.

The Gold Collection Campaign

As the government forged ahead with its plans to secure foreign exchange, a campaign to collect gold spread quickly among citizens as a way to show national unity in overcoming the financial crisis. After the Housing & Commercial Bank of Korea and the Korea Broadcasting System, the public television station, launched the campaign on January 5, 1998, six financial companies joined in to help gather 226 tons of gold valued at US$2.2 billion by March 14. About three tons (US$29 million) were bought by the Bank of Korea (BOK), the central bank, to add to its reserves, and the rest was exported. According to a report of the Ministry of Government Administration and Home Affairs, almost 3.5 million citizens took part in the campaign, representing about 23 percent of the 15 million total households at the time. On average, each participating household brought in 65 grams of gold. Some called the campaign a modern version of a sovereign debt repayment campaign under the waning Joseon Dynasty, when, in 1907, 40,000 citizens donated jewelry, grain, and other valuables, as well as quit smoking and drinking to be able to save money to contribute. The 1998 gold collection campaign was a rare show of unity and confidence that received wide publicity and praise from around the world and boosted the morale of the citizenry.

Escape from the Sovereign Default and Facing Other Challenges

The balance of payments and movements in the won/dollar exchange rate. During January–April 1998, the current account posted a US$14.33 billion surplus. However, exports were sluggish at best because of the economic downturn in Japan, Southeast Asia, and other key export markets and a 19 percent drop in the unit price of Korean exports, which was enough to offset the higher volume of goods exported. Trade financing remained difficult, and obtaining the raw materials needed for the production of export goods was as uncertain as ever. Imports fell sharply as well because of the slowing economy, which severely cut the demand for raw materials and capital goods. The current account surplus was helped by falling commodity prices outside Korea; the price of crude oil dropped from US$15.49 a barrel in January 1998 to US$10.20 in December.

The capital account recorded a US$1.5 billion surplus during the January–April period. Whereas foreign direct investment (FDI) showed a modest deficit of US$40 million, there was a US$7.47 billion net increase in foreign securities investments. The balance in other investment activities, which showed a US$7 billion deficit in December 1997, fell to less than US$6 billion during the first four months of 1998. This was caused mostly by improved roll-over and trade credit conditions amid ongoing discussions on debt extension and the infusion of the US$7 billion in financial assistance that Korea received from the International Monetary Fund (IMF) and other international financial institutions as part of the rescue package.

With the current account in the black and capital flows stabilizing, foreign exchange reserves grew substantially. Usable foreign exchange reserves, which stood at US$8.87 billion at the end of 1997, rose to US$30.76 billion in April 1998 (table 5.1). This level was reached ahead of the timetable set with the IMF—US$30 billion by the end of June 1998—by two months. The size of the reserves was also greater than the amount before the onset of the crisis. At the end of April 1998, total foreign liabilities stood at US$158.42 billion, down US$22.05 billion from the US$180.47 at the end of September 1997. Of the total, long-term liabilities accounted for US$120.24 billion or 75.9 percent. Short-term liabilities came to US$38.19 billion or 24.1 percent.

The Korean won/U.S. dollar exchange rate climbed to W 1,749.9 on January 24, 1998 in the wake of the worsening crisis in Indonesia, but dropped back to W 1,572.9 on January 31 with the successful conclusion of the debt extension talks in New York. Beginning in February, foreign stock purchases slowed, pushing the won/dollar exchange rate to W 1,707.3 per dollar on February 18. The continued progress in the short-term debt extension and the sovereign bond offering, coupled with sustained current account surpluses, helped drive down the won/dollar exchange rate to W 1,378.8 by the end of March and to W 1,338.2 by the end of April, a 5.8 percent drop from the W 1,415.2 rate at the end of 1997.

As the won began to show signs of stabilizing and the government reiterated its resolute commitment to muscular reform and restructuring, the leading international credit-rating agencies started to raise Korea's sovereign ratings. On January 21, Fitch lifted Korea's sovereign credit outlook from negative to positive and, on February 2, upgraded the rating from B– to BB+, a jump of five notches. Likewise, on February 17, Standard and Poor's raised Korea's rating three notches, from B+ to BB+. Moody's

Table 5.1 Trends in Targeted and Actual Foreign Exchange Reserves, End of Period, 1998
US$, billions

		1998						
Indicator	*1997*	*Jan.*	*Feb.*	*Mar.*	*Apr.*	*June*	*Sept.*	*Dec.*
Targeted usable foreign reserves[a]	n.a.	n.a.	n.a.	20.0	n.a.	30.0	35.5	39.1
Actual total foreign reserves	20.41	23.52	26.72	29.75	35.54	—	—	—
Usable foreign reserves	8.87	12.36	18.54	24.15	30.76	—	—	—

Source: Foreign Exchange Management Division, Ministry of Finance and Economy.
Note: n.a. = not applicable. — = not available.

a. Targeted reserves agreed to with the IMF during the fifth policy discussion, on February 7, 1998.

had Korea's sovereign credit rating one level below investment grade, at Ba1, since December 21, 1997. Thus, despite the rating upgrades, Korea's sovereign rating was still below the investment rating.

Challenges ahead amid a difficult global economic situation. By April 1998, Korea had managed to reduce its short-term external debt to US$38.2 billion and secure usable reserves totaling US$30 billion. The won/dollar exchange rate looked less ominous, at around W 1,300. The talk of sovereign default or moratorium was no longer taken seriously.

Nonetheless, the general economic situation outside Korea was not favorable. In Indonesia, inflation surged 33 percent during January–April 1998, and, at the end of April, unemployment reached 10 percent, with 9 million people out of work. The rupiah lost ground precipitously against the dollar, rising from Rp 5,470 per dollar at the end of 1997 to Rp 8,150 at the end of April 1998. Then, massive antigovernment protests and riots erupted on May 12–14, leaving 260 dead. The chaos in Indonesia, which had been triggered by economic hardship, cast a dark shadow over the whole of Asia. It could not be good for Korea.

Elsewhere in Asia, foreign exchange rates remained highly volatile. The Southeast Asian countries, as well as Korea and Taiwan, China, experienced sharp depreciations in their currencies. The Japanese yen weakened to ¥135 against the dollar in April 1998, the worst level since 1991. Only the exchange rate of the Chinese yuan against the dollar rose, to Y 8.62 in 1994, and remained steady at Y 8.29 beginning in 1997, although speculation was also rampant that a sharp depreciation of the yuan might be in the works.

The Japanese economy was experiencing a long slump under the weight of anemic domestic demand and distress in the financial sector; by mid-April, the Nikkei stock market index had dropped to 15,500, the lowest point of the year. A sharp depreciation of the yen might prompt a steep decline of the won or hurt Korea's export price competitiveness. Unstable Japanese financial markets could also prompt or accelerate loan callbacks from Korean borrowers. Amid the widespread gloom, the challenge facing Korea was to carry out bold reform and restructuring that could restore market confidence and relieve the debilitating credit crunch. Normal inbound FDI and access to credit from abroad might then resume.

Capital Market Liberalization and the Expansion of Foreign Investment

The Liberalization of Foreign Exchange Transactions

On March 30, 1998, the MOFE announced plans to overhaul foreign exchange controls and the FDI promotion system. There were several reasons for revamping foreign exchange controls. First, the existing rules and regulations based on a positive system, that is, a system of prohibition in principle and permission through exceptions, were outdated and needed major upgrading in light of the significantly liberalized trade and capital movements occurring since Korea had joined the Organisation for Economic Co-operation and Development. The removal of capital controls was also vigorously demanded by the IMF. Second, because of deepening global integration and diversification in private sector investment and trade, Korea's ex ante regulatory controls were neither effective nor desirable. Less restrictive ex post monitoring rules and regulations were needed. Third, the government recognized that a new foreign exchange transaction system was required to keep up with global standards in areas such as electronic transactions, money laundering, anticorruption, and foreign exchange fraud. Fourth, shortcomings in the foreign exchange control system that the financial crisis revealed had to be addressed. In particular, poor prudential oversight of financial companies on foreign exchange transactions, grossly inadequate monitoring of foreign exchange activities, and ineffective early warning systems for crises in foreign exchange required urgent action.

The MOFE plan called for several important changes. First, in foreign exchange transactions, the principle of a general prohibition, but with exceptions—that is, a positive system—was to be gradually changed to the principle of permission, but with exceptions—that is, a negative system. Current account transactions were to be fully permitted, but restrictions on limited activities concerning national security and criminal conduct were to remain in effect. Restrictions on most types of capital flows were also to be lifted. Second, steps were to be taken to minimize any problems that might arise from full foreign exchange and capital liberalization. In line with this, new systems were to be put into place to monitor unlawful money transfers disguised as travel expenses or overseas real estate investments. A new information-sharing system among the tax and customs authorities was also to be created. Third, to monitor the flow of foreign exchange effectively, the monitoring unit in the BOK was to be reinforced, and, to promote the effective operation of early warning systems in the case of potential market disruptions, the Korea Center for International Finance was to be established. Fourth, new safeguards that would take effect in the event of distress in the foreign exchange market were to be instituted. The government was to activate the safeguards by preventing temporary foreign exchange transactions during severe market disruptions and by introducing a tax on foreign exchange transactions or a variable deposit requirement to restrict speculative money inflows that could not otherwise be controlled.

Improving the Policy Framework for FDI

The government decided to adopt aggressive policy measures aimed at promoting FDI. The new posture made strategic sense in many ways. FDI differs from foreign borrowing in that dividends are paid out according to the earnings generated. Moreover, unlike portfolio investment, FDI mostly represents a long-term commitment by foreign investors. It also contributes to local job growth, promotes the sharing of technology and management expertise with local partners, and helps instill a global business culture.

There was, in fact, strong evidence in past experience that FDI had been the key to bringing new technologies and management expertise to Korea's semiconductor and chemical engineering sectors and that it boosted productivity (Kim June-Dong 1999). Moreover, foreign investment in the form of mergers and acquisitions (M&A) acted as a catalyst for restructuring by facilitating the takeover of poorly performing businesses and assets such as in real estate (MOFE 1998b). Because of the wide-ranging benefits FDI can bring, the competition for FDI has been intense among developing countries, but also among developed countries. FDI worldwide has been on the rise for many years. However, in Korea, FDI was being impeded by restrictive investment policies and widespread ambivalence and suspicion among the general public. The preferred approach was to borrow aggressively from foreign lenders. Table 5.2 shows inbound FDI to major economies in 1997.

Table 5.2 FDI among Major Economies, 1997
percent

Economy, group	*FDI stock/gross domestic product*	*FDI inflow/total fixed capital formation*
Korea, Rep.	7.7[a]	1.8
Malaysia	38.1	12.2
Singapore	81.6	27.3
Thailand	8.5	6.8
China	23.5	14.3
Hong Kong SAR, China	54.6	9.9
Japan	0.6	0.3
United Kingdom	21.5	18.6
Germany	9.9	2.3
United States	8.4	9.3
World	11.7	7.7
Advanced countries	10.5	6.5
Developing countries	16.6	10.3

Source: UNCTAD 1999.

a. Korea: 1996, 2.6 percent; 1997, 3.4 percent; 1998, 6.7 percent; 1999, 7.7 percent.

The essential goal of the government's plan to revamp the foreign investment promotion system was to remove barriers to inbound investment except in certain restricted sectors such as defense, broadcasting, and cultural heritage and assets. Telecommunications, shipping, and other sectors in which there were ongoing international negotiations were also restricted from full liberalization. The government administrative structure was to be reformed to encourage inbound FDI. For this purpose, steps were to be taken to clarify rules and regulations on foreign investors and give foreign investors automatic regulatory licenses and other administrative approvals after a fixed period. For foreign investors mulling investment in Korea, a one-stop service was to be established at the Korea Trade-Investment Promotion Agency. Efforts to attract foreign businesses were to be significantly expanded. This included giving a special designation to areas in which foreign investors showed a preference for the establishment of businesses and providing various tax incentives for high technology and the related service enterprises. In some cases, corporate or income taxes were to be lifted or reduced for up to 10 years.

Public Ambivalence toward FDI Liberalization

The sectors to be newly opened to unrestricted FDI were expanded as a result of the overhaul of the foreign investment promotion scheme. In April and May 1998, a total of 20 sectors, including securities trading, the management of golf courses, real estate rentals, investment advisory services, oil refining, and cigarette manufacturing, were opened to foreign investors. As a result of the government's liberalization measures, the business sectors fully closed or partially closed to foreign investors were cut to 13 and 18, respectively (in a total of 1,148 sectors), meaning that 98.9 percent of Korea's markets were now open to foreign investors. The scope and the conditions for hostile M&A by foreigners were partially loosened and expanded on April 16, 1998; this was followed by the full acceptance of all cross-border hostile M&A on May 25. In June 1998, the restrictions on the ownership of land by foreign investors were repealed.

Changing the mindset of the general public toward FDI and instilling a receptive attitude toward FDI were as challenging and important as changing the rules and regulations on foreign investment. The public's perception of FDI had never been positive, and many people raised the concern that foreign companies would indiscriminately raid Korean companies if there were no safeguards against hostile M&A. Some even flatly rejected the idea that any company that creates value and jobs in Korea should be welcomed irrespective of the company's national origin. For such people, the more convincing argument was that opening up local markets to foreign investors could cause leading Korean companies to become merely subcontractors for foreign companies and that the only way to create value and employment was to support the leading Korean companies and build up their market positions and brand power to a commanding level.

However, keeping foreign investors at bay through restrictive measures was certainly not the answer. As globalization took hold and markets began to integrate, companies started to interact simultaneously through both cooperation and competition. Protectionist approaches would mean missing the opportunity to enhance Korea's global competitiveness by embracing new technologies and management expertise. Protectionism did not make strategic sense, particularly at a time when countries were vying for ever-growing investment from abroad through favorable taxes and other incentives. Koreans had to change their attitude about FDI and make sure foreign investors felt welcome and at ease doing business in Korea.

Efforts to Attract FDI

The pace of the efforts to attract FDI picked up in 1998. In early April, President Kim Dae-Jung made a pitch for Korea as an ideal target of investment while attending the Asia-Europe Meeting in London. On April 27, the minister of finance and economy attended an investment forum hosted by the French Chamber of Commerce. Many meetings to invite foreign investors to do business in Korea were held in key cities, and foreign investors attended presidential trade promotion meetings in Korea. Private investor groups from Japan and Taiwan, China visited Korea in April and May, respectively, and European investors followed suit. The private sector also tried to bring new investment into Korea. These efforts were largely successful in polishing Korea's image abroad as a nation trying to shed its old ways, open its economy to the world, and offer foreign businesses and investors a level playing field within its borders. In a June 9 article, the *New York Times* praised President Kim Dae-Jung's commitment to reform and reported on the positive reception of his efforts among U.S. business leaders to attract FDI to Korea.

Laying the Groundwork for Structural Reform

Setting the Ground Rules for Restructuring

Korea faced the difficult task of carrying out unprecedented reform and restructuring in the corporate and financial sectors to restore investor confidence, relieve the market of the debilitating credit crunch, and address imbalances in foreign exchange markets. In the long run, the solution also lay in establishing a sound microfoundation for the postcrisis economy. In this respect, future prosperity depended greatly on the success of the efforts in reform and restructuring.

Five principles of corporate sector reform. On January 13, 1998, President-elect Kim Dae-Jung met with the heads of the Hyundai, LG, Samsung, and SK business groups—the four largest chaebols in Korea—and set out five principles of corporate restructuring. One motive for the president-elect to move swiftly on business restructuring even before taking office was to prod the chaebols to take the lead in the restructuring efforts and invite participation from the labor unions and others.

The five principles were rather straightforward. First, business transparency had to be drastically enhanced. Companies had to adopt consolidated financial reporting and raise their accounting and disclosure to global standards and practices. Second, the cross-debt guarantees that chaebol-affiliated companies provided to each other had to cease so as to ensure the financial independence of the companies in business groups and prevent one failing company from dragging down an entire business group because of the cross-debt guarantees. Third, the fundamental financial structure of companies had to improve. Companies had to reinforce their capital and financial soundness. Fourth, companies had to choose a core competence and strengthen their business ties with small and medium enterprises (SMEs). Under this principle, the chaebols had to cease their reckless expansion into new business areas and focus on businesses in which they held competitive strength. The chaebols also had to establish far more cooperative business relations with SMEs and not exploit the limited bargaining power of the SMEs. Technology transfers and financial support had to be actively encouraged. Fifth, corporate management and dominant shareholders had to be held strictly accountable for their actions. Dominant shareholders had to contribute to the efforts to raise capital and, if needed, offer debt guarantees supported by their own assets. The government would provide a program of corporate restructuring and eliminate obstacles to the implementation process.

In principle, corporate restructuring had to be undertaken by companies voluntarily. Financial companies were to enhance their business practices through strict evaluations and assign financial support in line with the seriousness of the efforts of companies to improve themselves. The theme running through the five principles of business restructuring was that companies must be managed on the basis of transparent and accountable practices in corporate governance, financial soundness, and competitive business structure. This had, in fact, been the goal since the 1970s, but it had somehow given way to debt-financed expansion.

The broad social consensus on the need to overcome the crisis. Following the agreement on the standby arrangement with the IMF on December 3, 1997, improving flexibility in the labor market emerged as a major policy challenge. The first step was the amendment of the Labor Standards Act to clarify the circumstances and procedures for layoffs, as well as legislation to introduce a system for dealing with temporary agency workers who were dispatched from subsidiary companies to their parent company. For their part, the labor unions saw this as an attempt to marginalize workers and make them bear an unfair share of the burden. The labor unions were clear that they would reject any government measures to improve labor flexibility at the expense of workers.

At a time when the entire nation had to come together and focus its efforts on overcoming the crisis, the positions labor unions took raised fresh concerns about what lay ahead. Similarly, foreign investors and others outside Korea were paying close attention to see how the thorny issue of labor rigidity would be dealt with by the new government. This was a first major test of Korea's commitment to overcoming the crisis through reform and restructuring (MOFE 1998b).

Soon after winning the presidential election, President-elect Kim Dae-Jung met with the heads of the two main union groups and asked them to join hands with businesses and the government to work together to overcome the crisis through social consensus and harmony. The labor unions initially resisted the proposition, but then changed their position on January 14, 1998. The next day, the Korea Tripartite Commission (KTC), which consisted of representatives of the unions, business, and the government, was officially launched.

On January 20, the KTC adopted a declaration of the principle of burden sharing in the effort to overcome the crisis. The declaration outlined several major agreements among the government, the labor unions, and businesses. First, the government was to implement measures to soften the effect of layoffs on workers and significantly augment public spending on social welfare and safety nets by the end of January. The government was also to submit a scaled-down budget for 1998 and put forth plans for the reorganization and downsizing of government ministries and agencies by mid-February. New measures aimed at improving corporate transparency were to be produced by the end of February. Second, companies had to embark on business turnarounds and restructuring, while preventing indiscriminate or unlawful layoffs. Companies also had to take the lead in improving business transparency and facilitating restructuring. Third, labor unions were to be open to more flexible wage and work-hour adjustments to minimize layoffs in distressed companies. Fourth, all labor disputes were to be addressed through dialogue and compromise, and the government had to adopt strong enforcement measures against illegal activities on work sites. Fifth, the KTC had to take into consideration the legislative schedule of the National Assembly in coming up with a comprehensive agreement on all major outstanding issues as soon as possible.

On February 6, the KTC came to a broad understanding on the outstanding issues and succeeded in issuing a joint declaration on voluntary restructuring and burden sharing. The joint declaration covered 10 broad areas through 90 specific provisions. The 10 broad areas were corporate transparency and accountability, speedy restructuring, price stability, employment, social safety nets, the union-management relationship, basic workfare rights, labor flexibility, the improvement of the current account in the balance of payments, and a proposal for people's integrity and other issues that were central to the interests of the government, businesses, and the labor unions. Issues that could not be settled through the joint declaration were listed in the addendum as tasks for the next round of talks and agreements.

The foundation for restructuring in the corporate and financial sectors. The government concluded the corporate and financial sector restructuring plan at the meeting of the Economic Policy Coordination Committee on April 14, 1998. The restructuring plan outlined key strategies and implementation steps. The context in which the new government plan was to be carried out was not rosy. Foreign exchange liquidity conditions had somewhat improved in the first quarter of the year, but the overall business environment, including the debilitating credit crunch, was deteriorating. Since the beginning of 1998, the monthly average number of bankruptcies had increased threefold over the monthly average in 1997. The BOK was injecting liquidity into the market, but the commercial banks were refraining from lending so as to focus on meeting BIS capital requirements. However, because of the underlying structural link between corporate distress and the soundness of financial companies, there was a clear limit to what the newly expanded credit facilities could achieve. A comprehensive, systemic program to bring about the desired changes was needed.

The government set several goals for the restructuring plan. In financial sector restructuring, the first objective was the recapitalization of banks and other financial companies so as to provide the level of liquidity the economy badly needed. The second was to improve the capital soundness of financial companies so that they could withstand losses from the nonperforming assets of failing corporate borrowers. The third was to transform financial companies fully into market-disciplined, high–value added, for-profit commercial enterprises under sound financial management.

In corporate sector restructuring, the first goal was to let failing companies close and to channel the limited pool of capital to companies with strong potential for viability. The second was to facilitate the disposal by companies of real estate assets and the acquisition by foreign investors of equity stakes in domestic companies. The third was to create an environment in which companies with a strong technological base and financial soundness could thrive and contribute to job creation and to the economy's growth potential.

The basic strategy for restructuring the financial and corporate sectors involved the following steps. First, needed measures for restructuring were to be implemented decisively and quickly. Without such actions, the early turnaround of these troubled sectors could not be expected or achieved. Second, the principle of accountability was to be maintained during the process of restructuring. Management, employees, and shareholders were to be asked to bear their fair share of the burden of responsibility for the distressed companies. Any use of public funds was to be linked to the level of commitment companies demonstrated. Third, another key strategy was the promotion of restructuring through market competition and discipline. Fourth, it was also stressed that the ultimate goal of restructuring was not to return to the precrisis years, but to transform and push the economy into a highly developed, advanced stage.

More than all the other goals, the early normalization of financial markets through speedy and resolute restructuring was critical. Distress and the losses already accumulated in the failing corporate and financial sectors were sunk costs. Thus, it was obvious that the more time one took to restructure or to dispose of the relevant companies, the costlier the process would be. Unless financial companies recapitalized quickly and relieved the credit crunch, a broad swath of the economy was going to suffer. Timing was of the essence, that is, the passage of time without action only meant the loss of the momentum needed for reform and restructuring.

The Implementation Plan for Financial Sector Restructuring

The government's implementation plan for financial sector restructuring consisted of several crucial steps, as follows:

- Sound financial companies were to be encouraged to raise their BIS capital ratios through self-initiated efforts and the disposition of troubled assets. They were to expand the scale of their business through mergers, capital increases, and partnerships with foreign investors. For ailing financial companies, mergers with sound financial companies and outright sales to new buyers were to be pursued. Regulators were to issue orders for mergers and sales if the businesses were deemed unable to make the turnaround on their own.
- Restructuring was to proceed based on market principles, but some of the unavoidable expenses arising from the clean-up of distressed assets and from depositor protection were to be supported through public funds.
- Financial sector restructuring was to cover the entire financial service industry, but priority was to be given to commercial banks so as to enable them to lead corporate sector restructuring. The pace of restructuring among nonbank financial companies was to be adjusted according to prevailing market conditions.
- The government stakes in Korea First Bank and Seoul Bank were to be sold off as soon as possible irrespective of the agreement that the government had reached with the IMF to achieve this outcome by November 5, 1998. The 12 banks with BIS capital ratios below the 8 percent minimum as of the end of 1997 were to seek approval from the Financial Supervisory Commission (FSC) on their turnaround

plans; those disapproved were to face M&A or the purchase of assets and assumption of liabilities. Banks meeting the minimum 8 percent capital requirement were to be extensively examined in terms of internal controls and risk management, together with the soundness of business operations. Mergers among large and sound banks were to be actively encouraged so as to enhance competitiveness.

- Restructuring for securities and insurance companies was to proceed on the basis that controlling shareholders would assume primary responsibility for the outcome. Companies with liabilities in excess of assets, low solvency margins, or low liquidity were to seek turnaround through recapitalization or merger. Companies with no real prospect of turnaround were to be sold off. Leasing companies were to be restructured under the control of their mother banks.
- Prompt corrective action was to be introduced to preempt financial distress. Financial companies were to be grouped into three to five categories depending on their overall soundness and to be subjected to prompt corrective action. New prudential regulations, including tougher loan-loss provisions and loan limits on single borrowers, were to be put into effect. Depositor protection was to be scaled down to partial coverage as a way to encourage market discipline.
- New measures aimed at boosting the stock market and promoting foreign investment as a way to encourage capital increases among financial companies were to be implemented. Public funds were to be used selectively only to assist those companies making genuine efforts to turn around. The fund for depositor protection was to be expanded through new debt issues and other government support so as to meet the anticipated demand arising from the closure of distressed financial companies.

The Implementation Plan for Corporate Sector Restructuring

For restructuring in the corporate sector, the government set forth the following goals:

- The top five chaebols were faithfully to carry out the five main restructuring tasks that had been set forth on January 13, 1998.
- Debt-equity ratios were to be improved to levels comparable with the levels of companies in the developed countries within two years. To attain this goal, measures aimed at encouraging capital increases were to be implemented. Short-term loans were to be turned into long-term loans so as to improve the underlying corporate debt structure. Debt repayments were to be promoted through sales of real estate and other assets.
- Support measures were to be made available to facilitate corporate restructuring. To further this goal, FDI was to be actively

> encouraged. FDI was to assume an important function in facilitating capital increases and in selling off the noncore businesses of domestic companies. Measures aimed at strengthening capital markets were to be implemented. By activating M&A and facilitating capital increases, capital markets were to assume a pivotal role in corporate restructuring.

Under the restructuring plan, the government established a corporate restructuring fund and incentive measures for the disposition of the real estate assets that many companies held. The corporate restructuring fund was to be created through the Korea Development Bank, jointly with the commercial banks, in June 1998, initially with W 1 trillion for a stock investment fund and another W 1 trillion for a debt rescheduling fund. Companies eligible for the restructuring fund were to be limited to SMEs so as to encourage the large chaebol companies to push for restructuring on their own through capital markets. The fund was to be managed by foreign management companies so as to utilize the managerial expertise of these companies.

With the real estate market in a deep slump in the wake of the financial crisis, there was a glut of properties for sale. So, property prices were falling sharply, but few buyers were in the market. As a way to prod companies to dispose of real property holdings, the government set up a real estate information center at the Korea Asset Management Corporation in May 1998. In June, the government began to hold real property exhibits open to both domestic and foreign investors. Foreign investors were allowed to acquire real property. The government also supported the Korea Land Corporation in creating a W 3 trillion fund for the purchase of real estate from companies for debt payment purposes.

The government decided to streamline the laws and regulations on asset-backed securities that help companies dispose of real estate. Along with this, it decided to give special tax breaks until the end of 1999 to companies that disposed of real property for the purpose of paying off their debt to financial companies or for the purpose of accelerating business restructuring.

Reinforcing the mechanisms for resolving heavily indebted and failing companies was urgent for successful voluntary business restructuring. The major creditor banks were therefore encouraged to create special task forces consisting of outside members to determine objectively and transparently the future of troubled companies. Banks that made steady progress with troubled corporate borrowers were also given priority in the purchase of subordinated bonds through public funds and in the provision of incentives for managers and employees.

To accelerate restructuring, the government forced large companies to enter into financial soundness improvement agreements with creditor banks. A special task force was set up at the Office of Bank Supervision

(OBS) in the BOK to encourage banks to accelerate the resolution of failing corporate debtors. For SMEs that were hit particularly hard by the crisis, the government also set up a task force at the OBS to lend a helping hand and ordered banks to create task forces directly under the bank presidents to assist SMEs. As a way to facilitate M&A, the government decided to allow the activities of corporate restructuring companies, which are restructuring vehicles that specialize in taking over troubled companies and turning them around. Steps were also taken to ensure regular communication and collaboration among government agencies, as well as to encourage progress monitoring in corporate restructuring.

Restructuring through Workouts

Under the agreement with the IMF and the World Bank, the government decided, in March 1998, to start workouts among debtor companies with a good prospect of turnaround as a way to aid and accelerate business restructuring. Until then, workouts between creditor institutions and debtor companies had been a new concept in Korea. In a workout, the debtor company typically submits a workout plan to its creditors to relieve debt pressure and earn time to turn the business around. The workout plans in Korea thus consisted of self-help efforts a debtor company was to undertake to achieve business restructuring and debt rescheduling. They were associated with relief measures the creditor banks granted for the turnaround efforts. Whereas companies outlined their restructuring steps in the self-help plans, such as business reorganization, capital write-downs, recapitalization, and employee downsizing, the creditor banks outlined the debt reduction and rescheduling, maturity extension, and fresh credit they were willing to grant. Any disputes between creditors and debtors were to be mediated through corporate restructuring committees made up of private sector specialists. Even though the corporate restructuring committees were not statutory entities, they were expected to act as honest and neutral mediators. The London approach was the model for Korea's workout scheme. Korea already had legal mechanisms, such as court receivership and composition for companies facing bankruptcy, but workouts were adopted because they were thought to be less time-consuming, less costly, and more rapid in facilitating debtor-creditor agreements for possible turnaround.

The Reform of Government Administration

On April 13, 1998, the Planning and Budget Committee submitted a government reform plan to the president. It proposed a major shift from control-oriented administration to performance-based administration and made the case that the role of the government should not be to row, but to steer and that market mechanisms should replace government mechanisms where possible. It argued that government administration centered on civil servants should be replaced by customer-first administration. It also argued that budgetary decisions should be made on the basis of performance and that the provision of public services need not be monopolized by the government, but could be shared with the private sector on a competitive basis.

On April 18, 1998, the government formed the Regulatory Reform Committee and decided to deregulate or streamline at least half the existing regulations. Regulatory reform was urgent in the effort to improve Korea's business and investment climate and economic vitality. It was needed if Korea was to become a place in which companies and investors, domestic and foreign, could do business and enhance the daily lives of ordinary citizens. The areas of focus were foreign investment regulations, anticompetitive business rules and regulations, and rules that restrict or hinder the economic activities of ordinary citizens. Directed by President Kim Dae-Jung to deregulate or do away with at least 50 percent of existing regulations, government ministries and agencies set about reviewing the 10,820 regulatory provisions on the books and deal with 5,401 regulations by year's end.

Progress in Restructuring, April 1998

The reforms and restructuring that had taken place between the introduction of the IMF standby agreement and April 1998 were mostly changes in the legal and regulatory framework. The changes that occurred during this period can be divided into changes across the financial, corporate, labor, and public sectors.

Progress in financial sector restructuring. The government injected public funds into Korea First Bank and Seoul Bank. At the end of 1997, the capital of both banks had become so eroded that it was in the negative: –2.7 percent for Korea First Bank and 0.97 percent for Seoul Bank. In consultation with the IMF, the government decided to inject public funds, turn the banks around, and then privatize them. The government's decision not to close the two banks arose largely because of the significant impact the closure of the two banks would have had on the broader economy. Korea First Bank had 4.9 million individual customers and dealt with 77,000 companies, while Seoul Bank had 5.6 million individual customers and 101,000 corporate customers. The government also determined that selling the banks off after bankruptcy would be costlier and less advantageous than turning around the banks first and then privatizing them. Thus, the government was to be a bridge until the two banks were ready for sale to buyers. On January 30, 1998, the two banks reduced their capital to the W 100 billion legal minimum level from W 820 billion. The government injected W 750 billion in assets into each bank, and the Korea Deposit

Insurance Corporation also injected the same amount of public funds. For the potential sale of the two banks to foreign buyers, a due diligence contract was signed on March 31 with Coopers & Lybrand and Samil, and due diligence was started on April 1. Then, on May 19, a contract was signed with Morgan Stanley to act as lead advisor for the sale.

In early February 1998, the OBS received the BIS capital ratios of commercial banks, excluding Korea First Bank and Seoul Bank, for the end of 1997. They showed that 12 banks had failed to meet the minimum 8 percent BIS capital ratio.[3] On February 26, orders for turnaround actions were issued to these 12 banks, and, by the end of April, these banks had submitted turnaround plans aimed at satisfying the minimum 8 percent requirement. The government and the IMF used the 8 percent threshold as the yardstick to determine whether a bank was in trouble. Initially, the computation of the BIS capital ratio was set for the end of March 1998, but, in January 1998, this was altered to the end of 1997. The change was made because even the sound banks were holding back on giving out fresh loans out of fear that they would not meet the 8 percent minimum requirement.

Amid the persistent credit crunch, some objected to the use of the 8 percent threshold as the yardstick for bank soundness. They argued, for example, that a BIS capital ratio of around 4 percent was sufficient for the smaller regional banks that did not engage in any international business. To be sure, the 8 percent bar was an arbitrary number, merely a threshold agreed to among banking supervisors in developed countries. Nonetheless, it was an important, internationally accepted threshold. As such, setting the bar below 8 percent was rejected as it would only undermine confidence in Korean banks and slow down the pace of the needed improvement in bank soundness.

The restructuring of merchant banks was well under way. In mid-December 1997, a total of 14 merchant banks were suspended from operations.[4] Hanareum Merchant Bank was created to take over and manage the assets of the merchant banks soon to be closed. In January 1998, a review committee made up of private sector experts was formed to assess the viability of merchant banks. The committee examined the capital soundness of all the merchant banks in operation and ordered the closure of 10 of them; on February 17, the business licenses of the 10 were revoked.[5] The remaining 20 merchant banks were ordered to submit second turnaround plans by February 7, and, on February 26, a second review of the merchant banks was completed on liquidity, capital adequacy, and management capability.[6] As a result of the second review, Hansol and Daegu had their business licenses revoked (March 16 and 31, respectively), and a further review was set for Daehan, Nara, and Samyang. On April 15, Samyang had its license revoked, but Daehan and Nara were set for a possible resumption of business. The remaining 15 merchant banks were to implement turnaround plans faithfully and conclude monitoring agreements on implementation with the OBS by March 21. However, First Merchant Bank was suspended from business on March 23 after the company's controlling shareholder gave up on capital restoration; on May 18, its business license was revoked.

Along with merchant banks, Shinsegi Investment Trust Co. was suspended from business operations on December 19, 1997 because of soured assets and the inability to carry on business as a going concern. The company's trust contracts were transferred to Korea Investment Trust Co. On February 17, 1998, Shinsegi's license was revoked, and Korea Investment Trust was selected as the Shinsegi liquidator.

As provided for under an agreement with the IMF, the government set up a special task force at the MOFE on March 7, 1998 to take charge of the oversight of bank restructuring. After the creation of the FSC on April 1, 1998, the task force was moved to the newly created commission on April 30 and renamed the bank restructuring unit. The creation of the FSC was followed by the integration of banking, securities, and insurance supervisory authorities into the Financial Supervisory Service on January 1, 1999. The FSC quickly took charge of financial sector restructuring as the government's financial supervisory authority.

Progress in corporate sector restructuring. At this stage, government actions on corporate sector restructuring were concentrated in the preparation of a new legal framework for restructuring. In February 1998, 10 laws were amended in support of corporate sector restructuring. The Act on External Audit of Stock Companies was amended. The amended act covered the legal and regulatory basis for consolidated financial statements beginning in fiscal 1999. To ensure the integrity of external audits, the creation of an auditor selection committee was made mandatory, and penalties for negligence were stiffened for independent outside auditors and companies and for in-house staff in charge of accounting.

The Monopoly Regulation and Fair Trade Act was also amended. On April 1, the limit on debt cross-guarantees among the affiliated companies of the 30 largest chaebols was set at 100 percent of the company's capital. A 3 percent penalty interest rate was to be applied to any amount in excess of the limit, and no new cross-guarantees were to be allowed for fresh loans. Moreover, all existing cross-guarantees were to be completely terminated by March 2000. However, the limitation on consolidated investments to other affiliated companies by the 30 largest chaebol-affiliated companies was repealed.

There were likewise amendments to the Corporate Tax Act. The noninclusion of interest expenses on any borrowing in excess of 500 percent of the capital of the company among the losses included in the calculations of taxable income amounts was originally scheduled to take effect in 2002, but was reset to take effect in 2000 instead. As a step to encourage debt-equity swaps through the amendment of the Banking Act, the ceiling on share ownership by a bank in a company was lifted from 10 to 15 percent.

The Regulation of Tax Reduction and Exemption Act was amended to allow SMEs full exemption (from the previous 50 percent) from the capital gains tax if the SMEs sold real property for the purpose of paying off debt. Other tax incentives for the disposition of real property as part of a merger or sale of business operations were also granted.

The Securities and Exchange Act was amended to give minority shareholders greater voice and authority to challenge management; the threshold was lowered from a 1.0 percent share in ownership to a 0.05 percent share in undertaking shareholder representative suits, from 1.0 to 0.5 percent to demand the removal of directors and the auditor, and from 3.0 to 1.0 percent for the right to examine company books. The appointment of outside directors to the board of directors of listed companies was made compulsory through the amendment of the Securities Management Committee Regulation.

The Foreign Investment and Foreign Capital Inducement Act was amended to give foreign investors significantly expanded freedom to engage in hostile M&A effective April 16, 1998. The mandatory takeover bid requirement—a safeguard designed to discourage hostile stock purchases—was repealed. As a way to give management an opportunity to fend off hostile takeover bids, the 10 percent purchase limit on treasury stocks was raised to one-third.

Changes to the Company Reorganization Act were made so that court receivership could be granted not if recovery was possible, but if the value as a going concern was greater than the value after liquidation. A cap on the permitted time for resolution was newly imposed to accelerate bankruptcy proceedings. The ratio of stock losses to be assumed by the controlling shareholder because of mismanagement was raised from two-thirds to more than two-thirds. The Composition Act and the Bankruptcy Act were amended to accelerate legal proceedings and resolutions.

Along with the government's preparation of a new legal framework for corporate sector restructuring, the OBS, on February 13, 1998, ordered creditor banks to enter into financial soundness improvement agreements with corporate companies with outstanding debt in excess of W 250 billion. In addition to steps designed to improve financial soundness, the agreement covered measures to be implemented to enhance corporate governance, business structure, and other key aspects of business restructuring.

A total of 64 large companies (chaebols) had submitted financial soundness improvement plans by the end of April. The execution of the plans was to be reviewed every six months by the creditor banks, and companies found to be making unsatisfactory progress were to be denied new loans and to be subjected to early callbacks on outstanding loans. On March 23, the OBS followed up with tougher guidelines for financial soundness improvements. The revised guidelines called for debt-equity ratios at or below 200 percent by 1999 (from the original target year of 2002). The chaebols strongly objected. The Federation of Korean Industries, which spoke for the chaebols, argued that the accelerated debt-equity reduction target would mean that 30 chaebols would have to pay off W 172 trillion or issue W 86 trillion in new stock issues as of the end of 1996, both incredible sums.

However, the situation was such that Korean companies would not be able to restore market confidence without achieving the 200 percent ratio, a widely used yardstick in international credit markets. The credit crunch would then persist, and the economy would continue to slump. For these and other obvious reasons, the government could not sit idly on the sideline and allow creditor banks and debtor companies to work out their differences at their own leisurely pace. Both the speed and the intensity of restructuring were enormously important to the government. It was decided that some flexibility would be given to specific chaebol-affiliated companies in meeting the 200 percent debt-equity ratio, but that the debt-equity ratios for each chaebol must average 200 percent.

Amid much confusion, restructuring in the corporate sector began in earnest in March 1998. A total of 505 listed companies had appointed 667 outside directors as of the end of March. Also as of the end of March, the chaebol companies had managed to cancel or terminate cross-debt guarantees totaling W 10 trillion, about a third of the total for the 30 largest chaebols. Daesang Group sold off a business operation (lysine production) to a German buyer for US$600 million, and Samsung Heavy Industries signed an agreement to sell its heavy equipment business to Volvo for US$720 million as of the end of April.

Labor market reform. On February 20, labor laws were amended as a follow-up on an agreement of the KTC. Through an amendment of the Labor Standards Act, layoffs that had been set to occur within two years from March 1997 were rescheduled to begin immediately. The controversial provisions on business spin-offs and sales to prevent deteriorating business conditions were also to include acutely adverse business circumstances as a criteria for layoffs. An advance notice of 60 days was to be given before the actual layoffs to the head of the labor union, along with explanations of the efforts undertaken to avoid the layoffs, as well as of the criteria for the distribution of the layoffs. Failure to supply the advance notice was to constitute an unlawful dismissal of workers.

Amendments to the Act on the Protection of Temporary Agency Workers took effect on July 1. The amended provisions excluded line workers at manufacturing sites and limited the affected workers to those with specialized skills or experience; a total of 26 types of jobs were to be subject to the amended provisions on worker outsourcing. The limited scope of the workers affected was designed to alleviate the concerns of labor unions that employers would rely excessively on or even abuse temporarily outsourced workers if the scope were too broad.

Improvements in employment protection and employee rights were also legislated. The Act on the Establishment and Operation of Public Officials' Councils, which allowed collective bargaining among civil servants, passed the National Assembly on February 17 and was slated to take effect on January 1, 1999. Because of mounting unemployment, amendments to the Employment Insurance Act were passed on February 20 and took effect on March 1. Under the amendments, the minimum payment duration for unemployed workers was extended from 30 to 60 days, and the unemployment insurance premium was raised from 1.5 to 3.0 percent. The Wage Claim Guarantee Act was passed on February 20 and went into effect on July 1. It consisted mainly of provisions on wage payments of three months and severance payments of three years through the Wage Claim Guarantee Fund if an employer became bankrupt or were otherwise rendered unable to pay workers overdue wages.

Downsizing the central government. Reorganization of the government was completed on February 28, 1998. Under the reorganization, the post of deputy prime minister, previously assumed by both the finance minister and the minister of land reunification, was eliminated, and several government ministries and agencies were merged, reshuffled, or downsized, or were given new mandates. As a result of the reorganization, the number of central government agencies was changed to 19 ministries and 16 agencies from 21 ministries and 14 agencies. Administrative organizations of the central government were significantly downsized. Among others, the Ministry of Finance and Economy (MOFE), which had been criticized as a dinosaur for wielding too much power, was downsized. Its budgetary authority was separated to set up the Planning and Budget Committee under the president and the National Budget Administration under the MOFE, and the financial supervisory authority was also detached to establish the Financial Supervisory Commission (FSC) under the prime minister. By establishing various presidential committees, the reorganization gave the president more streamlined authority to lead the government bureaucracy.

The Intensifying Credit Crunch and Mounting Unemployment

The Tightening of Fiscal and Monetary Policies

In April 1998, the government and the IMF were still adhering to the contractionary fiscal and monetary policies that they had agreed to in early December 1997. In the fourth policy discussion, on January 7, 1998, they agreed that, notwithstanding the slowing economy, the overnight call rate should remain around 30 percent to stabilize the won. Essentially the same stance was taken on interest rates at the fifth policy discussion, on February 7, with the expectation that the growth rate of gross domestic product (GDP) would be negative. The priority for the government and the IMF was to stabilize the won first and foremost.

However, as the risk of corporate defaults mounted and as banks curtailed credit to raise their BIS capital ratios, the credit crunch was worsening each day, and the prospect of massive corporate bankruptcies could not be ruled out. So, it was agreed by the government and the IMF that the support for export companies could be expanded as a way to relieve the mounting pressures. Accordingly, the BOK provided export credits on commercial terms, and measures aimed at facilitating imports of raw materials for export processing were to be implemented. In addition, because the economic downturn was more severe than originally anticipated, a government budget deficit for 1998 became all but unavoidable. It was therefore decided that the budget shortfalls would be dealt with through automatic fiscal stabilizers built into the economy rather than through any balancing measures by the government.

The first supplementary budget. The government submitted the first supplementary budget to the National Assembly on February 9. It was necessary to adjust for the expected tax revenue shortfalls of approximately W 6.8 trillion and the additional expenditures totaling about W 5.6 trillion, consisting of W 3.6 trillion for financial company restructuring and W 2 trillion for unemployment benefits. It was decided that the W 12.4 trillion in budget shortfalls would be covered through spending cuts and tax increases rather than through new debt. Approximately W 4 trillion was expected through tax increases, which was to be made up of W 3.7 trillion already budgeted through the amended traffic tax increases at the end of 1997 and W 300 billion in reduced exemptions in value added taxes and corporate taxes. Spending was to be cut by W 8.4 trillion through 10 to 20 percent pay cuts among civil servants and another 10 percent cut in administrative expenditures and in public projects. The supplementary budget was expected to achieve a balance, and the consolidated government budget deficit was estimated at 0.8 percent of GDP. The deficit may be viewed as expansionary spending, but, in reality, it was contractionary given that it took into account the substantial drop in tax revenues because of the slowing economy. Indeed, the fiscal impulse measure computed by the MOFE showed a negative 0.4 percent, which indicated that the budget was still contractionary.

The high interest rate policy. With the government and the IMF firmly set on stabilizing the won through a high interest rate policy, the overnight call rate started to rise from 12.15 percent on December 1, 1997. It then more than doubled, to 30.11 percent on December 24 and to 31.32 percent by the end of 1997. The yield on commercial paper (CP) at 91 days had climbed as high as 40.77 percent by year's end mainly because financial companies shunned purchasing it. There was no sign of any change in the high interest rate policy in February 1998. As a result, criticism began to surface that, although necessary for the stability of the won, persistently high interest rates could potentially threaten the long-term viability of companies, many of which were heavily burdened by a high level of debt and interest payments. Total corporate debt to financial companies (including debt guarantees) at the end of 1997 was estimated at W 484 trillion, and, assuming a 15 percent interest rate for 1998, the total interest payment by corporate borrowers came to W 70 trillion a year. With some signs of a stabilizing won in March and the successful conclusion of the sovereign bond offering in April, the government wanted to consult with the IMF on lowering interest rates and attempted, through various channels, to relay to the IMF its desire to cut the rates (MOFE 1998c). However, the IMF did not yield to the new proposal of the government, and the talks did not come to any concrete result.

The Worsening Credit Crunch and Instability in Financial Markets

Amid the continually deteriorating credit crunch, credit access for the corporate sector was nearly impossible. Some academics suggested that what was taking place was not so much a credit crunch as a drop in the available pool of credit as a result of a sharply contracting economy and the accompanying drop in the demand for credit (Ghosh and Ghosh 1999). But the prevailing view was that the market was, in fact, gripped by a severe credit crunch.

The underlying causes and effects of the credit crunch. Severe distress among financial companies was one obvious underlying reason for the shortage in credit. With the spate of merchant bank failures, there were fewer buyers for the CP that companies could issue. Moreover, amid the mounting loan defaults, banks were scrambling to raise their capital above the 8 percent minimum BIS requirement. One way to raise the ratio was to call back loans from companies that had high risk weight, while shoring up government debt securities that had low risk weight. Given the difficulties in the capital markets, capital increases through fresh debt or equity were all but ruled out.

The rising default risk among companies aggravated the credit crunch. Ever since the chain of large corporate bankruptcies in early 1997, there had been a heightened awareness in the market of the corporate default risk. There were early signs of corporate distress in 1996 when the interest coverage ratio fell sharply (see chapter 1). Because of the severely weakened won and the tight fiscal and monetary policies, the real economy was bound to suffer. When real estate prices began to collapse, there were concerns that even loans backed by collateral as secure as real estate could be at risk. Not surprisingly, financial companies hesitated to lend. The larger companies could try to issue debt to raise funds, but, for the smaller companies, this was not a viable alternative. The worry was that the smaller companies would collapse not because of insolvency, but because of illiquidity.

The times were in need of robust exports, but these were impeded by a dearth of trade financing. Importing the raw materials needed for export processing also proved difficult for exporters. In mid-December 1997, export credit, as well as import credit and financing, dried up, and inventories of some essential raw materials, such as crude oil and rubber, were barely sufficient for one month.

Responses to alleviate the credit crunch. The government came under heavy pressure to take steps to counter the intensifying credit crunch. Initially, the focus was on SMEs and exporters. On December 12, 1997, the BOK, fearing a run on banks in the aftermath of the collapse of several merchant banks and the freeze in the overnight call market, decided to provide emergency liquidity totaling W 11.3 trillion to avoid a bank run and raised the aggregate credit ceiling for SMEs from W 3.6 trillion to W 4.6 trillion.[7] Beginning on December 4, 1997, it also started providing liquidity so that banks could increase lending to exporters, against export bills of exchange, through the prior redemption of the monetary stabilization bonds held by banks.

On December 16, the government came up with countermeasures against banks that were shunning trade financing so as to raise their BIS capital ratios. By utilizing the export insurance scheme, the government could effectively reduce the BIS risk weight given to such loans from 100 to 10 percent. It expanded export insurance protection coverage to companies in composition or under court receivership and decided to give protection coverage for exports to 137 regions throughout the world that were considered risky and give insurance coverage for documents against acceptance between principal and subsidiary companies. It did the same for letters of credit for imports by guaranteeing them through the credit guarantee fund, which reduced the BIS risk weight from 20 to 2 percent.

The government reached an agreement with the U.S. government on December 29 on a US$1 billion program for imports of agricultural and livestock products. On February 5, 1998, an additional US$100 million was added to the program for imports of raw hides.

By mid-January 1998, the credit access and trade financing for exporters had improved somewhat as a result of the measures taken by the government. However, in the case of documents against acceptance and usance contracts, which represented about a third of total exports, the purchase of export bills of exchange continued to be shunned. Obtaining letters of credit for imports of basic raw materials was still difficult. These factors heightened the prospect that export production and the supply of even basic necessities might be severely disrupted in one or two months. The government therefore took additional steps to aid SMEs and exporters in January. On January 10, US$1 billion in Asian Development Bank loans were used to augment credit guarantee facilities for SMEs. On January 5, export companies were allowed to sell their export bills of exchange to foreign banks, and, on February 3, the term of deferred payments on imports was extended from 180 days to 360 days, until June 30.

On February 9, the MOFE followed up with the announcement of a series of new measures aimed at easing the funding difficulties among companies. The measures included allowing banks and securities companies to purchase CP at a discount; this had previously been handled mostly by merchant banks. Investment trust companies were allowed to set up special funds for investment in CP so as to stimulate greater demand for corporate CP. As a way to encourage bank lending, the government-controlled credit guarantee funds introduced guarantees for collateral-backed loans and removed the limits on collateral acquisition by banks. In a move designed to spur the corporate debt market, the government had the Korea Asset Management Corporation take over nonperforming loans from two guarantee insurance companies and temporarily allowed large corporate companies to issue new debt at a maturity of less than three years.

On February 11 and 12, creditor institutions voluntarily agreed that CP coming due in February and March 1998—estimated at about W 50 trillion—would be rolled over for two additional months. Then, on February 17, they agreed to give at least a six-month extension on loans for SMEs totaling W 25 trillion and coming due on June 30. This was a follow-up on the one-year extension given on February 2 to foreign-currency loans worth W 900 billion (US$530 million).

On March 11, the MOFE decided to offer special incentives to banks that were more willing to lend to the corporate sector. In supporting credit guarantees through credit guarantee funds and in depositing government funds, it was decided to take into account the corporate loans lent by banks. It was also decided to limit the purchase of the subordinated debentures issued by banks only to those banks that had a good track record in corporate lending. In tandem with these steps, the BOK decided, in assigning the aggregate credit ceiling, to take into account the corporate loans lent by banks. In March, the BOK added W 1 trillion to the aggregate credit ceiling following the previous December's W 1 trillion increase, thus bringing the total to W 5.6 trillion. Of the aggregate credit ceiling, 50 percent was rationed on new loans to the corporate sector.

In April, the MOFE announced additional measures to ease credit flows to companies. To encourage large companies to raise capital through the debt and equity markets, restrictions on initial public offerings were removed so that companies could make public offerings of stocks only by filing registration statements. Listing on the stock exchange was to be scrutinized with a particular focus on the transparency and accountability of corporate governance. Credit guarantees for SMEs were augmented as well. With W 2.9 trillion in new funding to credit guarantee institutions (US$1 billion from the Asian Development Bank loan and W 800 billion from the government budget), the total available for credit guarantees came to W 52 trillion. The government boosted the capital of the state-controlled Industrial Bank of Korea by W 1.5 trillion and increased SME lending by W 2 trillion. For their part, the banks set up special task forces controlled directly by the heads of the banks to deal with SME credit and funding problems.

Between January and March 1998, additional measures were taken to improve export and import financing conditions. On April 6, it was decided that US$1 billion from the World Bank loan would be used to help importers open letters of credit for raw material imports for export purposes, and the government decided to use US$300 million in foreign exchange reserves to help purchase export bills of exchange throughout April. The government committed US$3 billion, including US$1 billion from the Export-Import Bank of Japan, to supporting export financing. In addition, the Export-Import Bank of Korea was allowed to rediscount short-term trade bills that had been discounted by commercial banks; this had been handled exclusively by the BOK.

By April, the demand-supply situation in raw materials and agricultural products had improved noticeably. Aggressive government action had clearly paid off. Greater stability in foreign exchange markets and falling demand amid a contracting economy were also positive signs. However, conditions among the SMEs had not become much better because large companies demanded cash settlements for the raw materials and commodities they imported. The government decided to divert W 300 billion from the SME founding and development funds to helping SMEs with their cash payments for raw materials. The government also pulled W 150 billion out of the government reserved stock fund and raised the stockpile of key imports.

Fragile financial markets. Following the successful negotiations on the rollover of the short-term external debt of domestic financial companies toward the end of January 1998, the outlook for the won improved, and interest rates began to moderate somewhat. However, the overnight call rate still hovered around 20 percent on April 23, and the three-year corporate bond yield was stuck at around 18 percent. Because of the high interest rate policy adopted to stabilize the won, short-term interest rates remained at record levels well above the long-term rates. The Korea composite stock price index rebounded in January and February with a jump in stock purchases by foreigners because of the stabilizing won and the news of the short-term debt rollover. However, stock prices headed downward again in March and April as foreign investors pulled back.

The deposits of financial companies moved toward safer institutions, and this resulted in a concentration of deposits in these institutions. Moreover, short-term deposits were preferred over long-term deposits. Bank deposits in the form of short-term installment deposits at low interest rates dropped, but this was more than offset by sharp increases in time deposits at higher interest rates. Bank deposits in trusts also declined somewhat during this period. Deposits at merchant banks fell because many of these banks had closed. Meanwhile, investment trust companies and securities companies saw a large jump in deposits in short-term bond-type beneficiary certificates and CP, respectively. As a result, there was a noticeable discrepancy between M2 (monetary aggregate for broad money) and M3 (monetary aggregate for liquidity), the broad measures of the stock of money in the economy.[8] M2 grew 21.2 percent in December 1997 (year-on-year), but, by April 1998, it had slowed to 13.1 percent. M3 slowed from 15.9 to 14.2 percent during the same period.

Many companies continued to have difficulty securing funds because banks were lending only at a conservative pace. The outstanding loan amount in December 1997 fell sharply as banks called back their loans in an attempt to raise BIS capital ratios. The situation turned around in January 1998, when banks re-lent the loans they had called back in December, and large companies secured cash from prearranged overdraft facilities in anticipation of worsening funding difficulties. Between February and April 1998, banking account lending rose through increases in general lending for corporation and trade financing, though the discount on commercial bills fell sharply. However, the trust account lending of banks diminished again starting in February 1998. Overall, lending to large companies and SMEs declined in December 1997, but rebounded in January and February 1998. Lending then tumbled again in March, when the drop in lending to SMEs was much more precipitous than the drop in lending to large companies.

Unable to find funding from banks, many companies turned to bonds and equity. The value of corporate bond issues reached W 9.7 trillion during the first quarter of 1998 alone, but nearly all this amount, 99.1 percent, represented issues by large companies; the top five chaebols accounted for 87.5 percent. The discount on CP by merchant banks slumped after the closure of many merchant banks. The slack was taken up by banks and securities companies, among which the rise was valued at W 19.1 trillion during the first quarter of 1998. Most of the discounted CP was associated with companies at low risk of default. Of the discounted purchases by securities companies, the top five chaebols made up nearly 90 percent. The value of stock issues during the first quarter of 1998 totaled W 5.2 billion. However, most of the issues were aimed at raising capital among nonbank financial companies; for nonfinancial companies, the total came to only W 13.7 billion. Table 5.3 shows trends in key financial market indicators.

Table 5.3 Trends in Key Financial Market Indicators
% and won, billions

	1997	1998			
Indicator	*December*	*January*	*February*	*March*	*April*
Call rate, monthly average	21.29	25.34	23.43	22.47	21.31
KOSPI, monthly average, month-on-month[a]	390.3 (–21.0)	475.2 (21.7)	525.2 (10.5)	523.0 (–0.4)	444.2 (–15.1)
M2, average basis, year-on-year	21.1	16.1	13.8	13.7	13.1
M3, average basis, year-on-year	15.9	15.1	15.1	14.5	14.2
Bank loans, monthly increase	–5,993.9	4,869.1	1,693.1	102.3	610.1
Issuance of corporate bonds	7,410.8	3,409.5	3,156.7	3,125.7	1,630.5
Discounted CP, monthly increase	–4,010.6	6,660.2	5,270.3	7,150.5	536.2
Issuance of stocks, initial public offerings, new shares	149.4	0.8	17.7	1,531.1	632.9

Sources: Bank of Korea and Ministry of Finance and Economy.

Note: M2 = monetary aggregate for broad money. M3 = monetary aggregate for liquidity.

a. KOSPI = Korea composite stock price index. The numbers in parentheses show the percent change.

The Contracting Economy

As in December 1997, domestic demand continued to contract sharply during the first quarter of 1998. Activity in the construction sector spiraled downward, and imports of machinery and orders for domestically produced machinery slowed drastically. Wholesale and retail sales fell. Sales of consumer durables such as automobiles, construction materials, and special-purpose machinery saw a particularly pronounced drop.

Aside from semiconductors, shipbuilding, and few other sectors that were benefiting from robust export demand, production was slumping across the board. Despite the contraction in domestic demand, however, business inventories began to drop across broad sectors in February in tandem with the slowing production activities. The average manufacturing operation ratio was the lowest ever in February 1998, but it fell again in March to an average of 67.1 percent.

At the same time, consumer prices surged and put enormous pressure on households. In December 1997, prices jumped 2.5 percent over the previous month and continued to rise by 2.4 and 1.7 percent during the first two months of 1998, respectively. In March, the pace of the increase fell by 0.2 percent over February, but then rose by 0.4 percent in April, showing some signs of stabilizing. Housing prices declined, and the real estate market was in a severe downturn.

Inflation was fueled mostly by spiraling import prices because of the weakening won. With tight fiscal and monetary policies in effect and the economy in contraction, domestic demand continued to shrink. Wages and land prices were steady, and prices in dollar terms for crude oil and major raw materials were stable. So, the key determinant of inflation was the won/dollar exchange rate.

With the real economy in disarray and the credit crunch worsening day by day, bankruptcies surged. The ratio of dishonored checks and bills averaged 1.49 percent in December 1997. It fell somewhat in early 1998, but remained high. During March 1998, a total of 2,749 companies declared bankruptcy. The number of new companies, which used to outpace the number of bankrupt companies by a factor of 10, was only one to two times greater, heightening concerns that the industrial base was being severely weakened. The trends in the real economy during the first quarter of 1998 are summarized in table 5.4.

Growing Unemployment and the Government Response

With corporate bankruptcies on the rise, unemployment surged beginning in December 1997. The number of the unemployed, which moved to around 570,000 in November 1997, had jumped to 1.2 million by February 1998. The increase was particularly noticeable in the manufacturing and construction sectors. Social overhead capital and other sectors that usually boosted

Table 5.4 Economic Trends, January–March 1998, Year-on-Year
percent

	1997	*1998*		
Indicator	*December*	*January*	*February*	*March*
Industrial production	0.4	-9.4	0.4	-9.1
Domestic construction orders	-35.1	-20.0	-17.5	-28.7
Orders of domestically produced machines	-11.9	-30.5	-27.7	-50.1
Wholesale and retail sales	-4.9	-9.4	-12.8	-11.6
Average manufacturing operation ratio	75.7	69.8	69.6	67.1
Consumer prices	6.6	8.3	9.5	9.0
Housing prices, month-on-month	-0.5	-0.8	-1.3	-2.8
Unemployment rate	3.1	4.5	5.9	6.5
Number of unemployed, 1,000s	658	934	1,235	1,378
Nationwide ratio of dishonored bills	1.49	0.53	0.62	0.47
Number of bankrupt companies, monthly	3,197	3,323	3,377	2,749

Source: Ministry of Finance and Economy.

employment were also shedding workers. In February 1998, through the KTC, the government came up with responses to the growing threat of unemployment. Under the assumption that the unemployment rate would rise to 5 percent with the number of unemployed at 1.0 million, the government decided to provide W 5 trillion for the unemployed and pledged to come up with aggressive measures to deal with unemployment (table 5.5). However, employment statistics in January 1998 indicated that the annual average number of unemployed was likely to reach 1.3 million and 1.5 million in March and April, respectively, when young graduates entered the labor market. It was clear that additional actions by the government would be needed to deal with the pressing problem.

The number of the unemployed was projected to reach 1.3 million—200,000 unemployed without job experience and 1.1 million unemployed with job experience—in 1998 and to remain at a high level for some time. It was also estimated that 70 percent of the unemployed with job

Table 5.5 Government Unemployment Measures (I)

Measure	*Budget, won, billions*	*Persons, thousands*	*Description*
1. Job-maintenance support	451.2	548	
Work sharing	199.5	323	Supports for cuts in work hours and worker reassignments instead of layoffs
Other employment insurance activities	251.7	225	Promotion of employment among the disguised unemployed; support for job training within companies
2. Enhancing the job-seeking function	51.0	n.a.	
Expanding the job placement network	33.7	n.a.	Establishment of 20 job banks; expansion of regional branch offices, Ministry of Labor
Expanding the job information network	17.3	n.a.	Provision of computers (46) for job information
3. Expanding job training	625.4	265	
Training for the unemployed with job experience	179.9	112	Reemployment training for the unemployed; start-up training program
Training for the unemployed without job experience	45.5	65	Use of university facilities for job training; job adaptation training for the underprivileged
Training for the employed	401.0	88	Employment retention, vocation transfers, paid vocational training

(continued next page)

Table 5.5 Government Unemployment Measures (I) *(continued)*

Measure	*Budget, won, billions*	*Persons, thousands*	*Description*
4. Job creation	1,030.0	185	23,000 jobs
Support for commencing venture firms and small businesses	600.0	60	Financing venture firms and unemployed white-collar workers to start up businesses
Public works programs	400.0	75	Support for firms to replace foreign workers with Koreans
	30.0	50	Hiring among the unemployed for public sector works such as classifying government documents and thinning forests
5. Support for livelihood stabilization among the unemployed	2,844.5	739	n.a.
Increase in unemployment benefits	1,187.3	439	Expansion of unemployment benefit eligibility to workplaces with at least five workers; increase in unemployment benefits
Hiring the unemployed	55.2	20	Support for firms to hire the unemployed
Social care	1,602.0	280,000 households	Housing loans, livelihood stabilization loans
Total	5,002.1	1,962	There is some overlap in the totals

Source: Data of the Korea Tripartite Commission, February 1998.
Note: n.a. = not applicable.

experience were not covered by unemployment insurance and that, in any case, the duration of the insurance coverage would last only three to four months. It was therefore an urgent task to extend the coverage to those ineligible to receive any postemployment benefits and shore up the social safety net for the unemployed. Moreover, the shock from the massive layoffs in 1998 was widely expected to persist for at least three or four years. The government had to come up with comprehensive policy measures encompassing labor, social welfare, education, and the macroeconomy. President Kim Dae-Jung even referred to his cabinet as the unemployment response cabinet and called on the government to deal aggressively with the problem and substantially strengthen Korea's woefully inadequate social welfare systems. As a result, the minimum level of food, clothing, medical services, and education costs until children reached high school had to be supplied to unemployed people.

On March 26, the government held the third meeting of the Economic Policy Coordination Committee and finalized a package of measures designed to combat unemployment. Among other initiatives, the government called for systemic approaches in recognition of the need for policies tailored to the skill levels, ages, education, living standards, and careers of those in need. The priority was job stability, job creation, and social care for the unemployed. To minimize the loss of existing jobs, the government sought to boost the credit guarantees and funding for SMEs and thus help them restore business stability. The government offered subsidies (partial wage payments and full coverage for employee training) to encourage employers who sought to avoid layoffs. The efforts to avoid layoffs included work sharing through a 10 percent cut in work hours, temporary off days for pay (business closures should occur two days a month at minimum), a greater than 60 percent reassignment of existing workers in case of business realignment, and job training to help those currently employed stay employed.

For job creation, the government increased budget allocations. The budget for public sector projects and public works was reallocated from W 32 trillion to W 42 trillion in the first half of the year. About W 30 trillion allocated for the purchase of superior SME products by the Ministry of National Defense and other governmental agencies was put on a fast track as well. In the supplementary budget, the spending on social overhead capital was expanded by W 500 billion. W 600 billion was to be loaned by the state-controlled Korea Development Bank to enable the Korea Electric Power Corporation to embark on a new facility investment. The W 60 billion initially budgeted for public works programs was raised to W 511.9 billion in the supplementary budget, enough to provide W 500,000 a month to 128,000 unemployed for eight months. Fund allocations for special credit guarantees totaling about W 2 trillion for technology ventures and W 100 billion for information technology promotion were also budgeted.

In job training and job placement, reemployment training among about 80,000 workers who had been laid off and who were eligible for unemployment benefits was associated with trainee wages to be paid out at a rate of 50 to 70 percent of the minimum wage. Entrepreneur programs for about 10,000 white-collar unemployed who were 40 to 50 years of age were also initiated. For people with advanced education, but unable to find work, the government envisioned using university facilities for job training. Internships at large companies were encouraged. The costs of training or retraining, as well as wages, were to be covered by the Employment Insurance Fund. To facilitate job placement services, 20 new offices were to be established.

To improve the social care system, the government decided, in March 1998, to expand unemployment benefit eligibility criteria to workplaces with at least five workers and set the unemployment benefits at 50 percent of the wage received immediately before the layoff, but capped at W 1.05 million total a month. For the unemployed who were ineligible for unemployment benefits, low-interest loans to help households were made available. Half the national health insurance premium to be paid by the unemployed was to be paid out of the health insurance cooperative funds of the former workplaces of the unemployed for one year. For about 80,000 low-income unemployed households, special financial aid for living expenses, medical expenses, and education costs was granted. Fund allocations for the protection of the homeless were expanded.

Table 5.6 shows government unemployment measures by type of unemployment. As shown in table 5.7, expenditures for these programs were sharply expanded, to approximately W 7.9 trillion: W 5 trillion as agreed by the KTC, W 1.1 trillion made available through salary cuts among civil servants in the first supplementary budget the National Assembly had passed on March 25, and W 1.8 trillion for job creation (including W 600 billion for facility investment by the Korea Electric Power Corporation).

Table 5.6 Government Unemployment Measures (II)

Types of unemployment *Measures*

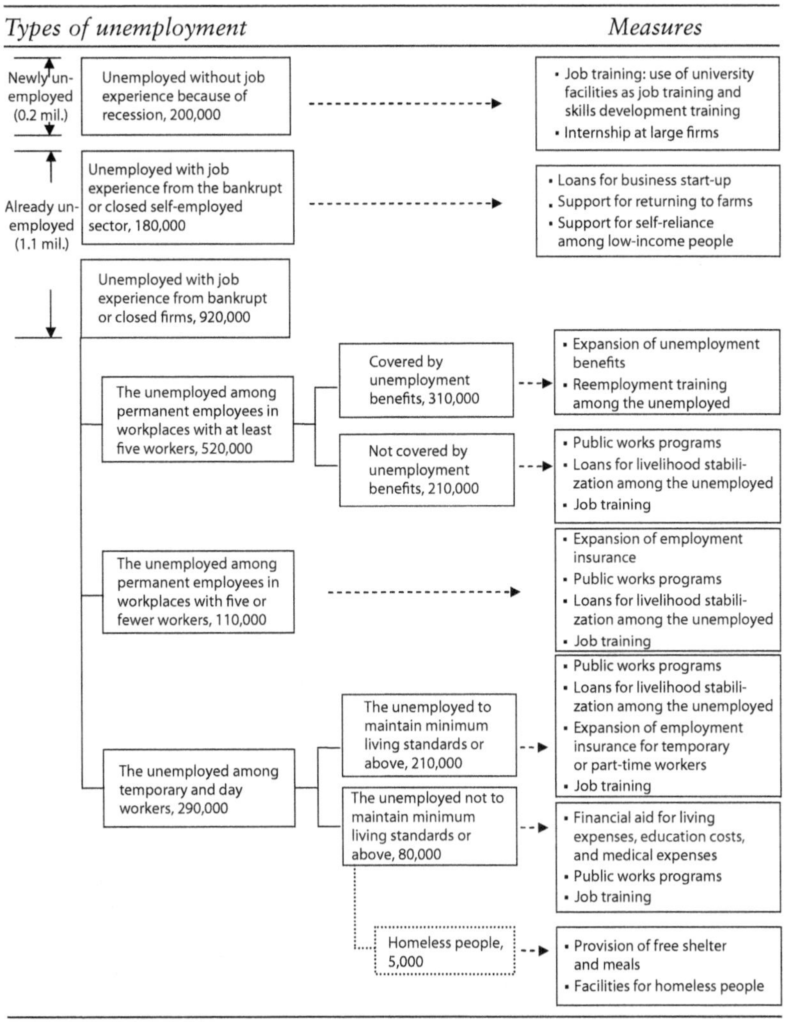

Source: Data of the third Economic Policy Coordination Committee, March 26, 1998.

Note: The government unemployment measures were drafted on the premise that there were 1.3 million unemployed workers in 1998, among whom 310,000 workers (24 percent of the total unemployed or 28 percent of workers who had already been unemployed) could not be covered by unemployment benefits.

Table 5.7 Funding and Expenditures: Government Unemployment Measures, April 13, 1998
won, billions

Measure	*Ministry*	*Budget*	*Expending*	*Funding and expenditure*
1. Funding in KTC agreements	Labor	4,995.1	191.3	
a. Government budget		253.6	30.1	Job adaptation training for underprivileged people, job placement
b. Employment insurance fund		2,014.4	138.7	Unemployment benefits, job training
c. Job training promotion fund		127.1	25.5	Skills development training
d. Long-term bearer bonds		1,600.0		Loans for livelihood stabilization (taking effect on April 15)
e. Government-guaranteed foreign loan		1,000.0		Proceeding with sublease contracts with the Korea Development Bank
2. Funding by salary reduction among government employees		1,111.9	383.7[a]	
a. Public works programs	Eight Ministries	511.9	387.3	Taking effect on April 20
b. Financial aid for living expenses	Health and welfare	200.0	66.7	Taking effect on April 20
c. Loans for livelihood stabilization	Agriculture and labor	200.0	100.0	Taking effect on April 15
d. Expansion of job training	Labor and education	100.0	32.6	Expansion of already-existing job training program
e. Credit guarantee fund contribution	SMBA	100.0	50.0	Planning contribution at the end of April

3. Funding for job creation		1,795.0	85.5	
a. Investment in electricity distribution facility of Korea Electric Power Corporation	MOFE	600.0		Deliberation of funding methods with the Korea Development Bank
b. Rollover of foreign currency denominated loans	MOFE	795.0	85.5	Rollover of all applied loans
c. Software venture firms	MIC	100.0		Support through Information Promotion Fund at the beginning of May
d. Increase in Housing Credit Guarantee Fund	MOFE	300.0		Proceeding with revision of the related law

Source: Data of the Economic Policy Coordination Committee and the Ministry of Finance and Economy.

Note: SMBA = Small and Medium Business Administration. MIC = Ministry of Information and Communication.

a. Planned first-stage expenditure.

Notes

1. The debt—estimated at US$24 billion as of the end of 1997—belonged to 33 domestic banks and nine merchant banks that were judged to be able to repay the debt given adequate time.

2. *Wall Street Journal*, April 2, 1998.

3. The 12 banks were Chohung, Chungchong, Chungbuk, Commercial Bank of Korea, Daedong, Donghwa, Dongnam, Hanil, Korea Exchange, Kangwon, Kyeonggi, and Peace.

4. The 14 suspended merchant banks were Cheongsol, Chungang, Coryo, Daehan, Hangdo, Hansol, Hanwha, Kyongnam, Kyungil, Nara, Samsam, Shinhan, Shinsegae, and Ssangyong.

5. Of the 14 suspended merchant banks, only four merchant banks, namely, Chungang, Daehan, Hansol, and Nara, escaped closure.

6. The ratio of capital to assets was to be 4 percent in March 1998, 6 percent in June 1998, and 8 percent in June 1999.

7. The BOK adopted the aggregate credit ceiling loans in March 1994 to facilitate the liquidity adjustment function of its lending facility. The BOK operates this lending facility by setting a ceiling on its refinancing credits to banks and allocating quotas under this facility to individual banks in accordance with prescribed criteria.

8. M1 = currency in circulation + deposit money (demand deposits at monetary institutions); M2 = M1 + quasi-money (time and savings deposits and resident's foreign currency deposits at monetary institutions); M3 = M2 + deposits at other financial institutions + debentures issued + commercial bills sold + certificates of deposit + repurchase agreements + cover bills.

6

Restructuring Led by Business Closures and the Push for Lower Interest Rates, May–June 1998

The Recognition of Economic Reality

In May 1998, the economy of the Republic of Korea was sinking into a vicious cycle consisting of a debilitating credit crunch and a sharp, broad-based contraction. Strikes by labor unions, which picked up noticeably in April, were further clouding the economic outlook. The falling Japanese yen, together with deteriorating economic conditions abroad, was intensifying the pressure on the economy. Overall, it seemed impossible to predict when the economy was going to hit bottom. Table 6.1 shows key economic indicators that the Korean government and the International Monetary Fund (IMF) had forecast immediately following the onset of the financial crisis. The indicators clearly suggest that the economy was faring much worse than had been anticipated.

Amid deepening gloom, rumors of a second financial crisis started to gain currency, and foreign news media began to give credence to the rumors, warning of dire consequences for the Korean economy. On March 30, 1998, SBC Warburg predicted that Korea would be hit by a second crisis some time in the second quarter of 1998 (Kim Kyeong-Won 1998). The *Economist* also reported, on May 8, that President Kim Dae-Jung had managed to save Korea from a sovereign default through his bold reform measures, but that the country faced the prospect of even more serious difficulties unless the political situation stabilized and the government accelerated the reform initiatives.

Because of the continuing uncertainties and a succession of adverse developments hitherto unknown to Korea, there was also a real risk of

Table 6.1 Forecasts of Key Economic Indicators by the Government and the IMF

Indicator	*December 3, 1997*	*January 7, 1998*	*February 7, 1998*	*May 2, 1998*
GDP growth, %	3	1–2	1 (or minus)	–1 (or below)
Inflation, %	5	about 9	9	less than 10
Current account, US$, billions	–4.3 (less than 1% of GDP)	3.0	8.0 (2.5% of GDP)	21–23 (7% of GDP)
Unemployment rate, %	3.9	5	6–7	n.a.
Persons unemployed, 1,000s	850	1,000	1,200–1,500	n.a.

Sources: MOFE 1997c, 1998d, 1998e, 1998f.
Note: GDP = gross domestic product. n.a. = not applicable.

grave policy mistakes. However, because of the huge potential cascading effects, there was little room for policy error. Government policy makers knew that economic policies could not be put on automatic pilot or instrument flight.

After April, nonetheless, usable foreign exchange reserves grew to exceed US$30 billion, and the short-term supply-demand conditions for the U.S. dollar began to improve markedly. Beginning in May, the government's key economic policy objectives were to stabilize the Korean won, stop and then reverse the cycle of the ever-contracting economy and the worsening credit crunch, and put the economy back on a growth track by laying firm foundations for a healthy future for corporate and financial companies.

This entailed several steps. First, the government had to pick up the momentum in restructuring efforts in the corporate and financial sectors so as to restore investor confidence at home and abroad. Second, new measures were needed to counter the credit crunch, which was likely to intensify in the course of restructuring. In particular, easing the credit shortage among small and medium enterprises (SMEs) and exporters and pushing for lower interest rates were crucial. Third, in the absence of well-functioning social welfare systems, the government had to beef up its responses to mounting unemployment; the support of the labor unions was crucial if the restructuring efforts were to have any chance of success.

The Focus of Corporate and Financial Restructuring on the Closure of Failing Businesses

Setting the Priorities and Building the Momentum of Reform

One salient shift that emerged from the sixth program review and policy consultation meeting between the government and the IMF, on May 2, 1998, was that the focus on preventing a sovereign default had given way to a focus on facilitating restructuring and shoring up the economy. At the meeting, several concrete benchmarks were set for restructuring, including completing the evaluations of bank recapitalization plans, drafting legislation for the creation of mutual funds as an investment vehicle by September 30, and repealing the equity investment cap in domestic companies by foreigners by December 31.

At its fifth meeting, on May 8, the Economic Policy Coordination Committee (EPCC) discussed the priorities in corporate and financial restructuring, as well as in the efforts to boost the economy. It was decided that it was better to push for corporate and financial restructuring simultaneously because the one could not be separated from the other. It was inevitable that the government would have to take part in financial restructuring. Because of the risk of the collapse of the financial system and the potential for huge, irreversible damage to the economy, the government recognized that it would have to inject public funds and take other unprecedented measures to facilitate financial restructuring. Corporate restructuring was, in principle, to be led by the companies themselves. For prompt and effective debt resolution, however, the creditor banks would have to take the lead because they were the creditors and the financial intermediaries of the companies. The government therefore decided that rapid bank restructuring had to be the primary focus and that corporate restructuring had to be led by the creditor banks.

The government also decided to put greater weight on restructuring relative to the stimulation of the economy because restructuring was considered about the only meaningful remedy for rising unemployment; that is, the fundamental cure to unemployment was to unfreeze and normalize credit markets, foster entrepreneurship, reinvigorate business enterprises, restore flexibility in the labor market, and rectify the deeply entrenched labor supply-demand imbalances.

Unemployment was certain to rise in the course of restructuring. Rather than implementing pro-employment policies, however, the government decided that continuing the W 7.9 trillion in initiatives already in the pipeline so as to mitigate the impact of unemployment was more important, particularly the on-the-job training and job placement programs.

In an attempt to add momentum to corporate and financial restructuring, the government created, on May 5, the Structural Reform Committee at the Financial Supervisory Commission (FSC) and charged it with the task of drawing up the basic outline of the government's restructuring plan and the steps in implementation. It was left to the committee to monitor financial market developments and corporate activities and prepare contingency plans. In short, the committee was to oversee and take charge of the government's restructuring efforts. The committee was headed by the chairman of the FSC and made up of four teams. In addition, the government created the Subcommittee on Reform and Restructuring—made up of the minister of finance and economy, the chairman of the Planning and Budget Committee, the chairman of the FSC, and the senior secretary to the president for economic affairs within the EPCC—to ensure coordination among various government ministries and agencies.

Having agreed to carry out reform and restructuring through the Korea Tripartite Commission (consisting of representatives of the government, labor, and business), the government issued a presidential decree on March 28 that gave statutory entitlement to the commission. However, when the government sought to convene the second tripartite meeting, the Korean Confederation of Trade Unions (KCTU) refused to attend, citing unsatisfactory progress in the reform of the *chaebols* (the large family-controlled and family-run groups that dominate business in Korea), unfair public sector restructuring, the need to repeal the Act on the Protection of Temporary Agency Workers, and unfair labor practices. As a result, the second tripartite meeting was delayed. The government and the ruling political party first urged the KCTU to return to the negotiating table at the commission, but the KCTU responded by staging work strikes for two days on May 27–28, forcing the government to convene the second tripartite meeting with businesses and the Federation of Korean Trade Unions, the other major national labor union group, on June 3. The KCTU soon relented and attended the second tripartite meeting, on June 10, after terminating a second work strike.

Forging Ahead with Corporate Restructuring

By May, several initiatives began to take shape in the implementation of corporate restructuring. First, the creditor banks had to expedite the process of determining the viability of distressed or failing companies and take the necessary follow-up actions. Second, corporate governance had to be drastically improved and strengthened to instill credible management transparency and accountability. Third, the government had to remove regulatory and other obstacles to corporate restructuring as it sought to step up support for corporate reform.

On May 15, 1998, the government completed the drafting of resolution plans for distressed companies. Under the plans, the corporate distress evaluation committee that each creditor bank had set up on May 9 to assess the viability and the prospects for the turnaround of distressed debtor companies was to complete its evaluation by the end of May. By the end of June, the special SME response task force at each bank was to complete the selection of the SMEs that were to be given full or conditional support. Then, by the end of July, the government was to produce a support scheme for corporate restructuring. In addition, as agreed to with the IMF, each bank was to establish a workout unit by the end of June. A creditor banks council—a coordination committee made up of representatives of the creditor banks who were to work out the differences among the banks—was to be established by the end of May. The banks were directed to bring in outside advisors or advisory groups to facilitate negotiations with the debtor companies and also seek outside investors. In an attempt to encourage the use of outside expertise, the government made available a technical assistance loan of the World Bank. The plan was to have agreements with the debtor companies on improvements in financial soundness completed by the end of July so that concrete actions could be undertaken in August.

However, restructuring failed to proceed as planned from the outset because the chaebol companies, which were supposed to embrace restructuring, did not show much enthusiasm. Neither did the creditor banks that, as their creditors, were supposed to push the chaebol companies into restructuring. The chaebol companies had already agreed to improvement plans on financial soundness with the creditor banks in February, but little had been accomplished since then. Indeed, the chaebols had attempted to attract huge capital infusions from foreign investors, though only a few, such as the Daesang Group and Samsung Heavy Industries, had any measurable success. The top five chaebols, believing they had already secured enough liquidity by issuing commercial paper (CP) and bonds in domestic capital markets, took a wait-and-see attitude; for all practical purposes, they were passive observers. Meanwhile, the banks acted as if their sole interest was to comply with the minimum capital requirements of the Bank for International Settlements (BIS) as quickly as possible. They therefore also failed to deal aggressively with the failing debtor companies and decide what their reaction would be toward these companies at a fundamental level. The creditor banks not only lacked the will to find a solution. In truth, they had neither the expertise nor the experience needed to lead in the restructuring of troubled debtor companies.

As President Kim Dae-Jung pointed out, Korea's economic reality made expeditious restructuring an absolute necessity. The government thus decided, on June 16, that there were limits to the steps the top five chaebols could take on their own and at their own pace, and it was therefore time for a bit of pushing and shoving by the government so as to put the companies on the right track. Likewise, the government judged that the financial companies were incapable of satisfactorily carrying out restructuring. It was decided that some guidelines would have to be mapped out.

Shifting gears, the government decreed that a determination of the viability—that is, the prospect of a meaningful turnaround—of large companies and SMEs would have to be completed by the end of June and that the restructuring of those large companies and SMEs considered viable would have to begin in earnest in July. Under the government guidelines, each of the eight major creditor banks, by July 15, was to select for workout at least two groups from among the 6th to the 64th largest business groups (chaebols) and 10 companies from among the other large independent companies with no affiliation. By the end of July at the latest, following consultations with the creditor banks and outside advisors, the top five chaebols were to announce concrete and specific restructuring plans.

To ensure steady progress, 210 financial companies, ranging from banks, merchant banks, and insurance companies to investment trust companies, were directed to conclude restructuring agreements by June 25 and create corporate restructuring coordination committees to preempt any conflicts of interest or disputes that might arise among the creditor financial institutions in the course of restructuring. It was also decided that the first phase of corporate restructuring should be completed by the end of September.

The government resolved to adopt measures to improve corporate governance significantly during the first half of 1998. The measures included (1) establishing tougher legal liability on controlling shareholders and introducing of cumulative voting to give minority shareholders a greater voice in electing directors; (2) assigning voting rights to institutional investors to enable them to monitor management more closely and provide more effective checks and balances; (3) allowing the incorporation of holding companies on a restricted basis to give companies a wider choice in corporate structures; and (4) lowering the minimum share ownership requirement from 0.05 to 0.01 percent for minority shareholder representative suits against management.

In addition, the government decided to bring about legal and regulatory changes it deemed necessary to encourage mergers and acquisitions (M&A) and thus quicken the pace of restructuring. It decided to seek amendment of the Commercial Act during the first half of 1998 to allow corporate spin-offs and shorten the time allowed for legal challenges from two months to one month. Tax laws were set to be amended in 1998 to grant spin-offs the same tax incentives available for M&A. Changes to the Securities and Investment Trust Act were to be undertaken in June 1998 to lay the statutory basis for the creation of corporate restructuring funds.

The Closure of 55 Companies

On June 18, creditor banks announced a list of 55 companies that they judged to be nonviable, along with corporate debtors that they considered distressed. The list was much longer than the 21 nonviable companies the creditor banks had announced earlier, on June 8. The June 18 list contained new companies affiliated with the top five chaebols. Earlier, the creditor banks had deliberately excluded such companies, arguing that the debt repayment of these companies was not in doubt because the debt was guaranteed by the other chaebol-affiliated companies. However, the government urged the banks to include companies belonging to the top five chaebols in the credit review on the basis of the soundness and the debt servicing ability of the companies on their own merits.[1] Under pressure from the FSC, the creditor banks reassessed the viability of their debtor companies. The list issued on June 18 was the result. The 55 companies to be closed by the creditor banks were identified through a review of 313 debtor and distressed companies that were each associated with one of the 64 chaebols or that were large independent (non-chaebol) companies.

A company was identified as a distressed debtor on the basis of an estimated future value calculated by assuming that interest rates were in the 12–13 percent range, not in the higher range that prevailed at the time. The key valuation factors encompassed financial statement items, such as fund flows, profit ratios, and soundness ratios, as well as sustainability indicators, such as industrial outlook, technology development, market share, and the feasibility of turnaround plans. The 55 nonviable companies included 20 companies associated with the top five chaebols, 32 companies associated with the 6th to the 64th largest chaebols, and 3 non-chaebol companies. The decision was made to establish business closure plans and execute them as quickly as possible. The creditor banks agreed to cut off all fresh credit from the companies on the nonviable list. No credit supports were to be allowed to avert the closure of the chaebol-affiliated companies. Only a discharge of the debt guarantee obligations of affiliated companies was allowed.

Financial Restructuring

Following agreements with the IMF and the World Bank, the government finalized the timetable for the restructuring of financial companies at the seventh meeting of the EPCC, on June 19, 1998. Due diligence on the assets of Seoul Bank and Korea First Bank by Coopers & Lybrand was about to be wrapped up. The two banks were to hold consultations with Morgan Stanley, the lead advisor, and then the sale to foreign buyers (financial companies) was to be completed soon thereafter, well before the original date set for the sale, November 15, 1998.

Due diligence on the 12 banks with BIS capital ratios below the minimum 8 percent had already been conducted. The 12-member Bank Evaluation Committee (consisting of certified public accountants, lawyers, and other experts) was to review the turnaround plans submitted by the 12 banks and send the evaluation reports to the FSC by June 27. The FSC was then to determine the steps in the clean-up process for the distressed banks by June 30. For the 12 banks with BIS capital ratios above 8 percent, another management and viability assessment was to be carried out by the end of August, and aggressive turnaround measures, including the replacement of top management and mergers, were to be adopted for the troubled banks identified through this process.

The restructuring of nonbank financial companies was to be carried out through reliance on capital infusions by the controlling shareholders; those companies deemed nonviable were to be closed without delay. If the capital of a leasing company had, in principle, become eroded, the company was to be shut down by the end of June unless controlling shareholders were able to shore up the company. The fate of Saehan Merchant Bank was to be determined by the end of June; other merchant banks were to be closely monitored during the business turnarounds. Those failing to make progress were to be closed in July. Action on insurance companies was to be undertaken following a review of business rehabilitation plans in August. Securities companies were to report their net capital ratios and asset-liability ratios by July. Their business rehabilitation plans were then to be evaluated by December to determine follow-up measures. Thus, under the timetable, the first round of restructuring among financial institutions was to be completed by the end of September 1998.

The injection of public funds. Corporate and financial restructuring required enormous sums of money. Corporate companies had to reduce their debt ratios drastically to improve their financial structure in a meaningful fashion. However, it was important to secure the needed funding through the market. Making government funds available to failing companies would have delayed the pace of the restructuring carried out by the companies themselves, invited moral hazard, and brought additional harm to the economy.

Financial companies were obliged to dispose of nonperforming assets promptly and raise fresh capital to comply with the minimum BIS capital requirements. As in the case of corporate companies, it was crucial that financial companies also raise the necessary capital on their own through the markets. However, when this became impossible, government support was deemed unavoidable. There were several reasons for this. Unlike other businesses, financial companies acted as intermediaries for funds and in the settlement of financial transactions and thus supported real economic activities. If restructuring failed, and financial companies were rendered impotent in carrying out their credit intermediation role, the problems would quickly spill over to the entire economy and bring about systemic failures. No modern commerce could function if credit could not flow through financial companies. This was the reason that the United States had to use public funds to deal with the savings and loan debacle in the 1980s and that Finland, Norway, and Sweden all took similar steps in the 1990s to cope with financial crisis.

The prospect that a major capital increase would become available to Korean financial companies was dim, given, among other factors, the depressed stock market, the depressed real estate market, and falling investor confidence. Large infusions of fresh capital from foreign investors were also unlikely. At the end of June 1998, the share prices of financial companies were well below the book values of the companies, and the only foreign capital investment at the time was poured into Korea Exchange Bank by Germany's Commerzbank.

The conditions were such that financial companies were limited in their ability to solve their own problems. The government had to step in. There was no other alternative. However, the magnitude of the bailout required easily exceeded the capacity of the annual government budget. The practical approach, then, was to issue government guaranteed bonds to raise the necessary funds, while relying on government coffers to cover the interest expenses.

At the sixth meeting of the EPCC, on May 20, the government estimated the amount of public funds that would be required, and the methods to be used to raise the funds were determined. About W 50 trillion would be needed: W 25 trillion for the purchase of nonperforming assets, W 16 trillion for the capital infusions, and W 9 for the substitute payment of deposits. Including the W 14 trillion in government guaranteed bonds already used to finance the capital infusions at Korea First Bank and Seoul Bank, the substitute payment of deposits for failed merchant banks, and the purchase of nonperforming assets, the total package came to about W 64 trillion.

The W 50 trillion bailout was to be raised through government guaranteed bond issues by the Non-Performing Asset Management Fund of the Korea Asset Management Corporation and by the Deposit Insurance Fund of the Korea Deposit Insurance Corporation (KDIC).

The estimate that W 25 trillion would be needed for the purchase of nonperforming assets (loans) was derived as follows. The overall value of the nonperforming assets on the books of financial companies had been W 68 trillion at the end of March 1998. If the loans likely to turn sour in the near future were included, the total value of the troubled assets would rise to W 118 trillion. Of this amount, assets worth W 68 trillion had to be cleaned up. However, among the rest of the troubled assets, it was likely that some loans would become nonperforming and would have to be written off in the course of corporate restructuring. It was possible that the sale of some corporate assets and investments from abroad might help reduce the amount of troubled assets. It was concluded that approximately W 100 trillion would be needed to clean up all the bad loans. Using mark-to-market valuation, the W 100 trillion in bad assets recorded on the books of financial companies was worth about W 50 trillion, meaning W 50 trillion in loan write-downs for financial companies. The prognosis was that about half the W 50 trillion in bad assets could be sold off or otherwise cleaned up by the financial companies themselves and that the remaining W 25 trillion in bad assets could be purchased and resolved by the Korea Asset Management Corporation.

The estimated W 16 trillion needed for capital infusions was derived as follows. First, the overall capital infusion was estimated at W 39 trillion. W 15 trillion in loan-loss provisions that had already been reserved could be deducted from the W 50 trillion in losses that financial companies were to incur because of the clean-up of the W 100 trillion in bad loans, leaving W 35 trillion in net losses that needed to be recapitalized. Financial companies required an additional W 4 trillion to comply with the BIS capital requirements. Of the W 39 trillion that had to be recapitalized, it was projected that approximately W 20 trillion could be raised by the financial companies on their own through fresh subordinated debt and equity issues, leaving W 19 trillion. With the deduction of the W 3 trillion already injected into Seoul Bank and Korea First Bank, the final recapitalization amount came to W 16 trillion.

The W 9 trillion in new debt for the substitute payment of deposits was based on the W 5 trillion already paid out in the course of cleaning up the merchant banks and the W 4 trillion likely to be needed to clean up savings and finance companies, credit unions, and securities companies. For banks in grave distress, the plan was to utilize M&A or purchase of assets and assumption of liabilities (P&A), whereby a healthier bank would purchase the assets and assume the liabilities of the failing bank to save on the cost of the substitute payment of deposits to be made by the KDIC.

The closure of five banks. On June 19, the government put the finishing touches on the financial restructuring plan. Under the new plan, a two-year grace period was to be given to banks for phase-by-phase compliance with BIS capital requirements (table 6.2). For the smaller local banks and other banks that did not extend corporate loans in excess of a certain amount (for example, W 5 billion) and that had abandoned international banking activities, less restrictive BIS capital requirements were to be put into effect.

Table 6.2 BIS Ratio Requirements, End of Period, 1999–2000
percent

Action	*March 1999*	*March 2000*	*December 2000*
Conducting international banking activities	6	8	10
Giving up international banking activities	4	6	8

Source: FSC 1998a.

The reason for the gradual implementation of BIS capital compliance was that the BIS capital ratios of the banks had already fallen sharply because of the weight of spiraling nonperforming loans, and the capital markets were in tatters. The overriding concern was that the banks would therefore resort to calling back loans or cutting off fresh lending altogether rather than boosting capital. The credit crunch could then only worsen.

For the 12 banks falling short of the 8 percent minimum BIS capital requirements, the 12-member Bank Evaluation Committee was to assess the general health of the banks in capital adequacy, asset soundness, profitability, liquidity, management capability, and future plans to raise capital to meet BIS capital requirements. The committee was then to recommend each bank to the FSC for approval, conditional approval, or disapproval.

The FSC decided to undertake separate actions for these three classes of banks. From the approved banks, the FSC demanded quarterly implementation reports on turnaround plans and decided to impose punitive measures, including capital write-downs, replacements of management, or mergers if the implementation did not keep pace with the plans. Banks that received conditional approval were directed to submit turnaround plans within one month of the date of the conditional approval and then, after getting a green light from the FSC, to proceed with implementation. For the disapproved banks, the follow-up actions included closing through merger orders or a P&A. A bank that received either a conditional approval or a disapproval but voluntarily sought a merger with a healthier bank was to be excluded from the government action.

The government preferred either M&A or a P&A as the method of resolving failing banks so as to minimize the adverse impact on the economy. Liquidation, M&A, or P&A can be employed to clean up a distressed bank. Liquidation was associated with heavy up-front costs, such as large payouts to depositors and disruptions to household and corporate customers. Liquidation was also likely to have a significant impact on financial markets. Because M&A involve a voluntary negotiation, the process can become protracted and raise many difficult issues, such as maintaining a workforce. As a general rule, in the process of the P&A of a failing bank, deposits (liabilities) are transferred to a healthy bank to protect depositors, but the assets (loans) are divided into two categories: performing loans, which are usually taken over, and nonperforming loans, which are resolved through sales, write-offs, or other dispositions.

On the morning of June 29, 1998, the FSC convened a meeting to deliberate on the final report of the Bank Evaluation Committee and announce its decisions on the 12 banks that had fallen short in meeting the 8 percent minimum BIS capital requirements (FSC 1998b). The FSC gave conditional approval for the turnaround plans submitted by seven banks that were deemed capable of making a comeback, but rejected the plans by five others that were considered to have little or no chance of survival.[2] The FSC ordered the seven conditionally approved banks to submit implementation plans for turnaround within one month, by the end of July. The five rejected banks were to be closed and absorbed into healthier banks through a P&A.[3] Good banks were invited to become acquiring banks in the process. The selection of these banks was based on the recommendation of the FSC, which took into account the following: (1) The BIS ratios of the banks had to be above 9 percent. (2) The banks could resume normal operations in the near future through recapitalization after the acquisitions. (3) They could achieve economies of scale by enlarging their market shares and expanding branch networks.

A number of steps were taken by the government to pave the way for a smooth resolution of the five rejected banks. One was to encourage, among the acquiring banks, the continued employment of as many nonmanagement employees as possible. To ensure that the acquiring banks were not overburdened by assuming the assets and liabilities of the rejected banks, the KDIC took over any liabilities in excess of the healthy assets of the rejected banks. The asset management entity also provided put-back options so that the acquiring banks would be protected from any assets that soured after the takeover by being able to sell such assets back to the entity within a fixed time period.

As the restructuring of corporate and financial companies intensified, the government established contingency plans for a variety of potential scenarios during June and August. The scenarios included a surge in the incidence of corporate bankruptcies and the resulting cascading impact, the sudden disruption of credit flows to companies resulting from bank mergers, and problems over interbank funding. However, these measures failed to restore calm or order to financial markets. One reason was that the contingency plans did not prepare for the sabotage of the electronic banking network by angry bank employees who had been laid off.

Plans for the restructuring of nonbank financial companies were also developed during May and June 1998 (FSC 1998c). For securities and insurance companies, the government first established a benchmark for sound management. For securities companies, prompt corrective action based on operational net capital ratios and asset-liability ratios went into effect in May. For insurance companies, the FSC decided to use a solvency margin as the key indicator of business soundness and, on May 11, ordered 18 life insurance and four non–life insurance companies that were at or below the minimum level of solvency margin or that had been deemed unsound or heavily indebted (as of March 1998) to submit turnaround plans.[4] In the same month, the FSC ordered leasing companies and investment trust companies that were said to be on the verge of insolvency to submit turnaround plans. The FSC also suspended the business operations of Saehan and Hangil merchant banks on May 15 and June 12, respectively. Similarly, the MOFE revoked the business licenses of Coryo Securities and Dongseo Securities on June 1. (These securities firms had already been suspended.)

Public Sector Restructuring

Following the reform and reorganization of several state-run research institutes in May 1998, the Planning and Budget Committee announced, on July 3, privatization plans for state-owned companies. Efforts to improve the efficiency of state-run companies by privatizing those that were primarily commerce-oriented had been on the drawing board for a long time. For instance, in 1993, the government had pushed for the privatization of 58 state-run companies and the merger or closure of 10 others. The Act on the Improvement of Managerial Structure and Privatization of Public Enterprises had also been passed earlier, in 1996–97.

However, no meaningful privatization had ever materialized. There were several reasons for the decades-long impasse. The conventional thinking was that only large companies would be the primary beneficiaries because they alone were able to bid for the state-run companies, and economic power would therefore become further concentrated in the hands of a few chaebols. It was also of concern that any large stock issues of the newly privatized companies would upset the stock market. Resistance to change by the state-run companies out of self interest, a lack of the strong political leadership needed to overcome the resistance, and no clear national consensus had also contributed to the long impasse.

This time around, the government's approach was to hold open public hearings with an eye to building a broad national consensus and to persuading the labor unions that were involved in the state-run companies and that were vehemently opposed to privatization. Excluding financial companies, a total of 11 companies (within 26 parent companies) were targeted for privatization. Of these 11 companies, POSCO and four other companies that could be quickly privatized were to be put on a fast track and sold off between 1998 and 1999.[5] The Korea Gas Corporation, KT&G, and four others that needed more time for the necessary preparations were to be privatized in phases.[6]

In June 1998, the government announced reorganization proposals for local governments following the completion of the downsizing and reorganization of the central government. Since the 1980s, the number of local government employees had been growing 4.6 percent a year and, by the end of 1997, accounted for a third (291,673) of all government employees. The government plan primarily called for a substantial reduction in the number of administrative units.

Lowering Interest Rates and Easing the Credit Crunch

Turmoil in Global Financial Markets

In mid-May 1998, unrest in Indonesia was turning into bloody street protests. In Japan, the slow pace of the financial sector clean-up and a deepening recession were taking a heavy toll on the economy. The Japanese yen, after tumbling in April, continued to slide in May. Then, on June 8, the yen broke through the psychologically important ¥140 mark against the dollar and, on June 15, reached ¥146, the highest level in eight years. International investors, who tended to look at Asia as a bundle, interpreted the events in Indonesia and Japan as a cue to retreat from Asia. Soon, currencies weakened sharply against the dollar, sovereign debt yields spiraled upward, and stock markets tumbled in Korea, in Malaysia, in Taiwan, China, and in Thailand. Stock markets in China and Hong Kong SAR, China plummeted amid widespread expectations of currency depreciations against the dollar, even as China reiterated its pledge not to lower the value of the yuan relative to the dollar, and Hong Kong SAR, China made clear it would stick to the currency board system.

In the meantime, the situation in the Russian Federation was also deteriorating. Amid continuing political instability and rising budget deficits, the Russian ruble was falling, stock markets were sliding badly, and foreign investors were starting to withdraw from Russia. Worries over Brazil were mounting as well, further fueling uncertainty and fear in global financial markets. Table 6.3 shows the fluctuations in key financial indicators among Asian economies during the second quarter of 1998.

Table 6.3 Changes in Key Financial Indicators, Asian Economies and Russian Federation, April 16–June 16, 1998
percent

Indicator	*Korea, Rep.*	*Japan*	*Indonesia*	*Malaysia*	*Hong Kong SAR, China*	*Russian Federation*
Exchange rate	1.9	10.3	48.5	8.2	–0.1	0.4[a]
Stock index	–38.3	–7.3	–22.3	–30.2	–32.7	—
Spread of overseas-issued benchmark sovereign bonds	27.2	9.6	37.5	20	—	31.5

Sources: MOFE 1998f, 1998g.
Note: — = not available.
a. Change in May 1998.

The worsening conditions outside Korea weighed heavily on the exchange rate of the won against the dollar. However, the depreciation of the won was narrower than that of other Asian currencies because of Korea's trade surplus, inflow of foreign capital, and increasing dollar-denominated deposits by local companies. Nonetheless, ominously, while the won was falling against the dollar, it was strengthening against the yen, putting Korean exporters at a comparative disadvantage against their Japanese competitors. This was a troubling development because Korea's top 15 export goods that competed directly with Japanese counterparts, including semiconductors, automobiles, and ships, accounted for about 40 percent of the total value of Korea's exports.

Worse still, export growth, which had been rising, reversed direction in May and began to decelerate, raising fresh speculation about whether the won was becoming overvalued. The question now was no longer whether the won was rebounding from its collapse in the wake of the financial crisis, but whether the won had to mirror the depreciating Japanese yen to maintain the international competitiveness of Korea's exports. In terms of goods imported from Japan and used later, as components or otherwise, in exports by Korean companies, the estimate was that Korea's export competitiveness would not be harmed badly if a 10 percent depreciation of the yen was matched by a 3 to 5 percent depreciation of the won. Among Korean exporters and in foreign exchange markets, the expectation was that this threshold would be about W 1,000 for ¥100. However, the won/yen exchange rate had not quite reached W 1,000/¥100 during June.

The unfavorable developments among Asian economies pushed up yields on the sovereign bonds issued by Korea to overseas investors and made it more difficult and costly to raise fresh funds from abroad. Nonetheless, it was estimated that, even in the worst-case scenario, the capital withdrawal by foreign investors would amount to only about US$15 billion (MOFE 1998h). This was well within the absorption capacity of Korea given its reserves (US$36.2 billion as of June 16, 1998), as well as the additional borrowing scheduled to take place in the near future (US$2 billion from the IMF, US$2 billion from the World Bank, US$1 billion from the Asian Development Bank, US$2 billion from the Export-Import Bank of the United States, and US$2 billion in syndicated borrowing by the Export-Import Bank of Korea). Instability in international financial markets—triggered partly by the faltering yen—further squeezed trade credit and exacerbated the tight credit conditions many resident Korean companies already faced, forcing these companies to boost their foreign currency deposits at home.

Drafting a Differentiation Strategy

A flexible exchange rate policy and adequate foreign exchange reserves. Because Asia was more or less viewed as a single block by most foreign investors, it made sense for Korea to set itself apart through strategies that differentiated Korea from other countries in the region. The Korean government therefore decided to step up business restructuring and manage its foreign exchange rate policy by allowing flexibility so the exchange rate would remain in tune with market movements. The government also decided to pursue liberalization in foreign exchange and capital movements through a drive to attract foreign capital and rebuild the confidence of foreign investors in Korea.

There was no disagreement on the need to restore investor confidence at home and abroad by allowing the market to decide the appropriate value of the won. However, while the won faced pressure for currency appreciation because of the excess supply of dollars, it was also becoming clear that the won had to be depreciated if Korea's export goods were to remain competitive against the weakening yen. So, the exchange rate could not simply be left to the markets. The basic stance of the government was that it would defer to the market, but would try to contain the yen/won exchange rate at ¥100/W 1,000 or lower. The concern was that the economy already faced extremely sluggish demand at home and would falter yet again if the won strengthened against other currencies, thereby hurting Korean exports. Adding to foreign exchange reserves was another way Korea might set itself apart from the struggling Asian economies and help restore the confidence of foreign investors, while absorbing the excess dollars in foreign exchange markets. At the end of June 1998, Korea's usable foreign exchange reserves amounted to US$37.04 billion, exceeding the level agreed to with the IMF.

The liberalization of foreign exchange transactions. In June 1998, the government announced foreign exchange liberalization measures. They were to take effect in two phases: one in April 1999 and one in January 2001. During the first phase, except for a few types of transactions, current account transactions related to ordinary external business activities by companies were to be fully liberalized. With a few exceptions, restrictions on payments that were conducted through foreign exchange banks, such as company payment netting and third-party payments, were to be lifted. However, restrictions on current account transactions by individuals were to remain in effect to prevent capital flight to safe havens.

In respect of capital account transactions, company overseas borrowing at maturities of less than one year were to be allowed. Nonresidents were to be allowed to make deposits and open won-denominated trust accounts at maturities of more than one year. Similarly, restrictions on overseas real estate investments and branch operations by corporate and financial companies, as well as the issuance of securities denominated in won or foreign currencies in domestic markets by nonresidents, were to be repealed. In addition, the foreign exchange business was to be opened to financial companies that met certain requirements in capital, manpower, and computer capability. Licensing for the establishment and the activities of such businesses was to be replaced by registration with the MOFE. The bona fide (real demand) principle in foreign exchange and derivative transactions was to be abolished.

During the second phase of the liberalization, a number of provisions were targeted for repeal or significant deregulation. First, in respect of current account transactions, only restrictions in place on international criminal activities, money laundering, gambling, and economic sanctions imposed by the United Nations were to stay in effect. Restrictions on individuals remaining in effect after the first phase were to be repealed, including the ceilings on overseas travel expenses, donations, emigration expenses, and withdrawals of domestic assets by nonresident nationals. Second, in respect of capital account transactions, the positive regulation system was to be converted into a negative one. Corporate overseas deposits and credit extensions were to be liberalized, and the obligation to repatriate overseas claims was to be lifted. Investment in overseas securities without involving a domestic brokerage was allowed, and deposits in won and investment-in-trust products at a maturity of less than one year were allowed for nonresidents. Trading in derivatives without going through foreign exchange business companies was to be liberalized as well. Individual capital account transactions, such as overseas deposits and borrowing, credit extensions, and real estate investment, were also fully liberalized.

In consideration of possible difficulties arising because of comprehensive foreign exchange liberalization, new measures were to be implemented to shore up prudential supervision over the foreign exchange transactions of corporate and financial companies.

Another plan was to create an electronic network at the Bank of Korea (BOK) to monitor foreign exchange transactions and establish the Korea Center for International Finance to maintain systems to provide early warning of any foreign exchange crisis.

As a precaution against the occurrence of critical situations such as natural disaster, war, or a drastic change in the economic environment, a number of safeguards were to be instituted, including the ability to suspend external transactions temporarily, concentrate the means of payment, require prior approval for certain kinds of capital transactions, or establish variable deposit requirements. In essence, the government sought to overhaul the legal and regulatory systems involved in dealing with foreign exchange. The National Assembly passed the government-proposed amendments on September 16, 1998.[7]

Prior to these changes, the government had taken a number of steps to repeal or eliminate altogether several foreign exchange restrictions. Amid worries over the adverse impact of the weakening yen and the worsening external environment on the ability of domestic corporate and financial companies to raise funds from foreign lenders, the goal was to reaffirm

Korea's commitment to economic reform and restore the confidence of foreign investors in Korea. So, beginning on May 25, 1998, the government accelerated measures to open the market for certificates of deposit, repurchase agreements, and other short-term financial products, such as bills issued by merchant banks. On the same day, restrictions on the purchase by foreign investors of shares listed on the Korea Stock Exchange, the stock market of Korea Securities Dealers Automated Quotations, beneficiary certificates, and options and futures on stock indexes were all repealed. For investment in the shares of public corporations, however, the equity investment ceiling was raised to 30 percent for foreign investors (3 percent for an individual foreign investor). Beginning on July 1, foreign borrowing and debt issues at a maturity of longer than one year, as well as trade financing by the domestic corporate sector, were deregulated. In addition, nearly all the restrictions on foreign exchange transactions by foreign investors that were connected with inbound investment were repealed.

The efforts abroad: economic diplomacy. President Kim Dae-Jung's visit to the United States in early June 1998 was a meaningful one. By reiterating Korea's firm resolve to carry out economic reform, President Kim sought to set Korea apart from other Asian economies in the eyes of foreign investors. For their part, U.S. policy makers and legislators, even the media, extended an enthusiastic welcome to President Kim.[8] Tangible benefits for Korea quickly ensued, including (1) steps to reach a bilateral investment treaty with the United States; (2) further negotiations on the terms and conditions for drawing funds, if necessary, from the second line of defense that was to be provided by major developed countries; (3) resumption of investment guarantees by the U.S. Overseas Private Investment Corporation for investments in Korea; and (4) a push for the conclusion of a bilateral open skies agreement and the promotion of strategic tie-ups between U.S. and Korean airlines. The Export-Import Bank of the United States agreed to provide US$2 billion in trade credits. In investor meetings held in New York and other major markets, pledges were made for investments in Korea worth US$2.15 billion. The establishment of a joint Korea–United States committee on software cooperation and an industry consortium for industrial cooperation were also agreed to.

Progress was reported with other countries aside from the United States. At the May 22–24 Asia-Pacific Economic Cooperation meeting of finance ministers, Korea secured US$1 billion in loans from the Export-Import Bank of Japan to be executed by the end of the month. On May 26, the board of directors of Commerzbank voted to invest W 350 billion in the Korea Exchange Bank.

The continuing current account surplus and falling short-term debt. Korea posted a current account surplus of US$4.07 billion in May and US$3.32 billion in June 1998, mostly because of surpluses in the trade balance on the back of sharp drops in imports. Export growth slowed during the May–June period from a year earlier as a result of a downturn in the Asian markets, as well as falling prices for semiconductors, petrochemicals, and other key Korean export items. The persistent credit crunch and other difficulties faced by many export companies weighed on Korean exports. Likewise, import amounts fell on weakening domestic demand, the depreciating won, and sluggish commodity prices worldwide.

The capital account recorded a US$90 million surplus and a US$430 million deficit in May and June, respectively. The net outflow of investment in securities and a jump in short-term debt repayment accounted for the capital account deficit during the period despite two separate inflows from the IMF (US$1.25 billion and US$620 million). The net outflow of investment in securities resulted from the fact that, while foreign stock purchases faltered and Korean bond holdings abroad dropped, domestic banks raised their holdings of foreign securities during the period.

At the end of June 2008, Korea's total external liabilities stood at US$155.17 billion. Of this total, long-term debt represented US$121.33 billion or 78.2 percent. Short-term debt accounted for US$33.84 billion or 21.8 percent of the total, which was lower than the 23 percent in May. Public sector debt came to US$34.62 billion, up from the previous month because of the withdrawal of funds that had been provided by the IMF and others. However, the external debt of the financial sector and the private sector fell relative to the previous month, to US$79.76 billion and US$40.79 billion, respectively.

The Push for Lower Interest Rates and Relief from the Credit Crunch

Usable foreign exchange reserves had climbed above US$30 billion by the end of April 1998, and a sense of normalcy was returning to foreign exchange markets. Thus, when the government and the IMF held the sixth policy review and consultation, on May 2, the government set about shifting its focus in the second half of the year from the stabilization of the foreign exchange rate to stimulating the real economy.

Support for SMEs and exporters and lowering interest rates. As the pace of restructuring in the corporate and financial sectors began to pick up in May, the market was in the grip of fear that the Keopyung and Donga groups, along with several other large business groups, were on the verge of collapse. Strikes and street protests by the KCTU on May 1 added to the general sense of instability and volatility. With the outlook for Asian economies sharply deteriorating amid a mounting crisis in Indonesia and the falling yen, foreign investors also showed obvious signs of hesitation about investing in Korea. Even talks of a crisis looming in June began to gain currency.

Conditions worsened: the crunch in credit intensified, share prices continued to slide, and the real estate market went into a freeze. Fortunately, the won was showing greater stability than other Asian currencies. The government believed there was enough economic room for interest rate cuts. The overnight call rate fell sharply, from 18.04 percent at the end of April to 14.41 percent by the end of June. The benchmark three-year corporate bond yield also dropped, from 17.7 percent to 16.0 percent. The high short-term, low long-term interest rates that resulted from efforts to stabilize the won had shifted to low short-term, high long-term interest rates by late June. The bank loan rate and deposit rates headed lower. During June, the interest rate on overdrafts hovered around 18.5 percent, while the interest rate on general loans reached 16.4 percent. The rate on one-year time deposits stayed close to 15.5 percent. Table 6.4 shows the market interest rates that prevailed from March to June.

The downward trend in interest rates despite the volatile financial market conditions at home and abroad was boosted by the relative strength of the won and the low interest rate policy the government was pursuing together with the IMF. Since early May, the BOK cautiously lowered interest rates through open market operations. For its part, the FSC moved aggressively to rein in financial companies claiming high-yield investment products and put a stop to exaggerated advertisements aimed at luring new customers. It also took steps to keep banks and investment trust companies from outbidding each other on investment yields. On May 25, the government lifted the restrictions on short-term investment products so as to promote foreign portfolio investment and lower market interest rates.

During May and June, the credit crunch persisted, and companies continued to face funding difficulties. In May, the average amount of reserve money with the BOK came to about W 19 trillion, which left the central bank with room for an extra W 4.5 trillion before the amount reached the W 23.5 trillion that it had agreed to with the IMF at the end of June. Assuming a money multiplier of 11 at the time, the W 4.5 trillion could

Table 6.4 Trends in Market Interest Rates, March–June 1998
percent

Indicator	*March 31*	*April 30*	*May 9*	*May 20*	*May 31*	*June 10*	*June 20*	*June 30*
Call rate, 1 day	22.05	18.04	18.01	17.34	16.71	16.34	15.55	14.41
Yield on three-year corporate bonds	18.28	17.70	17.70	18.10	17.82	16.81	16.00	16.00

Source: Bank of Korea.

have been transformed into about W 50 trillion in credit that the banks could have provided to the market. However, the banks chose to put the surplus money into risk-free repurchase agreements or the monetary stabilization bonds issued by the central bank rather than boosting the credit available to companies (BOK 1998a). So, the reserve money the BOK was providing to the market was finding its way back to the central bank.

SMEs were hit especially hard by the freeze in the credit markets. Whereas top-tier lenders with comparatively high BIS capital ratios such as Kookmin Bank and Housing & Commercial Bank boosted their lending, troubled lenders such as Korea First Bank and Daedong Bank shunned giving out fresh credit. Government efforts to alleviate the debilitating credit crunch focused on helping out healthy SMEs. Facilitating trade credit and expanding the availability of credits for housing were other key priorities.

A range of measures were implemented in support of SMEs during May and June. First, extensions of maturity were granted for existing loans. Beginning in May, the BOK stepped up the supply of credit to commercial banks and enabled commercial banks to provide one-year extensions of maturity on US$7 billion in loans denominated in foreign currencies. On May 15, the minister of finance and economy and the heads of financial companies held a meeting at which they agreed to give a six-month extension of maturity on W 22.3 trillion in SME loans.

Second, state-owned banks and commercial banks with comparatively high BIS capital ratios agreed to boost SME lending. Following the May 15 meeting, the banks announced the voluntary SME credit support measures described in table 6.5.

Third, the government changed the method of supplying SME credit support in mid-June so that the SME Foundation and Development Fund could make the loan decisions and let the individual lending banks oversee post-loan management. Up to that point, the SME fund selected the companies to be recommended for loans, and the banks extended the loans to the recommended borrowers after a credit review and then also assumed the risk. This was soon changed because the banks had to set aside additional capital for the risks assumed so as to comply with the BIS capital adequacy requirements. However, as the incidence of corporate bankruptcies rose, banks started to avoid even government policy funds to limit their exposure to borrower risks. The SME support fund was estimated to contain W 1.8 trillion in 1998.

Fourth, steps were taken to boost the pool of money available for debt guarantees. Since June 1998, the demand by SMEs for credit guarantees had risen steadily and was projected to reach approximately W 13 trillion at the end of the year. However, since the onset of the crisis near the end of 1997, the number of corporate bankruptcies had skyrocketed, and the payments by subrogation had already reached W 1.1 trillion by the end of May 1998. Because the payments by subrogation were going to continue

Table 6.5 Announcements of SME Credit Support by Banks
won, billions

Bank	*Announced support*	*Actual support, May 28*	*Remarks*
Kookmin	1,000	22	Deliberating connected support with credit guarantee agency for partial guarantee
Hana	300	n.a.	Support since June 1
Korea Long-Term Credit	200	140.5	n.a.
Shinhan	500 (US$100 million)	38.5 (US$67 million)	Scheduled for active support through an increase in the ceiling decided by branches since June 1
KorAm	300	7	Support since May 28
Industrial Bank of Korea	2,000	n.a.	Support since June 1
Chohung	200	13	Expected support since June 1
Commercial Bank of Korea	200	48	Expected support since June 1
Korea First	660	380	n.a.
Hanil	2,000	460	n.a.
Seoul	300	12	Expected support since June 1
Korea Exchange	1,000	270	n.a.
Dongwha	200	17	Expected support since June 1
Boram	300	n.a.	Support since June 1

Source: MOFE 1998g.
Note: n.a. = not applicable.

to rise, the pool for debt guarantees at the end of the year was estimated at about W 8.7 trillion, which was not sufficient to cover the W 13 trillion that would be needed for SMEs. Guarantees on secured debt were therefore to be limited to new SME loans beginning on June 1. Furthermore, the credit guarantee institutions were to raise W 4 trillion in additional funds through the more active collection of payments by subrogation and other efforts. Extra funds were also to be raised by securing public financial support. It was decided that regional cooperative financial bodies should be established jointly by credit guarantee institutions and creditor banks with the goal of providing coordinated support to SMEs. A partial guarantee scheme was to be set up in phases so as to facilitate loss-sharing between lenders and the credit guarantee institutions.

Fifth, a new incentive was to be instituted whereby banks with better performance in SME lending were to be given priority in deposits of temporary government budget surpluses and receive favorable rationing by the BOK in the aggregate credit ceiling. Despite these and other efforts by the government, funding difficulties persisted among SMEs.

The government and the IMF agreed to allocate US$2 billion in excess of the target in foreign exchange reserves to support imports of raw materials. Since May 1998, the support for import-export financing had grown to US$5.3 billion. This consisted of US$3 billion in support by commercial banks to finance imports of raw materials (US$1billion from the World Bank loan and US$2 billion from foreign exchange reserves), US$2 billion in support by the Export-Import Bank of Korea for short-term import-export financing (US$1 billion from the loan of the Export-Import Bank of Japan and US$1 billion raised independently by the Export-Import Bank of Korea), and US$300 million in commercial bank discounts on SME export bills of exchange (from foreign exchange reserves). The government set its sights on raising import-export financing for up to 80 percent of total imports and exports, but fell short of the goal in May. For the first four months of 1998, export and import financing covered 63.3 percent of total exports and 57.4 percent of total imports; in May, the respective ratios reached 61.6 and 63.2 percent. Import-export financing for bills at sight was an active area because of the advantages of short-term duration (7 to 15 days), low credit risk, and freedom from long-term commitments. Meanwhile, import-export financing for usance and documents against acceptance bills was sluggish because of the long-term duration (90 to 180 days) and the need for collateral or letters of guarantee. Beginning on June 1, to remedy the situation, the Export-Import Bank of Korea decided to make US$2 billion raised through its own efforts available to large companies short on trade credit. In addition, the number of companies eligible for export insurance was expanded, and the credit guarantees of the credit guarantee institutions were to be given priority in trade financing so as to shore up the ability of SMEs to put up collateral for credit.

Since the onset of the crisis, housing prices had plummeted, and the number of unsold housing units had climbed. In response, the government decided, in 1998, to focus on alleviating the problem of unsold housing units. In May, tax incentives were provided such as an exemption on capital gains and a reduction in registration and acquisition taxes. On May 20, the Housing & Commercial Bank started a special W 900 billion lending program for home builders struggling because of the significant stock of unsold housing units.

Financial market developments. During May and June, with the exception of trade bill discounting, bank lending fell, including lending through discounts on commercial bills, overdrafts, and general loans. One obvious reason for the drop was the declining demand for credit within the contracting economy. But the primary reason was that commercial banks had curtailed the credit going to companies in light of the heightened credit risk prevailing in the corporate sector. Banks also sharply cut back on overdrafts to companies as the banks struggled to meet target BIS capital ratios by the end of June. Lending trends among the major banks indicated that credit was being cut more sharply for SMEs than for large companies.

Overall, bank lending fell during the second quarter of 1998. However, direct financing—that is, companies raising capital directly by issuing debt and equity to investors—actually showed a modest upward trend during the same period. The monthly average in debt issues during the second quarter came to W 1.6 trillion, down from the more than W 3 trillion monthly average in the previous quarter. The top five chaebol companies accounted for 61.1 percent of the issue amount, whereas the SMEs made up only 1 percent. Equity issues during the second quarter jumped noticeably from the first quarter, but this was mostly caused by capital increases through equity issues by banks and the top five chaebol companies. Discounts on CP by merchant banks plummeted because many of the merchant banks had closed, but the discount by securities companies climbed. The top five chaebols also accounted for most of the CP issued.

In line with the fund flows in the financial sector during the second quarter, discrepancies between the leading monetary aggregates deepened. During April, the growth of M2 (monetary aggregate for broad money—see endnote 8 in chapter 5) slowed to a low of 13.1 percent. The pace then picked up, and the growth reached 18.1 percent in June as some of the money held in bank money-in-trust accounts flowed into bank savings deposit accounts. However, the banks, rather than directing the increased deposits to corporate borrowers, put the deposits in monetary stabilization bonds and other risk-free investments. Despite a sharp increase in fund flows into securities companies and investment trust companies, M3 (monetary aggregate for liquidity—see endnote 8 in chapter 5) showed a 14.2 percent increase in June, a relatively stable level. Securities companies mostly put the increased funds into discounts on the CP issued by large companies.

Stock indexes nosedived during May and June, reflecting imbalances in the supply and demand conditions in the stock markets as more companies issued equity to raise capital. The stock markets also came under pressure from deteriorating external conditions such as the weakening yen and the violent labor unrest. Table 6.6 shows key financial market indicators during the second quarter of 1998.

Table 6.6 Key Financial Market Indicators, Second Quarter, 1998
won, billions

Indicator	*April*	*May*	*June*
Total bank loans, month-on-month[a]	610.1	-1,757.2	-6,488.4
Issuance of corporate bonds	1,630.5	1,446.7	1,987.5
Issuance of stocks (initial public offering and new shares)	632.9	1,295.5	1,696.2
Discounted CP, month-on-month	536.2	4,844.2	2,093.1
M2, year-on-year, %	13.1	14.8	18.1
M3, year-on-year, %	14.2	14.1	14.2
Korea composite stock price index, monthly average	444.2	356.3	313.3
Foreign investment in stocks	128.5	-74.0	-333.2

Sources: Bank of Korea and Ministry of Finance and Energy.

Note: M2 = monetary aggregate for broad money. M3 = monetary aggregate for liquidity.

a. Including trust accounts, except discounted CP and adjusted decreases in loans because of the disposal of bad loans, and excluding loans by the domestic branches of foreign banks, Chughyup Bank, Nonghyup Bank, and Suhyup Bank.

The Contracting Real Economy and Deepening Labor Unrest

Falling Industrial Production and the Stabilization in Inflation

Domestic demand continued to fall during the second quarter of 1998. Construction orders for housing and office buildings in the private sector were on a downward spiral. The case was the same in public sector demand. Similarly, orders for domestically produced and imported machinery were shrinking. In wholesale and retail sales, orders for durable goods such as automobiles and refrigerators were drying up. Worse still, in May, as domestic demand continued to slide, exports started to weaken.

Sluggish domestic demand and the slump in exports led to falling industrial production in automobiles, machine equipment, metals, timber, wood products, bags and shoes, and clothing. Producer shipments continued to drop amid declining demand at home and abroad. Because of the drop-off in industrial production, producer inventories also dwindled despite the reduced shipments. The manufacturing operations ratio was stuck at low levels, and most industries, with the major exception of semiconductors, shipbuilding, office equipment, and petrochemicals, were operating at well below capacity.

Inflationary pressures began to show signs of stabilizing in the second quarter of 1998. Consumer prices continued to drop in May over the previous month, and the trend persisted as consumer real income stagnated. Table 6.7 shows trends in key indicators in the real economy during the second quarter of 1998.

Rising Corporate Bankruptcies and Unemployment amid Growing Labor Unrest

The number of corporate bankruptcies remained high during the second quarter of 1998 (table 6.8). The ratio of newly established companies to bankrupt companies in the seven largest cities persisted at extremely low levels and darkened the prospects for employment. During the period, unemployment surged, rising to 6.7 percent in April, when the number of the unemployed was 1.43 million. The figures reached 6.9 percent, with 1.49 million unemployed, in May and 7 percent, with 1.53 million unemployed, in June.

The surge in unemployment stemmed from widespread contraction across industries throughout the economy, from manufacturing and construction to the service sectors. The ratio of jobs offered to jobs sought remained at 0.2 to 0.3, indicating a brewing unemployment crisis.

As corporate bankruptcies multiplied and the number of the unemployed grew by between 40,000 and 50,000 a month, labor unrest began

Table 6.7 Economic Trends, Second Quarter, 1998, Year-on-Year
percent

Indicator	*April*	*May*	*June*
Industrial production	–11.4	–11.1	–14.0
Domestic construction orders	–58.6	–61.6	–45.6
Orders for domestically produced machines	–46.7	–40.6	–43.6
Wholesale and retail sales	–15.5	–16.5	–15.3
Average manufacturing operation ratio	67.5	67.3	66.3
Consumer prices, month-on month	0.4	–0.5	–0.4
Housing purchase prices, month-on-month	–2.8	–2.4	–1.5

Source: Ministry of Finance and Economy.

Table 6.8 Trends in Bankruptcies, Second Quarter, 1998

Indicator	*April*	*May*	*June*
Ratio of dishonored bills, %[a]	0.42	0.45	0.42
Bankrupt firms, number			
Monthly	2,462	2,070	1,825
Daily average	95	86	73
Ratio of newly established firms to bankrupt firms, seven largest cities[b]	2.3	2.1	2.5

Sources: MOFE 1998i, 1998j, 1998k; BOK 1998b.
a. Value basis after adjustment for electronic settlement.
b. Seoul, Busan, Daegu, Gwangju, Incheon, Daejeon, and Suwon.

Table 6.9 Trends in Labor Disputes, 1997 and First Half of 1998
number of cases

		1998					
Indicator	*1997*	*Jan.*	*Feb.*	*Mar.*	*Apr.*	*May*	*June*
Labor strikes	78	1	6	10	31	34	42
Labor disputes	612	18	21	83	176	323	392
Agreed wage growth, %	4.2	-0.1	-0.2	-0.7	-1.5	-2.9	-2.9

Sources: MOFE 1998i, 1998j, 1998l, 1998m.

to intensify. This coincided with the accelerating restructuring in the corporate and financial sectors. Following the strike by the labor union at Kia Motors in April, the KCTU joined hands with university students to stage violent street protests on May 1. The KCTU also announced plans for large multiple street protests in the seven largest cities on May 16 demanding government actions on unemployment, but failed to carry out the plans.

On May 27, union members at Hyundai Motor Company went on strike, and several umbrella unions under the KCTU, the public industries union, and the metal industries union also staged strikes at their worksites until the next day. The scale of the strikes was smaller than feared, but the strikes nonetheless dealt a major shock to markets at home and abroad because they coincided with the sharply depreciating Japanese yen and the plunging stock markets. The strikes were also particularly troublesome because they were perceived as a prelude—a warning shot—of more to come, irrespective of the scale of the protests.[9] Labor disputes, which had appeared to be at a lull, surged noticeably beginning in the second quarter of 1998 (table 6.9).

In response, the government expanded the Employment Insurance Fund by W 557.0 billion. Thus, the cost of unemployment measures increased from W 7.9 trillion to W 8.5 trillion in early June. In addition, as projections of the number of the unemployed reached 1.5 million, the government began, once again, to incorporate new unemployment measures in the supplemental budget.

Notes

1. Press release by the FSC chairman on the corporate viability review, June 17, 1998.

2. The seven approved banks were Chohung, Chungbuk, Commercial Bank of Korea, Hanil, Kangwon, Korea Exchange, and Peace. The five rejected banks were Chungchong, Daedong, Donghwa, Dongnam, and Kyeonggi.

3. Chungchong was merged into Hana, Daedong into Kookmin, Donghwa into Shinhan, Dongnam into Housing & Commercial, and Kyeonggi into KorAm.

4. The 18 insurance companies were BYC, Chosun, Daishin, Donga, Doowon, Handuk, Hanil, Hankook, Hansung, Kookmin, Korea, Kukje, Kumho, Pacific, Shinhan, SK, Taeyang, and Tong Yang; the four non–life insurance companies were Dongbu, Haedong, Hankuk Fidelity & Surety, and Korea Guarantee.

5. The four other companies were Korea General Chemical Corporation, Korea Heavy Industries & Construction Company, Korea Technology Banking Corporation, and State-Compiled Textbook Company.

6. In addition to Korea Gas Corporation and KT&G, the four other companies were Daehan Oil Pipeline Corporation, Korea District Heating Corporation, Korea Electric Power Corporation, and KT Corporation.

7. The name of the law was changed from the Foreign Exchange Management Act to the Foreign Exchange Transactions Act.

8. Bill Clinton, the president of the United States, expressed his respect for President Kim Dae-Jung as a global democratic leader, and an article in the *Washington Post* on President Kim's visit was titled "Welcome Hero!"

9. *Maeil Business Newspaper*, May 28, 1998.

7

Completion of First-Phase Restructuring and Policies Aimed at Boosting Potential Growth, July–September 1998

Economic Outlook and Policy Challenges, Second Half of 1998

The Gloomy Economic Outlook for the Second Half of 1998

In May 1998, the Bank of Korea (BOK), the central bank, projected that the provisional growth in the gross domestic product (GDP) of the Republic of Korea in the first quarter of the year would slow to negative 3.8 percent, the first negative growth since 1980. During the quarter, private consumption fell to negative 10.3 percent, while investment in plant and equipment fell to negative 40.7 percent. The worse-than-expected GDP growth in the first quarter prompted many to speculate that a prolonged recession was imminent in Korea. The argument was that the precipitous drop in investment in plant facilities and equipment did not bode well for Korea's long-term potential growth and that the restructuring of corporate and financial companies getting under way would aggravate the already debilitating credit crunch, making a painful recession all but inevitable.

A comparison of economic forecasts put out in June with earlier forecasts indicates that inflation and the balance in the current account had improved, but that the growth outlook was deteriorating (see table 7.1). The fact that the economic slump had persisted for more than two years and increasingly looked like a long-term trend made the large drop in growth appear even more threatening.

Table 7.1 Macroeconomic Forecasts by Domestic and Overseas Institutions, 1998
percent

Indicator	*MOFE*	*KDI*	*BOK*	*IMF*	*OECD*
Economic growth	–3.9	–4.4	–4.0	–5.0	–4.7
Private consumption	–11.1	–11.0	–12.3	–10.0	–11.0
Plant and equipment investment	–39.9	–43.1	–42.0	–42.1	–40.4[a]
Construction investment	–19.6	–21.1	–25.2	–21.0	—
Exports	16.7	16.2	16.8	12.7	20.0
Imports	–17.4	–17.1	–23.7	–19.3	–16.0
Consumer prices	8.7	7.7	8.7	Below 8	6.0[b]
Current account, US$, billions	32.6	36.3	33.0	34.9	11.4[c]

Sources: OECD 1998; MOFE 1998n.

Note: MOFE = Ministry of Finance and Economy. KDI = Korea Development Institute. IMF = International Monetary Fund. OECD = Organisation for Economic Co-operation and Development. — = not available.

a. Total fixed capital formation.

b. GDP deflator.

c. Ratio to GDP.

Indeed, the economy faced many downside risks in the second half of 1998. The most serious threat was the persistent credit crunch caused by the weakening financial intermediation system. As the risk of corporate bankruptcy spiraled upward and banks scrambled to meet the 8 percent minimum Bank for International Settlements (BIS) capital requirements, banks were refusing to direct their funds to corporate borrowers, but were, instead, putting their money back into the central bank.

Consumer spending was falling at a pace that was more rapid than the drop in disposable incomes, pushing down the propensity to consume and dampening domestic demand. The free-falling investment was more onerous because it could hurt the economy's growth potential. It was estimated that a 1 percent drop in investment would reduce the potential growth by 0.12 percent in the first year and by 0.25 percent in the second year. As exports slowed, imports also declined consistently, raising the prospect of sharply contracted international trade for years to come.

Because consumption, investment, and exports were tumbling simultaneously, the industrial base was quickly losing its vitality. Table 7.2 describes the slumping industrial landscape. Unemployment was poised for a sharp jump, and it was taking longer for laid-off workers to find new

Table 7.2 Signs of the Eroding Industrial Base, First Half of 1998

Industry	*Industry trend*	*Business trend*
Consumer electronics	• Decrease in the operation ratio because of sluggish domestic and export demand • A large number of bankrupt sales agents	• Sharp reduction in production lines • Manpower loss and rapid increase in the number of bankruptcies among small and medium consumer electronics firms
Electronic components	• Rapid fall in production because of sluggish domestic and export demand • Lower operation ratio relative to end product firms • Rapid decrease in investments in plant and equipment	• Serious slump among small and medium electronics components firms because of the rapid rise in the prices of imported raw materials • Disposal of the electronics components business by medium firms
Motor vehicles	• Decrease in the sales of all types of cars except compact cars • Fall in the operation ratio to around 40% • Likelihood of collapsing production networks because of bankrupt auto-parts makers	• Fall of credibility because of the delay in the disposal of bankrupt firms • Large loss because of labor disputes • Decrease in potential growth because of manpower losses
Machinery	• Slump because of the decrease in investments in plant and equipment in manufacturing • Contraction in exports because of sluggish Asian markets • Rapid fall in the operation ratio to around 60%	• Difficulty in exiting because of the adverse environment for asset sales • A large number of bankrupt machine tool companies

(continued next page)

Table 7.2 Signs of the Eroding Industrial Base, First Half of 1998 *(continued)*

Industry	*Industry trend*	*Business trend*
Steel	• Sluggish export demand and depressed domestic demand • Rapid fall in the operation ratio to about 60% • Increased financing difficulty and large increase in the number of companies operating at a net loss	• Increased market disorder because of delays in the disposal of bankrupt steel companies • Solving oversupply problems regarded as an industry hot issue
Plastic processing	• Depressed production because of sluggish domestic demand • Facility overcapacity because of the fall in the operating ratio • Financing difficulty because of the long bill settlement period	• Neutralization of the exchange depreciation effect because of the weakening leverage in negotiations on exports • The sale of idle facilities at a loss
Textiles	• Decrease in production because of sluggish sales • Overdiscounted sales for cash • Fall in the operation ratio to around 50%	• Problems in profitability because of low-price competition • Weakening among sound firms because of overcompetition and the survival of uncompetitive firms
Construction	• Recession because of the decrease in investment and demand • Reduction in public sector construction because of budget shortages	• Restructuring and mass layoffs • 30% of general construction companies are operating at a deficit

Source: Choi 1998.

jobs. The prospect of increasingly restless unemployed workers becoming involved in major social unrest could no longer be readily dismissed. It was estimated that, since the onset of the financial crisis, workers who had lost their jobs were remaining unemployed for five or six months. The employment outlook for the second half of 1998 was even more negative. Worse still was the fact that nearly three-quarters of all laid-off workers were receiving no unemployment benefits.

Korea also faced many downside risks in the external environment. In mid-June, the Japanese yen looked more settled than it had been before, but markets were rattled by the growing likelihood of a sovereign default in the Russian Federation, and financial markets in the emerging countries were reeling because of mounting volatility and uncertainty. In short, the external situation was not at all favorable for the success of efforts to induce an increase in the foreign capital Korea so desperately needed to revive the economy.

To be sure, there were some encouraging signs in the second half of 1998. One was the improved conditions for foreign currency liquidity despite the continued distress in global financial markets. This effectively removed any talk of a second financial crisis in Korea. Indeed, conditions had sufficiently improved so that the government could start taking aggressive steps to cut interest rates and address pressing domestic economic problems.

Unlike in the past, bold corporate and financial restructuring in May and June led to a significant, genuine clean-up of troubled assets and in other areas of distress, which helped to breathe new life into financial intermediation, alleviate the credit crunch, and reinvigorate businesses. The confidence of foreign investors in Korea and in the direction the country had taken in managing the economy was on the rebound; it was being recognized that Korea was pursuing a market-oriented economic system. Another positive factor was the summit diplomacy of President Kim Dae-Jung and the persistent engagement with reform and a wider market opening on the economic front, which solidified the foreign perception that Korea was undertaking serious efforts to put the economy back on track. The result was unequivocal expressions of support for Korea not only by the Asian Development Bank, the International Monetary Fund (IMF), the World Bank, and other major international institutions, but also by countries and regions as diverse as China, the European Union, Japan, and the United States.

The Need for Restructuring and Stimulative Economic Policies on Parallel Tracks

In May, the government put a priority on restructuring and started to close down nonviable corporate and financial companies (see chapter 6). Because of the gloomy economic outlook for the second half of 1998, a debate surfaced over whether restructuring should remain a priority or whether it should be undertaken in parallel with the implementation of an economic stimulus package.

There was no doubt that restructuring was absolutely crucial in addressing and correcting the structural weaknesses that had long eroded Korea's long-term economic competitiveness. But restructuring also took time. It was therefore being argued that the contraction in domestic demand, coupled with slowing exports, posed a serious threat to Korea's potential growth and made a robust economic rebound less likely. The proper course of action, the proponents of a pro-stimulus, pro-growth policy argued, was to carry out restructuring, while simultaneously adopting aggressive economic stimulus measures.

However, the case for an uninterrupted restructuring-first strategy was also compelling given the risk that prolonged, half-baked restructuring, combined with stimulus measures, would fail to revive the economy. According to this view, only swift and bold restructuring would effectively resolve the credit crunch, help raise the long-term competitiveness of domestic business firms and financial companies, and improve the economy's potential for growth going forward. Another argument in favor of the restructuring-first strategy was the difficulty of sustaining the momentum for restructuring in the face of a reinvigorated economy. The fear was that the pressure for change would dissipate, along with the momentum for restructuring, if restructuring was put on a back burner.

Indeed, it was probable that the urgency of restructuring would diminish if the economy recovered vigorously, business sales jumped sharply, and the credit situation improved. Given the likelihood that a severe economic contraction would result from the massive restructuring the government envisioned and that a protracted recession would lead to additional stress, there was significant potential for a general backlash against restructuring, which would make it difficult for the government to forge ahead with its plans. The issue of whether restructuring and economic stimulus measures should be pursued simultaneously was not merely an academic one.

As a first step toward overcoming the financial crisis, the government took swift and forceful action to close down nonviable and failing companies and embraced a high interest rate policy as a key part of its economy-wide restructuring effort. The intent was to send an unequivocal signal to the market, in particular to foreign investors, that Korea was serious about reform and restructuring. The result was a return to a more stable exchange rate between the Korean won and the U.S. dollar and growing confidence in Korea among foreign investors. However, this came at the cost of a crushing credit crunch and unprecedented corporate failures that put heavy strains on the economy. The massive layoffs that took place in the course of restructuring provoked angry protests by labor unions and, at times, seriously tested the willingness of the people to support the painful changes the government sought. In the end, what was needed was not a debate about prioritizing restructuring or a stimulus, but striking an appropriate balance and understanding the mutually reinforcing relationship between restructuring and stimulus. This was, in fact, the path the government chose in the second half of 1998 to revive the economy.

Policy Challenges: Completing the First Phase of Restructuring and the Push toward Economic Stimulus

At their seventh program review and policy consultation meeting, on July 24, the government and the IMF came to the understanding that the government would have to take the following steps: (1) build on the success and achievements to date and continue to boost the confidence of foreign investors in the health of the Korean economy, (2) expand the social safety net to alleviate the economic hardships associated with unemployment and provide support to stimulate domestic demand, and (3) step up corporate and financial restructuring to pave the way for stable future growth.

Although external conditions improved somewhat, the reality was that Korea still faced an adverse situation in financial markets abroad, as amply demonstrated by the financial crisis unfolding in Russia. In particular, exports and imports continued to shrink, and steps had to be taken to bolster Korea's import-export position and maintain a favorable current account balance. Bringing in more foreign investors and more capital was paramount given the contribution these would make to the stability of the won and the overall economy.

The tight fiscal and monetary policies had to be eased to shore up the economy and foster the potential for growth. Among fiscal policy measures, state-supported credit guarantee institutions and government-owned banks had to be bolstered through additional capital injections to enable them to expand the pool of credit available to companies and help reduce the credit crunch. More aggressive social overhead capital spending, temporary tax credits for investment, and lower special consumption taxes on durable goods were also called for to encourage more robust consumer spending and business investment. In monetary policy, it was thought that an expansion of the money supply, a lowering of interest rates, and the provision of targeted credit support for exporters and small and medium enterprises (SMEs) were needed.

The government had to beef up its efforts to address unemployment so as to maintain social cohesion and the public's tolerance for the pain inflicted by restructuring. A key part of the challenge was expanding the social safety net through additional fiscal expenditures and enhancing the effectiveness of existing unemployment programs. The government felt compelled to wrap up the first round of corporate and financial restructuring by September 1998 because this was the pledge it had made to the public. Because the deepening credit crunch was taking a heavy toll on businesses and fueling unemployment, the next three to four months were considered critical for the economic recovery the government envisioned. The optimistic forecast was that economic growth would turn positive in 1999 and reach a level close to potential by 2000 if the government could manage to deal successfully with these and other tasks that lay ahead in the near term.

The Completion of the First Round of Restructuring

When Russia declared a moratorium in August 1998 and jolted international financial markets, it became more urgent than ever for Korea to differentiate itself from other troubled economies and buttress the confidence of overseas investors. At home, the top priority for the government was to ameliorate the stifling credit conditions facing companies. To achieve this, ending the vicious cycle of mutually reinforcing stresses in the corporate and financial sectors was a must. So, the government resolved to finish the first round of corporate and financial restructuring by the end of September 1998.

Wrapping Up the First Round of Financial Restructuring

By July, the government had set about accomplishing the following: (1) completing the resolution of the five failing banks that were to be closed and implementing business turnaround plans for the seven banks that had received conditional approval for restructuring, (2) examining the business soundness of banks with capital ratios above the 8 percent minimum BIS capital requirement and pushing business improvement initiatives, and (3) coming up with a blueprint for the restructuring of nonbank financial companies, including merchant banks, securities companies, investment trust companies, and insurance companies.

Support measures for financial restructuring. At the 10th meeting of the Economic Policy Coordination Committee (EPCC), on September 2, 1998, policy makers laid out several principles for government support and relief in financial restructuring. First, government financial support must be matched by self-help efforts such as the downsizing of the workforce and of branch operations to boost productivity and profitability, the selling off of assets, and the bringing in of foreign investors and shareholders.

Second, stakeholders must equitably bear the burden of the losses and the pain of restructuring, including capital write-downs, the loss of equity, and the replacement of the top managers who had been responsible for business failures.

Third, cleaning up the balance sheets of financial companies would proceed through several steps: (1) Comprehensive plans for reducing nonperforming loans and preventing new bad loans would be mandatory. (2) Loans classified as substandard or worse were to be sold off to the Korea Asset Management Corporation (KAMCO) for full resolution. (3) Loans classified as precautionary were to be turned around through workouts among the debtor companies. (4) Other loans to highly leveraged companies were to be cleaned up through debt-equity swaps and mutual fund support.

Fourth, financial support would be provided in a quick and adequate manner so as to facilitate effective turnarounds among financial companies. The government directed banks that fell short of the 8 percent minimum BIS capital requirement to raise the capital ratio to 10 percent within two years (see chapter 6). However, the two-year target had the effect of encouraging banks to curtail new lending sharply in an effort to boost their capital ratios, thereby aggravating an already stifling credit crunch and threatening to prolong it (table 7.3). To ease the credit crunch, sufficient financial support by the government was needed to enable banks to meet the 10 percent capital requirement immediately, not within two years. A swift injection of sufficient public funds into the banks was also considered necessary to turn the banks around so that the funds could be recovered as soon as possible.

Fifth, expanded bank lending to companies was to be established as a precondition for government financial support so as to ensure an adequate supply of credit for SMEs in the course of restructuring.

The closure of five failing banks. When the announcement of the closure of five failing banks was made on June 29, the business operations of the banks went into complete paralysis. Led by the unions, the bank employees vehemently resisted the closures and refused to show up for work. Worse still, they sabotaged the computer systems of the banks. The government urged them to return to their posts, but to no avail, and the paralysis continued for nearly two weeks. Predictably, these actions triggered much anguish among bank customers and heightened the risk that

Table 7.3 Comparison between the BIS Ratio and the Growth in Banking Account Loans, Year-on-Year
percent

Indicator	*1996*	*1997*	*January–June 1998*
12 banks with BIS ratios of 8% or more	18.0	17.6	11.7
14 banks with BIS ratios of less than 8%	15.9	7.5	4.0

Source: MOFE 1998o.
Note: Numbers are rounded to the nearest 10th.

corporate customers would not be able to execute payment settlements and, as a result, default on their debt obligations.

In response, the government ordered full cash payments for checks issued by the failing banks and the exemption of the bills and debt instruments of the customers of the banks from delinquency. In addition, the penalties normally levied for delays in money transfers for tax, utility, and other routine automatic payments were suspended at the failing banks until the end of July. Special services for corporate customers were to be set up at the banks to deal with the bottleneck caused by the failures.

The government encouraged the acquiring banks to retain as many of the employees of the failed banks as possible, especially the lower-level workers. However, in the end, only about 2,800—32 percent—of the 8,950 employees of the five failing banks were retained and reemployed. (The total was 10,000 if temporary staff are included.)

To minimize the risk that the acquiring banks would become overwhelmed because of the additional burden of distressed assets, the Korea Deposit Insurance Corporation (KDIC) stepped in to make up the W 5.8 trillion difference between the liabilities and high-quality assets of the acquiring banks and provided the acquiring banks with a six-month put-back option for any troubled assets that might sour after the takeovers. Capital of W 1.3 trillion was injected into the acquiring banks on the basis of August 31 bank business evaluations to keep the BIS capital ratio of the acquiring banks from falling after the takeovers. In addition, KAMCO injected W 1 trillion for a 100 percent purchase of the nonperforming assets of the failed banks and another W 1.2 trillion for a 50 percent purchase of the nonperforming assets of the acquiring banks. As a result of these actions, the takeovers of the failed banks were more or less completed by the end of September.

Mergers and capital increases at the seven banks that had conditional approval. The Financial Supervisory Commission (FSC) ordered Chohung Bank and the six other banks that had received conditional approval for turnarounds to submit turnaround implementation plans by the end of July. The FSC proposed to examine the feasibility of the implementation plans by August and then conduct quarterly reviews of progress on the turnaround implementation plans. Banks that failed to comply with the turnaround plans were to be ordered to take action. Tough turnaround actions were to be ordered of banks demonstrating unsatisfactory progress, and these banks were to be induced for possible merger.

Large-scale banks were considered crucial if Korean banks were to compete effectively with large internationally active banks, support vigorous corporate business and investment at home, and make investments in advanced information technologies for the banking business. The government therefore believed it was necessary to encourage consolidation and enlargement in the banking sector.

For the seven banks that had received conditional approval for turnaround, restructuring proceeded as follows. The Commercial Bank of Korea and Hanil Bank agreed to merge and submitted regulatory filings to the FSC on August 25. The government injected W 3.3 trillion in public funds into these banks for recapitalization and used an additional W 2 trillion for the purchase of nonperforming assets. The rationale was that these steps would prevent more distress in these two banks and help them achieve synergy through the merger. As a way to ensure the participation of the shareholders of the banks in the equitable distribution of the associated losses, the FSC ordered, on September 14, capital write-downs from W 1 trillion to W 100.2 billion at the Commercial Bank of Korea and from W 830 billion to W 80.6 billion at Hanil Bank.

Chohung Bank and Korea Exchange Bank each submitted plans for turnaround involving capital provided by foreign investors. In response, the FSC ordered the two banks to come up with more specific and realistic turnaround plans incorporating precise analyses of the likelihood of finding foreign investors and the possibility of mergers. It set a deadline of August 31, 1998. The FSC also demanded that there be measurable progress under the revised turnaround plans and that a written pledge be given by the banks that all senior managers would resign if they failed to secure foreign investors or find merger partners by October.

For banks that sought turnarounds involving capital provided by foreigners, public funds were to be supplied through the purchase of subordinated bonds from these banks for the purpose of recapitalization. For the purchase of nonperforming assets, KAMCO injected W 1.2 trillion into Chohung Bank and W 900 billion into Korea Exchange Bank at the end of September. Commerzbank had executed its investment in Korea Exchange Bank in July.

Chungbuk Bank, Kangwon Bank, and Peace Bank drafted turnaround plans based on capital increases. In August, the capital of these three banks was reduced to the minimum required under the Banking Act. Under the plans submitted, Chungbuk Bank and Peace Bank were each to boost their capital by W 120 billion by the end of October, while Kangwon Bank was to boost its capital by W 100 billion. The turnaround plan of Peace Bank was received with the understanding that it would no longer engage in international banking or give out loans greater than W 5 billion. With Kangwon Bank, the understanding was that it would seek a merger with Hyundai Merchant Bank after a capital increase had been completed. KAMCO spent W 300 billion at the end of September 1998 to purchase the nonperforming assets of these three banks.

Mergers and capital increases among banks with BIS capital ratios higher than 8 percent. The 12 banks with BIS capital ratios exceeding 8 percent at the end of 1997 were to receive prompt corrective action following capital reexaminations during the first half of 1998 if the capital ratios had fallen below the 8 percent threshold.[1] However, all had capital ratios in excess of the minimum 8 percent. A follow-up examination was set for September to determine if any further actions, including prompt corrective action, were needed. The FSC ordered Jeju Bank, which had already shown signs of distress, to write down its capital and then to recapitalize subsequent to an examination. Boram Bank and Hana Bank announced a merger on September 8. This was followed by a merger announcement between Kookmin Bank and Korea Long-Term Credit Bank, on September 11. These mergers were aided through government financial support for recapitalization and the purchase of bad assets. Shinhan Bank decided to boost its capital by W 150 billion on September 17, 1998. Korea First Bank and Seoul Bank were both pursuing foreign buyers. For the disposition of nonperforming assets, KAMCO injected public funds totaling W 498.9 billion into Seoul Bank on July 23 and W 606.6 billion into Korea First Bank on July 31.

Restructuring nonbank financial companies. The restructuring of merchant banks, insurance companies, and other nonbank financial companies was to be led primarily by the respective controlling shareholders. However, the government resolved to deal swiftly with these companies and close them if they were found to be nonviable or faced insolvency. The business licenses of a total of 14 merchant banks were revoked between the onset of the financial crisis and the end of June 1998. The assets and liabilities of these banks were transferred to Hanareum Merchant Bank, the bridge merchant bank the government had set up to resolve the troubled merchant banks. Business at two other merchant banks was also suspended thereafter. The FSC ordered the suspended merchant banks Hangil and Saehan to transfer their assets and liabilities to Hanareum Merchant Bank on July 24. On August 12, the Ministry of Finance and Economy (MOFE) revoked the business licenses of these banks. On July 30, the KDIC injected W 827.2 billion in Hanareum Merchant Bank for the substitute payment of deposits.

Among securities companies, either the net operating capital ratios or the asset-liability ratios of Dongbang-Peregreen Securities, KLB, Korea Development Bank (KDB), SK, and Ssangyong were below 100 percent as of the end of June 1998. When KLB Securities laid off all its employees with severance packages on July 3, the FSC determined that the company could no longer carry on its business and ordered it to suspend operations on July 6. On July 25, the FSC ordered the suspension of the business of KDB Securities, which had decided voluntarily to seek liquidation. On August 21, the FSC ordered four other securities companies to submit turnaround plans. After an internal review of the turnaround plans of the four companies, the FSC suspended business at Dongbang-Peregreen and, on September 25, gave conditional approval to SK and Ssangyong for turnarounds.

On August 14, the FSC ordered Hannam Investment Securities and Hannam Investment Trust Management to suspend business in the wake of severe liquidity difficulties resulting from massive customer fund withdrawals. Then, on August 26, the FSC ordered Hannam Investment Trust Management to transfer its customer trust assets to Kookmin Investment Trust. By the end of September, Dongbang-Peregreen Investment Trust had voluntarily liquidated, and three other investment trusts—Boram, Eutteum, and Coryo Investment—were in the process of voluntary business liquidation.

The restructuring of insurance companies was also under way. The FSC reviewed the turnaround plans of the 18 life insurance companies and four non–life insurance companies that were found to have fallen short of the required solvency margin requirements as of the end of March 1998. After taking into account the relatively strong solvency margins and the high likelihood of rehabilitation, the FSC ordered seven life insurance companies and two non–life insurance companies to submit turnaround implementation plans, including quarter-by-quarter execution measures, within one month.[2] The FSC noted that seven other life insurance companies had drafted turnaround plans that were likely to be implemented successfully, but that the solvency margins were somewhat low, and this could adversely affect the turnaround plans. So, the FSC opted to order these companies to provide supplemental and more specific measures in the turnaround plans within one month.[3]

Effective August 11, the FSC suspended the business of four life insurance companies that faced difficult turnarounds given their effectively insolvent financial positions and that had drafted turnaround plans that were not likely to succeed.[4] It sought to earn time to resolve all the outstanding matters such as the protection of policyholders and to take the steps needed to minimize additional financial losses. Then, on August 21, the FSC ordered the purchase of assets and assumption of liabilities (P&A) of Kukje by Samsung, BYC by Kyobo, Taeyang by Hungkuk, and Coryo by Korea First.

It was determined that Hankuk Fidelity & Surety and Korea Guarantee Insurance, two non–life insurance companies, would face difficulties in achieving successful turnarounds, but a sudden demise of the two companies was likely to cause major disruption in markets. So, the decision was made to push for business normalization with the goal of a merger of the two companies by the end of November. In September, it was decided to provide financial support for the redemption of the outstanding claims on the companies.

The government established Korea Non-Bank Lease Financing Company in July 1998 as a bridge leasing company to resolve failing leasing companies that could not continue in business. The parent companies of five leasing companies experiencing large losses came up with ₩ 20 billion in legal capital.[5] A bridge savings and finance company was set up on September 16 to clean up distressed and nonviable savings and finance companies. The normalization of failed credit unions through self-turnaround or mergers was to be encouraged, but liquidation was also set in motion if a turnaround was not likely.

The institutionalization of prompt corrective action. Prompt corrective action took effect on September 14, 1998, for the first time following the legislative amendment of the Act on the Structural Improvement of the Financial Industry. Prompt corrective action is a prudential tool that grants regulators the authority to step into troubled financial institutions—for example, institutions failing to maintain a certain level of capital as provided under the law—and order corrective measures to restore financial soundness. It was first used in Denmark in the 1970s and has since become widely accepted as a legitimate prudential tool for regulators. It was also adopted in the United States through the passage of the Federal Deposit Insurance Corporation Improvement Act of 1991.

Under prompt corrective action, the FSC can issue (1) management improvement orders to banks and merchant banks with BIS capital ratios falling below 2 percent, (2) management improvement requests if the ratios fall between 2 and 6 percent, and (3) management improvement recommendations if the ratios are between 6 and 8 percent. The steps the FSC may take or demand under prompt corrective action include admonitions and warnings to senior managers and employees, recapitalization, asset disposition, stock write-offs, the suspension of senior managers, the transfer of businesses, and mergers and acquisitions (M&A). If a financial company receives a prompt corrective action from the FSC, it must inform the FSC how it intends to address the matter, seek FSC approval of a management improvement plan, and implement the plan under FSC supervision.

The outcome of the initial round of financial restructuring and future tasks. A first benefit of the initial round of restructuring in the financial sector was the positive effect on the turnaround efforts of financial companies. Many banks, in particular, managed to dispose of bad assets on a large scale and significantly clean up and strengthen balance sheets. As a result of substantial recapitalization efforts, they also raised their BIS capital ratios above 10 percent. More important, by boldly closing down nonviable financial companies, the government sent a strong signal to the market that financial companies could fail and be forced to close. It thereby dealt a blow against the moral hazard associated with the idea that the government would not allow financial companies to fail.

Second, as the soundness of the banking sector improved, the financial sector found some breathing room from the stifling credit crunch and was able to pave the way for economic revival. As creditor banks resumed more normal balance sheet positions, they were able to act more forcefully and more swiftly in restructuring distressed debtor companies.

Third, the initial round of restructuring succeeded in sending a powerful message to foreign investors and analysts who had been skeptical of Korea's true intentions and the level of commitment to restructuring. The upbeat assessments and the praise offered by foreign investors and market watchers in regard to Korea's success in reform and restructuring emerged during a series of Korea Forums, the investor relations meetings the government held in 17 major cities in seven countries from late September to early October 1998.

Despite the early success, policy makers were keenly aware of the need to press on with the reform and restructuring in the financial sector. There were still many daunting challenges. First, if closing down failing financial companies and cleaning up the balance sheets of distressed financial companies represented hard reform and restructuring, then, henceforth, soft reform was needed through the establishment of a new financial management system not only by building better financial skills and techniques, but also by constructing financial infrastructure in governance, accounting rules, and supervision that was in line with global best practices and standards.

Second, as odd as it sounded, Korea's financial companies had to be reborn and reengineered as strictly commercial, for-profit business enterprises. There had to be a shift in focus to productivity and profitability rather than the size of the customer deposits or the assets under management and the number of branches. Reducing the entry barriers in the financial service industry, promoting M&A (especially by foreign investors), and letting financial companies fail were all considered crucial. The Banking Act had to be amended to improve bank ownership and management structures fundamentally and hold managers accountable for business decisions. Preventing *chaebols*—the large family-controlled and family-run groups that dominate business in Korea—from turning financial institutions into their private piggy banks was important, but equally important was the need to establish ownership structures that encouraged management accountability and business efficiency.

Third, deepening the pool of highly skilled finance professionals and transforming the financial industry into an internationally competitive engine for the growth of Korea were paramount.

Corporate Restructuring Centered on Business Turnarounds

The closure of 55 nonviable companies was completed in June, and the government now shifted the focus of restructuring to helping companies turn around their businesses. The method of support to be extended by the government varied depending on the size of the companies selected for restructuring. For example, the top five chaebols agreed with their main creditor banks to embark on voluntary business restructuring soon after the financial crisis erupted. However, no real outcome or progress resulted from this voluntary pledge. So, the tasks before policy makers in the restructuring of the top five chaebols were (1) to review agreements on improvements in financial soundness and ensure that the companies stay on track with their promises and pledges, (2) to beef up the Fair Trade Commission to ensure that no illegal intragroup business support took place and to encourage business reorganization based on core business competence, and (3) to ensure the swift implementation of the Big Deal, which involved swaps of business units among the top chaebol companies.

For other chaebols (from the 6th to the 64th largest chaebols) and large independent (non-chaebol) companies, the plan was to initiate, along with creditor banks, workouts aimed at turnarounds. The SMEs were divided into three groups: a priority support group, a conditional support group, and an other group. Whereas the priority support group was to receive stepped-up financial assistance, the conditional support group was to receive assistance through the workouts with creditor banks.

The blueprint and timetable for corporate restructuring were set as follows. For the top five chaebols, each of the main creditor banks established its own loan monitoring team on July 2, 1998. The creditor banks also set up a council of creditor banks to coordinate and facilitate the restructuring of the chaebols under their watch. It was envisioned by the government that a basic framework for the corporate restructuring of these chaebols would be ready by the end of September. It was decided that (1) due diligence on the assets and liabilities of the targeted companies should be conducted in October and November, (2) the parties involved should iron out any differences and set up the basic restructuring framework, and (3) the financial soundness improvement agreements, including the much publicized Big Deal, should be drawn up by the end of December.

For the 6th to the 64th largest chaebols and large independent (non-chaebol) companies, the workout team that the creditor banks had created in June was to take the lead in drafting the outline for business turnaround plans by the end of September. The council of creditor banks was to coordinate the actions of creditor banks. Due diligence on the assets and liabilities of the targeted companies, as well as other concrete steps, was to be conducted and completed in October and November so that specific turnaround measures could be undertaken in December. The implementation of turnaround plans for SMEs was to be led by the special SME task force team of the creditor banks that had been set up in May. Because the number of creditor banks involved with SMEs was fairly small and easily manageable, it was decided that the principal creditor bank should coordinate the restructuring actions among all the banks in each case.

Restructuring the Top Five Chaebols

Poor progress in voluntary restructuring. In April 1998, the 64 largest business groups, including the top five chaebols, reached an agreement on financial soundness improvement with creditor banks. But little progress was made because the agreement lacked specific benchmarks that could be used to measure the progress in implementation. There was virtually no expectation that the financial soundness improvement plan would actually lead to movement forward. For example, the top five chaebols made the pledge in May that they would cut their debt-equity ratios below 200 percent by the end of 1999. Unfortunately, no change in the debt levels occurred. The promise was not kept.

As of June 1998, the amount of bank lending to large companies was declining, but the drop was smaller relative to the corresponding decline among SMEs. On the other hand, the number of corporate bond and commercial paper (CP) issues by large companies continued to rise, particularly among the top five chaebols. This suggested that the earlier promises of the top five chaebols concerning restructuring and financial soundness improvement plans were unlikely to be kept and that a new set of financial soundness improvement targets with specific and measurable intermediate benchmarks was needed.

There were shortcomings in the corporate governance of chaebols that had to be addressed in a meaningful fashion. One was the practice of packing the boards of directors of the chaebols with outside, supposedly independent members, most of whom were widely known university professors or licensed professionals, but who possessed little knowledge of the business affairs of the companies they served and, as a result, took no active part in management decisions. Another problem was that these independent outside directors constituted only about 10 percent of the corporate directors in Korea. The number and the proportion of independent outside directors had to be expanded in the makeup of Korea's corporate boardrooms, and these people had to be provided with a wider range of corporate information. Especially, the majority of the nominating committees of auditors should be composed of outside directors.

There were also structural cracks in the chaebols. The chaebols spanned practically all industries and, like fleet convoys, included numerous companies that could not be rationalized or justified in terms of factory utilization, debt ratios, or profitability. There was an urgent need for the chaebols to restructure, dispose of uncompetitive businesses, and reorganize along core areas of strength. Instead, the chaebols continued to maintain failing companies by taking over the worthless convertible bonds these companies issued or by engaging in other unlawful intragroup supporting activities such as providing free access to real property. Policy makers recognized that these sorts of uncompetitive no-arm's-length intragroup activities had to be stopped by way of the significantly beefed-up Fair Trade Commission, Korea's competition authority.

In an effort to put an end to the fleet-convoy-like chaebol structures, the government decided to terminate, by March 2000, all cross-debt guarantees among the chaebol companies. Four of the top chaebols, in fact, announced that they would do this by May 1999. (The exception was the Hyundai Group.) However, the pledge to end cross-debt guarantees immediately raised suspicions because no concrete steps were undertaken to carry it through. The pledge was also met with skepticism because the top five chaebols were slower to act on their promises than the smaller chaebols. For the top five chaebols to keep their promises in a practical sense, they had to take immediate and aggressive steps such as allowing no new rollover of debt guarantees and setting specific benchmarks to realize their pledges to terminate the cross-debt guarantees.

The agreement between the government and the top five chaebols. The top five chaebols were dragging their feet and resisting government attempts at meaningful reform and restructuring. It became clear that the government and the business community had to come to an agreement about the need for restructuring. To this end, President Kim Dae-Jung hosted a luncheon with senior members of the Federation of Korean Industries (FKI), which spoke for the chaebols, on July 4, 1998. At the luncheon, President Kim noted that the international community had praised Korea for its reform and restructuring efforts, but expressed concern over the slow pace of change and the lack of real progress. He pointed out that Korea now had to counter the growing perception in the international community that it was reluctant to restructure. More important, he let it be known at the luncheon that the pace of restructuring in the corporate sector would now pick up in earnest. In a plea to the business community, President Kim conceded that the government alone could not carry out the needed restructuring and that success more or less depended on the commitment and the participation of the chaebols in the endeavor. He also stressed that a candid dialogue between the government and businesses was a requirement for the economic revival of the country.

The luncheon produced an agreement to hold regular meetings to be chaired by Minister of Finance and Economy Lee Kyu-Sung and FKI Chairman Kim Woo-Choong. The two sides also agreed on the following at the conclusion of the luncheon: (1) the government and businesses would act in concert to expand exports; (2) the government would promptly carry out restructuring among financial companies and establish measures as needed to facilitate the financing of SMEs and exports; (3) the business community would reaffirm its commitment to the five principles of restructuring (see chapter 5) and take steps to accelerate corporate restructuring; (4) business groups would have to end the practice of providing assistance to affiliated companies through unlawful intragroup trading and would have to resolve failing businesses and help build a fair and competitive market environment for all; (5) the government and businesses would work together to address the problem of unemployment; (6) the government would endeavor vigorously to help relieve SMEs from the credit crunch, and big businesses would endeavor to build cooperative relations with SMEs as equal partners; (7) the government would put its public expenditures on a fast track for early release and consult with the IMF on raising the government's consolidated deficit to 4 percent of GDP; (8) the government would aggressively push for the privatization of state-owned companies and enterprises and repeal or relax half the regulations currently in effect by the end of the year; and (9) the government and businesses would, through the agreement, renew their commitment to restructuring and would endeavor to create a positive business environment for all.

The government and businesses held an initial joint meeting on July 26 as a follow-up to the July 4 meeting. The meeting on July 26, which began at four o'clock in the afternoon and continued until half past eleven o'clock the same day, produced the following agreements: (1) For the purpose of resolving and eliminating the cross-debt guarantees currently in effect by March 2000, the top five chaebol companies were to establish phase-by-phase debt reduction targets until March 1999 and to endeavor to reduce the average debt-equity ratio to below 200 percent by the end of 1999. Specific benchmarks were to be set to ensure measurable progress. (2) Only individuals able to contribute to business and management decisions were to be appointed to boards of directors as outside directors. The proportion of outside directors was to gradually increase, and audit committees headed by outside directors were to be introduced. (3) The government was to investigate unlawful intragroup trading among chaebol companies vigorously. Businesses were to endeavor in earnest to end the long-established practice of providing illegal financial assistance and other forms of subsidy to affiliated companies. Uncompetitive companies should be restructured through business swaps, and the government would support the voluntary restructuring efforts of companies. (4) The government and businesses were to expand export financing through appropriate means so as to reverse the declining trend in exports and examine the possibility of expanding financing for exports on a deferred-payment basis. An export support committee was to be created. It would be headed by the minister of commerce, industry, and energy. It would help resolve the difficulties exporters were facing and identify the steps to be taken to support export businesses. (5) Lawful layoffs must be respected, but work-sharing efforts were to be undertaken to minimize layoffs. The government and businesses were jointly to explore ways to increase the employment of workers with advanced education.

Meanwhile, the FSC established a timetable for the top five chaebol companies to meet the financial soundness improvement agreements.

Under the plan put forth, the creditor banks were (1) to request any modifications in the financial soundness improvement agreements by the end of July; (2) to establish a council of creditor banks for each of the top five chaebols by the end of August; (3) jointly with local accounting firms, to conduct due diligence on the chaebols from August to mid-September; and (4) to develop draft proposals for financial soundness improvements by mid-November that included input from outside advisory groups. The financial soundness improvement plans were to be finalized by mid-December. For this purpose, adjustments and negotiations between the councils of creditor banks and the top five chaebols were to begin November 15.

On July 2, 1998, the FSC adopted a new regulation that limited the amount of CP and privately placed bonds that financial companies could hold. The purported aim of the new regulation was to prevent the top five chaebols from monopolizing the credit market, cutting off credit flows to SMEs, or exposing financial companies to the risk of excessive concentration. Under the new regulation, the amount of CP that banks and investment trusts could purchase from the same corporate issuer was restricted to 1 percent of the assets under trust management. For CP issued by companies belonging to the same chaebol, the limit was 5 percent of the trust assets. It was also decided that any holdings in excess of the 1 and 5 percent ceilings must be reduced to the ceilings by the end of January 1999. The limit on holdings by investment trusts of privately placed bonds was lowered from 10 to 3 percent of the trust assets. In addition, the scope of lending by insurance companies to affiliated companies in the same business group—set at 5 percent of the total assets—was expanded to cover not only loans, but also other loan-like credit extensions such as the purchase of CP and privately placed debt. On September 16, the amount that funds managed by investment trusts could invest in the same marketable securities (excluding stocks) was toughened from 10 percent per securities offering to 10 percent per issuing company.

The Big Deal among the top five chaebols. The need for a big deal—a term used during the crisis years to refer to restructuring through swaps or exchanges of business assets among chaebols—emerged soon after Korea received rescue funds from the IMF. It was reported that Samsung Economic Research Institute proposed, in a report in December 1997, that the major chaebols swap or exchange businesses that were either unsustainable or generating losses with businesses that were more well suited to the strategic goals and core strengths of the chaebols. This idea was circulating in business circles as well. On December 16, 1997, an article titled "Are Business Swaps among Chaebols Possible?" in the *Korea Economic Daily* even quoted senior managers at the Hyundai and Samsung business groups who acknowledged the need for a big deal.

A big deal was seen as a way to rectify the duplication in investment and the overinvestment across wide industrial sectors in which chaebols engaged and to give the chaebols the opportunity to concentrate on their core strengths. It offered a way to end the fleet-convoy-like or one-for-all, all-for-one management structure of the chaebol companies and give the companies managerial independence. Moreover, under a big deal scheme, mergers of a marginal business with a well-matched company made strategic sense because investments that had already been made could be utilized and marginal companies would not have to be allowed to fail.

The case for restructuring through a big deal was compelling, but it was not certain whether the government could play a dominant role in the process. One major concern was that the government would be exposed to charges of favoritism and bias. This criticism was based on the perception that the government would be creating new, powerful monopolistic industries and leaving too much economic power in the hands of a few chaebol families. Moreover, given the huge scale of the businesses and enterprises involved, it was not clear whether the government could tackle issues such as asset valuation and due diligence in the short period of time available. Conflicting asset valuations, job cuts, and corporate culture were other obvious sources of trouble and delay. Finally, if the Big Deal were to succeed, the chaebols would have to view the restructuring through the Big Deal as a means of advancing their long-term self-interests and their strategic goals in terms of competitiveness and synergy.

For these reasons, the new administration that took office in early 1998 decided to focus, first, on improving the financial soundness of businesses and stick to the five principles of corporate restructuring (see chapter 5). Actually, the Big Deal became a pending issue on June 10, 1998, when Kim Joong-Kwon, chief presidential secretary, remarked in a morning lecture that big deals among the large chaebols would be announced in the next several days, adding that one chaebol had vehemently resisted, but had then relented and capitulated on June 9.

This seemingly offhand announcement was followed by a meeting between President Kim Dae-Jung and the heads of the FKI on July 4, during which both sides professed the desire to see the companies carry out the Big Deal voluntarily on their own terms. The government decided to lay the legal and regulatory groundwork for the Big Deal so as to support it and expedite the process. This included various tax relief measures for business asset swaps, the resolution of cross-debt guarantees, and debt-equity swaps.

Despite the July 4 meeting, there was no sign that the chaebols were making any serious attempt or headway on the Big Deal for the rest of the month. Because of the slow progress, the government decided to draft its own set of guidelines that described industries that were appropriate for the Big Deal and a desirable timetable. The goal was to create a propitious environment for the Big Deal and help maintain the pace and momentum of restructuring. It was also agreed that the FKI would have to take the lead in coordinating actions among the concerned companies and addressing any conflicts arising among them. The government held a second meeting with businesses on August 7, at which an outline of the industries and companies identified by the Ministry of Commerce, Industry, and Energy as participants in the Big Deal was presented and discussed, including the factory utilization, profitability, debt structure, and global outlook of the industries. Table 7.4 shows a summary of the 10 industries the ministry targeted for the Big Deal.

It was also agreed at the August 7 meeting that a task force on restructuring should be set up at the FKI to propose remedies for companies that were heavily indebted or losing export competitiveness. The government and the FKI agreed to meet again before the end of August.

On August 14, the vice chairman of the FKI came to the following agreements with the heads of restructuring units at the top five chaebols: (1) Business swaps would proceed on the principle of mutual benefit and competitiveness; it is under this principle that businesses propose conditions for the support of the government. (2) Industries to be considered for the swap would consist primarily of the 10 businesses that the government proposes. (3) Letters of understanding on business swaps would be exchanged among the companies involved by the end of August at the latest. (4) Where differences arise on the valuation of the assets to be swapped, the basis for negotiation would be the valuation produced by the external valuation firm designated by the parties involved. (5) The methods of swap may involve M&A, a P&A, stock transfers, or other agreements reached between or among the parties involved. (6) If the liabilities exceed the assets, the parties involved would propose debt forgiveness, debt restructuring, interest rate adjustments, reduced tax liabilities, and so forth to the FKI, which would then forward the proposals to the government for deliberation. (7) The parties involved in business swaps would exchange the good faith information necessary for decision making. (8) If the government fails to deliver its pledged support for a finalized swap agreement, the agreement would be null and void.

In an effort to facilitate the negotiations, the FKI set up a restructuring task force. After much back and forth, the FKI announced, on October 10, that an agreement had been reached, as follows:

1. Petrochemicals, aerospace: These businesses were to be separated from the chaebols and transferred to newly incorporated companies. The shares of these companies would be distributed equally among the chaebols concerned. The companies would be headed by independent management. Foreign investors may become controlling shareholders.
2. Rolling stock manufacturing: The manufacturing facilities of Daewoo, Hanjin, and Hyundai were to be merged into a newly incorporated

Table 7.4 Ten Industries Targeted in the Big Deal

Industry	*Major companies*	*Production capacity*	*Operation ratio, %*	*Global market prospects*
Automobile	Hyundai, Daewoo, Kia, Samsung	4.2 million	40–50	Global oversupply
Semiconductors	Samsung, Hyundai, LG	2 billion units (16 M D-RAM)	80	Oversupply until the beginning of 1999
Liquid crystal displays	Samsung, Hyundai, LG	14.4 million units	100	Expecting recovery from beginning of 1999, and world markets controlled by Korea and Japan
Steel	Coke furnace: POSCO; Electric furnace: five companies, including Inchon Steel	41.17 million tons	Coke furnace: 90; electric furnace: 70–80	Continuing recession until 1999
Petrochemicals	Eight companies, including SK and LG	4.92 million tons	80–90	Oversupply until the economic recovery of China and Southeast Asian countries
Shipbuilding	Four companies, including Hyundai	9 million gross tons	About 100, excluding Halla	Full operation until 2000

(continued next page)

Table 7.4 Ten Industries Targeted in the Big Deal *(continued)*

Industry	*Major companies*	*Production capacity*	*Operation ratio, %*	*Global market prospects*
Power plant equipment	Korea Heavy Industries & Construction, Hyundai, Samsung	Fire: 3,300 MW Nuclear : 1,500 MW	—	Small increase in fire power plant
Aerospace	Four companies, including Samsung Aerospace	Parts assembly such as engine, wing, and body	—	Expecting difficult period because of the decline in military demand
Manufacturing, rolling stock	Daewoo, Hyundai, Hanjin Heavy Industries & Construction	1,500 cars (based on electric rail cars)	70	Securing production orders until the end of 1998
Cement	Seven companies, including Ssangyong Cement Industrial Co.	61.71 million tons	67	Expecting difficult period until 2000

Source: Hankook Ilbo (daily newspaper), August 8, 1998.
Note: — = not available. D-RAM = dynamic random access memory (chips); MW = megawatts.

company. The share distribution and management would be decided by October 6. The company would be opened to controlling ownership by foreign investors.

3. Ship engines, power plant equipment: Samsung's ship engine business and power plant equipment business would be transferred to Korea Heavy Industries & Construction. Whether there would be a merger of the power plant equipment businesses of Hyundai Heavy Industries and Korea Heavy Industries & Construction would be decided by October 6.
4. Semiconductors: The ownership shares and the management following the merger of LG Semicon and Hyundai Electronics would be decided by October 6.
5. Oil refineries: Talks would be ongoing on the takeover of Hanwha Energy by Hyundai.

Under the timetable set for the Big Deal, the new management of the affected companies was to produce restructuring plans, including the steps to be taken for the disposition of redundant investments and employees, debt reductions, and other turnaround measures. By mid-October, the creditor banks were to evaluate the feasibility of the restructuring plans for each specific industry, including financial support measures. The companies and the creditor banks also decided to finalize all procedures by mid-December and to determine, by the end of October, when due diligence would be undertaken.

Workouts for the 6th to the 64th Largest Chaebols

According to the first phase of the workout plan finalized by the EPCC on July 15, 1998, eight banks were to select roughly 16 business groups from the 6th to 64th largest business groups (chaebols) for workouts.[6] Approximately 80 additional large independent companies not belonging to chaebols were to be chosen for workouts during the first phase. It was decided that each of the eight creditor banks would seek advice from outside advisory groups, begin preparations with the companies selected for workouts in August, and produce workout plans by December. By September, the eight creditor banks had selected 35 companies for workouts within 13 of the 6th to 64th largest business groups (chaebols). A total of 22 large independent (non-chaebol) companies were also selected for workouts.[7]

The Restructuring of SMEs

By the end of June, the special SME task force that had been created in each creditor bank had evaluated a total of 22,199 SMEs with outstanding bank debt in excess of W 1 billion and had completed a three-stage screening process. As a result of the screening, 7,851 companies (35.4 percent of the total) were selected for priority support, while 12,926 companies (58.2 percent) were selected for conditional support. At the end of June 1998, outstanding SME bank loans totaled approximately W 114 trillion. Of this amount, loans to the SMEs subjected to the creditor screening process represented about W 68 trillion or 60.5 percent. A breakdown of these loans indicated that roughly W 23 trillion (34.2 percent) was associated with the SMEs that had been selected for priority support, and about W 40 trillion (58.1 percent) with SMEs tagged for conditional support. About W 5 trillion (7.6 percent) was associated with the rest of the SMEs.

Thus, SMEs were to be given differentiated support after the three-stage evaluation. For the priority support group, the creditor banks were to provide steady financing to achieve quick turnarounds. A total of approximately W 7.6 trillion and US$500 million were to be made available to this group. For SMEs in the conditional support group, there was a risk that the chance of a turnaround would quickly diminish if the companies were left on their own. So, the workouts were urgent for these companies. To ensure stable business operations during the workout process, the creditor banks decided to provide W 2.8 trillion in fresh financing, in addition to loan maturity extensions and other support measures. For the third group (companies belonging to neither group), each creditor bank was to determine its actions independently.

Expanding the Market Instruments for Restructuring

On September 16, the government enacted the Securities Investment Company Act that established the legal framework for the incorporation of securities investment companies as mutual funds and corporate restructuring vehicles. This was followed by the creation of corporate restructuring funds on September 24, to which a total of 25 banks, including the KDB, contributed approximately W 1.6 trillion. Restructuring funds can be classified into debt rescheduling funds that convert short-term debt into longer-term debt (two or three years), equity investment funds that acquire stocks for recapitalization, and hybrid funds that do both. The newly created corporate restructuring funds consisted of one debt rescheduling fund and three hybrid funds (table 7.5).

The funds were to be managed by foreign asset managers because no domestic asset managers had the necessary expertise to ensure that the funds would be managed independently and without political interference or other unsavory meddling.

The government passed the Asset-Backed Securitization Act on September 16, 1998, which supplied the legal and regulatory framework for the securitization of the bonds, land, and other assets held by financial companies and KAMCO. The new law was squarely aimed at making it easier for these entities to securitize assets and improve financial soundness.

Table 7.5 Corporate Restructuring Funds
won, billions

Type of fund	*Size*	*Asset management company*
Debt rescheduling fund		
Seoul Debt Rescheduling Fund	600.0	Rothschild
Hybrid funds		
Hangang Restructuring Fund	333.3	Scudder Kemper Investment
Mugoongwha Restructuring Fund	333.3	Templeton Asset Management
Arirang Restructuring Fund	333.4	State Street Bank & Trust
Total	1,600.0	

Source: Korea Development Bank.

It also provided for the securitization of mortgage-backed securities and long-term mortgage financing.

On September 14, the government promulgated the amendment of the Act on the Structural Improvement of the Financial Industry that granted the FSC the authority to issue orders for M&A, P&A, and other restructuring measures. The scope of the distressed financial companies into which either the government or the KDIC might inject capital and take equity shares was also expanded. The amended law significantly simplified the procedures for mergers, capital write-downs, and other similar restructuring measures for financial companies relative to the procedures set out under the Commercial Act or the Securities and Exchange Act.

This was followed by the amendment of the Depositor Protection Act on September 16 so as to expand the types of financial companies eligible for protection by the KDIC. The ceiling on the deposit insurance premium rate was raised to 0.5 percent of the deposits to be insured to increase the funds available for protection. The amendment provided for an expansion in the scope of the financial companies to which the KDIC may provide fund support to facilitate the resolution of distressed financial companies. The amendment was preceded by a revised decree on deposit insurance protection on July 25 that reduced the amount of principal and interest to be protected from December 1997 to the end of 2000. Under the revised regulations, both the principal and interest were to be protected up to W 20 million for all deposits made after August 1, 1998 and until the end of 2000. For amounts greater than W 20 million, only the principal was to be protected. Beginning in 2001, only W 20 million in principal and interest was to be protected.

On September 16, the amended Securities Investment Trust Act took effect. By repealing provisions that capped equity ownership by individual shareholders and related parties, it enabled the controlling shareholders of investment trusts to aid restructuring through recapitalization.[8] In an effort to help improve the prevailing corporate governance dominated by the controlling shareholders, investment trust companies were allowed to exercise voting rights in companies in which they held shares.

New Policies for the Growth of the Bond Market

Korea had always exercised prudent fiscal management. At the end of 1997, the outstanding balance of government bonds stood at W 28.5 trillion or about 6.8 percent of GDP, compared with 20.7 percent in Germany. 49.7 percent in Japan, 50.4 percent in the United Kingdom, and 69.7 percent in the United States at the end of 1996. However, in the course of managing the financial crisis, the government was likely to issue substantially expanded debt. Including the bonds for the deposit insurance fund, the size of government bond issues was expected to reach W 16 trillion in 1998 and W 22 trillion in 1999.

To establish an efficient financial system, Korea had to nurture a well-developed capital market, including bond markets, along with robust banks. This was what had prompted the World Bank to recommend to the government that a task force be formed to draft proposals aimed at improving the bond markets. The task force, consisting of 12 experts, started its work on February 18, 1998, and reported its proposals in August 1998.

First, the task force proposed that (1) the three-year treasury bond issue be expanded so that it could become a benchmark treasury bond; (2) government debt, beginning with the three-year treasury bond, be issued regularly on the first or second week of each month to improve the predictability of government debt issues and help establish a benchmark interest rate; (3) various government debt issues, such as grain bonds, be consolidated into the government debt management fund bonds and streamlined; (4) the government debt management fund bonds be renamed treasury bonds to enhance their recognition in the market; and (5) the method used in debt issues be converted to the fungible issue method so as to strengthen the liquidity of treasury bonds.

Second, primary bond dealers were to be recognized for the sale of treasury bonds. As an initial measure in instituting a new system, treasury bond dealing by banks was to be allowed. The intent was to enhance the liquidity—the convertibility into cash—of treasury bonds and to amplify the underwriting capability in the primary market, as well as the market-making ability in the secondary market, which were prerequisites in creating a primary dealer system. The new system was to take effect in 1999 after the necessary arrangements had been made, such as the establishment of standards for the selection of primary dealers.

Third, the bidding system was to be improved so that part of the debt issues could be allotted to the general public and individuals could invest in government debt issues through their agents. The bidding for government bonds was to be changed to an electronic bidding system by relying on the computer network used by financial companies (BOK Wire).

Fourth, proceeds from the sale of government bonds were to be managed by financial companies, or short-term debt was to be issued to ensure that there was no discrepancy between regular bond issues and the government's need for funds, thereby avoiding temporary surpluses or deficits on the treasury account. In addition, the Korea Stock Exchange was to provide information on the real-time yields on benchmark treasury bonds to investors. To improve the credibility of the credit ratings on treasury bonds, foreign credit-rating providers were to be encouraged to establish branch operations in Korea. In August 1998, the Korea Investors Service agreed on a business tie-up with Moody's.

Tax Measures for Restructuring

Tax incentives and support measures for business restructuring were laid out by the government under certain principles. The first principle was that tax measures would be general in nature. In the past, it was not uncommon for tax benefits to be given to specific companies or individual businesses. However, in the era of the IMF and the World Trade Organization (WTO), selective measures favoring only certain companies or sectors were neither tenable nor acceptable. This meant that all tax measures had to be extended and generalized to all companies that met established criteria. The method of support also had to be switched from permanent tax benefits to temporary relief or deferred tax payments.

The second principle was that obstacles to restructuring would be eliminated. Tax support for restructuring was not meant as a privilege or a favor, but as a tool to resolve tax obstacles that hindered restructuring. For instance, there were obvious cases in which companies disposing of some of their assets for the sole purpose of restructuring were subject to harsh tax liabilities even though the asset disposition could not be justified as a profit-making enterprise. With respect to the appropriate method of tax support, the imposition of acquisition and registration taxes that merely increased the cost of transactions was to be waived. Meanwhile, tax liabilities arising from capital gains, such as the special surtax and the corporate tax, were to be deferred.

The third principle was that tax measures should help strengthen the business fundamentals of the recipient companies so that their value as going concerns would increase as a result of the government tax support. The tax measures were not to be used in the case of nonviable companies or of mergers that spread distress from one company to another.

The fourth principle was that taxation should be equitable. Some differences in the way support was provided were unavoidable, but this still raised questions about the fairness of the measures. Thus, it was imperative that the government take appropriate steps to minimize tax inequities. It also made sense that government tax support should not be so generous that it rewarded incompetent managers or provided perverse incentives to managers to seek government handouts. Such moral hazard had to be avoided.

Under these principles, the government amended the Regulation of Tax Reduction and Exemption Act on September 16, 1998 to promote restructuring among corporate and financial companies. Corporate companies, financial companies, and entities that facilitated restructuring were to be eligible for tax support. The types of corporate restructuring covered included reorganizations such as mergers, spin-offs, or the incorporation of going businesses; business restructuring such as sell-offs of business units, asset swaps, and business conversions; and improvements in financial structure such as through debt redemptions, asset sales, recapitalization, and asset contributions from business owners.

The restructuring of corporate companies could take the form of voluntary actions by creditor banks (such as reorganization, business restructuring, and improvements in financial structure and business management) or actions (such as a P&A) imposed by regulators. Special entities created to assist in restructuring, such as corporate-type investment trusts (mutual funds), corporate restructuring vehicles, special-purpose vehicles, and bridge loans, could also be used.

Because of the wide range of the business restructuring being undertaken and the different forms available, covering them all effectively under any single set of tax measures was difficult, if not impossible. In corporate restructuring alone, it was obvious that individual companies had their own unique sets of issues and problems and that their dealings with creditor banks were diverse. The fact that tax support measures were revised and reinforced twice already, in December 1997 and February 1998, suggested the great variety of issues involved and the arduous task the government faced. Table 7.6 lists tax measures that had taken effect as of September 1998 in support of business restructuring.

Expanded Unemployment Measures and Labor Union Resistance to Restructuring

Labor Union Resistance to Restructuring

As the pace of restructuring picked up with the closure of 55 companies and five banks in June and the announcement of privatization plans on July 3, the resistance of labor unions began to intensify, and tensions

Table 7.6 Tax Support Measures, by Type of Restructuring

Type		*Tax support*	*Date amended*
Reorganization	M&A	Deferred tax payment of the corporate tax on capital gains from M&A	Dec. 1997
		Exemption from the registration tax	Feb. 1998
	Spin-offs	Deferred tax payment of the corporate tax and the special surtax on capital gains	Dec. 1997
		Exemption from the acquisition tax and registration tax	Dec. 1997
	Integration	Deferred tax payment of the special surtax	Dec. 1997
	Change of company	Deferred tax payment of the special surtax	Dec. 1997
Business restructuring	Transfer of firms	Shareholder guarantee liabilities included among deductible expenses	Feb. 1998
		From gross income, exclusion of corporate profits accrued from liability exemptions	Feb. 1998
	Sale of business units	Deferred tax payment of the special surtax for sellers	Feb. 1998
		Exemption from the acquisition tax and registration tax for acquirers	Feb. 1998
	Asset swaps	Deferred tax payment of the corporate tax and special surtax	Feb. 1998
		Exemption from the acquisition tax and registration tax	Feb. 1998
		Expanding support for multilateral swaps	Sept. 1998
	Business conversion	Deferred tax payment of the special surtax	Dec. 1997

(continued next page)

Table 7.6 Tax Support Measures, by Type of Restructuring *(continued)*

Type		*Tax support*	*Date amended*
Improving financial structures	Debt redemption	In selling of real estate for debt redemption, exemption of the special surtax	Dec. 1997
		Exemption from the acquisition tax and registration tax for acquirers	Apr. 1997
	Asset sales	For the disposer of real estate for restructuring, a special surtax reduction of 50%	Feb. 1998
		For the acquirer of real estate for restructuring, a special surtax reduction of 50%	Sept. 1998
	Owner's property contribution	A capital gains tax reduction of 50–100%	Feb. 1998
		Profits from contributions not included in gross income	Feb. 1998
		Exemption from the acquisition tax and registration tax	Feb. 1998
	Redemption of borrowing	In paid borrowing at the present value and exempted from the payment of the difference between the actual payment and the book value; for corporate companies, exemption gains not included in gross income, and, for financial companies, this exemption included in deductible expenses	Sept. 1998
	Capital increase	Tax deduction of the capital increase for SMEs	Aug. 1997

Restructuring, financial companies	M&A	Tax exemption of fictitious dividends and clearance income (same application for the transfer of a whole business)	Aug. 1997
		On transferring overlapping assets due to M&A, a special surtax reduction of 50%	Dec. 1995
		On transferring whole business, a deferred tax payment of the special surtax	Aug. 1997
	P&A	Inclusion of actual asset value less than market value in deductible expenses	Sept. 1998
		For acquirers and failing financial companies, exemption from the special surtax and securities transaction tax	Sept. 1998
		For acquirers, exemption from the acquisition tax and registration tax	Sept. 1998
Establishing entities to aid restructuring	Mutual fund	In case of giving dividends of 90% or above of dividend income, dividends deducted from income	Sept. 1998
		In transferring stock, exemption from the securities transaction tax	
	Securities investment company for corporate restructuring	Inclusion of 50% of securities investment among deductible expenses	Sept. 1998
		For individual investors, capital gains for stock transactions and separate dividend income exemption from global income tax	Sept. 1998
	Companies specialized in securitizations	Exemption from the acquisition tax and registration tax	Sept. 1998
		A special surtax reduction of 50%	Sept. 1998

Source: Jang 1999.

mounted. The labor unions associated with the failed banks began to join forces and express their anger publicly in various venues, at Myeongdong Catholic Cathedral, for example. Union members working in public corporations also geared up for collective protests following the announcement of the government's privatization plans.

Workers at Busan Subway struck on July 3. The Korean Federation of Hospital Workers Unions and the Korean Metal Workers Unions, along with other unions, went on strike on July 9. The labor union at Hyundai Motor Company demanded, on June 30, that the company withdraw its plan to lay off 4,830 employees and then went on a 48-hour strike on July 6 and struck again from July 14 to 16.

The heads of the Federation of Korean Trade Unions and the Korean Confederation of Trade Unions held a joint press conference on July 10 to announce that they were working together. They also declared that they would no longer take any part in the Korea Tripartite Commission (KTC) and staged a strike on July 15.

At the July 10 press conference, the two labor leaders made the following demands: (1) The government must immediately suspend and cease all forceful or arbitrary restructuring and provide job guarantees to workers being laid off at restructured companies and failed banks. In addition, the principles, the criteria, and the direction of restructuring in the public and financial service sectors must be negotiated through the KTC. (2) The government and employers must immediately cease unlawful layoffs and provide meaningful job protection and unemployment measures. The KTC must promptly investigate the alleged illegal labor practices at 63 workplaces and prosecute business owners guilty of committing labor abuses. (3) The government must order the return to work of all workers laid off unlawfully and ensure the end of arbitrary pay cuts and suspensions, rapidly deteriorating collective bargaining processes, and other abuses by companies. (4) The government and the National Assembly must restore the stature of the KTC as the site of negotiations among the government, businesses, and labor unions and enact special legislation on the KTC.

On July 12, in response to these demands of labor, the government acknowledged that the level of consultation and negotiation on restructuring through the KTC was unsatisfactory and renewed its pledge to be more faithful to the commitments it had made in regard to the KTC. In an effort to implement rapid measures to strengthen its role, the KTC, on July 13, created a subcommittee to be charged with the related tasks. The government promised strict enforcement and criminal prosecutions of companies for any unlawful or abusive labor practices. It promised to apply the same principle with regard to unlawful activities by labor unions. The government demanded that the labor unions call off the July 14–15 strikes, but it pledged to hold ministerial-level consultations to facilitate the work of the KTC.

The news media urged restraint on the labor unions and argued that the nationwide strikes only delayed the necessary restructuring, fueled uncertainty in financial markets, undermined the competitiveness of the country's exports, scared off foreign investors, and brought enormous harm to Korea's efforts at economic recovery from the financial crisis. The argument was also heard that the actions of labor would only encourage more layoffs and result not in collective benefit, but collective disaster. The news media made the case that strikes did not represent a solution, but a rejection of the only sensible course of action for a country in dire straits.

The mounting pressure facing labor unions more or less reflected public sentiment at the time. Nonetheless, the strikes persisted until a turning point was reached on July 23, when the chairman of the KTC and the leaders of the two national union groups reached a tentative understanding on ongoing issues except for the restructuring in the financial and public sectors and the layoffs at Hyundai Motor Company. Table 7.7 shows the trends in labor disputes during the third quarter of 1998.

Layoffs at Hyundai Motor Company. The layoffs at Hyundai Motor Company prompted considerable apprehension among the public because it was the first major downsizing by a large company in the name of discretionary action. Many feared that it would not only set a precedent, but also provoke concern about the extent of the layoffs and the likely responses of the company's labor union, one of the strongest in the country. No one was sure of the outcome. The company estimated that, of the 46,000 workers on its payroll, 18,000 were redundant, and that even after taking into account voluntary retirements, about 8,000 workers would have to be subjected to employment adjustments. On May 18, 1998, the company notified the company labor union of its decision to lay off 8,198 workers. On June 30, following additional voluntary retirements, the company notified the Ministry of Labor of its decision to lay off 4,830 workers.

Hyundai Motor Company pushed for discretionary layoffs during July and August; the company's labor union responded by staging five strikes that the authorities deemed illegal, and the company twice shut down workplaces. The government sought to mediate the crisis, and efforts were undertaken to mitigate the situation, including through voluntary

Table 7.7 Trends in Labor Disputes, Third Quarter, 1998
number of cases

Indicator	*July*	*August*	*December*
Labor strikes	24	12	13
Application of labor dispute mediation	207	42	45
Agreed wage growth	−2.4	−2.4	−2.8

Sources: MOFE 1998p, 1998q, 1998r.

retirements and unpaid leaves. The company reconsidered and notified only 1,569 workers individually on July 30 that they would be laid off. After more ups and downs, the two sides came to an understanding on August 24 that (1) the list of 1,569 workers to be laid off would be scaled back to 277; (2) management would make the selection of the workers to be laid off, but the company would endeavor to help the affected workers find new employment; (3) the workers to be laid off were to receive a lump sum severance payment equivalent to about seven to nine months of ordinary wages; and (4) the 1,261 workers to be spared from layoffs were to go on unpaid leaves for a year and half and then undertake a six-month program of training.

The compromise struck by Hyundai and the labor union was praised by some as a successful result of negotiation, particularly because the discretionary layoff plan was achieved through talks with the most aggressive labor union at the country's largest workplace. However, others severely criticized the process, lamenting the unlawful, often violent strikes the labor union staged and the government's appeasement and failure to uphold the discretionary layoff system, which had been legislated and agreed on at the national level. It was also argued that the settlement established a bad precedent by reinforcing the perception that the labor market was extremely rigid and that management always yielded to the violent protests of workers. Another controversy revolved around the number of layoffs. While some argued that the 277 layoffs paled in comparison with the 1,569 layoffs the company had announced on July 30, others argued that the negotiations nonetheless produced the positive effect of removing idle workers through voluntary retirements and unpaid leaves. Table 7.8 summarizes the workforce adjustment at Hyundai Motor Company that the Ministry of Labor reported at the time.

Bank workforce downsizing. By September, tensions and frictions had mounted on the issue of downsizing and layoffs in the banking sector. The FSC demanded workforce reductions at the seven banks that had received conditional approval for turnarounds, as well as Korea First Bank and Seoul Bank, as part of restructuring and in exchange for the injection of public funds. As a basis for downsizing, the FSC proposed the criterion of operating profit per bank employee and noted that the average per domestic bank employee was W 150 million in contrast to the W 260 million per employee at foreign banks such as Bank of America, Chase Manhattan Bank, and HSBC. The FSC demanded that the workforce at the banks be downsized to bring the average among domestic bank employees in line with that of the more competitive foreign banks by the end of 1999. Under the FSC criteria, nine banks had to cut the size of their workforce by approximately 40 percent (based on the workforce size as of the end of 1997). Banks that could not survive without bailout funds from the government revised their turnaround plans to incorporate the

Table 7.8 Workforce Adjustment at Hyundai Motor Company, August 24, 1998
number of persons

					Downsizing workforce, 10,166			
			Maintaining employment 8,564		*Workforce adjustments through negotiation 8,746*			
Total workers	*Necessary workers*	*Redundant workers on payroll*	*Salary reduction*	*Substituting subcontractors*	*Unpaid leave*	*Voluntary retirement*	*Layoff*	*Natural turnover*
			6,842	1,722	2,018	6,451	277	1,420
46,132	27,402	18,730						

Source: Labor-Management Cooperation Division, Ministry of Labor.

40 percent workforce reduction the FSC demanded and sent the revised plans to the FSC in early September.

The labor unions in the financial industry, including the nine banks, had originally accepted 20 to 30 percent workforce reductions. They reacted angrily to the higher target set by the government and threatened early on to stage massive strikes. During negotiations on September 15 with the presidents of the nine banks, members of the labor union went so far as to lock in the bank heads after the talks failed to resolve the differences. The standoff ended when the government sent riot police to the scene to rescue the bank officials. As the deadline for the first round of financial sector restructuring neared, the labor unions at the nine banks came to an agreement with bank management after an 18-hour negotiating session that had begun at 7 p.m. on September 28. Under the agreement, the workforce could be downsized by 32 percent counting from the end of 1997 to the end of 1998. Because the nine banks had already dismissed 7,936 employees between January and August 1998, 10,006 employees were subject to layoff as a result of the new agreement.

A New Labor and Management Culture

In an era of globalization characterized by open markets and free competition, it is imperative that Korean companies provide global markets with low-cost, high-quality products. If a business is to maintain price competitiveness, labor costs must be flexible. Otherwise, companies will lose their competitiveness and disappear under the competitive pressure of markets. Labor is also the source of value generation. It is the quality and eagerness of the labor force that ultimately raise labor productivity and contribute to the success of business enterprises.

If a society fails to maintain social cohesion and is staggering under conflict and uncertainty about the future, investment ceases because investment is essentially about the future. Investment then naturally moves to where the future is more certain and safer. Sluggish investment translates into slow economic growth and a declining economy.

Korean companies and Korean labor unions had to recognize these simple realities, which pointed to the need to establish a new relationship between labor and management that would facilitate flexibility in the labor market and expand growth potential, social stability, and harmony. The distrust and the confrontations that had characterized labor relations in the past had to be banished for good and replaced by mutual trust and respect. In reaching for this goal, what mattered was fairness, efficiency, and broad participation in common endeavors.

Responsible for social integration and stability, the government also had a role in shaping the social understanding of the relationship between labor and management. A consensus had to be based on a shared sense of fairness that both sides had to respect. In negotiating solutions, the party in a superior position had to refrain from abusing its power. The party in the inferior position should not persist in meaningless stubbornness. Both sides had to exercise self-control and be accountable for their actions. A system had to be developed to ensure the equitable sharing of pain and of any gains that might result from the shared pain. In an era of global competition, labor and business had to innovate and reinforce their core competitive strengths continually.

On August 15, Independence Day, President Kim Dae-Jung called for the rebuilding of the nation with a view to establishing a democracy and a market economy. He proposed six goals. One was the creation of a new labor and management culture based on harmony and cooperation. He proposed that mutual trust and reconciliation, backed by shared pain and benefits, should become the basis for the new relationship between labor unions and companies.

Expanded Unemployment Measures

Unemployment was expected to rise in the second half of 1998. In June, the number of people in employment was 20.18 million, up slightly from early in the year (January–February), but down 5.6 percent from the same period a year earlier. The drop in employment was particularly noticeable in manufacturing and construction. The monthly increase in the number of the unemployed rose to as high as 300,000 early in the year, but had fallen to about 40,000 by June. The number of the unemployed was 1.53 million in June, when the unemployment rate was close to 7 percent. People with prior work experience made up 93.3 percent of the unemployed.

According to projections by the Korea Development Institute, the slowing economy was likely to cause sharp increases in unemployment from an estimated 6 percent early in the year to 7.9 percent in the second half of the year and possibly as high as 8.3 percent in the fourth quarter. The institute also projected that the average period spent between jobs among the unemployed would rise from four or five months to seven or eight months. Worse still, the institute predicted that the proportion of unemployed white-collar workers would jump as restructuring intensified and that unemployment among college graduates and other highly educated job-seekers would spike in the foreseeable future.

As the employment outlook deteriorated and the resistance of labor unions intensified, the government decided to adopt additional unemployment measures. At the ninth meeting of the EPCC, on August 10, the government reaffirmed its goal of creating jobs by rapidly concluding the necessary restructuring and improving the competitiveness of the economy. However, it also took note of the inevitable increase in unemployment and decided that it must utilize the occasion to develop the ability of the unemployed to participate in a knowledge-based high-technology economy of the 21st century. The government decided that (1) expenditures on job creation had to be boosted through expanded public works projects, social overhead capital spending, and support for regional economic development; (2) the social safety net needed to be supplemented by extending employment insurance to all workplaces and guaranteeing and protecting minimum living standards among laid-off workers; (3) job training had to be significantly improved and augmented in preparation for the postrestructuring economic rebound; and (4) unemployment measures had to become more well tailored to reflect the wide variety of unemployed workers, including part-timers, women, youth, and highly educated white-collar workers. The budget for the new unemployment measures in the second half of 1998 was to be raised by W 1.71 trillion, from W 8.46 trillion to W 10.17 trillion so that benefits could be extended among 2.92 million individuals.

Unemployment reached 7.6 percent in July, rising by 122,000 over the number in June, to 1.65 million. Employment in agriculture saw a modest increase, while manufacturing and construction experienced a larger drop. Other sectors generally saw a broad drop in employment. In August, unemployment reached 7.4 percent or 1.58 million unemployed, down by 73,000 from the previous month. This was the first decline in unemployment since November 1997. There was more good news in September, when unemployment fell to 7.3 percent, and the number of the unemployed dropped to 1.57 million. The drop in September was mostly caused by an increase in consumer demand associated with the traditional thanksgiving holidays and the expanded public works projects. However, the job offer ratio—the ratio of jobs available to job-seekers as a broad measure of the health of the job market—continued to move between 0.21 and 0.28, suggesting that the market was still tight.

The Russian Moratorium and the Fate of the Won

The Russian Crisis and Distress in International Financial Markets

The Japanese yen, which had resumed its downward trajectory toward the end of July, fell to ¥147 against the U.S. dollar on August 11, the lowest rate since August 20, 1990. In China, a massive flood was likely to trim the country's economic growth rate by at least 1 percentage point. In Hong Kong SAR, China, a speculative attack on the currency by hedge funds triggered a drop in the stock market to 6,780—the lowest point since July 23, 1993—on August 11. The slide in Hong Kong SAR, China was brought under control only after the authorities intervened aggressively to buoy the market and the currency, which was clearly an unusual move in the context of an economy that had long taken deep pride in a laissez-faire attitude toward the market.

The declaration of a moratorium in Russia and the sharp decline of the ruble. Amid mounting volatility across markets in East Asia, the Russian government, on August 17, declared a moratorium that (1) suspended principal payments for 90 days on foreign loans with maturities greater than 180 days, (2) suspended principal and interest payments for 90 days on short-term zero-coupon Russian treasury bills (GKO bonds) held by foreign investors, and (3) replaced the existing short-term government debt through new bond issues. The Russian government banned trading in short-term government debt and new foreign purchases of short-term debt until it could restructure the foreign debt. It significantly expanded the trading band for the ruble against the dollar from the Rub 6.1 to Rub 6.3 range to the Rub 6.1 to Rub 9.5 range, which effectively devalued the Russian currency by approximately 33.7 percent.

A confluence of adverse developments at home and abroad led the Russian government to declare a moratorium. For two years, in 1996 and 1997, Russia posted fiscal deficits that amounted to about 6 to 7 percent of GDP. In 1998, the government's fiscal position sharply deteriorated because of low tax collections and a drop in oil prices. The government attempted to find additional tax revenues to shore up the precarious fiscal position, but the parliament resisted the move. Meanwhile, foreign exchange reserves became badly depleted, declining from US$24 billion in mid-1997 to about US$17 billion shortly before the declaration of the moratorium. This was insufficient to cover even the US$23 billion in foreign debt coming due in the second half of 1998.

The ruble showed some signs of stabilizing after the IMF and others pledged emergency support on July 13. But two days later, on July 15, the currency began to slide again and hit the daily floor until the date of the moratorium. On August 13, the ruble hit Rub 6.4 against the dollar. The price of Russian bonds plummeted as foreign investors, fearing a massive devaluation of the ruble, dumped Russian investments. During the days leading up to the moratorium, the yield on Russian treasury bills skyrocketed to as high as 150 percent. The stock market fell 4.8 percent between August 10 and 14, and, for the year, the market lost about 72.4 percent.

The spread of the Russian crisis. Because of Korea's limited foreign trade with Russia, the problems in Russia were initially expected to have a limited impact on the Korean economy. Exports to Russia made up only about 1.1 percent of the total. Korea's foreign direct investment and construction projects in Russia also made up less than 1 percent of the total. The exposure of Korean financial companies to Russian debt was estimated at US$2.77 billion, of which US$1.64 billion represented credit arranged between the two governments that was not likely to be affected by the moratorium because it was to be repaid in kind. However, the rest—investments by securities and investment trusts—was likely to lead to losses.

Although the direct impact of the Russian crisis appeared to be limited, the indirect impact proved far more devastating as the contagion spread to Latin America and the developed markets. In the credit markets, the prices of the sovereign bonds of the emerging countries collapsed, and the spread widened enormously. The spread on Korea's Foreign Exchange Stabilization Fund bonds—issued at 355 basis points on April 8, 1998 (due for redemption in 2008)—had jumped to 1,000 basis points by August 31. Similarly, the spread on Brazilian government bonds (due for redemption in 2008), at around 377 basis points on April 8, had spiraled to 1,444 basis points by August 31. At the beginning of September, the spread on debt of some emerging countries, including China, Korea, and Thailand, showed some signs of narrowing, but that of other emerging countries, including Brazil, Indonesia, Mexico, and Russia, worsened (table 7.9).

Another casualty of the Russian crisis was Long-Term Capital Management (LTCM), a hedge fund the bets of which in the market proved widely off the mark as a result of the crisis. LTCM reportedly tried to undertake arbitrage trading in spreads between the government bonds of emerging economies, including Russia, and the government bonds of advanced economies, including the United States, and suffered losses totaling US$4 billion. Alarmingly, LTCM had been making highly leveraged investments to maximize returns. Thus, there was a real risk that a disorderly collapse of LTCM would lead to the insolvency of several major lending institutions. This concern prompted the Federal Reserve Bank of New York to intervene and lead an effort to provide US$3.73 billion in emergency funding to LTCM, on September 24.

In the midst of the LTCM crisis, stock markets crashed not only in emerging markets, but also in developed markets. When the Russian Parliament rejected a candidate for prime minister that the market supported, stock markets worldwide fell again, 3.20 percent in Frankfurt, 1.41 percent in Madrid, 1.99 percent in Milan, and 1.54 percent in Paris. In the United States, the Dow Jones Index dropped 512.61 points on August 31, the second largest loss ever up to that time. The NASDAQ market also declined steeply, by 140.43 points, the largest single loss for the market. Market turmoil grew and spread to other markets. On September 10, the Brazilian market fell 15.0 percent, and the Mexican market 9.8 percent. This was followed in Asia the next day by a 5.1 percent drop in Tokyo and close to a 3.5 percent drop in Hong Kong SAR, China.

In currency markets, the dollar showed some downward volatility beginning in September in the wake of soured lending in Latin America and the slowing U.S. economy. Expectations were also growing that the U.S. Federal Reserve would accelerate interest rate cuts in the wake of the pressures brought about by LTCM. At the Federal Open Market Committee meeting on September 29, the Federal Reserve reduced the federal funds interest rate by 0.25 percentage points, to 5.25 percent. Earlier, on September 9, Japanese monetary authorities had cut a key overnight target

Table 7.9 Trends in Spreads on Emerging Market Treasury Bonds, April–September 1998
basis points

Date, indicator	*Korea, Rep. 2003*[a]	*Korea, Rep. 2008*[a]	*Thailand 2007*	*China 2006*	*Malaysia 2006*	*Philippines 2008*	*Mexico 2008*	*Brazil 2008*	*Indonesia 2006*	*Russian Federation 2007*
Issuance interest rate[b]	8.75	8.88	7.75	7.75	7.13	8.88	8.27	9.38	7.75	10.00
Credit rating	Bal/ BB+	—	Bal/ BBB	A3/ BBB+	Baa2/ BBB+	Bal/ BB+	Ba2/ BB	B1/ BB–	B3/ CCC+	B3/ CCC
Apr. 8	329	345	300	130	265	325	289	388	560	—
Apr. 15	283	315	300	120	265	317	299	370	490	493
Apr. 30	301	341	285	110	275	333	305	399	600	495
May 29	430	435	340	140	325	385	335	502	825	635
June 30	485	485	440	155	440	410	367	581	860	957
July 31	395	435	450	190	440	410	340	537	850	1,112
Aug. 26	675	790	825	365	850	800	657	1,194	1,575	3,869
Aug. 27	800	900	850	365	850	850	826	1,434	1,725	4,524
Aug. 28	945	959	860	365	850	960	759	1,365	1,725	4,797
Aug. 31	975	1,000	950	445	950	975	865	1,444	2,100	4,807
A. Sept. 16	785	735	775	300	1,100	750	647	1,276	1,610	4,708
B. Sept. 30	745	715	650	275	1,125	750	702	1,371	1,750	4,406
B–A	–40	–20	–125	–25	25	0	65	105	140	298

Source: International Finance Division, Ministry of Finance and Economy.
Note: — = not available. The years under the countries in the column heads indicate redemption years.
a. Foreign Exchange Stabilization Fund bonds.
b. Some numbers are rounded to the nearest 100th decimal place.

rate to around 0.25 percent. The Canadian central bank followed suit on September 29 with a 0.25 percentage point interest rate cut, from 6.00 percent to 5.75 percent. The Bank of England was also expected to cut its benchmark rate in early October. France and Germany were not expected to make rate cuts ahead of the launching of the European Monetary Union in 1999.

As the financial crisis spread rapidly across markets (Asia, Latin America, Russia, and developed markets), the outlook for the global economy looked increasingly grim. Data Resources Inc. (now part of Global Insight) projected that global economic growth would slow to 1.7 percent in 1998, compared with 3.1 percent in 1997 and 1.9 percent in 1999. More downbeat forecasts had the estimated growth rate at 1.0 percent in 1998 and negative 1.6 percent in 1999. Pressures then began to mount on the G-7 countries to act decisively and in concert to restore global economic growth by strengthening domestic demand, containing the risk of contagion, and supporting the economic recovery of the crisis-stricken countries.

Supply-Dominating Conditions in the Foreign Exchange Market

There was an expectation that the supply of dollars would be ample in Korea in the second half of 1998 relative to the first half of the year. The current account surplus in the first half was US$22.4 billion, but most of the surplus was used to pay off foreign debt and held in deposits by businesses. There was also an additional inflow of US$12.8 billion from the IMF and other financial institutions. Because they were credited to usable foreign exchange reserves, however, this had little impact on the dollar demand-supply conditions in foreign exchange markets.

The projections of a current account surplus of US$12.6 billion and corporate foreign currency deposits of US$11.9 billion meant that additional demand for dollars by businesses was likely to weaken in the second half of 1998. This heightened the risk that a significant portion of the dollars in the trade surplus would be sold off in the markets. Another consideration was that the supply of dollars looked set to increase because of the inflow of foreign investment capital and the proceeds from the sale of overseas assets by domestic companies. The risk of a surfeit of dollars was real. Table 7.10 summarizes the demand-supply conditions on foreign exchange markets as measured by the MOFE. There was some imbalance and some pressure in the won/dollar market in favor of a stronger won, which would hurt exporters.

By the end of June, however, the won was trading at W 973.85 per ¥100, much stronger than the W 1,000 per ¥100 that the market generally expected. When July came, the appreciation of the won persisted, while the yen continued to depreciate. The government therefore faced

Table 7.10 The Prospects of Demand and Supply in Foreign Exchange, 1998
US$, billions

Indicator	*1998*			
	1st half	*2nd half*	*Total*	*1999*
Current account	22.4	12.6	35.0	13.0
Capital account	1.1	7.0	8.1	1.0
Public sector, such as IMF financial support	12.8	1.9[a]	14.7	-6.4
Private sector, such as trade credits	-11.7	5.1	-6.6	7.4
Errors and omissions	-2.9	—	-2.9	-3.0
Overall balance of payments	20.6	19.6	40.2	11.0
Change in usable foreign exchange reserves	28.2	10.0	38.2	3.0
Usable foreign reserves at the end of period	37.0	47.0	47.0[b]	50.0

Source: Ministry of Finance and Economy.
Note: — = not available.
a. Borrowing of US$4.7 billion and redemption of US$2.8 billion.
b. The targeted year-end foreign exchange reserves agreed to with the IMF amounted to US$41 billion.

the delicate task of anchoring the won in a favorable range. Among other reasons, the government did not want to see a sharp volatility movement of the won because of the resulting sudden large inflows of foreign capital. So, it came to an understanding with the IMF that, in addition to smoothing operations, the BOK would intervene with strings attached: it would buy only up to US$250 million a week or up to US$1.5 billion during a three-month period.

The government also encouraged state-owned companies such as Korea Highway Corporation and Korea Housing Corporation to hold their bond offerings at home instead of abroad. Nonetheless, by the end of July, the yield on domestic corporate bonds had fallen to 12.5 percent, closely matching the 11 to 12 percent associated with borrowing abroad.

Despite the efforts by the government, the won continued to appreciate against the U.S. dollar at least until early August. In mid-August, the won/dollar exchange rate returned to the level of early July even after the shock unleashed by the Russian moratorium. The won/yen exchange rate fell after mid-August, but not as much as the won/dollar rate. By early September, the yen had begun to show signs of gaining on the dollar and stabilizing the won/dollar exchange rate, pushing the won/yen exchange rate to about W 1,000 per ¥100. The stronger yen brought some respite to Korea's export companies. Table 7.11 shows key exchange rate movements during the third quarter of 1998.

Stabilizing foreign exchange markets. Despite the turmoil in international financial markets that was precipitated by the Russian moratorium, the won was gaining traction and stabilizing. Because of the excess supply of dollars, foreign exchange reserves in Korea also grew (see table 7.10). The volatility of the won/dollar exchange rate was similar to that of exchange rates in the major advanced economies.

No major problem was anticipated with regard to Korea's ability to service its foreign debt. At the end of September 1998, Korea's foreign liabilities totaled US$151.87 billion, of which long-term debt accounted for US$121.20 billion, and short-term debt US $30.67 billion. The foreign debt (principal) due between the fourth quarter of 1998 and the first half of 1999 came to US$23.75 billion: US$18.66 billion long-term debt and US$5.09 billion short-term debt. The assumption in determining the private sector short-term foreign debt to be redeemed was that most of the

Table 7.11 Foreign Exchange Rates, Third Quarter, 1998

Date		*W/US$*	*W/¥100*	*¥/US$*
July	1	1,374.70	994.18	137.92
	7	1,346.00	963.32	138.65
	15	1,294.60	922.57	140.50
	28	1,218.60	854.83	141.33
	31	1,236.00	860.72	144.65
August	3	1,227.40	847.21	145.63
	11	1,347.00	920.71	147.25
	18	1,330.20	909.41	144.87
	27	1,308.50	900.79	141.87
	31	1,331.80	941.53	140.55
September	3	1,343.90	972.15	134.25
	7	1,331.70	1,064.00	131.95
	11	1,367.30	1,022.66	130.70
	21	1,388.10	1,039.78	134.47
	30	1,373.60	1,023.93	136.66

Source: Korea Financial Telecommunications and Clearings Institute.

debt was related to trade financing and thus revolving. For the short-term foreign debt of financial companies, the assumption was that the debt would be repaid on which the maturity had been extended through negotiations, and about 90 percent of the rest would be rolled over.

The approximately US$24 billion that was due in the first half of 1999 was well within the manageable range given Korea's continued current account surpluses in 1998 and 1999, the borrowing from the Export-Import Bank of Japan and the World Bank, and the increases in foreign direct investment (see table 7.10). Moreover, foreign exchange reserves stood at US$43 billion at the end of September.

However, the spread on Korea's Foreign Exchange Stabilization Fund bonds was past the 700-basis-point mark in September, making it virtually impossible to secure long-term funds from overseas markets. The spread on short-term borrowing did not show much change, but the roll-over ratio was growing slightly worse. As long-term debt became all but inaccessible and short-term financing became more difficult, there was concern that Korea might encounter real difficulties in redeeming foreign debt.

One obvious worry was the risk that international financial markets would trigger the withdrawal of funds from Korea. Because of widespread distress stemming from the Russian moratorium, markets were vulnerable to risks. Another serious worry was that a prolonged global economic slowdown would severely hamper Korea's ability to export goods and aim for an economic rebound. The possibility that foreign investors would conclude that Korea's reform efforts were not genuine and the likelihood of a sudden collapse among the heavily leveraged chaebol companies could not be easily dismissed. At the moment, the supply of the dollar was stronger than the demand, but preparations had to be undertaken to face the worst-case scenario because the situation could easily reverse.

Preparations for the worst-case scenario. The government decided to take several steps to prepare for the worst-case scenario. First, it drafted contingency plans so that it could effectively deal with ongoing global financial instability and the economic downturn. Second, it sought to step up its efforts to encourage exports and boost flagging domestic demand.

Stabilizing the exchange rate was at the top of the agenda. The government decided to take advantage of the imminent passage of the Foreign Investment Promotion Act to attract foreign investment and lower the cost of foreign borrowing by relying more on secured borrowing (for example, through the use of asset-backed securities). In addition, the government wanted to ensure smooth funding from the IMF and the World Bank and promote a consortium of international financial institutions to create backup credit facilities against a variety of contingencies.

Emergency measures were also put into place. If external market conditions deteriorated sharply, the government would seek a maturity extension on a US$2.8 billion Supplemental Reserve Facility loan from the IMF that was coming due in December and secure US$8 billion of the US$23.3 billion pledged by 13 developed countries as a second line of defense against the Korean financial crisis. The government encouraged banks to seek rollovers as their foreign debt came due and left open the possibility of government involvement in facilitating rollovers on the foreign debt of domestic financial companies. In the case of foreign debt owed by domestic nonfinancial companies, the government urged that reliable information about the debt servicing capacities of these companies be collected through the due diligence being undertaken because of the agreements to improve the financial soundness of chaebol companies; the government decided to take relevant steps through the banking supervision authority.

Fortunately, there was no shock—such as a demand by foreign lenders for a large-scale loan redemption—during the third quarter of 1998 despite the worsening external situation. Calm also prevailed in foreign exchange markets, removing the need for the execution of the emergency measures the government had prepared. There was no more discussion about securing funds from the second line of defense the developed countries had promised in the wake of the onset of the financial crisis.

Policies for Robust Growth

The Agreement on Macroeconomic Policies with the IMF

The focus of the policy program with the IMF had been on accumulating foreign exchange reserves and stabilizing the won in the wake of the financial crisis. At the policy review and consultation meeting in the third quarter of 1998, the government and the IMF agreed to shift the focus to alleviating the credit crunch and stimulating domestic demand. The government envisioned that the money supply could be expanded and that interest rates could fall more to help mitigate the credit crunch. Even though the outlook on growth was grimmer and prices looked more stable, the targets in money supply did not drop proportionately compared with the targets set for the second quarter. The target for reserve money was maintained at the previous level, and the target for M3 (monetary aggregate for liquidity—see endnote 8 in chapter 5) was raised only slightly. It was also agreed that the fiscal deficit could be expanded from 1.7 to 4.0 percent of GDP in the second supplementary budget.

The Second Supplementary Budget

The government had decided, by mid-June, to draft a supplementary budget and submit it to the National Assembly on July 30. The supplementary budget provided for W 11.5 trillion in additional spending and allowed the deficit to reach 4 percent of GDP. On the tax revenue side, however, it appeared that there would be a shortfall of about W 5.5 trillion even if tax collection improved and the additional tax revenue from supplementary government spending were taken into account. Given the expected revenue shortfall, the amount of extra expenditure came to approximately W 6 trillion.

The resources of the supplementary budget were to be mobilized through proceeds from the sale of state-owned enterprises (W 2.9 trillion), budgetary adjustments (W 700 billion), and government bond issues (W 7.9 trillion). With W 6 trillion in extra spending, the total government budget came to W 80.1 trillion, up 12.2 percent over the 1997 budget.

The major expenditures were targeted at unemployment benefits (W 1 trillion), contributions to credit guarantee institutions to support SME restructuring and export activities (W 500 billion), recapitalization of the KDB and the Industrial Bank of Korea (W 1.2 trillion), and a capital injection into the Export Insurance Fund and the Export-Import Bank of Korea (W 300 billion). Also targeted were a raft of social overhead capital projects (W 1.2 trillion) that had been effective in creating jobs, underwriting municipal bonds to support local and regional governments (W 1.6 trillion), and interest payments on government bonds (W 200 billion).

However, before the deliberations on the supplementary budget could be concluded at the National Assembly, heavy torrential rains from August 5 to 19 caused major damage. According to the Central Disaster Relief Center, there were 206 deaths and 35 missing (and assumed dead). The number of flood victims was estimated at 150,000, and property damage was extensive, including houses, roads, bridges, cropland, and livestock. It was being estimated that the damage from the rains was at record levels, and many analysts predicted that the economic growth rate would drop by 1 percentage point as a direct result. Coming on the heels of the financial crisis, the damage was particularly devastating among the people. The fear that more difficulties lay ahead was more or less confirmed when the BOK announced, on August 27, that the GDP growth rate for the second quarter of 1998 had slowed to a shocking negative 6.6 percent, the lowest rate since 1980. Worse still, private consumption had fallen 11.7 percent, the most significant decline since 1970. These figures heightened the sense of crisis and cast a pall on the daily lives of the people.

The massive rain and flood damage and the sharply deteriorating economic outlook made it all but certain that additional money would have to be allocated to deal with the problems at hand. Estimates of the costs associated with the flood damage came to about W 1 trillion. Likewise, tax revenues, especially revenues from the value added tax and customs duties, were expected to fall by approximately W 3 trillion because of reduced economic activity, the tax deferrals among flood victims, and decreased imports.

The second supplementary budget, including additional spending related to the summer floods and the lower tax revenues, passed the

National Assembly on September 2. In the budget, the increase in expenditures was enlarged by W 700 billion, to W 6.7 trillion. The shortfalls in tax revenues were expanded by W 2.8 trillion, to W 8.3 trillion. The expected W 15 trillion deficit was to be covered by the sale of stakes in state-run companies and other proceeds (W 2.6 trillion), spending cuts (W 700 billion), and new bond issues (W 11.7 trillion). The new consolidated budget deficit was expected to rise from 4 to 5 percent of GDP.

Tax Packages for the Economic Stimulus

The government put into effect a series of tax measures designed to help the struggling economy. On July 10, the special consumption tax applicable to luxury goods such as automobiles and household appliances was cut by 30 percent. In August, the temporary 10 percent tax credit that was to apply until June 1999 on investments by manufacturing companies was expanded. Whereas the former tax credit was limited to investments to replace obsolete equipment and enhance production and energy-saving activities, the new tax credit covered all new investment in plant and equipment. As a way to shore up the falling revenue base, the government increased the tax rate on interest income and the traffic tax. In light of the extremely high interest rates that prevailed following the onset of the financial crisis, the tax rate on interest income (including the resident tax) was raised from 22 to 24.2 percent. The traffic tax was also raised by W 100 per liter of gasoline and by W 80 per liter of diesel.

More Aggressive Monetary and Credit Policies

There were three primary tasks facing monetary policy in the third quarter of 1998, as follows: (1) expand the money supply, push for a reduction in interest rates, and stimulate domestic demand so as to prevent further decline in the real economy and protect the growth potential of the economy; (2) improve the access to consumer credit and financing so as to ensure that the expansive monetary policies would lead to more robust consumer spending and investment; and (3) continue to provide support for SMEs, exporters, and the housing sector, all of which had suffered heavily from the credit crunch since the onset of the financial crisis.

The push for lower interest rates and easier consumer credit. By July 1998, the demand-supply conditions of the dollar had improved and the won had begun to show an appreciating trend. In response, the BOK intervened in the open market. This led to a sharply lower overnight call rate. Although Russia's declaration of a moratorium in August injected new fears and exerted pressure in financial markets, the won/dollar exchange rate continued to show relative calm, and the overnight call rate had dropped to 9.97 percent by August 4 and to 8.59 percent by the end of the month.

When the central banks in the United States and other major developed countries cut their benchmark interest rates on September 30, the BOK followed suit with a cut in the open market operation rate from 8.1 to 7 percent. This caused the call rate to drop to the 7 percent range. The yield on corporate bonds fell from 15.5 percent on July 1 to 11.7 percent at the end of August. It bounced back somewhat in September, but fell to 11.9 percent at the end of September.

The weighted average interest rate on bank loans shifted downward in May, but stood at about 14.3 percent at the end of September, still significantly higher than the precrisis rate. It was only in November that the rate began to drop to the precrisis level of around 12 percent. The primary reasons for the slow decline in the bank lending rate relative to market rates were (1) deposits made during high interest rate periods represented a relatively high proportion of bank deposits, and (2) there was still a high premium associated with the risk of corporate default.

The government decided to use the US$2 billion loan secured from the Export-Import Bank of the United States during President Kim Dae-Jung's visit to that country in June for the purpose of financing imports of facility equipment and urged the KDB to expand lending for investment in equipment. It decided to encourage private consumption to keep the economy from sliding deeper into recession and shift the focus to improving consumer credit and financing as a way to help ease the credit crunch that many businesses faced. As part of this effort, the government increased the supply of credit for housing purchases and encouraged banks to provide financing for purchases of durable goods by enabling credit guarantee institutions to offer special credit guarantees to selling agencies. The government encouraged banks to step up their purchases of bills issued by installment finance companies so as to help credit flows and support the securitization of such bills and similar assets.

Credit support for SMEs, exporters, and housing purchases. As a way to help ease the credit crunch that many SMEs and exporters faced, the government expanded the credit guarantees available to these companies. Funds allocated through the government budget and loans from the Asian Development Bank were used during the first half of 1998 to boost credit guarantee financing significantly. The funding proved inadequate because of a rapid increase in payments by subrogation, and, as a result, the reserve power of credit guarantee providers was expected to face a major shortfall in the second half of 1998. In response, the government decided to allocate W 500 billion from the second supplementary budget and US$1 billion from the World Bank loan for two credit guarantee funds by the end of the year with the goal of expanding credit guarantees to about W 10 trillion (about W 5 trillion in fresh credit guarantees) for SMEs and exporters, especially those involved in the workout process. The BOK also lent a helping hand by raising the aggregate credit ceiling for SMEs from W 5.6 trillion to W 7.6 trillion beginning on September 1, 1998.

Export financing was targeted so as to ease the financing difficulties of exporters. Trade financing usually involved making lines of credit available to exporters based on past export performance or documentation such as export letters of credit. Trade financing for SMEs could be facilitated by BOK support through the Aggregate Credit Ceiling Facilities. Accordingly, the BOK decided to expand trade financing through its Aggregate Credit Ceiling Facilities beginning July 1. In August, it simplified the procedures for obtaining trade financing. On August 28, the credit guarantee providers expanded the eligibility for credit guarantees for trade financing from SMEs to large companies except the 30 largest chaebols and raised the guarantee amount from one-third to one-half of annual export sales.

A thorny issue was the demand for trade financing by large companies receiving credit guarantees for trade financing, which were allowed in the WTO rules. However, because the BOK took part in trade financing by providing credit at below-market interest rates and because such BOK support otherwise resembled export subsidies, which represented a violation of WTO rules, the demand of the large companies for direct support was initially rejected. The government also had to take into account its agreement with the IMF that it would support only the SMEs. Following discussions on the issue among the relevant authorities on August 18, the decision was reached that, rather than giving direct support for trade financing to large companies, the Korea Export Insurance Corporation was to provide guarantees for discounts on the trade bills of large companies, and the maximum amount to be made available for discounting was to be fine-tuned. The KDB was to set up a trade bill discounting service with about W 1 trillion at interest rates in the 13 to 15 percent range, much lower than the 17 percent market rate. In August 1998, the export finance support ratio and the import finance support ratio were 67.4 and 60.9 percent, respectively.

As housing prices continued to fall and the number of unsold housing units increased, the government decided to make more financing available for housing purchases. Table 7.12 shows the trends in housing prices and unsold housing units.

In July 1998, W 1.7 trillion was made available for the National Housing Fund, and W 600 billion for a housing fund created by a consortium of private sector commercial banks, including Housing & Commercial Bank and Kookmin Bank, to support housing purchases. On September 26, the National Housing Fund and the commercial banks decided to expand housing loans by W 2.0 trillion and W 1.65 trillion, respectively. The Korea National Housing Corporation lent its support to the struggling housing market by spending W 300 billion to purchase unsold housing units and rent them out until they could be sold off when the market improved. Housing & Commercial Bank also decided to make loans up

Table 7.12 Housing Prices and Unsold Housing Units, December 1997–July 1998

	1997	*1998*		
Indicator	*December*	*March*	*May*	*July*
Monthly housing price growth, %	-0.5	-2.8	-2.4	-0.4
Unsold housing units, 1,000s	88.9	97.2	108.4	116.4

Source: MOFE 1998s.

to W 200 billion available to businesses and individuals acquiring unsold housing units for leasing purposes.

The Credit Crunch and the Staggering Economy

Despite interest rate cuts and other expansive monetary policies during the third quarter of 1998, the credit crunch persisted, and there was no sign that the economy was poised for any noticeable rebound. Part of the reason was that economic uncertainty deepened amid the unprecedented restructuring of corporate and financial companies, which diluted or weakened the effectiveness of government policies. Another reason was that it took time for government policies to have an impact throughout the economy.

Bank lending continued to shrink during the third quarter as it had during the second quarter. As a result, finding credit was as difficult as ever for most SMEs. In contrast, the top five chaebol companies fared much better by raising funds through bonds and CP. In essence, bank lending shrank because banks were curtailing the additional extension of credit so that they could comply with the minimum BIS capital requirements and the high default risk of their corporate customers. The corporate debt issued, especially by large companies, had picked up sharply since July as companies scrambled to raise funds before tougher rules on funding took effect in the course of corporate restructuring for financial soundness and because borrowing costs had fallen at home relative to overseas, making it more attractive to issue debt at home. In particular, corporate debt issues became even more concentrated among large companies after guarantee insurance companies ceased the guarantee business on corporate bond issues in August, prompting primary bond markets to shift from secured to unsecured bonds that were issued mostly by large companies.

During the third quarter, the debt issued by the top five chaebols made up 78.8 percent of the total. If other blue-chip companies such as Korea Telecom and POSCO are included, the share of major companies in total debt increased to close to 90 percent. Stock issues jumped sharply in September, mostly because of recapitalization efforts following the injection of public funds during the first round of bank restructuring. The discounted purchase of CP by banks and investment trusts fell noticeably in August following the imposition, on July 25, of a ceiling on the amount of CP the banks and investment trusts could acquire from the same issuers. However, the slack was also picked up by merchant banks, which were exempted from the purchase restrictions. Discounting by securities companies of the CP issued by the top five chaebols dropped following the imposition of the CP possession ceiling.

In the stock market, the Korea composite stock price index climbed to 365.2 on July 20, buoyed by falling interest rates and aggressive buying by foreign investors. However, the index had fallen by the end of the month on pressure from the weakening yen. Share prices struggled throughout August because of a combination of developments at home and abroad such as the falling yen, the business suspension of the Han Nam Investment Trust, and the Russian moratorium. Stock prices at the end of September had changed little over the previous month.

The developments in financial markets were reflected in key monetary aggregates. Discrepancies in the monetary aggregates became apparent as the movements among financial assets picked up in response to financial restructuring and the introduction of deposit insurance and low interest rates. The growth of M3 (monetary aggregate for liquidity—see endnote 8 in chapter 5) was on a slow downward trend in the third quarter relative to the 15.9 percent in December 1997. Despite the persistent credit crunch that was reducing bank lending, the sharp increases in corporate debt issues by large chaebol companies were most likely responsible for the slower growth in M3. However, M2 (monetary aggregate for broad money—see endnote 8 in chapter 5) grew at a rapid pace as banks cut back funding through short-term high-cost instruments such as certificates of deposit and repurchase agreements and, instead, turned for funding to low-cost time deposits. Funds in bank trust accounts, which were not subject to deposit insurance, also moved to regular time deposit accounts. Table 7.13 shows the trends in key financial indicators.

The Continued Sluggishness of the Economy

The economy continued to struggle in the third quarter of 1998. The pace of the slowdown moderated somewhat in September and seemed poised for a reverse. On the domestic demand side, investment declined noticeably. Orders for domestically produced machinery continued to contract, but the pace of the contraction slowed. Construction permits for industrial and commercial facilities plummeted, albeit at a more modest speed, in September.

Table 7.13 Trends in Key Financial Indicators, Third Quarter, 1998
won, billions

Indicator	*July*	*August*	*September*
Total bank loans, month-on-month	339.8	–4,059.7	–1,710.4
Issuance of corporate bonds	6,057.4	6,629.0	6,729.0
Paid-in capital increases and initial public offerings	426.7	31.8	3,903.2
Discounted CP, month-on-month	5,868.1	881.5	2,502.2
Korea composite stock price index, monthly average	327.8	312.8	312.2
Foreign investment in stocks	41.1	–59.6	142.9
M2 growth, %	20.0	20.8	21.0
M3 growth, %	14.0	14.0	13.3

Sources: Bank of Korea and Ministry of Finance and Economy.

Note: M2 = monetary aggregate for broad money. M3 = monetary aggregate for liquidity.

The sale of durable consumer goods such as automobiles and home appliances was extremely sluggish throughout July and August, but picked up somewhat in September on the rising sales of compact cars.

Industrial production also fell amid falling domestic demand and weak exports in July and August, but looked more upbeat in September. Outbound shipments for export slowed in July and August, and shipments for domestic consumption continued to fall. In September, export shipments picked up on the back of rebounding exports of automobiles and semiconductors. Despite the drop in shipments, the reduction in industrial production led to a corresponding decline in inventories. The average manufacturing operation ratio plummeted to a low of 64.6 percent in July, but rebounded for the first time in 1998 in September, to 70.5 percent.

The ratio of dishonored checks and bills during the third quarter indicated that the number of defaults increased in July as corporate restructuring gained momentum, but came down in August. The number of bankrupt companies continued to fall, dropping from 3,323 in January to 1,085 in September. The ratio of newly established companies to bankrupt companies in the seven largest cities improved from 1.1 in January to 4.2 in September. Table 7.14 shows key economic indicators during the third quarter.

Table 7.14 Economic Trends, Third Quarter, 1998, Year-on-Year *percent*

Indicator	*July*	*August*	*September*
Industrial production	–14.0	–12.8	–1.7
Domestic construction orders	-47.0	-41.3	-50.4
Orders for domestically produced machines	-26.6	-25.3	-14.6
Wholesale and retail sales	-17.5	-16.3	-11.6
Average manufacturing operation ratio	64.6	65.1	70.5
Nationwide ratio of dishonored bills	0.50	0.41	0.31

Source: Ministry of Finance and Economy.

Table 7.15 Economic Projections for 1998 and 1999

Indicator	*1997*	*1998*[a]	*1999*[a]
Economic growth rate, %	5.5	–5	2
Current account, US$, billions	-8.2	37.0	18.0
Export growth rate, %	5.0	-2.5	1.0
Import growth rate, %	-3.8	–30	16
Consumer price increase, %	4.5	8	5

Source: MOFE 1998t.
a. Approximate projections.

As the economy spiraled downward, the government saw a need to lay out mid- to long-term economic recovery plans to the public and maintain an upbeat outlook. On September 2, 1998, at the 10th meeting of the EPCC, the minister of finance and economy put forth a projection that economic growth would rebound from negative 5 percent in 1998 to positive 2 percent by 1999 and resume a level close to the potential growth rate by 2000, provided economic reform stayed on track and aggressive macroeconomic policies were pursued to reinvigorate the economy.

The current account balance was expected to turn in a large surplus in 1998 because of anemic domestic demand. For 1999, the current account surplus was forecast to continue despite a modest rebound in imports. Consumer prices behaved well and were projected to drop to the 5 percent level in 1999. Table 7.15 sums up the key projections made at the time.

Notes

1. The 12 banks were Boram, Busan, Daegu, Hana, Housing & Commercial, Jeju, Jeonbuk, Kookmin, KorAm, Kwangju, Kyongnam, and Shinhan.

2. The seven life insurance companies were Daeshin, Hanil, Hansung, Kumho, Shinhan, SK, and Tong Yang. The two non–life insurance companies were Dongbu and Haedong.

3. The seven companies were Chosun, Donga, Doowon, Handuk, Hankook, Kookmin, and Pacific.

4. The four life insurance companies were BYC, Coryo, Kukje, and Taeyang.

5. The five companies were Busan, Central Lease, Daegu, Kwangeun, and Seoul.

6. The eight banks were Chohung, Commercial Bank of Korea, Hanil, Korea Development, Korea Exchange, Korea First, Seoul, and Shinhan.

7. Among others, the 13 business groups included Donga, Keopyung, Kohap, and Shinho. The large independent companies included Dongbang T&C, Dongwha Duty Free Shop, Hanchang, and Ildong Pharmaceutical Co.

8. Ownership by an individual shareholder (and related persons) was capped at 15 percent for investment trusts operating in Seoul and 30 percent elsewhere. Ownership was also capped at 10 percent if a shareholder (and related persons) held equity in two or more investment trusts.

8

Getting the Economy Back on Track and Quickening the Pace of Restructuring, October–December 1998

Policy Challenges and the Shifting Economic Landscape

Changing the Global Economic Environment

The trouble in the Russian Federation continued to roil markets worldwide in October. The International Monetary Fund (IMF) and other international forecasters were predicting a slowing global economy (table 8.1).

Amid mounting economic concerns, concerted international efforts were undertaken on multiple fronts to deal with the uncertainties in financial markets. First, a broad consensus on the need for cuts in interest rate was reached. The U.S. Federal Reserve cut the interest rate on September 29 and, on October 15, cut the federal funds rate and the rediscount rate by a quarter of a percentage point. Other central banks in the developed countries soon followed suit.

Second, serious efforts to prevent financial crises in the emerging countries and stabilize international financial markets were beginning to be initiated. In early October, at the IMF and World Bank Group Annual Meetings of the Boards of Governors, discussions took place on revamping the international financial architecture. When signs pointed to a brewing crisis in Brazil, U.S. President Bill Clinton proposed, at the G-22 meeting in early October, that the IMF provide contingent lines of credit to countries susceptible to financial contagion and that the World Bank and regional

Table 8.1 Projections of World Economic Growth for 1998 and 1999
percent

Source	*1998*	*1999*
IMF	2.0	2.5
Wharton Econometric Forecasting Associates	2.2	2.8
Data Resources Inc.	1.7	1.9

Source: MOFE 1998u.
Note: The historical trend rate of world economic growth is estimated at around 4 percent.

financial institutions provide credit guarantees so that capital could flow back to emerging countries. After protracted debates, the U.S. Congress passed, on October 21, legislation authorizing participation in a capital increase of US$18 billion to the IMF. Japan also announced the New Miyazawa Initiative to provide US$30 billion—US$15 billion for short-term funds and another US$15 billion for mid- to long-term funds—to support Asia's economic recovery.

Third, as these actions gained momentum, the Japanese yen/U.S. dollar exchange rate, which had traded at around ¥130 in September, had fallen to ¥116 by mid-October, a 13 percent appreciation. This was partly caused by the slowing U.S. economy despite the interest rate cuts and the distress stemming from the Long-Term Capital Management fiasco (see chapter 7), which prompted short-term money to rush into Japanese markets.

In the Republic of Korea, the first round of restructuring among financial companies was coming to a close, and this restored a measure of calm and stability in financial markets. However, the Korean market was in the grip of a debilitating credit crunch, and the overall situation continued to be dire. Production, consumption, investment, and exports were all contracting, and unemployment continued to show a stubbornly high rate.

The Policy Implications of the Changing Environment

Korean foreign exchange markets were still caught up in the distress generated by the exchange crisis in Russia, and the spread on Korea's Foreign Exchange Stabilization Fund bonds had widened sharply. For some time, this made it all but impossible for Korea to raise money through overseas investors and lenders. Brazil and Russia were on the brink of what increasingly looked like a financial crisis, and it was not clear that Korea would be able to return to international credit markets with hopes of a more favorable borrowing environment any time soon.

In the face of mounting adversity, the government had to aim at several goals. First, it had to maintain the stability of the demand-supply conditions for the dollar. Although usable foreign exchange reserves totaled US$43.37 billion at the end of September, the level still warranted close monitoring. This was especially important because of the US$2.8 billion due in December 1998 and the US$9.7 billion due in 1999 to the IMF. The government also faced the arduous task of differentiating Korea from deeply troubled emerging economies in the minds of foreign investors and raising the country's sovereign ratings.

Second, because the global economic slowdown was all but certain and domestic consumption and investment were in a downward spiral, macroeconomic policy had to focus on expanding exports and preventing a further contraction in domestic demand. To achieve these tasks, government spending had to be significantly augmented, and the efforts to lower interest rates and alleviate the credit crunch had to be stepped up. More effective assistance to small and medium enterprises (SMEs) and exporters, along with more sector-specific support, was also needed.

Third, the pace of restructuring had to accelerate and the outcome had to be successful because of the shaky confidence of international investors regarding the health of the Korean economy and because only the first phase of restructuring had been completed.

Fourth, in response to the difficulties that the unemployed had to undergo during the cold winter and the shortcomings and weaknesses that had been identified in the implementation of the unemployment measures, the government endeavored to make genuine, meaningful support available to the unemployed.

Instability in International Financial Markets and the Government Response

Concerted Action on the Global Economy

The leaders and finance ministers of the G-7 declared in their communiqué on October 30 that the main thrust of their macroeconomic policies would shift from controlling inflationary pressure to creating an environment more favorable to growth. As a follow-up, the U.S. Federal Reserve lowered the federal funds rate to 4.75 percent and the rediscount rate to 4.50 percent on November 17. In Europe, the central banks of Spain and the United Kingdom cut their short-term rates from 4.25 to 3.75 percent and from 7.50 to 7.25 percent, respectively. In late October, the central banks of Denmark and Italy cut their rates from 4.75 to 4.65 percent and from 5.00 to 4.00 percent, respectively. In contrast, France and Germany announced that they intended to hold their rates steady at 3.3 percent. Japan already had extremely low interest rates, but, on November 16, announced a stimulus package totaling ¥24 trillion. US$41.5 billion was allocated to deal with the crisis brewing in Brazil, and the related actions were initiated on December 12. The IMF provided US$18 billion; the Inter-American Development Bank and the World Bank provided US$4.5 billion each; and 20 developed countries provided US$14.5 billion.

At the IMF and World Bank Group annual meeting, the discussions on international financial system architecture highlighted the weaknesses in national and international financial systems that had been revealed through the Asian and Russian crises. These weaknesses may be summarized as follows: (1) Insufficient market information, flawed legal institutions and organizations, lack of transparency and accountability, and other shortcomings of governance had undermined the effective functioning and efficiency of markets. (2) A transparent, uniformly applicable set of internationally accepted system principles or standards was needed. (3) Sound economic and financial structures, consistent macroeconomic policies, effective financial supervisory bodies, and the orderly and well-sequenced liberalization of capital accounts were needed to reduce capital market volatility. (4) When markets became volatile, there was a general withdrawal of funds from emerging markets without regard for the diversity of the issues and prospects facing these markets, and this could needlessly fuel a contagion.

In general, the discussions on revamping the international financial architecture centered on five key elements: transparency, the soundness of the financial system, the involvement of the private sector in crisis prevention and resolution, the orderly liberalization of capital accounts, and the promotion of internationally accepted standards and codes of good practice.

In the case of transparency, it was argued that national authorities needed to improve the level of transparency of macroeconomic policies such as fiscal policies and provide accurate macroeconomic statistics as the IMF had recommended. To ensure sound financial systems, responsible lending practices (including risk assessment), effective governance structures, and tighter financial supervision were proposed. For private sector involvement, it was argued that outflows of short-term capital from a private sector—namely, foreign banks—that is inevitably bailed out through the official supports of the IMF and others were encouraging moral hazard. The private sector had therefore to be bailed in to prevent and resolve crises. For orderly capital account liberalization, the IMF noted that it was desirable in principle, but that the sequence of liberalization should also be carefully considered in light of problems that could arise from the erratic short-term movement of capital. With respect to the emphasis on internationally accepted standards and practices, the IMF was urged to play a leading role in promoting more transparent fiscal and monetary policies, developing and propagating standards on economic statistics, and monitoring markets. A consensus was also reached on the need for an expanded role for the work of international standard-setting bodies such as the Basel Committee on Banking Supervision on, for example, banking supervision, accounting, auditing, bankruptcy, and corporate governance.

The Difficulties of Emerging Economies in International Financial Markets

As interest rates in the G-7 countries headed lower, stock markets worldwide, which had been badly bruised by the Russian moratorium, began to surge in mid-October. Markets rallied in late November after the U.S. Federal Reserve Board cut its interest rates three times and the IMF announced its rescue plans for Brazil. By mid-December, share prices in New York had rebounded to the levels of July. However, the dollar continued to slide against other major currencies. The yen/dollar exchange rate, in particular, reached ¥116 per dollar in mid-October, but was hovering between ¥110 and ¥120 by December. As markets stabilized in late November, emerging countries, many of which had been shut out of the global credit markets in the wake of the Russian moratorium, hoped to resume borrowing on these markets. Table 8.2 shows the spreads in secondary markets on the sovereign bonds of several emerging economies.

However, several potential risks still loomed. In particular, there was a good chance of a weakening yen because of the slow economic recovery in Japan, and markets were still skittish over worries prompted by the Brazilian and Russian crises. At the same time, Korea had not been able to restore the confidence of foreign investors about the issue of whether it would fail in reform and restructuring. It also faced steep spreads on its Foreign Exchange Stabilization Fund bonds. Korea's sovereign rating was still below investment grade. On the other hand, the roll-over ratio on short-term foreign borrowing by Korean domestic banks had improved from 80 percent in November to above 90 percent in December. Overall, the outlook for market conditions between November 1998 and the first half of 1999 was improving, but there were many downside risks that warranted the concern of policy makers.

Difficulties in Access to International Credit Markets and the IMF Loan Payoff

By November, the IMF had disbursed US$18 billion of the US$21 billion it had planned to lend to Korea. Of this US$18 billion, US$12.5 billion was accounted for by the Supplemental Reserve Facility, and, of this amount, US$2.8 billion was due in December 1998 and US$9.7 billion was due in 1999. The IMF conveyed to the Korean government its strong desire to have the amount due in December paid off as scheduled. The explanation given was that Korea's foreign exchange reserves had already exceeded US$41 billion in August, which was ahead of schedule because this was

Table 8.2 Trends in Spreads on Emerging Market Treasury Bonds, Fourth Quarter, 1998
basis points

Indicator	*Korea, Rep. 2003*	*Korea, Rep. 2008*	*Thailand 2007*	*China 2006*	*Philippines 2008*	*Mexico 2008*	*Malaysia 2006*	*Brazil 2008*	*Indonesia 2006*	*Russian Federation 2007*
Issuance interest rates[a]	8.75	8.88	7.75	7.75	8.88	8.63	7.13	9.38	7.75	10.00
Credit ratings	Ba1/ BB+	—	Ba1/ BBB–	A3/ BB+	Ba1/ BB+	Ba2/ BB	Baa3/ BBB+	B2/ BB–	B3/ CCC+	B3/ CCC
Sept. 30	745	715	650	275	750	702	1,125	1,371	1,750	4,406
Oct. 15	675	635	625	275	660	607	1,000	1,104	1,850	5,105
Oct. 30	575	550	550	250	560	589	890	1,140	1,350	4,074
Nov. 16	475	480	440	250	460	517	665	974	1,000	4,398
Nov. 30	425	445	360	225	445	494	620	865	750	3,422
Dec. 15	420	447	385	250	450	517	635	1,089	1,090	4,312
Dec. 31	340	375	375	240	425	514	620	1,135	1,120	4,200

Source: International Finance Division, Ministry of Finance and Economy.

Note: — = not available. The dates under the countries in column heads indicate redemption years.

a. Some numbers are rounded to the nearest 100th decimal place.

the target for the last month of the year. The IMF noted that future debt payments could be deferred if the financial market situation deteriorated and Korea encountered financing difficulties.

Because the repayment of the Supplemental Reserve Facility on time according to the schedule would send a positive message to international investors and help enhance the perception of foreign investors with regard to Korea, the government saw the debt payment as an opportunity. Nonetheless, the money might also be needed at home if external conditions unexpectedly deteriorated. So, the government decided to examine the issue thoroughly, consider if full payment, partial payment, or full deferment was the better course, and negotiate with the IMF once a decision had been reached.

According to an assessment undertaken by the Ministry of Finance and Economy (MOFE) regarding the demand-supply conditions of the dollar, Korea's usable foreign exchange reserves were likely to be in the US$46 billion–US$47 billion range by the end of 1998 and in the US$50 billion–US$51 billion range in 1999 even if the debt payment was made to the IMF. These estimated amounts were judged sufficient in the context of Korea's foreign trade situation, expected capital flows, and external debt coverage ratio.

The IMF Debt Payment and the Agreement on a Currency Swap with Japan

Even though there was a steady pool of dollars in the foreign exchange reserves, there was always the possibility that unexpected external shocks could suddenly put the economy in a perilous position again. This was the thinking behind the decision reached by the Korean government on November 26 concerning the repayment of the IMF loans. First, the government decided to (1) seek approximately US$10 billion as a backup facility to supplement foreign exchange reserves; (2) step up its monitoring of the availability of dollars among large companies; (3) consult closely with credit-rating agencies to explore ways to upgrade Korea's sovereign rating; (4) in consultation with the IMF, pay back the US$2.8 billion due in December 1998 and the US$1 billion due in January 1999; and (5) discuss with the IMF the loan payments due beginning in February 1999.

Accordingly, the government explained to the IMF in early December its plan to pay off the loans due in December 1998 and January 1999 and notified the IMF of its decision to make the loan payments due in December 1998. Regarding the plan to borrow up to US$10 billion in backup funds, the government decided that it would seek US$5 billion through the New Miyazawa Initiative and secure the other US$5 billion through borrowing supported by the guarantees of international institutions or through consortium loans. However, the plan to raise money through international institutions was soon scrapped after the foreign reserve position had improved.

In October, the government proposed a plan for a currency swap between the central banks of Korea and Japan as a means to generate backup support. In December, Japan and Korea agreed on a US$5 billion package, and, on January 15, 1999, the finance ministers of the two countries finalized the agreement. Under the agreement, the Bank of Korea (BOK)—the Korean central bank—could swap Korean won for U.S. dollars held by the Bank of Japan if difficulties arose in obtaining foreign currency for funding purposes. The money exchanged was to be used for trade financing, support for SMEs, and other domestic economic needs. This was a major development. The agreement enabled Korea to improve significantly the short-term foreign currency situation and paved the way for swap agreements with other Asian economies.

Enhanced Economic Diplomacy and Raising Korea's Sovereign Ratings

Amid turmoil in international financial markets, one of the surest ways for the government to raise the confidence of investors and markets was to differentiate Korea from other troubled economies. Because international investors tended to perceive most economies as either high risk or low risk, it was crucial for Korea to be perceived as a low-risk market. The government therefore sought to upgrade its standing among major credit-rating agencies by highlighting its economic reforms and the outlook for economic recovery. In October, the minister of finance and economy visited Moody's and Standard and Poor's in the United States and made the argument that the prospects for Korea's growth were improving. A government delegation visited Fitch in the United Kingdom for the same purpose.

The credit-rating agencies noted that the amount of nonperforming and other troubled assets held by Korean financial companies had been underestimated and predicted that the cost of the government bailout would exceed W 64 trillion: W 180 trillion according to Moody's and W 85 trillion according to Standard and Poor's. They commended Korea for the progress it had achieved in the reform of the *chaebols*—the large family-controlled and family-run groups that dominate business in Korea—and the effort to reduce chaebol debt, but also emphasized the unfinished work ahead and the persistently high debt-equity ratios of the chaebol companies. There were some doubts about whether the Korean economy would, in fact, be able to turn around and grow rather than shrink in 1999. For Moody's, one particular concern was whether relations with the Democratic People's Republic of Korea would improve markedly going forward.

The three major credit-rating agencies maintained their previous ratings until October. In November, they dispatched their rating teams to the Republic of Korea for a first-hand look at the situation. Then, on

December 19, Moody's announced that it would put Korea up for review for a possible rating upgrade in relation to its foreign currency debt. In the meantime, it gave Korea's won-denominated government debt, not subject to review, an investment grade rating of Baa1.

During consideration of a possible rating upgrade, the necessary due diligence usually takes up to three months to complete. Moody's planned to send its sovereign rating team to Korea in early 1999. Then, on December 22, Fitch announced that Korea would be considered for a rating upgrade. So, the developments on the rating front were positive for Korea. Table 8.3 shows key credit ratings through December 1998.

Throughout the fourth quarter of 1998, the government engaged in aggressive economic diplomacy in its effort to seek external support. President Kim Dae-Jung held summit meetings with his counterparts in Japan in early October and in the United States later the same month, and he took part in the Asia-Pacific Economic Cooperation meetings in mid-November and in the ASEAN+3 meetings (the members of the Association of Southeast Asian Nations, plus China, Japan, and Korea) in mid-December. As a result of the Korea-Japan summit meeting, Korea reached 10 agreements with Japan, including a US$3 billion loan facility through the Export-Import Bank of Japan, the resumption of regular meetings at the ministerial level, early adoption of an agreement on the avoidance of double taxation, and mutual cooperation on aerospace businesses. At the Korea–United States summit meeting, the United States reaffirmed that it would consistently support the economic recovery of Korea. At the ASEAN+3 meetings, it was agreed that China, Japan, and Korea would be regular participants. The ASEAN+3 countries also adopted President Kim Dae-Jung's proposal for the formation of vision groups for fresh initiatives to reinvigorate intraregional investment and trade through the region's private sector businesses.

Maintaining the Optimal Exchange Rate

For the fourth quarter, the capital account posted a US$1.52 billion deficit, but the current account showed a surplus of US$8.91 billion, meaning that the supply of foreign exchange was well in excess of the demand. However, exports of goods had been on a downward trend since May. With the balance of payments in surplus, the size of usable foreign exchange reserves grew in the fourth quarter (table 8.4). By the end of December, even after the loan repayment of US$2.8 billion to the IMF, usable foreign exchange reserves stood at US$48.51 billion.

At the end of 1998, Korea's total external liabilities stood at US$148.7 billion, down US$3.17 billion from the US$151.87 billion at the end of September. The liabilities were also down US$10.5 billion from the level at the end of 1997. Long-term liabilities represented US$118.01 billion, about 79.4 percent of the total. Short-term debt was US$30.7 billion.

Table 8.3 Trends in the Republic of Korea's Sovereign Ratings by Major Credit-Rating Agencies

Standard and Poor's		*Moody's*		*Fitch*		*Debt repayment capacity*	*Grade*
AAA		Aaa		AAA		Strongest	Investment grade
AA+		Aa1		AA+			
AA		Aa2		AA		Very good	
AA–	Before Oct. 23, 1997	Aa3		AA–	Before Nov. 25, 1997		
A+	Oct. 24, 1997	A1	Before Nov. 27, 1997	A+			
A		A2		A	Nov. 26, 1997	Good	
A–	Nov. 25, 1997	A3	Nov. 28, 1997	A–			
BBB+		Baa1		BBB+			
BBB		Baa2	Dec. 11, 1997	BBB	Dec. 11, 1997	Adequate	
BBB–	Dec. 11, 1997	Baa3		BBB–			
BB+	After Feb. 17, 1998	Ba1	After Dec. 21, 1997	BB+	After Feb. 2, 1998		Speculative grade
BB		Ba2		BB		A little uncertain	
B–		Ba3		BB–			
B+	Dec. 23, 1997	B1		B+			
B		B2		B		Uncertain	
B–		B3		B–	Dec. 23, 1997		
CCC+		Caa		CCC+		Highly uncertain	
D		C		C		Highest uncertainty	

Source: Korea Economic Daily, November 5, 1998.
Note: The data are based on credit ratings on bonds denominated in foreign currencies.

Table 8.4 Trends in Foreign Exchange Reserves, Fourth Quarter, 1998
US$, billions

		1998		
Indicator	*Year-end 1997*	*End of October*	*End of November*	*End of December*
Total foreign reserves	20.41	48.83	50.02	52.04
Usable foreign reserves	8.87	45.27	46.47	48.51

Source: Foreign Exchange Division, Ministry of Finance and Economy.

The won/yen exchange rate was also becoming more favorable. Because the yen was strengthening, the won/yen exchange rate moved past the W 1,000 mark per ¥100, giving much-needed relief to Korean exporters. At the end of 1997, the won was trading at W 1,087.82 per ¥100, but, by the end of 1998, it was trading at W 1,053.47, gaining about 3.3 percent on the yen. In 1997, the won had depreciated approximately 33.2 percent against the yen. In terms of the dollar, the won had appreciated below the W 1,300 mark per dollar after November 18, below W 1,250 in early December, and to W 1,193 on December 21. On a year-to-year basis, the won gained against the dollar, from W 1,415.2 at the end of 1997 to W 1,207.8 by the end of 1998, appreciating some 17.2 percent. In 1997, the won had depreciated 40.3 percent.

As exports weakened and the won strengthened against the U.S. dollar, it was feared that exports would suffer heavily if the won/dollar exchange rate moved below the W 1,200 mark. As the supply of dollars persisted, maintaining an exchange rate that helped sustain exports emerged as a crucial challenge for the government. The critical government policy difficulty was the identification of the best way to deal with the oversupply of dollars and the potential disruption in foreign borrowing caused by the ever-shifting conditions in international financial markets.

The Push for Market Liberalization

The government put into effect the Foreign Investment Promotion Act on November 17. The law significantly enlarged the incentives for inbound foreign direct investment. The number of foreign high-technology businesses eligible for tax incentives rose from 265 to 464. Then, 70 additional service industries, including Internet services, were added to the list, as were companies that had set up business operations in specially designated foreign investment zones. Foreign investment zones were defined as areas in which (1) foreign investment exceeded US$100 million; (2) the foreign investment ratio was 50 percent or higher, and the number of newly hired workers was more than 1,000; or (3) the foreign investment exceeded US$50 million, and the number of newly hired workers was 500 or higher.

The duration of full tax exemptions was set at seven years for the corporate tax, the income tax, and the tax on dividend income and at a 50 percent reduction for the next three years (all of which are national taxes). Exemptions up to eight years were provided for the acquisition tax, the property tax, the aggregate land tax, and the registration tax (all of which are local taxes). The lease period for the use of government-owned land was extended from 20 to 50 years, and the annual rent was set at 1 percent or more of the price of the land to be used.

For the 13 industries still closed to foreign investors (of the 1,148 total industries), the government decided to expand to 100 percent the plan to allow foreign direct investment of up to 50 percent in the book and periodical publishing business beginning in 1999. Among the 18 industries that were partially opened to foreign investors, the government decided to open alcohol extracting and outport shipping fully. From July to November, the government also held three separate negotiations with the United States on a bilateral investment treaty. Some of the key stumbling blocks in the negotiations were the appropriate safeguards for capital transactions, the reduction on screening quotas for domestic motion pictures, and the removal of investment barriers on telecommunication business and the wholesale trade in imported beef. Some progress was made in certain areas, but, in others, such as lowering the screen quotas, the differences proved more difficult to resolve.

Quickening the Pace of Restructuring

Consultations on Restructuring with the IMF

One feature of the consultations between the government and the IMF at their eighth review and consultation meeting, on October 27, was that a cover letter was used to highlight the success Korea had achieved in restructuring the corporate and financial sectors. The cover letter was to be sent out to publicize to foreign investors the rapid pace of the progress in Korea, help differentiate Korea from other economies in trouble, and boost the confidence of foreign investors in the health of the Korean economy. The government also sought to emphasize that, as soon as possible, it planned to sell off its stake in the troubled commercial banks it was rescuing and that its bailout was only a temporary measure aimed at resuscitating the banks in accordance with general market principles.

The government decided that the prudential standards for financial companies should be strengthened so as to quicken the pace of the restructuring of troubled corporate and financial companies. For instance, provisions made against loans classified as substandard or worse were not to be counted as part of tier-2 capital. In addition, new regulations limiting large extensions of credit to controlling shareholders and interlinked business groups were to take effect earlier than originally planned. By incorporating in its Letter of Intent to the IMF the pledge the top five chaebols had made to terminate cross-debt guarantees among affiliated companies in different business lines by the end of 1998, the government sought to counter the skepticism of those foreign investors who thought the chaebol reform had not gone far enough.

Restructuring the Top Five Chaebols

The top five chaebols accounted for nearly 30 percent of the nation's output and had been the driving force behind Korea's economic growth. Compared with the progress in the restructuring of the 6th to 64th largest business groups (chaebols) and large independent (non-chaebol) companies, however, the restructuring of the top five was moving at a snail's pace.

In terms of amount, the voluntary restructuring efforts through sales of assets and recapitalization by the top five chaebols represented W 8.08 trillion from March to mid-October, compared with W 8.01 trillion for the 6th to 30th largest business groups. Yet, the total debt of the 6th to 30th largest business groups as of June was W 68.88 trillion, while the total debt of the top five chaebols was W 145.92 trillion. Moreover, the US$29 billion the top five chaebols promised to raise from foreign investors in May through asset disposition and convertible debt issues did not materialize; only US$4.6 billion—or 15.7 percent of the original goal—had been met as of October 20. For these reasons, the government considered the restructuring of the top five chaebols the most urgent priority.

Therefore, the government urged the top five chaebols to adjust their restructuring plans by the end of the year and requested that they finalize concrete plans for the seven business swaps known as the Big Deal (see chapter 7), as well as the reorganization of business structures, the termination of cross-debt guarantees, and improvements in the financial structure of the chaebols. These measures were to be implemented within the framework of the financial soundness improvement plans the chaebols had agreed to with their creditor banks.

The push for the Big Deal among the top five chaebols. The Federation of Korean Industries (FKI) announced, on October 7, plans for the restructuring and reorganization of the industrial sectors in petrochemicals, aerospace, rolling stock, ship engines, power plant equipment, semiconductors, and refineries. In power plant equipment, the original plan had called for the consolidation of the sector into a single business entity. However, this time it looked as if the two leaders in the sector, Hyundai Heavy Industries and Korea Heavy Industries & Construction, might go separate ways. The consolidation plans for the semiconductor sector also looked uncertain.

The government responded on October 12 that it would force workouts and business closures beginning in December if the chaebols failed to come up with meaningful restructuring plans for the semiconductor and power plant equipment sectors by the end of November. It saw no problem with the restructuring plans drafted by the chaebols for the rolling stock, ship engine, petrochemical, aerospace, and refinery sectors. Following the tough stance by the government, the FKI renegotiated with the chaebols and then presented modified plans. Under the modified plan in the rolling stock sector, a single company was to be formed (shares of 40 percent for Hyundai, 40 percent for Daewoo, and 20 percent for Hanjin) instead of the original plan for two separate companies, such as Hyundai and a company resulting from the merger of Daewoo and Hanjin. Hyundai Heavy Industries was to turn over its power plant equipment business to Korea Heavy Industries & Construction. In semiconductors, Hyundai Electronics and LG Semicon agreed to seek an independent evaluation and consult with Arthur D. Little on which firm should assume control of the consolidated business. It was agreed that the firm receiving the more favorable assessment from the outside consultant would take over the consolidated business by the end of November and that the equity would be divided at 70 and 30 percent on this basis.

The progress in restructuring by the top five chaebols. During the fourth meeting between the government and the chaebol representatives, on October 22, a discussion took place on the five principles of restructuring (see chapter 5). The government pointed out that corporate transparency and accountability would be greatly facilitated through an improved regulatory framework such as combined financial reporting, which is similar to consolidated reporting, and that the main task going forward would be to implement the necessary changes aggressively. The government also stressed that little progress had been made in reducing the high level of corporate debt and reorganizing the chaebols around the most competitive core business units. Moreover, to ensure that cross-debt guarantees were completely terminated by March 2000 and that business reorganization around the core competencies would be achieved, the government argued that an intermediate schedule for the elimination of cross-debt guarantees, such as the end of 1998 or mid-1999, had to be set and that, as a priority, cross-debt guarantees among affiliated companies in different business lines had to be eliminated.

The creditor banks, for their part, decided to cut off credit to 25 failing companies in the top five chaebols in October. This was a follow-up to the elimination of the credit to 20 companies the creditor banks had decided to close in June. By business group, Daewoo lost four companies, Hyundai six, LG five, Samsung six, and SK four.

On December 7, President Kim Dae-Jung presided over a meeting of representatives of the government, the chaebols, and the creditor banks. At the meeting, the participants drew up implementation plans for the restructuring of the top five chaebols. Under the agreement that was reached at the meeting, the Hyundai Group was to concentrate on automobiles, construction, electronics, heavy industries, chemical industries, and financial and other services and push for the separation and independent management of the group's companies. As a mid- to long-term goal, the automobile business was to be converted into an independent business group. The number of companies under the group's control was to be reduced from 63 to around 30. Samsung was to concentrate on electronics, financial services, trading, and other services as the group's core businesses and reduce the number of its affiliated companies from 66 to around 40. For Daewoo, the core businesses were automobiles, heavy industries, trading, construction, financial services, and other services. The number of the group's affiliated companies was to be cut from 41 to around 10. The LG Group was to focus on chemicals, energy, electronics, telecommunications, financial services, and other services, and the number of affiliated companies was to be reduced from 53 to around 30. For the SK Group, the core businesses were energy, petrochemicals, information and telecommunication, construction, logistics, and financial services, and the number of affiliated companies was to be cut from 42 to 20. The top five chaebols were also to institute independent management and strict transparency and accountability.

The business groups and the creditor institutions were to finalize the implementation plans for the seven areas of reorganization under the Big Deal scheme and incorporate the plans in their financial structure improvement plans by December 15. It was agreed that the decision on whether Hyundai or LG would take over the semiconductor businesses of the two groups would be made by December 25 according to the recommendation of the independent outside consultant. The dispute was not resolved at first because LG objected to the recommendation of the independent consultant. However, LG relented on January 6, 1999, and Hyundai was able to assume control of the semiconductor business. In addition to the Big Deal in the seven areas, Samsung was to leave its automobile business to Daewoo and receive Daewoo's electronics business in return. Both groups agreed to finalize the agreement by December 15.

The top five chaebols agreed to terminate cross-guarantees by March 2000 and to dissolve all guarantees among affiliated companies in different business lines by the end of December. Through the financial soundness improvement plans, the top five chaebols agreed to reduce their debt to a level that would enable them to borrow at normal market interest rates in international credit markets. An agreement was also reached to develop revised financial soundness improvement plans by December 15 so as to lower the debt level in a meaningful fashion by the end of 1999. Under the agreement, the proceeds from the sale of noncore business units and other self-help activities—involving approximately W 20 trillion among the top five chaebols—were first to be used to pay off chaebol debt to financial companies.

As a way to strengthen the competitiveness of the core business units of each business group, the creditors were to organize debt-equity swaps and other support measures. If foreign capital was deemed necessary, the debt-equity swaps were to be accompanied by foreign capital inducements. The chaebols were to name outside directors and institute audit committees so as to improve management transparency significantly, cease illegal intragroup trading, and take steps to prepare for the implementation of combined financial reporting beginning in the 1999 fiscal year.

On December 17, four of the top five chaebols finalized financial soundness improvement plans, including business reorganization schemes, with the creditor banks. Daewoo finalized its agreements two days later, on December 19. The chaebols set the target debt-equity ratio at 199 percent by the end of 1999 to comply with the 200 percent ratio that the government demanded. However, the results in 1998 were not promising. Other than Samsung's 276 percent, all other groups reported debt-equity ratios in excess of 340 percent. Daewoo's debt-equity ratio reached 527 percent, even worse than the 473.6 percent at the end of 1997. Moreover, none of the chaebols could show much progress from their efforts at voluntary restructuring or attracting foreign capital. Daewoo and Hyundai groups fared especially poorly. The chaebols did show some progress in their efforts to dissolve cross-debt guarantees, the disposition of ancillary business units, and the instilling of effective corporate governance.

Restructuring the 6th to 64th Largest Business Groups and SMEs

The restructuring of the 6th to 64th largest business groups (chaebols) and other large independent (non-chaebol) companies proceeded by means of workouts, court receiverships, or self-imposed turnarounds. Eight companies belonging to three business groups (Anam, Dongkook Trading, and Ssangyong) in the 6th to 64th business groups were selected for workouts between October and December. The total had reached 43 companies in 16 business groups by the end of December after 35 companies in 13 business groups that had been selected prior to September were added. Among large independent companies, the total reached 34 at the end of December, including Choongnam Textiles and 11 companies chosen between November and December. Four companies belonging to the Tongil Group were excluded from workouts because of the objections of the controlling shareholders over loss sharing. As a result, the number of companies selected for creditor-led workouts totaled 73 at the end of December: 39

companies in 15 business groups (chaebols) and 34 large independent companies. Of these, 31 companies in 12 business groups, excluding the Anam, Dongkook Trading, and Ssangyong groups, and 20 large independent companies, including Dongbang, Dongbo Construction, Dongwha Duty Free Shops, and Shin Woo Corporation, had finalized workout plans by the end of December.

Among the 6th to 64th largest business groups, Haitai, Hanil, and Tongil were set to be restructured under court receivership. The 41 other groups were to embark on self-imposed turnarounds. Among these, Daesang, Doosan, Hanwha, Hansol, and Hyosung embraced aggressive restructuring and were able to restore their business health relatively quickly. However, they were the exceptions; most groups simply took a wait-and-see attitude, hoping to avoid any painful downsizing. Hanwha folded BASF Urethane, Hanwha Energy, and NSK Precision. Doosan merged seven affiliated companies, including Doosan Donga, Doosan Industrial Development, Doosan International Corporation, and Oriental Brewery Company into Doosan Incorporated and then sold off Oriental Brewery. Hansol sold a paper factory in a provincial area, and Hyosung merged its four key business units—Hyosung Corporation, Hyosung Industries, Hyosung Living Industry, and Hyosung T&C—into a single entity. Daesang sold off its lysine business unit and merged four other business units, including its trading, construction, and beverage companies.

By the end of 1998, the 6th to 64th largest business groups did not include 15 groups that had gone bankrupt during 1997 and 1998. The resolution of the groups that had gone bankrupt in 1997 (Chonggu, Dainong, Hanbo, Halla, Hanshin Engineering & Construction, Jinro, Kia, Sammi, NewCore, and Soosan Heavy Industries) and in 1998 (Bosung, Doore, Hwaseung, Kukdong Engineering & Construction, and Nasan) was therefore an urgent matter. In particular, the resolution of Hanbo Steel and Kia Motors attracted considerable attention at home and abroad.

In August 1997, Dongkuk Steel and POSCO made a joint bid for Hanbo Steel for W 2 trillion, but the bid failed because of irreconcilable differences with creditors. Several international bids had been offered through mid-December, but no successful bidder emerged. One of the main reasons for the failed bids was the Corex furnace (for coal ore reduction) that was shunned by bidders as uncompetitive and unattractive.

In April, the government, the creditors, and the court-appointed receiver decided to hold an open auction for the Kia Group. However, the conflicting positions taken by lawmakers, labor unions, civic groups, and suppliers, as well as the divergent interests among Kia creditors, made a quick resolution extraordinarily difficult. Then, in July, interested ministry representatives, the heads of the creditor banks, and the receiver agreed on several key steps for the Kia Group. Under this plan, Asia Motors and

Kia Motors were to be resolved simultaneously. In light of the adverse economic impact on the region of the closure of Kia's Kwangju factories, it was decided that the factories would not be relocated. Because Asia Motors and Kia both had wide-ranging assets and multiple creditors, it became obvious that debt claims on the two companies had to be rescheduled and settled as a key part of the resolution. For the selection of the new owner, it was agreed that technological capability, the impact on exports and employment, and the ability to pay for the takeover would all have to be considered. The sale of the affiliated companies, the new relationship between labor and management, and bold restructuring measures were planned so as to ensure the successful purchase of the two companies by a new buyer. The creditor banks also decided to provide additional credit support to ensure the continuation of the normal business operations of the two companies.

The receiver conducted two separate auctions: one on July 15, and one on September 21; however, both failed to produce a winning bidder. At the third auction, on October 12, Daewoo Motor, Ford, Hyundai, and Samsung made bids. Ford was quickly ruled out after it proposed a takeover price below the face value of the shares of Asia Motors. In the end, on October 19, Hyundai emerged as the winner. After completing due diligence on November 18, Hyundai demanded additional debt reduction by the creditors for the takeover. On December 1, Hyundai was able to complete the deal after a W 219.4 billion reduction in the liabilities of Kia Motors and Asia Motors. The takeover was finalized on March 15, 1999 after Hyundai had made a payment of W 1.17 trillion for the shares of Asia and Kia.

In the restructuring of SMEs, companies with outstanding loans in excess of W 1 billion were divided into three groups—a priority support group, a conditional support group, and an other group—in June. SMEs with outstanding debt of less than W 1 billion were also divided into the same three groups in November. By December, SMEs had been grouped as shown in table 8.5. For companies with more than W 1 billion in liabilities, changes in the grouping occurred because of the closure of some companies and because of the restructuring of some companies in the conditional support group. Table 8.6 summarizes the support measures provided for companies in the priority support group and the conditional support group from July to December.

Of the 20,748 companies selected for conditional support, 14,231 that were small in the scale of business and dealt with one or two lenders were directed to reduce their debt, sell assets, and recapitalize in return for any fresh credit from creditor institutions as part of their restructuring endeavor. By the end of 1998, 11,189 companies had completed the restructuring agreement, and 2,796 companies were in negotiations. For the 765 large companies that dealt with multiple lenders, workouts under joint supervision by creditors were to be arranged. By the end of 1988,

Table 8.5 Three Classifications for Restructuring SMEs, Year-End 1998
number of companies

Classification	*W 1 billion or more in debt*	*Less than W 1 billion in debt*	*Total*
Priority support group	8,859 (40.4)	5,789 (37.3)	14,648 (39.1)
Conditional support group	11,903 (54.2)	8,845 (57.0)	20,748 (55.4)
Other group	1,182 (5.3)	871 (5.6)	2,053 (5.5)
Total	21,944 (100)	15,505 (100)	37,449 (100)

Source: MOFE 1999a.
Note: The numbers in parentheses are percentage shares.

Table 8.6 Financial Support for SMEs, Second Half of 1998
won, billions

Support	*Priority support group*	*Conditional support group*	Total
New loans	8,247.2	9,301.9	17,549.1
Loan maturity extension	5,360.9	8,652.1	14,013.0
Conversion to medium- and long-term loans	49.4	515.8	565.2
Prime lending rate	5,593.7	5,261.9	10,855.6
Other (debt-equity swaps and so on)	71.2	52.1	123.3

Source: MOFE 1999a.

of 246 companies slated for workouts, 88 had wrapped up restructuring agreements with creditors.

Accounting Reform and the Introduction of Holding Companies

The government instituted a number of new measures to improve management transparency and strengthen corporate governance in the wake of the crisis and the emergence of cracks in Korea's corporate sector. As part of this effort, during the fourth quarter of 1998, the government paved the way for the introduction of an accounting system that was more consistent with international standards. The Securities and Futures Commission, on

October 21, adopted the combined financial reporting system for large business groups and decided to implement it beginning January 1, 1999. The new accounting system made it possible for more highly consolidated financial reporting on large business groups that were effectively under the control of the chaebol families and their associates.

On December 11, the Financial Supervisory Commission (FSC) amended the corporate accounting standards and established supplementary accounting standards for financial businesses in line with prevailing international standards. (See table 8.7 for a summary of the changes to Korea's corporate governance that took effect after the onset of the financial crisis.) It decided to put these new standards into effect beginning with the 1999 accounting year. Under the old accounting system, companies were often able to distort financial statements easily because the accounting rules made the manipulation of income and expenses straightforward. For financial companies, the reality was that financial disclosures were geared toward satisfying regulatory reporting requirements rather than providing useful and meaningful information to investors and shareholders. Moreover, it was not uncommon for financial companies to report financial results according to standards that were different from the standards for other business entities.

In April, the government unveiled a plan to introduce holding companies. It put the plan into effect after public hearings and amendments to the Monopoly Regulation and Fair Trade Act, in January 1999. Korea had banned holding companies in 1987 to prevent excessive business diversification and the concentration of economic power among a few chaebols. As a result, the chaebols resorted to creating vacuous posts such as the group chairman's office or the planning and coordination office that had no legal basis or authority in an effort to control their sprawling business empires. In introducing the holding company system, the government had to contend with many thorny issues, including whether holding companies should be allowed to accumulate debt, whether minimum share ownership rules in subsidiaries should be set for the parent companies, whether sub-subsidiaries should be permitted, and whether both financial and nonfinancial subsidiaries should be permitted to exist under the same parent company. Under the amended Monopoly Regulation and Fair Trade Act, the debt ratio was set at 100 percent and the minimum equity in a subsidiary unit was set at 50 percent. Holding companies were barred from holding financial and nonfinancial subsidiaries together. Sub-subsidiaries were to be barred in principle.

The Finishing Touches in the First Phase of Financial Restructuring

The primary task of the government during the fourth quarter of 1998 was to complete the first phase of the restructuring of financial companies

Table 8.7 Improvements in Corporate Governance, Year-End 1998

Indicator	*Content*	*Laws and regulations*
	Strengthening outside control	
Activation of the mergers and acquisitions market	• Repeal of restrictions on hostile mergers and acquisitions and complementation of defensive methods against mergers and acquisitions attack	
	- Repeal of mandatory tender offering	Securities and Exchange Act
	- Repeal of ceiling on equity investments of large business groups	Monopoly Regulation and Fair Trade Act
	• Deregulation of foreign mergers and acquisitions - Repeal of ceiling on foreign stock investment - Narrowing of scope of stocks purchased by foreign investors with the permission of the minister of finance and economy (from firms with assets of W 2 trillion or above to firms in defense industry) - On foreigners' purchasing stocks, easing of requirements of preapproval of board of directors (change in minimum purchase shares from 10% to 1/3)	Foreign Capital Inducement Act
	• Introduction of the corporate spin-off system and simplification of mergers and acquisitions procedures	Commercial Act
Strengthening of the bank monitoring function	• Dissolution of cross-debt guarantee - Prohibition of new loans issued through cross-debt guarantees - Termination of existing cross-debt guarantees until March 2000	Monopoly Regulation and Fair Trade Act
	• Financial soundness improvement plans agreed to by 64 large business groups and creditor banks	Enforcement Rule on Supervision of Banking Business

(continued next page)

Table 8.7 Improvements in Corporate Governance, Year-End 1998 *(continued)*

Indicator	*Content*	*Laws and regulations*
	Strengthening internal control	
Strengthening of outside director and standing auditor system	• Mandatory designation of outside directors in listed companies - At least one outside director before general shareholder meeting in FY1998 - At least 25% of total directors from general shareholder meeting in 1999	Listing Regulation of Securities
	• Exclusion from outside directors list those persons having effective relationships with majority shareholders or the firm	Listing Regulation of Securities
	• Delisting of firms that violate mandatory designation of outside directors	Listing Regulation of Securities
	• For listed firms with assets of W 100 billion or more, mandatory designation of standing auditor	Securities and Exchange Act
Easing of requirements for the exercise of rights by minority shareholders	• Easing of shareholding requirement for filing representative suits (threshold lowered from 1 % in ownership to 0.01 %)	Securities and Exchange Act
	• Easing shareholding requirements for requesting dismissals of director and auditor (threshold lowered from 1% in ownership to 0.5%), but 0.25% for firms with capital of W 100 billion or more	Securities and Exchange Act
	• Easing of shareholding requirement for reading accounting books (threshold lowered from 3% in ownership to 1%), but 0.5% for firms with capital of W 100 billion or more	Securities and Exchange Act
	• Introduction of submission proposal to general shareholder meeting (3%)	Commercial Act
	• Introduction of cumulative voting for director designation	Commercial Act

Repeal of restrictions on voting rights of institutional investors	• Free exercise of voting rights of shares under trust property of banks, investment trust companies, and other financial companies, but restriction of voting rights of shares of their affiliated firms	Securities Investment Trust Business Act
Strengthening of responsibilities of controlled shareholders	• Establishment of clauses related to the faithful performance of duties by directors • Establishment of clauses related to implementation officer's (de facto director) responsibility	Commercial Act
	Establishment of transparent accounting system	
	• Revision of financial reporting standards and establishment of the supplementary accounting standards of financial businesses	Supervisory Regulation of FSC
	• Introduction of combined financial statements to large business groups since fiscal year 1999	Act on External Audit of Stock Companies
	• Mandatory establishment of committee to designate outside auditors for listed companies and affiliated companies in business groups	Act on External Audit of Stock Companies
	• Allowing of class action suits to be filed against outside auditors and strengthening penalties	Act on External Audit of Stock Companies

Source: Author's compilation.

without disruption. The government first had to execute the financial support measures it had put together in September. It also had to keep pressing Chohung Bank, Korea Exchange Bank, and other banks with Bank for International Settlements (BIS) capital ratios below 8 percent to expedite turnaround efforts and achieve quick rehabilitation. For banks with BIS capital ratios higher than 8 percent, but found to be showing signs of distress, the FSC had to undertake prompt corrective action. The sell-off of Korea First Bank and Seoul Bank also had to be concluded. Facilitating the purchase of assets and assumption of liabilities for four failing life insurance companies and resolving failing leasing companies were also on the government's to-do list.

As the reform and restructuring of the hardware aspects of the financial sector gradually came to a close, the time was ripe for the government to lay the groundwork so that the financial service sector could become Korea's strategic growth industry of the 21st century. In this endeavor, many argued that the global competitiveness of Korea's financial companies had to be significantly upgraded and improved through encouragement for the application of advanced financial techniques, risk management, and customer-tailored services. This was widely referred to as software reform in Korea. For this to succeed, new mindsets and a resolve to favor change within the financial sector were crucial.

It was urgent that the financial companies that had been unavoidably nationalized in the course of reform and restructuring become privatized as quickly as possible and that they be run by competent managers. For this to occur, the governance structures on which financial companies relied had to be revamped and upgraded. At the same time, the safety and soundness of the financial system had to be drastically enhanced, while prudential regulations and supervision over financial companies had to be brought into conformity with global standards and best practices.

The injection of additional public funds. On November 6, the Korea Asset Management Corporation (KAMCO) purchased the troubled assets being held by a number of financial companies, including two regional banks (Jeonbuk and Kwangju), two securities firms that had been approved for business turnarounds (SK and Ssangyong), and five life insurance companies (Handuk and four others that were to be resolved: BYC, Coryo, Kukje, and Taeyang). KAMCO paid W 261.6 billion, while the book value of the assets was W 496.9 billion. On December 29, KAMCO also acquired the troubled assets being held by the Korea Development Bank (KDB), the Industrial Bank of Korea, and three cooperatives (agriculture, fisheries, and livestock). In this case, KAMCO paid W 1.90 trillion, while the book value of the assets was W 4.53 trillion.

The Korea Deposit Insurance Corporation (KDIC) paid W 228.8 billion to four life insurance companies on November 20 for losses they had incurred in assuming the liabilities of four failing life insurance companies.

On December 28, the KDIC put up W 1.19 trillion for the recapitalization of banks that had assumed the assets and liabilities of five failing banks so as to keep the capital ratios of the acquiring banks at the levels before the purchase of assets and assumption of liabilities (as of the end of June 1998). It provided W 329.5 billion to support the merger of Boram Bank and Hana Bank and paid W 14.1 billion to the customers of Dongbang-Peregreen and KLB Securities for deposits protected under the law. On December 29, the Public Capital Management Fund purchased subordinated bonds valued at W 591.7 billion issued by acquiring banks to cover the losses the banks had incurred through the transfer of the assets of the five failed banks. It likewise invested W 500 billion in subordinated debt issued by KorAm Bank and others for the outstanding support they had provided to SMEs, and it invested another W 360 billion in subordinated bonds issued by the Industrial Bank of Korea to strengthen that bank's capital position.

The government took steps to recapitalize government-owned banks not only through cash infusions from the budget, but also through the provision of state-owned property. Between September 15 and November 10, the government made a cash injection of W 1.35 trillion in the KDB, along with W 100 billion for the Export-Import Bank of Korea and W 200 billion for the Industrial Bank of Korea. The government transferred government-owned shares in KT&G and POSCO that were valued at W 1.5 trillion to the Industrial Bank of Korea. On December 31, the government transferred to the KDB shares worth W 3.367 trillion, which included shares of the Korea National Housing Corporation. The Export-Import Bank of Korea received government-owned shares worth approximately W 450 billion.

These actions brought about the significant recapitalization of state-owned banks and boosted the ability of these banks to return to international capital markets to raise funds. In the midst of the persistent credit crunch, the steps also strengthened the ability of the banks to contribute to the resolution of problems in the banking sector. Table 8.8 summarizes the use of public funds by KAMCO, the KDIC, and the government in support of the restructuring of financial companies.

Normalization efforts for banks with capital ratios below 8 percent. Some progress had been made by banks with capital ratios lower than 8 percent to strengthen their capital positions. Chohung Bank failed to keep its promise to find foreign equity investors and turn its sagging business around by October. In response, the FSC, on November 27, ordered Chohung to come up with a tougher and more aggressive turnaround plan within a month. On December 17, Chohung asked for government bailout funds. In return, it proposed a merger with Kangwon Bank, new management, and other turnaround steps. Kangwon bank was to push for a self-imposed turnaround under the guidance of the business group at

Table 8.8 The Use of Public Funds for Financial Restructuring, November 1997–December 1998
won, billions

	KDIC					*Public finance*			
Entity	*Subtotal*	*Capital increase*	*Contribution*	*Deposit payoffs*	KAMCO	*Subtotal*	*Capital increase*[a]	*Purchase of subordinate bonds*	*Total*
				November–December 1997					
Banks	n.a.	n.a.	n.a.	n.a.	5,375.6	5,339.3	970.0	4,369.3	10,714.9
Commercial banks	n.a.	n.a.	n.a.	n.a.	4,221.2	3,082.3	n.a.	3,082.3	7,303.5
Regional banks	n.a.	n.a.	n.a.	n.a.	274.1	908.0	n.a.	908.0	1,182.1
Specialized banks	n.a.	n.a.	n.a.	n.a.	880.3	1,349.0	970.0	379.0	2,229.3
Merchant banks	30.0	30.0[b]	n.a.	n.a.	1,755.5	n.a.	n.a.	n.a.	1,785.5
Total	30.0	30.0	n.a.	n.a.	7,131.1	5,339.3	970.0	4,369.3	12,500.4
				January–December 1998					
Banks	12,065	6,286	5,779	n.a.	11,339.4	10,988.6	9,536.9	1,451.7	34,393
Commercial banks	12,065	6,286	5,779	n.a.	7,239.8	2,446.6	1,500	946.6	21,751.4

Regional banks	n.a.	n.a.	n.a.	n.a.	2,019.3	110.4	n.a.	110.4	2,129.7
Specialized banks	n.a.	n.a.	n.a.	n.a.	2,080.3	8,431.6	8,036.9	394.7	10,511.9
Merchant banks	12,682.1	n.a.	n.a.	12,682.1	n.a.	n.a.	n.a.	n.a.	12,682.1
Securities	14	n.a.	n.a.	14	56.4	n.a.	n.a.	n.a.	70.4
Insurance	1,153.5	n.a.	1,153.5	n.a.	1,371.4	n.a.	n.a.	n.a.	2,524.9
Savings and finance companies, credit unions	1,909.3	n.a.	n.a.	1,909.3	n.a.	n.a.	n.a.	n.a.	1,909.3
Total	27,823.9	6,286	6,932.5	14,605.4	12,767.2	10,988.6	9,536.9	1,451.7	51,579.7

Source: MOFE and FSC 2000.

Note: n.a. = not applicable.

a. Including the contribution of government shares.

b. Investment in Hanareum Merchant Bank.

Hyundai, its controlling shareholder. However, due diligence performed on the bank revealed that its net worth had fallen to negative W 270 billion, prompting the FSC to issue a strongly worded warning to the bank to restore its positive net asset position. To accomplish this, Kangwon Bank ended up taking over Hyundai Merchant Bank after a series of ups and downs. Chungbuk Bank failed to find a foreign partner or replenish its depleted capital (see chapter 7) and ended up merging with Chohung Bank in 1999.

Korea Exchange Bank set about boosting its capital by W 1 trillion and returned to normalcy by itself. Under the turnaround plan Korea Exchange Bank had proposed, Commerzbank, which had invested W 350 billion in the bank in July, was to invest another W 250 billion (approximately US$200 million), while the BOK, as a large shareholder, was to invest W 330 billion. Korea Exchange Bank also expected to get W 100 billion from its managers and employees, as well as W 320 billion from shareholders. However, the plan did not materialize in 1998 because the bank was unable to secure the BOK investment. Then, on February 1, 1999, the BOK invested W 700 billion in the Export-Import Bank of Korea and, in a roundabout way, had this bank invest W 336 billion in Korea Exchange Bank.

On October 27, Peace Bank wrote off its capital from W 273 billion to the legally required minimum of W 100 billion and then added W 120 billion—W 15 billion from money set aside for the bank employees retirement fund and W 105 billion from public stock offerings—to its capital.

The business review the FSC conducted up to the end of September on banks with BIS capital ratios higher than 8 percent determined that three small regional banks—Busan, Jeju, and Kyongnam—were in an unsound business condition. Jeju Bank had already received a management improvement order from the FSC in April, but had failed to turn the situation around. In October, it was able to increase its capital by W 30 billion. Busan Bank and Kyongnam Bank, both cited for management improvement recommendations by the FSC on October 16, received approval from the FSC for turnaround plans that included replacing management and increasing their capital ratios.

Finding a foreign buyer for Korea First Bank. Morgan Stanley, which had been chosen to act as advisor for the sale of Korea First Bank and Seoul Bank in May, held talks with 49 potential foreign bidders beginning in September to meet the November 15 deadline it had agreed to with the IMF. On October 7, it provided the terms of the sale to prospective foreign bidders. However, only Citicorp, HSBC, and a consortium led by Newbridge Capital expressed serious interest in a takeover.

Under the terms of the sale Morgan Stanley proposed to the prospective buyers, (1) new shares were to be issued and sold off by the two Korean banks for the sale, (2) the KDIC would cover losses arising from the disposal of any nonperforming assets for up to three years after the takeover (but only up to a ceiling of W 3.3 trillion), and (3) the government would guarantee the principal and interest payments of the bonds issued by KDIC to cover 80 percent of the losses. The government would also guarantee the book value and certain returns on the shares taken over from the two banks. However, the government would decide the timing of the sale of shares, and any gains in excess of the book value were to be returned to the government.

Despite these efforts, the November 15 deadline for the sale of the two banks came and went. When HSBC and Newbridge Capital eventually expressed strong interest in acquiring Korea First Bank, the government decided to proceed first with the sale of that bank and entered into negotiations on the terms of the sale that the two prospective foreign bidders proposed on December 26. After comparing the two bids, the FSC and Morgan Stanley determined that the offer by Newbridge Capital was more favorable. With a particular focus on the amount of goodwill and to minimize the put-back options on the assets to be taken over by the new buyer, the FSC, on December 26, started negotiations with Newbridge Capital and signed a letter of intent for the purchase of Korea First Bank at 2:00 p.m. on December 31.

Key terms of the sale were as follows: (1) Bad assets and certain liabilities were to be transferred to the bad bank that the government was about to establish for this purpose, and the losses from the separated assets were to be assumed by the government to help Korea First Bank turn around as a clean bank. (2) Assets that soured within a year of the takeover were to be allowed to be transferred to the bad bank (the put-back option). (3) Additional transfers to the bad bank were to be allowed up to the second year, but with certain restrictions on the amounts to be transferred. (4) The recovery of the expenses that had been incurred by the government was to take place as the business of the bank improved and as the bank increased its value as a going concern. (5) The government was to hold on to 49 percent of the total stakes and receive warrants worth 11 percent of the government stakes as a premium for the sale.

The terms of the sale of Korea First Bank drew criticism. Because Newbridge Capital was essentially a private equity fund in pursuit of the highest returns possible for its investment, some argued that the terms would not enable the government to lay the groundwork for a more developed banking sector through the introduction of advanced banking management into Korea First Bank as the government had originally envisioned. It was said, furthermore, that the financial benefits of the takeover and the value of the goodwill offered were so low that they were not even sufficient to recover what the government had already put into the bank. Finally, the government came under attack for giving a 100 percent put-back option to Newbridge Capital and for retaining uncertain liabilities that it might continue to have to hold well into the future.

The local news media speculated that the government rushed the sale of Korea First Bank despite the unattractive terms Newbridge offered because it had missed the November 15 deadline it had agreed to with the IMF and thus wanted to have the deal wrapped up by the end of the year. Meanwhile, foreign news media mostly took the view that the sale of Korea First Bank was an important milestone and that it would be a major catalyst for future reform and restructuring in Korea.

Restructuring nonbank financial companies. During the fourth quarter of 1998, the government planned to liquidate KDB Securities and three investment trusts: Boram, Dongbang-Peregreen, and Eutteum. On November 11, it revoked the business licenses of Kukje and three other life insurance companies. On November 25, Hankuk Fidelity & Surety Co. merged with Korea Guarantee Insurance Co. and became newly incorporated as Seoul Guarantee Insurance Co. In the leasing sector, the leasing contracts of the KwangEun and Seoul leasing companies were brought under the Korea Non-Bank Lease Financing Company in November. Busan, Central, and Daegu leasing companies followed suit in December. Table 8.9 gives a snapshot of the restructuring of financial companies in 1998.

Contemplating amendment of the Banking Act to improve bank governance. The government sought to draft amendments to the Banking Act in an effort to improve the legal framework for the independent management of commercial banks. Under the Banking Act, individual investments in a nationwide bank were limited to 4 percent of the total equity; for the smaller regional banks, the ceiling was set at 15 percent. The ownership limits on Boram, Hana, and KorAm banks had been specified at the time they received approval to engage in the banking business. Under agreements reached with the IMF in December 1997, an equity stake of up to 10 percent could be obtained (15 percent for a regional bank) if certain conditions were satisfied. Further acquisitions (in excess of 10, 25, or 33 percent) were possible with the approval of regulators. However, domestic investors were to be allowed to acquire bank equity up to the same level allowed to foreign investors. For each of the 30 largest chaebols, bank ownership in excess of 4 percent (15 percent for regional banks) was limited to only one bank at any one time.

Under the old governance framework, (1) a search committee made up of non–executive directors recommended to the board of directors a candidate or candidates for the post of a bank's chief executive officer based on a two-thirds vote; (2) candidates for the position of bank auditor were screened and selected in the same manner; (3) the members of a bank's board of directors consisted of executive and non–executive directors, and the number of non–executive directors was to be larger than the number of executive directors; and (4) large shareholders were to recommend the nomination of 70 percent of the non–executive directors, and the board of directors was to nominate the remaining 30 percent.

Table 8.9 Restructuring Financial Companies, 1998
number

Entity	*End of 1997*[a]	*Restructuring and newly established in 1998*	*End of 1998*
Bank	33	License revocation: 5 (Daedong, Dongnam, Donghwa, Kyungki, Chungchong); merge:[b] 3 (Hanil + Commercial Bank of Korea, Hana + Boram, Kookmin + Korea Long-Term Credit)	25
Merchant bank	30	License revocation: 16 (Samsam, Kyongnam, Coryo, Kyungil, Shinsegae, Ssangyong, Hangdo, Cheongsol, Shinhan, Hanwha, Hansol, Daegu, Samyang, First, Saehan, Hangil)	14
Securities company	36	License revocation: 3 (Coryo, Dongseo, KDB); business suspension: 3 (HanNam, KLB, Dongbang-Peregreen); newly established: 1 (Samsung Investment Trust Securities)	34[c]
Investment trust company	31	License revocation: 4 (Shinsegi, Dongbang-Peregreen, Boram, Eutteum); business suspension: 2 (HanNam, Coryo)	27[c]
Insurance company	50	License revocation: 4 (Kukje, BYC, Taeyang, Coryo); merge: 1 (Korea Guarantee Insurance + Hankuk Fidelity & Surety)	45
Leasing company	25	License revocation: 5 (Seoul, KwangEun, Central, Busan, Daegu)	21
Savings and finance company	231	License revocation: 22; merge: 2; newly established: 4	211
Credit union	1,666	License revocation: 69; merge: 14; newly established: 9	1,592
Total	2,102	License revocation: 123; merge: 22; business suspension: 5; newly established: 14	1,969

Source: Financial Supervisory Commission.

a. Excluding bridge companies and branches of foreign financial companies.

b. Merge refers to the number of companies closed because of a merger.

c. Based on the criterion of license revocation.

Under this governance structure, bank managers could be selected without any backing from shareholders. In fact, except for a few banks controlled by foreign investors or the largest shareholders, the selection of bank management was heavily influenced by the government or others with political power. For this reason, most bank managers were preoccupied with currying favor among those officials who dictated their fate rather than with running a business enterprise and generating profits. As a result, bank managers, in many instances, were passive spectators in business affairs and failed to run their banks as profit-seeking businesses.

Following the first round of restructuring among financial companies, the fundamental transformation of banks as profit-seeking commercial entities was initiated. The government proposed to repeal the existing cap on bank ownership in principle, but limit the debt-equity ratio of controlling shareholders to below 200 percent so as to secure the participation of financially sound investors. It also sought to level the playing field for domestic investors by allowing them to become controlling shareholders regardless of the level of the shares in banks held by foreigners. As a way to prevent abuses and negative side effects because of the existence of controlling shareholders, lending restrictions on controlling shareholders were expanded to include all direct and indirect lending. Cross-lending among the controlling shareholders of separate banks was also barred, and the credit limit on the largest shareholders was set at 50 percent of the bank equity held by shareholders. In addition, banks were barred from acquiring shares in any companies affiliated with controlling shareholders, and no officers or employees of a company belonging to controlling shareholders were allowed to hold positions at the banks concurrently or to receive employment in the banks for three years after leaving a company belonging to controlling shareholders. The main purpose of these regulations was to prevent controlling shareholders from abusing their positions and using financial companies as their personal piggy banks.

To encourage independent bank management, as provided for under the Commercial Act, the banking regulations regarding the search committee for the chief executive officers of banks, the composition of non–executive directors of bank boards of directors, and other governance issues were to be eliminated in principle. Moreover, to protect the interests of the public in bank management, the rules and regulations regarding the number of directors and the fixed tenure of members of the board of directors were to remain on the books. Moreover, the role of minority shareholders was to be enhanced in the exercise of checks and balances, and individuals responsible for bank failures or incompetence were to be barred from senior management positions.

In the course of public debates on the merits of the proposals for banking reform, opposition arose because it was felt that the chaebol families would be the primary beneficiaries of the new bank ownership rules and that they would be able to turn banks into personal vaults. It was also feared that compromising the separation between financial capital, which tended to safeguard the public interest, and industrial capital, which tended to represent self-interest, would cause serious problems in the economy. On November 3, the MOFE convened a meeting of the Advisory Committee on Financial Policy and decided to suspend the amendments it had proposed to improve bank management and ownership. In the face of the fierce opposition to the proposed changes, the government ultimately realized that it was more prudent not to push through questionable remedies.

It was expected that the government had ample time to dispose of the stakes it had acquired in banks in the course of restructuring. Moreover, it was hoped that, because of strong financial supervision and the successful reform of the chaebols, the resistance to banking reform would eventually diminish. The task of reforming governance and ownership in banking thus had to wait for another opportunity.

Establishing Financial Supervision in Line with Global Standards

To establish an effective financial supervision system on a par with global standards, the government set about reforming the financial supervision system. The following reform measures were taken by the government up to the end of 1998:

Shifts in the framework for financial supervision

- Banking supervision based on the Basel Core Principles for Effective Banking Supervision
- A shift in the methods of financial supervision
    - From direct regulation to capital adequacy and other indirect regulation
    - From positive-list regulation to negative-list regulation
    - From abstract, expedient supervisory standards to objective and transparent standards
    - From institution-specific supervision to function-oriented supervision
    - From unconsolidated to consolidated supervision, encompassing parent, subsidiary, and overseas branch operations
    - From regulation-focused to service-oriented oversight

Strengthening of prudential standards

- Implementation of prompt corrective action
    - The provision of a legal framework for the enforcement of the Act on the Structural Improvement of the Financial Industry, March 1997

  - Implementation of prompt corrective action in regard to banks, securities firms, insurance companies, and merchant banks, beginning in May 1998
  - Additional stringent measures, September 1998
- Improvement of the evaluation of the management of financial companies
  - Adoption of CAMEL (five categories of performance: capital adequacy, assets quality, management, earnings, and liquidity) for bank ratings, October 1996
  - Addition of sensitivity to market risks to the CAMEL (thus, CAMELS) for bank ratings, in 1998
  - The improved management evaluation of securities firms, insurance companies, and investment trust companies, beginning in January 1999
- BIS capital ratio requirements
  - Introduced in July 1988 to ensure the effective management of credit risk; took effect for Korean banks in 1992
  - Recommendation that banks with BIS capital ratios lower than 8 percent raise the ratio to 6 percent by March 1999, to 8 percent by March 2000, and to 10 percent by December 2000; for regional banks with no international business, the ratio was to rise to 4 percent by March 1999, to 6 percent by March 2000, and to 8 percent by December 2000
  - Merchant banks to raise the ratio to 8 percent by June 1999
- Stricter prudential regulations on the management of foreign exchange
  - Oversight of the management of the foreign exchange among financial companies was assigned to the FSC by the BOK, January 1999
  - Quarterly reviews of foreign exchange liquidity ratios among banks switched to monthly reviews to help ensure that short-term assets (maturity less than three months) covered at least 70 percent of short-term borrowing; overseas branches and offshore accounts were added to the review, July 1998
  - Funding at least 50 percent of long-term assets (maturity more than one year) through long-term borrowing, August 1998; 100 percent, beginning in July 1999
  - Foreign-currency-denominated asset-liability maturity gap requirements (seven-day basis: higher than 0 percent; 30-day basis: lower than –10 percent), introduced in January 1999
- Improved asset classification
  - Beginning on July 1, 1998, precautionary loans were redefined as loans delinquent for one to three months rather than three to six months; loans delinquent for longer than three months were reclassified as substandard loans

  - More stringent provision requirements for loan losses and write-offs, July 1998
  - Adoption of forward-looking criteria in loan classification to reflect more accurately the future ability of borrowers to service their debt, 1999
- Improvement of loan management practices among financial companies
  - Amended Banking Act presented for legislative approval, November 1998
  - See table 9.2 (chapter 9) for details
- Implementation of risk-based supervision
  - New guidelines on risk management by the FSC, 1998: principles of risk management, the role of management, risk management structure and procedures, and establishment of firm-specific internal controls
  - Reinforced supervision of risk management by the FSC, 1998: checklist for each risk area by examiners, expanded risk weight in evaluating and rating financial companies, and new indexes for estimating risks under off-site surveillance
  - Risk estimation and management using internal models (the BIS standard or value at risk models): to be implemented initially with large banks because of the cost of building the necessary electronic information systems; one-year grace period to be given for other financial companies

Improvement of accounting transparency
- Introduction of mark-to-market accounting among financial companies
  - Banks, securities firms, investment trust companies, merchant banks, consumer finance companies, and credit unions: to take effect beginning in the first half of the 1998 fiscal year
  - Savings and finance companies: beginning with the close of the 1998 fiscal year
  - Insurance companies: beginning with the close of the 1999 fiscal year
- Supplementary accounting standards for financial service firms amended by the FSC, 1998

Management accountability
- Improved management disclosure systems, October 9, 1998, under FSC supervisory regulations
  - Expansion of periodic disclosure items to the levels demanded by the International Accounting Standards; expanded ongoing disclosure items
  - Increase in the frequency of periodic disclosure from once a year to twice a year

- Expanded disclosure to be applicable to merchant banks, savings and finance companies, consumer finance companies, credit unions, and foreign bank branches

- Creation of effective disciplinary mechanisms for the management of financial companies, 1998, the FSC
  - Civil and criminal penalties aimed at controlling shareholders and directors for direct or indirect management failures after business failures or distress
  - Monetary fines and penalties to be levied on the managers and employees responsible for business failures or distress
  - Similar liabilities and penalties aimed at outside auditors and supervisors for improper audits

Effective supervision and examination of financial companies

- Strengthened off-site surveillance of financial companies
  - The Office of Bank Supervision in the BOK revamped its off-site surveillance in October 1996, and the supervisory authorities of insurance and securities firms conducted continuous off-site surveillance; however, no early warning system utilizing electronic data or distress indexes indicating potential problems was developed
  - Organizational changes: specific divisions were made responsible for electronic data collection, continuous surveillance, and management guidance to facilitate continuous off-site surveillance
  - Preparations for electronic systems designed to identify early distress signs and to become operational in 1999
- Improvement of the examination handbook and the examination database

The Push for Public Sector Reform

During the fourth quarter of 1998, the main thrust of public sector reform was on improving government organizational structures and functions, the reform of state-run enterprises, and regulatory reform. For the reform of organizational structures and functions, the government conducted a management evaluation of central government ministries and agencies. The goal of the management evaluation was (1) to introduce the concept of the strategic management of public administration and improve public sector competitiveness, (2) to redesign the public administration so that it would be a service-oriented administration and raise customer satisfaction, and (3) to improve the efficiency of the public administration through the fine-tuning of government functions on the basis of the evaluation.

The evaluation lasted for approximately four months, from November 1998 to February 1999. In an effort to ensure the fairness and objectivity of the evaluation, the government turned to 19 private sector management consultants. The extent of the evaluation ranged from the assessment and analysis of government functions, the rating of customer satisfaction, the appropriateness of organizations and the workforce, and the extent of open hiring and the positions to be filled through the private sector.

The government also sought to streamline various public commissions. As of October 1998, there were 372 commissions that had been sanctioned by presidential decree or by law. Thirty key administrative commissions, such as the Fair Trade Commission and the FSC, and 22 commissions related to fund management were excluded from the effort. Therefore, 320 were subjected to reassessment and streamlining. Of these, 117 were to be terminated, and 28 were to be consolidated.

The privatization of state-owned companies was also undertaken. In September, Namhae Chemical Company, a subsidiary of Korea General Chemical Corporation, was sold to the National Agricultural Cooperatives Federation for W 300 billion. This was followed by the sale of State-Compiled Textbook Co. to Daehan Printing & Publishing Co. for W 44.7 billion in November, the first privatization of a parent company. In December, 5.8 percent of POSCO held by the government and the KDB were sold as American depositary receipts on the New York Stock Exchange for US$350 million. In addition, Korea Telecom finally listed its shares on the Korea Stock Exchange in December, laying the groundwork for full privatization and bringing long-awaited relief to small investors who had bought shares in the company from the government in 1994.

The government eyed, in April, the repeal of 50 percent of existing regulations, limits on new regulations, and doing away with those regulations not supported by active legislation. In 1998, under the related guidelines, 35 government ministries, agencies, and regulatory authorities repealed 5,430 regulations—48.8 percent of the 11,125 in effect—and streamlined or simplified 2,411 regulations after an extensive review by the Regulatory Reform Committee.

At the MOFE, 255 regulations—about half of the 509 under its authority—were repealed. In repealing regulations, the MOFE was guided by several principles. First, ex ante regulations that hindered productive economic activities were to be removed, but ex post regulations that ensured the stability of the economic system were to be reinforced. Regulations that hindered productive economic activities included restrictions on prices, market entry and exit, the scope of businesses, asset management, the internal management of private business enterprises, overseas business activities, and foreign currency and capital transactions. Regulations that ensured the stability of the economic system included, but were not limited to rules and regulations on financial soundness, off-site supervision, prompt corrective action, and disclosure regimes.

Second, among the ex ante regulations, those related to foreign currency and capital transactions were to be gradually streamlined and fine-tuned. Rules and regulations that restricted the flow of inbound foreign investment and the business activities of companies in which there was foreign investment were to be repealed. Restrictions on outbound hard currencies were to be lifted gradually.

Third, the transparency of and the rationale for regulations were to be significantly improved. Ambiguous rules were to be clarified and made objective, redundant provisions were to be eliminated, and excessive regulatory intrusion was to be drastically curtailed.

Beginning on June 1, 1998, the government also instituted a preview of new regulations, as well as existing regulations that were being made more restrictive. Over about seven months in 1998, the Regulatory Reform Committee examined 573 regulations that were to be introduced or made tougher among the existing 94 laws and 33 enforcement decrees and rules and recommended the withdrawal of regulations in 51 cases and the revision of regulations in 112 cases.

Policies Aimed at Economic Revival

Consultations on Macroeconomic Policy with the IMF

In the face of anemic consumption and investment and amid sluggish exports dampened by the slowing global economy, the government held the eighth review and consultation meeting with the IMF, on October 27. At the meeting, the IMF agreed to let Korea resume its authority and discretion in monetary policy and shared the government's view that economic growth would be positive in 1999. In regard to the money supply in the fourth quarter, the restrictive supply stance was to be terminated, and a more accommodating stance was to be adopted. It was hoped that these shifts would lift the confidence of foreign lenders. Moreover, the IMF agreed with the government's positive growth outlook for 1999 despite its earlier forecast, in early October, of negative 1 percent growth. This signaled the willingness of the IMF to support more aggressive macroeconomic actions by the government to stimulate the economy.

The Push for Pro-Growth Economic Policies

At the 11th meeting of the Economic Policy Coordination Committee, on October 20, the government decided to take aggressive pro-growth measures in the fourth quarter, including expansionary monetary policies, lower interest rates, and expedited fiscal spending. Efforts aimed at easing the credit crunch were to be stepped up to coincide with the completion of the first phase of financial sector restructuring; additional support was to be given to SMEs and exporters; and new measures were to be adopted to buoy the housing and real estate markets.

Lowering interest rates and accelerating government spending. On October 1, the Monetary Policy Committee of the BOK decided to maintain its stance on steadily falling interest rates for the fourth quarter. To avoid the risk that large government debt issues would spark higher interest rates, the BOK also decided to expand market liquidity by purchasing monetary stabilization bonds and repurchase agreements from financial companies that could potentially encounter liquidity shortages after buying up government debt.

On another front, the government decided to step up business restructuring with the goal of alleviating the credit crunch. The downsizing and reassigning of the workforce at banks were to be completed by the end of October. In addition, the government hoped to wrap up the efforts under way to facilitate business workouts and eliminate the uncertainty associated with problems in the corporate sector so as to create an environment in which financial companies could expand business lending with greater confidence.

For accelerated fiscal spending, vice-minister-level economic officials were to hold meetings to review the execution of fiscal spending and run an on-site monitoring team made up of personnel from the Budget Office and other government agencies to ensure the quick implementation of government expenditures. Local governments were also to draft their own supplementary budgets expeditiously, complete their lists of recipients of public support by October, and take other accelerated administrative steps.

Enhancing the effectiveness of stimulus packages. Steps undertaken to enhance the effectiveness of the stimulus packages at the 11th meeting of the Economic Policy Coordination Committee emphasized areas in which policy measures were most likely to have comparatively strong effect. Beginning on October 1 with offers of credit for purchases of housing and durable goods, the government sought to encourage business agreements between consumer finance companies and sellers of durable consumer goods in an attempt to boost consumer spending.

The government decided to promote investment in promising areas such as information and telecommunication, tourism, and venture businesses. For this effort, the government expanded the list of companies eligible for temporary tax credits for investment (until June 1999) so that, besides manufacturing, service industries such as tourist hotels and business support services were also included. The assets eligible for tax credits were expanded beyond manufacturing equipment to all major business assets.

Several steps were taken to promote investment in venture capital companies. Thus, individual investors were allowed to deduct 20 percent of the invested amounts from their global taxable incomes and to exempt the capital gains arising from transfers of stocks. Likewise, the Regulation of Tax Reduction and Exemption Act was amended, and a special fund of about W 1 trillion was to be established that utilized postal savings for investment in information technology and other knowledge-intensive industries.

For the promotion of public infrastructure investment, the government decided to rewrite extensively the Act on Inducement of Private Investment to Social Overhead Capital in line with international standards. In particular, build-operate-transfer methods, among other new approaches, were to be allowed for a variety of construction projects. The investment returns of up to 18 or 20 percent prevailing in many competing countries were to be allowed; usual local returns at the time were around 13 percent. About W 500 billion in start-up capital in an infrastructure fund was to be made available for project financing.

Trade financing had not yet rebounded to precrisis levels, but trade by money remittance was on the rise, suggesting some improvement in trade financing. Table 8.10 shows the export and import financing ratios in 1997 and 1998.

In December 1998, in a move aimed at easing the credit crunch among SMEs, the BOK began to evaluate bank SME lending, including aggregate credit ceiling loans, operating funds, export bills, and import letters of credit; it redirected aggregate credit ceiling loans allocated to banks with sluggish lending so as to allocate them to banks with more aggressive SME lending. The MOFE put a US$1 billion loan from the World Bank into credit guarantee institutions and decided to expand the amount of credit guarantees available to SMEs by W 2.5 trillion per month until the end of the year to help relieve the credit crunch many SMEs faced. With the goal of drawing out the US$3 billion from the Export-Import Bank of Japan some time in December, the government concluded the borrowing agreement with the National Assembly's consent for the government guarantee for repayment, thus paving the way for a US$1.3 billion credit support for SMEs.

Table 8.10 Ratio of Export and Import Credit, 1998
percent

Indicator	*1997 December*	*1998 Q1*	*Q2*	*Q3*	*Q4*
Ratio of export credit[a]	44.7	62.4	66.2	70.5	63.9
Ratio of import credit[b]	38.1	59.9	61.7	63.6	60.7

Source: Financial Policy Division, Ministry of Finance and Economy.

a. Ratio of the purchase amount of export bills + secured export advances to exports.

b. Opening amount of the ratio of import letters of credit to imports.

Support for the Unemployed

A look at the measures the government adopted to address the problem of unemployment for about six months, from March 26 to October 17, suggests that there was some progress. During the period, W 7 trillion of the approximately W 10 trillion set aside for unemployment benefits and support was expended on 1.95 million unemployed. The recipients of the government unemployment aid can be divided into public works programs for 360,000 unemployed, training for 230,000, unemployment benefits for 340,000, and loans to 60,000.

Because of a sudden spike in the number of the unemployed, the government had to expedite unemployment protection spending without much preparation. This enabled a relatively large number of people to receive unemployment benefits, but opened the government to the criticism that some of the expenditures were ineffective or wasteful. In response, the government set about improving the effectiveness of the programs already in place rather than adding new, untested programs. For example, in the face of the criticism that the public works projects open to unqualified persons such as people younger than age 15 or older than age 65 and to housewives undermined the effectiveness of the projects, the government narrowed the age requirements from 15–65 to 18–60 and limited the eligibility to people who were registered unemployed or were registered as seeking work. In response to the charge that some public works programs were unproductive, the government redirected a portion of the spending to more productive activities such as the construction of a new national address system and the electronic conversion of maps in underground facilities, family registration documents, and land registration maps.

The government stepped up the monitoring of training providers and facilities to minimize substandard worker training and sought out model programs that could be promoted. Training in simultaneous interpretation, hotel management, and other service sector activities was expanded so as to focus on training in promising new service areas. A pilot program using vouchers for worker training was conducted from September to December in three cities (Cheonan, Cheongju, and Daejeon) and was expanded after the results demonstrated the program's effectiveness in offering trainees the option to select the desired areas of training and in promoting competition among training providers.

The progress was found to be satisfactory with the results of the W 127 billion allocation in the second half of 1998 for six public works projects targeted at 42,000 persons with advanced educational attainment, but unable to find work. The Ministry of Labor therefore pushed for new programs that could commence by the beginning of November. Meanwhile, expenditures aimed at providing jobs to 170,000 of the 400,000 college graduates in 1999 had already been incorporated into the 1999 fiscal budget. To help launch the program in the early part of the following year, the government produced extensive information guides on the program and distributed them at various work sites and universities.

Recognizing that there was an acute lack of employment opportunities for unskilled low-income job-seekers during the winter, the Ministry of Health and Welfare drafted plans to guarantee money for basic household necessities for low-income families, including food, clothing, and medical and educational services. Additional measures were taken to prevent the unemployed from becoming homeless and encourage food services for the homeless. Assistance was boosted for entities involved in conducting job searches to help homeless persons return to their families and engage in productive activities. Medical services and lodging facilities for the homeless were supported.

The Return of Stability to Domestic Financial Markets

Beginning in October 1998, domestic financial markets showed signs of stabilizing. Interest rates were falling sharply, and stock prices were surging. The overnight call rate, which hovered around 7 percent in October, had dropped to around 6 percent by December. The yield on corporate bonds fell from around 9 percent in November to around 8 percent in December. Bank lending rates began to drop below the precrisis level and averaged around 11.3 percent in December.

However, bank lending continued to show a downward trend during the fourth quarter, mainly because of declines in bank lending through trust accounts and credit from overdraft facilities. Nonetheless, discounted commercial bills, trade financing, and ordinary loans showed an upward trend despite the economic downturn. Lending to large companies dropped, while lending to SMEs rebounded. This was caused by several factors, including the reduced credit risk of SMEs as a result of business restructuring, aggressive credit guarantees, the improved capital positions of banks following the conclusion of the first round of bank restructuring, the expanded aggregate credit ceiling of the BOK, and a sharp drop in interest rates.

Corporate bond issues continued to increase in the fourth quarter over the previous quarter. Bond issues by the top five chaebol companies decreased to 62.1 percent, while corporate bond issues by large independent (non-chaebol) companies increased as a result of restructuring. In equity issues, capital-raising through stock issues jumped significantly in the fourth quarter as the restructuring of banks and corporate companies gained momentum. However, the issuance of commercial paper (CP) dropped noticeably in the fourth quarter as a result of new restrictions on the holdings by financial companies of the CP of the same company, which forced some issuers to redeem debt.

As financial assets moved around in and out of financial circles, the divergence in the trends in the monetary aggregates become apparent. In December, the growth of M3 (monetary aggregate for liquidity—see endnote 8 in chapter 5) showed a slight drop from the previous month as bank lending fell, though this was offset by the expanded credit supply from nonbank financial companies, including investment trusts that aggressively absorbed corporate bonds. Meanwhile, M2 (monetary aggregate for broad money—see endnote 8 in chapter 5) jumped 21.5 percent as money flowed from certificates of deposit and repurchase agreements into deposits.

The stock market surged during the fourth quarter. When market interest rates fell and the yen appreciated against other key currencies in October, the market outlook brightened significantly and prompted foreign investors to buy up shares. With the sovereign rating outlook improving in December and conditions on the stock market looking more favorable, many individual investors also jumped into the market. Table 8.11 shows key financial market indicators during the fourth quarter.

The Slowing Pace of the Economic Downturn in the Real Economy

The pace of the economic downturn began to slow in the fourth quarter. Construction was still mired in a deep freeze, but the drop in the orders for domestically produced machinery sharply moderated in November. Both wholesale and retail sales began to drop at a slower pace in September and moderated sharply beginning in November.

Table 8.11 Trends in Basic Financial Indicators, Fourth Quarter, 1998
won, billions

Indicator	*October*	*November*	*December*
Bank loans, month-on-month increase	–1,988.7	–1,836.8	–3,779.4
Issuance of corporate bonds	8,233.8	7,941.0	5,623.5
Issuance of stocks, initial public offerings, and capital increases	2,312.7	511.5	3,004.0
Increase in discounted CP increase, month-on-month	–187.3	–2,545.4	–16,417.6
M2 growth, year-on-year, %	26.4	26.1	21.5
M3 growth, year-on-year, %	13.5	13.1	12.4
Korea composite stock price index, monthly average	358.8	429.2	524.7

Sources: Bank of Korea and Ministry of Finance and Economy.

Note: M2 = monetary aggregate for broad money. M3 = monetary aggregate for liquidity.

Industrial production rebounded in November as exports increased and the drop in domestic demand moderated. The average manufacturing operation ratio rebounded in September. Consumer prices were more stable in the fourth quarter, but still showed an average annual rate of increase of 7.5 percent. The sharp rise in average annual consumer prices, despite the economic slowdown, was mostly caused by the large depreciation of the won since the onset of the financial crisis and the price pressures from the higher traffic tax on oil products.

Because of rising employment in the agriculture-fishery and manufacturing sectors, the unemployment rate in October showed a modest drop from August, but headed up as soon-to-be college graduates entered the job market. The ratio of dishonored bills and checks dropped beginning in October. For the month of October, the nationwide average ratio of dishonored checks and bills came to 0.2 percent, down from 0.31 percent in September. In December, the ratio fell to 0.12 percent, the lowest level since September 1996. Table 8.12 shows key economic indicators for the fourth quarter of 1998.

In short, the financial markets at home began to show signs of stabilizing in the fourth quarter of 1998, and the pace of the economic downturn began to moderate. By mid-November, some were expressing cautious optimism that the Korean economy might be nearing the end of the tunnel and poised for a rebound. Local news media were reporting that the

Table 8.12 Major Economic Indicators, Fourth Quarter, 1998, Year-on-Year
percent

Indicator	*October*	*November*	*December*	*1998*
Domestic construction orders	–52.2	–35.7	–45.2	–42.5
Orders for domestically produced machinery	–25.4	–5.1	0.9	–30.5
Wholesale and retail sales	–13.2	–8.1	–3.6	–12.7
Industrial production	–9.3	0.3	4.8	–7.3
Average manufacturing operation ratio	69.1	69.6	71.1	68.1
Consumer price, monthly	0.3	–0.3	–0.2	7.5
Unemployment rate[a]	7.1	7.3	7.9	6.8
Nationwide ratio of dishonored bills	0.20	0.20	0.12	0.38

Source: Ministry of Finance and Economy.
a. Before seasonal adjustment.

increases in the prices of stocks, the value of the won, and the prices of Foreign Exchange Stabilization Fund bonds might be signals of the early phase of an economic rebound. They also reported from the Guro Industrial Complex that factory orders were on the rise, more businesses were hiring new workers, and there were more start-up businesses. The challenge for 1999 was to forge ahead with expeditious and effective reform and restructuring amid the uncertain conditions at home and abroad and validate these early signs of optimism.

9

Restoring Financial Stability and Realizing Positive Economic Growth, January–June 1999

The Economic Policy Agenda for 1999

Conditions at Home and Abroad

For the government of the Republic of Korea, the year 1999 was going to be the stepping-stone to positive growth after the sharp economic contraction of the previous year. The year would see a bolstering of Korea's economic constitution so that the economy could resume growth at a pace close to full potential by the year 2000. In many aspects, it was a transition year. With the new millennium on the horizon, it was time to lay out a compelling forward-looking vision for the future of the country.

However, many challenges at home and abroad awaited Korea in 1999 as had been the case the previous year. The global economy was expected to grow only in the 1 to 2 percent range as it did in 1998, and global trade was projected to expand only at around 4 percent. Should another crisis break out in Brazil or the Russian Federation, the risks and uncertainties lurking in the emerging countries were going to become more menacing.

With regard to the challenges at home, the Korean economy had benefited significantly from deep and wide-ranging corporate and financial sector restructuring, as well as from the labor market reform and reorganization and the streamlining of public institutions that had taken place in 1998. However, if corporate and financial restructuring in 1998 was the hardware reform, what lay ahead was the software reform, akin to building a new operating system for all economic agents. Moreover, the government's reform efforts in the past had been accompanied by pain and conflict, and the general expectation for 1999 was not that different.

The stabilization in consumer prices and the other signs of a rebounding economy in the last quarter of 1998 raised the prospect of positive growth in 1999. There was growing optimism that there would be improvements in financial markets and needed relief from the credit crunch. Moody's was contemplating a rating upgrade to investment grade for Korea, and the outlook on the sovereign credit rating looked more promising. Yet, there was a consensus that, even if growth resumed, it would fall well short of the economy's growth potential. This meant that the job market would worsen, and unemployment would become more entrenched in the economy. The drop in real incomes and the continued corporate restructuring during the first half of 1999 were going to depress consumer and investor confidence.

The Policy Agenda for 1999

This was the context in which the government had to carry out several important tasks in 1999. First, the reform and restructuring efforts, which, to date, had focused primarily on the hardware aspects of the economy, had to lead to concrete, meaningful results. In regard to rules and regulations, a culture of economic freedom, but strict accountability and responsibility, had to take root and become embedded in the psyche of the people. The guiding principles in this endeavor had to be in accord with global standards and practices. The soundness of the financial system had to be restored and strengthened to prevent future crisis, and the financial service industry had to be transformed into a strategic growth industry for the economy in the 21st century. The corporate sector had to operate within a steady financial structure and transparent management in pursuit of innovation and global competitiveness.

Second, an effective stimulus had to be provided to the economy, and positive growth had to be the goal. In the midst of a slowing global economy, domestic demand had to be propped up through healthy consumption and investment and an optimal mix of monetary, fiscal, and foreign exchange policies. The government had to take fiscal steps during the first half of the year to boost falling private sector demand and adopt monetary policies to help revive the real economy in the second half of the year, when the pace of credit flows was expected to become more vigorous through improved financial intermediation.

Third, as joblessness worsened, additional measures had to be taken to enhance the effectiveness of the government's response to unemployment and to create cooperative management-labor relations. The job market was not likely to see a drastic turnaround during the first half of the year, and the general consensus was that, given past experience, unemployment would probably not fall to the 2–3 percent range even following a full economic recovery.

Fourth, the groundwork had to be laid for a knowledge-based economy for the 21st century. Unlike the past, when inputs of capital and labor drove economic growth, the economy now had to advance to a new level in which knowledge and, in particular, technology would be the source of dynamism and growth. Innovators and specialists had to be nurtured, and new foundations and infrastructure had to be laid to promote knowledge-based industries.

Through the successful implementation of these policies, an economic growth rate of 2 percent was thought to be well within reach in 1999. The expectation was that the economy would expand and rebound to positive growth during the first half of the year and then register solid growth in the remainder of the year. Unemployment would probably rise somewhat during the first half of 1999, but recede in the second half of the year as the economy gathered momentum. Inflation was expected to drop to about 3 percent as the Korean won strengthened and wages stagnated. The current account balance was likely to produce a sizable surplus, but at a lower level than in 1998 as the economy picked up steam and imports surged again. Table 9.1 shows projections for growth, inflation, and the current account balance for 1999.

Consultations with the International Monetary Fund on the Macroeconomy

The ninth program review and policy consultation meeting between the government and the International Monetary Fund (IMF), in March 1999, called for economic growth of 2 percent for 1999. It was possible that the economy could expand at a much more rapid pace if conditions improved at home and abroad. To be sure, this was a far more upbeat prediction than the one put forth at the review and consultation meeting in the fourth quarter of 1998 according to which the economy would simply rebound into positive territory. The inflation forecast had been lowered from 5 to 3 percent. The current account surplus was likely to narrow significantly, but remain substantial. Because of factors at home and abroad that could easily throw off the projections of a surplus, numerical estimates were

Table 9.1 Macroeconomic Projections for 1999

Indicator	*1997*	*1998, estimated*	*1999, projected*
Economic growth, %	5.5	–5.5	2.0
Consumer price, %	4.5	7.5	3.0
Current account, US$, billions	–8.2	40.0	20.0

Source: MOFE 1998v.

not specified. Given the economic prospects, the government and the IMF agreed at the March meeting that the goal of economic policies should be to (1) sustain recent improvements in confidence and provide support for the emerging recovery in domestic demand, (2) advance financial and corporate restructuring so as to strengthen the foundations for the resumption of sustained growth, and (3) ensure that the social safety net was adequate to ease the hardships among the unemployed.

The government and the IMF shared the view that Korea was recovering from the crisis more quickly than had been expected and that restructuring was taking place at a satisfactory speed. It was agreed that the quarterly review and consultation meetings between the government and the IMF should be switched to semiannual meetings in January and July. The IMF also agreed to extend US$250 million as part of the original assistance package, bringing the total loan assistance from the IMF to US$19.25 billion or 91.7 percent of the US$21.0 billion that the IMF initially pledged to Korea at the onset of the financial crisis.

Forging Ahead with Restructuring

A Strong Financial System: The Agenda for 1999

The primary focus of financial restructuring in 1998 had been protecting the economy from imploding under the weight of the financial crisis. The government sought to restore soundness by resolving ailing financial companies and recapitalizing badly shaken ones. At the same time, the government wanted to introduce a new legal framework for prudential regulation and supervision, along with corporate governance that would be globally accepted and reflect international best practice.

In 1999, financial restructuring was to be focused on building a strong financial system on the foundations that had been established during the previous year. Such a financial system should be efficient in allocating resources to the most productive uses, capable of absorbing shocks emanating from inside and outside the country, and sufficiently stable to shield the market from uncertainty and volatility. In building this system, efficient financial markets, competitive financial service companies, an effective system of supervision, and well-developed financial infrastructure had to be created simultaneously. Financial markets had to be able to operate in a free and competitive environment. Only then could effective market discipline be established and enforced. Information had to flow smoothly to facilitate the productive use of capital and enable the monitoring of business firms by the market. Capital markets had to evolve to achieve a better balance in Korea's bank-based financial system.

To gain competitive strength, domestic financial service firms had to run their businesses as commercial, profit-seeking undertakings based on sound and profitable business strategies. They had to develop the ability to provide sophisticated customer-tailored services and continue to grow in size and business scale. Prudent risk management, effective internal controls, and transparent and responsible governance structures had to take root. Even as the number of financial service firms dropped because of mergers and acquisitions, a competitive market environment had to be maintained at all times through easy entry and exit.

In removing the weaknesses in the financial system, the government had to toughen lax financial supervision and reinforce the market oversight system to bring both much closer to global best practices and standards. The deposit insurance protection system had to be run so as not to encourage moral hazard implicitly because, under a fully insured deposit protection system, depositors would pay little or no attention to the risks of depositing their money in failing banks and thus potentially fuel distress in the banking system.

In revitalizing financial infrastructure, the creation of a legal and regulatory framework in harmony with international standards was a priority. Deepening the pool of highly experienced finance professionals and ushering in a new professional culture in the financial service industry were necessary. All this mattered because sound fiscal and monetary policies depended on a strong financial system. Flexibility had to be embedded in economic policy making so that the economy would be better able to absorb internal and external shocks as economic conditions shifted at home and abroad.

The government decided to push for a number of policy initiatives in 1999 to help build a strong financial system. First, the underlying strength of the financial service industry had to be reinforced significantly. The clean-up of ailing or failing financial companies therefore had to continue. The sale of Korea First Bank and Seoul Bank had to be wrapped up, and the resolution of distressed and failed life insurance companies and other companies in nonbanking sectors had to be expedited. The W 23 trillion in public funds left over from 1998 was expected to be used to cover losses arising from the sale of Korea First Bank and Seoul Bank, as well as losses among the assets assumed by five banks as part of the restructuring.

Banks had to adopt a profit-seeking, commercial orientation. The government made clear that it would not interfere in the internal management of Chohung and Hanvit, two failed banks that the government had nationalized, but would establish transparent management goals and, if these were not reached, take appropriate follow-up actions.

Second, capital markets had to be reinvigorated. Only through dynamic capital markets can large companies raise needed capital and small and medium enterprises (SMEs) obtain bank credit more easily. Capital market development was crucial to the growth and success of start-up companies in technology. Well-developed capital markets help shield the banking sector from the brunt of shocks to financial markets and the broader economy.

The government saw 1999 as an opportunity to bolster capital markets substantially and decided to buttress the role of institutional investors as a first step. As a way to encourage technology start-ups to raise capital in established markets, the government separated initial public offerings from listing, relaxed listing requirements, and decided to nurture the growth of the markets of Korea Securities Dealers Automated Quotations (KOSDAQ) for small cap technology companies. In addition, it decided to open a futures market by April to help bond traders and investors more effectively hedge risks in bond investing and promote bond markets. Fresh efforts to turn the yields from three-year government bonds into benchmark treasury yields were set to be undertaken. Tax incentives were to be used to promote asset-backed securities, and a special company was to be established for the securitization of mortgage-backed securities. Investor relations and road shows to help market participants and investors gain a better understanding of Korean companies were also planned.

Third, financial supervision had to be stepped up and significantly strengthened. Through the creation of an integrated supervisory authority, the Financial Supervisory Service (FSS), which had been set to launch on January 1, 1999, the government hoped to push for effective financial supervision, especially in regard to prudential supervision, such as through limits on lending to large shareholders and their affiliates, limits on the exposure of single borrowers and groups of borrowers, new loan classification criteria, prompt corrective action, and prudential regulations for foreign exchange liquidity and exposure that had been introduced or reinforced in 1998.

Fourth, the government decided to shore up financial infrastructure. This would include efforts to provide better training and education in advanced financial management, enhance the outside recruiting of finance professionals, and establish performance-based compensation and other rewards. Credit-rating providers and credit bureaus had to do a better job in the markets; confidence in the accuracy of accounting documents had to improve; and independent auditors had to command much greater credibility and authority in the markets. Among yield-based financial products, the mark-to-market valuation of bonds had to be expanded, and the principle of yield-based dividends had to take root among investors. In addition, the risk management systems of financial companies had to be significantly upgraded, and the credit histories of individuals and corporate customers had to be managed more carefully so that credit could be extended without collateral. The role and function of outside directors in corporate boards had to be augmented to provide appropriate checks and balances in management. A new system for the public disclosure of management practices and personnel within financial companies had to be devised to enable minority shareholders, depositors, investors, and other interested parties to monitor and discipline management efficiently.

The Push to Turn Around Distressed Financial Companies

Restructuring banks. During the first half of 1999, cleaning up troubled financial companies remained a priority of the government. The Financial Supervisory Commission (FSC) determined that, among banks with Bank for International Settlements capital ratios below the minimum of 8 percent, the recapitalization plan by Chungbuk Bank was unrealistic, declared it a distressed bank, and ordered it to merge with another bank in February. Kangwon Bank took over Hyundai Merchant Bank in the same month. In March, Chohung, Chungbuk, and Kangwon banks agreed to a merger supported by a capital injection of over W 2.3 trillion by the Korea Deposit Insurance Corporation (KDIC), while the Korea Asset Management Corporation purchased nonperforming assets totaling W 45.3 billion.

The Bank of Korea (BOK), the central bank and the controlling shareholder of Korea Exchange Bank, injected W 336 billion into the latter through the Export-Import Bank of Korea on April 21. Commerzbank acquired preferred shares valued at W 260 billion in the same bank. Together with additional share purchases from ordinary shareholders, Korea Exchange Bank managed to raise W 1.02 trillion from private sector investors. Peace Bank managed to raise W 570 billion in paid-in capital, along with W 220 billion from the KDIC and additional capital from private sector investors. The recapitalization of Korea Exchange Bank and Peace Bank was thus off to a good start. The capital ratio of Jeju Bank had initially exceeded 8 percent, but the bank had been struggling to bounce back after its business soundness deteriorated; it managed to increase its capital by W 65 billion on March 31. Busan and Kyongnam banks each increased their capital by W 150 billion on June 29.

Negotiations on the sale of Korea First Bank to Newbridge Capital were ongoing, but there were difficulties because of disagreements over the size of the loan-loss provisions. There was a concern that protracted negotiations over the sale of Korea First Bank, which was already in a financially precarious situation, would raise the cost to the government of the eventual clean-up. Due diligence by the FSS indicated that, at the end of March, the liabilities of Korea First Bank exceeded the bank's assets by W 1,876.9 billion. In June, the FSC declared Korea First Bank a distressed bank and decided to inject public funds to raise the bank's capital ratio to around 10 percent.

On February 22, the FSC signed a memorandum of understanding with HSBC on the sale of Seoul Bank. Under the terms of the document, the sale was to be consummated after Seoul Bank had been cleaned up by separating and transferring problem assets to a bad bank. The government was to hold 30 percent of the bank shares. In the event of the sale of the shares to HSBC, the government was guaranteed to receive subscription rights equivalent to 19 percent ownership, thus effectively giving the government a 49 percent total stake in the new bank. The terms of the sale called for HSBC to cover 70 percent of the cost of raising the bank's net asset value to an appropriate level. HSBC agreed to pay the government US$200 million in the form of a facilitation payment for the takeover of Seoul Bank. Assets that had soured within a year of the takeover were to be sold off to a bad bank. As a way to ensure independent business management, the government agreed to give HSBC full management control. Many analysts noted that the terms of the sale of Seoul Bank were more advantageous than the terms of the sale of Korea First Bank.

Restructuring nonbank financial companies. The restructuring of nonbank financial companies was under way. The government revoked the business licenses of Hannam Investment Securities on January 6, KLB Securities on March 15, and Dongbang-Peregreen Securities on April 9. In the restructuring of merchant banks, Korea International Merchant Bank was merged with Korea Exchange Bank on January 1. The following month, Hyundai Merchant Bank was merged with Kangwon Bank. In June, the license of Daehan Merchant Bank was revoked after the bank became insolvent and unable to pay off depositors.

The restructuring of six life insurance companies—Chosun, Donga, Doowon, Handuk, Kookmin, and Pacific—began in earnest in March after the rehabilitation plans of the companies were judged unworkable. The liabilities of these companies far exceeded the assets. As a way to ensure a minimum injection of public funds and maximum employment, the government opted for mergers and acquisitions rather than the purchase of assets and assumption of liabilities. It also created an implementation committee to restructure life insurance companies and enhance transparency and objectivity throughout the restructuring process.

In March 1999, the FSC imposed management oversight on Korea Life Insurance. On June 8, 1998, Korea Life had signed a letter of intent for US$1 billion in investment with MetLife, a major U.S. insurer. However, after due diligence revealed that the company's liabilities exceeded the company's assets by W 2.9 trillion (20.1 percent of the value of the assets), the investment by MetLife was all but ruled out. Nonetheless, declaring the insurer a failed financial company was going to cause policy cancellations by the company's policyholders, trigger a sharp devaluation of the company, and bring chaos to the local insurance industry. So, recapitalization through an open sale was deemed more prudent. The government opted to impose management oversight out of concern that the company's management, if left intact, risked continuing a pattern of mismanagement and generating greater asset losses.

The FSS conducted due diligence on the assets and liabilities, as of March 1, 1999, of Seoul Guarantee Insurance Co., which had been created by merging two guarantee insurance companies in November 1998. The due diligence revealed that the company's liabilities surpassed the assets by W 3.79 trillion; unpaid insurance claims were valued at W 3.4 trillion, while the liquid assets represented only W 1.08 trillion. The company was clearly insolvent. However, an evaluation committee under the FSC determined that business normalization was possible within several years if outside funding was provided by the government and others and if there was an upturn in the overall business cycle. It was also considered important that the creation of a new guarantee insurance market as an alternative to Seoul Guarantee amid the rising demand for credit guarantees from low-income households and SMEs was not likely in the short run. So, the government decided to revive Seoul Guarantee as soon as possible. The FSC designated Seoul Guarantee a distressed financial company in June. The KDIC contributed W 1.25 trillion in investment, and the Korea Asset Management Corporation decided to defer the settlement of payments for certain receivables until the end of March 2001. The outstanding shares of Seoul Guarantee were written off and retired.

The establishment of effective financial supervision. The government consolidated the banking, securities, and insurance supervisory authorities and brought them under the roof of the FSS on January 1, 1999. Several other important changes in supervision took place during the first half of the year. For instance, a new European Union solvency margin system was introduced for life insurance companies in May and for non–life insurance companies in June. Under the new system, insurance regulators could issue prompt corrective action for insurance companies with low solvency margins: supervisory action could take the form of management improvement recommendations for companies with solvency margins between 50 and 100 percent, management improvement requests for companies with solvency margins between 0 and 50 percent, and management improvement orders for companies with solvency margins below 0 percent.

In accordance with the revised Banking Act and the related enforcement decree on lending rules that were set to take effect on April 1, the financial supervisory regulations on lending rules were revised to take effect on May 24 so as to incorporate conventional international standards on the ceiling on the credit extensions allowed for borrowers. Table 9.2 summarizes the revised lending rules and regulations.

Reinvigorating capital markets. Promoting growth in institutional investment was critical to reinvigorating and advancing capital markets. In the United States, mutual funds and pension funds made up a large share of the investors in the securities market. In contrast, in Korea, banks, insurance companies, and investment trusts accounted for most investments in securities. Pension funds represented a tiny share of investment activities, and

Table 9.2 Summary of Revised Lending Rules and Regulations

Indicator		*Before amendment*	*After amendment*	*Effective date*
Equity capital definition		Paid-in capital, reserves, and other surplus	Tier 1 capital and tier 2 capital (as defined under the Basel Accords)	April 1, 1999
Loans subject to the lending rules		Credit (loans and payment guarantees)	Credit exposure (credit, securities holdings, and all transactions involving credit risk)	April 1, 1999
Lending ceilings	To a single person (and related parties)	• 45% of equity capital (15% for loans and 30% for payment guarantees)	• 20% of equity capital	January 1, 2000
	To a single business group	• 45% of equity capital • Applicable to loans extended to a business group consisting of companies controlled by a business group owner or related parties or their affiliated company	• 25% of equity capital • Applicable to loans extended to a single borrower (and related parties who share credit risk)	January 1, 2000

Loans in excess of a certain amount	• FSC-designated ceilings (up to five times equity capital) • Applicable to a huge sum of loans extended to a single person or a single business group that collectively exceed 15% of equity capital	• Up to five times equity capital • Applicable to a huge sum of loans extended to a single borrower that collectively exceed 10% of equity capital	April 1, 1999
To a large shareholder[a]	• The lower of ceilings specified in a relevant presidential enforcement decree or equity contributions made by such a large shareholder; but, in either case, up to a limit of 45% of equity capital	• The lower of an amount specified in the relevant presidential decree up to a limit of 25% of equity capital or equity contributions made by such a large shareholder	January 1, 2000

Source: Author's compilation.

a. A shareholder and related parties whose combined shareholdings are equal to or exceed 10 percent of the total voting shares of a bank (15 percent for regional banks).

mutual funds were introduced in Korea only in 1998. Moreover, the prevailing practice among most private sector companies was to set aside corporate pension or severance funds in the form of provisions for retirement benefits on their own balance sheets or to keep the funds with insurance companies in various types of group retirement pension insurance plans.

During the first half of 1999, the government sought to improve the corporate pension system, foster the growth of mutual funds, supplement employee stock ownership schemes, and reform the way savings and investments were managed through bank trusts. In regard to the corporate pension system, the government granted regulatory approval to insurance companies in March to issue retirement pension insurance that offered defined benefits through pension payouts. The government planned to amend labor laws to allow the introduction of pension products and services akin to the U.S. 401(K) plans and others that involved defined contributions.

To foster the growth of mutual funds, the government decided to examine the possibility of introducing open-ended mutual funds earlier than it had originally planned. Mutual fund management companies were to be required to have start-up paid-in capital of W 7 billion, have a minimum of five asset management specialists each, and register with the FSC. However, some of the requirements were later relaxed to make it easier to set up a mutual fund. To encourage employee stock ownership plans, the government opted to explore an approach involving cutting short the mandatory stock-holding period from seven years to three to five years.

In revitalizing bank trust services, one key goal was to ensure that dividend payouts were based on actual investment yields. As of November 1998, the government had already required that provisions for debt valuation losses be incorporated in the computation of trust investment yields. For all bank trust and investment trust products created after November 15, 1998, a mark-to-market valuation was to be used. In addition, beginning in January 1999, no new subscription for development trusts—a type of money-in-trust that guaranteed the principal and interest—was allowed. Beginning on January 1, 2000, banks offering trust services were to set up internal controls to minimize conflicts of interest between normal banking accounts and trust accounts in organization management, asset management, and information flows.

To help companies gain easier access to capital markets, the government decided to separate initial public offerings from listing in the stock exchange and relax listing requirements. As a way to foster growth in bond markets, the government was also to adopt, in July 1999, the primary dealer system in the trade in government debt securities. An upgraded securities trading and settlement platform was to be launched by February 1999. To encourage more active bond trading, the market for repurchase agreements was to be expanded. Growth in the markets for repurchase agreements depended on the existence of standardized contracts and systems for delivery versus payment. After preparations by the appropriate agencies, the new system was to be launched in August 1999.

The credit-rating industry had to be significantly improved and strengthened. Following the introduction of the ongoing credit-rating system in January 1998, the government required credit ratings for guaranteed corporate bonds and the bonds issued by state-owned enterprises and financial companies, which had previously been exempted from the requirement to obtain credit ratings for debt issues.

In May 1999, the government came up with plans to stimulate high-yield bond markets; in October, it allowed high-yield bond funds to be used to help investment trust companies attract new funds into bond markets. It also began revamping secondary bond markets through the creation of interdealer brokers and a system for delivery versus payment.

Through the opening of the Futures Exchange on April 23, corporate and financial companies had new tools to hedge against interest rate and foreign exchange risks. However, because the Futures Exchange had been set up in Busan, while most traders and brokers were based in Seoul, criticisms were raised about the resulting inefficiencies and needless costs. The Futures Exchange first undertook trading in U.S. dollar futures and options, certificate of deposit interest rate futures, and gold futures. In September, trading in government bond futures was added.

On May 4, the government announced a package of measures aimed at fostering the growth of the KOSDAQ markets to help promising SMEs and technology start-ups raise capital more easily and at lower cost. For large companies with W 100 billion or more in paid-in capital, listing requirements were loosened so that companies that had exhibited positive cash flows in recent years or companies that had received foreign investments could be exempted from requirements in debt-equity ratios and capital erosion recognition. As a way to encourage small and medium high-technology companies to list on the KOSDAQ markets, the government stepped up efforts to help some 750 promising technology companies list on the KOSDAQ. The rules and regulations on public offerings were revised to expand the new mandatory proportion of shareholders to more than 20 percent and to bar the sale of shares by controlling shareholders and related parties for six months following the listing of shares on the KOSDAQ markets. To promote the trade in the shares of companies that had been delisted from the Korea Stock Exchange or KOSDAQ markets or that had been unable to meet listing requirements, an over-the-counter bulletin board market for the trade in shares of unlisted companies was planned for the end of 1999 or during the first half of 2000.

The Progress in Corporate Restructuring

The primary goal of corporate restructuring in 1999 was to meet the implementation schedule of the five principles of corporate restructuring (see chapter 5). To rebuild financial soundness, large companies had to reduce their debt-equity ratios to 200 percent by the end of 1999 and completely eliminate cross-debt guarantees by the end of March 2000. The top five *chaebols*—the large family-controlled and family-run groups that dominate business in Korea—had to participate in the Big Deal business swaps (see chapter 7) and reduce the number of their affiliated companies so as to restructure around their core lines of business. Large independent (non-chaebol) companies had to execute workouts without interruption.

Corporate disclosures and accounting standards had to improve drastically through the establishment of an organization to institute accounting standards that conformed more closely with international standards and practices. For advanced corporate governance, new best practices and standards had to be established using guidelines such as the Principles of Corporate Governance of the Organisation for Economic Co-operation and Development (OECD). Should any of these critical reform efforts falter, Korea was likely to experience a difficult economic recovery and face skeptical foreign investors.

Restructuring the top five chaebols. On January 15, the top five chaebols submitted quarterly implementation plans to the main creditor banks for the restoration of the financial soundness of the chaebols. These plans invariably pushed the self-help timetables for the restoration into the second half of the year and shifted the focus of the downsizing of the chaebol-affiliated companies from outright sales to external investors to mergers within each chaebol group. The creditor banks identified these and other shortcomings in the plans and demanded that the chaebols produce more aggressive proposals by mid-March.

As the restructuring of the top five chaebols continued, the funding problems of the Daewoo Group resurfaced in March after troubles had flared up the previous year. Daewoo Corporation, the main business unit of the group, was encountering difficulty collecting payments for its exports and securing fresh credit. Then, on April 13, Standard and Poor's downgraded the credit rating of the Daewoo Corporation from B to B–. The reality was that the cash problems of the Daewoo Group were only going to grow more serious unless there was expeditious restructuring. Yet, Daewoo had shown little progress in restructuring even by the first quarter of 1999.

As the situation rapidly deteriorated, Kim Woo-Choong, the chairman of the group, announced additional restructuring measures on April 19. Under the plan he announced, the businesses of the group were to be consolidated into three core business units (automobiles, trading, and finance), and W 9 trillion was to be raised by selling off the shipping unit of Daewoo Heavy Industries & Machinery, the commercial automobile unit of Daewoo Motor Company., and the Hilton Hotel in Seoul, which the group owned. Initially, these measures were met with an upbeat reception by the market, and the shares of some Daewoo companies surged. However, as questions began to mount about whether the plan was realistic and could actually be carried out, market sentiment quickly soured. In May, Korea Investors Service and National Information & Credit Evaluation, two local credit-rating companies, downgraded the commercial paper (CP) and bonds issued by Daewoo-affiliated companies to below investment grade. During the first half of the year, several investment trusts and other creditors refused to roll over the group's maturing CP and bonds. By June, the cash flow at the group had reached a critical point.

Meanwhile, the prospect for slashing the debt-equity ratio of the business group at Hyundai to 199 percent dimmed because of the lack of additional action after the group's acquisition of Kia Motors and LG Semicon. Hyundai announced a new set of restructuring measures on April 23 to shore up its faltering financial outlook. Under the measures, the number of affiliated companies shrank from 79 to 26 by the end of the year. In addition, the group's W 79 trillion debt, which surged with the acquisition of Kia Motors and LG Semicon, was to be cut to W 45 trillion through the sale of business units by the end of the year so that the group could comply with the 199 percent debt-equity ratio it had originally pledged.

The progress of the top five chaebols in business restructuring during the first half of 1999 can be summed up as follows:

- Hyundai's debt ratio reached 340.8 percent, which was lower than the 374.0 percent the group had planned to achieve. The group sold off W 1.51 trillion in assets and increased its capital by W 5.89 trillion, which was equivalent to 95.9 percent of the target amount of W 7.71 trillion. It also brought in US$859 million from foreign investors and disposed of 21 affiliated companies.
- Daewoo's debt ratio was 588.2 percent, which was higher than the target of 512.4 percent. It sold off assets valued at W 510 billion and added W 60 billion to its capital, which was about 28.6 percent of the W 1.99 trillion it had targeted. It brought in US$25 million from foreign investors and severed ties with 11 affiliated companies.
- Samsung's debt ratio was 192.5 percent, compared with the 233.8 percent it had set out to achieve. It sold off assets valued at W 1.61 trillion and added W 3.42 trillion to its capital, which was 236.2 percent of the W 2.13 trillion it had aimed for. It attracted US$1.22 billion from foreign investors and cut loose 15 affiliated companies.
- LG's debt ratio was 246.5 percent, which was lower than the 285.8 percent it had targeted. It disposed of assets valued at W 2.38 trillion and increased its capital by W 360 billion, which was about 110.5 percent of the W 2.48 trillion it had aimed for. It managed to obtain US$150 million in foreign investment and disposed of eight affiliated companies.

- SK cut its debt ratio to 227.3 percent; it had aimed for 313.7 percent. It raised W 970 billion by selling off assets and increased its capital by W 580 billion, which totaled 407.9 percent of W 380 billion it had targeted. It attracted US$363 million from foreign investors and disposed of six affiliated companies.

As part of the Big Deal, negotiations continued between the Samsung Group and the Daewoo Group after they had agreed, on December 7, 1998, to swap Samsung Motors and Daewoo Electronics. However, little headway was made. The proposed deal collapsed in June 1999 over differences in the valuation of Samsung Motors. As a result, Samsung Motors immediately applied for court receivership, and Daewoo Electronics was set for a creditor-led workout in August. In the semiconductor business swap, the price of the deal was agreed on, at W 2.56 trillion, in April 1999, and the consolidated company was launched in October. For the aerospace business swap, due diligence on the assets of Daewoo Heavy Industries & Machinery, Hyundai Space & Aircraft, and Samsung Aerospace was completed in March 1999, and the combined Korea Aerospace Industries was launched in October 1999. In the power plant equipment and ship engine sectors, due diligence began in March 1999, and, by November, Hyundai and Samsung had agreed to hand over their businesses and facilities in the power plant equipment sector to Korea Heavy Industries & Construction, while, in the ship engine sector, the three groups decided to create a separate business unit under the control of Hyundai Heavy Industries and Samsung Heavy Industries. In the manufacture of rolling stock, Daewoo, Hanjin, and Hyundai came to a consolidation agreement on May 3, 1999 and launched Korea Railroad Vehicles on July 1. In the oil refinery business, Hanwha Energy and Hyundai Oil Refinery agreed on stock swaps on April 2, 1999 and consummated the deal in late August, the first fully completed business swap under the Big Deal. Hyundai Petrochemical and Samsung General Chemicals agreed to merge and bring in investment capital from Mitsui & Co. of Japan. However, the deal collapsed in February 1999 after the companies could not agree to the conditions of Mitsui.

Restructuring the 6th to 64th largest business groups and SMEs. Workouts among the 6th to 64th largest business groups (chaebols) and large independent (non-chaebol) companies continued during the first half of 1999. Four companies in the business group of Shindongbang, four companies in the Miju Group, two companies in the Singsong Group, and Korea Industrial Co. were selected for workouts. Anam Electronics was rejected because of its poor prospects for a turnaround. KG Chemical and a subsidiary, Daljae Chemical, were also rejected because of the unsatisfactory efforts of the controlling shareholders. Three companies of Kangwon Industries, four Kohap companies, and three companies of Dongkook Trading merged. Two companies in the Shin Woo Group, two Miju companies, and two companies of

Dongbo Industrial Co. merged. Hanchang Chemical succeeded in bringing in foreign investors and completed its workout ahead of schedule. Table 9.3 summarizes the progress with workouts during the period.

As of the end of June, there were positive developments among the 76 companies that had finalized workout plans. The amount of debt restructuring and rescheduling represented W 20.5 trillion among the banks. Including the additional W 12.8 trillion for nonbank financial companies, the total debt restructuring and rescheduling represented W 33.6 trillion. Of this total, deferred debt payments came to W 25.8 trillion, and debt-equity swaps to W 3 trillion, which represented a 93.5 percent execution rate for the planned workouts. New funding support totaling W 1.6 trillion was also provided during this period.

As of the end of June, the 75 companies that had finalized workout plans had agreed to self-turnaround measures valued at W 9.8 trillion. Of this amount, self-executed restructuring actions represented W 2.7 trillion, or a 27.1 percent execution rate. Given the target amount of W 3.6 trillion by the end of June, the success rate was 73.6 percent. The main reason for the shortfall was the sluggish disposition of real estate and other business assets.

The 15 business groups that had finalized workout plans as of the end of June controlled 248 companies, of which 38 were set to be worked out. Of the remaining 210 companies, 12 were set to continue as going concerns, and 198 were to be dissolved or terminated through sales (82), liquidation (48), mergers (47), or court receivership and composition (21). As of the end of June, 78 companies, or 39.4 percent of the total, had been dissolved.

Of the large independent (non-chaebol) companies set for workouts, 17 having at least two affiliated companies controlled a total of 101 companies. Of the affiliated companies, 33 were to carry out workouts, 17 were to carry on in business as before, and 51 were to be dissolved; 17 of these last had already been terminated by the end of June 1999.

SMEs were also being restructured during the first half of 1999. Of the three SME groups creditor banks had selected for restructuring, the number of SMEs in the priority support group had grown since the beginning of 1999 as creditor banks stepped up their efforts to identify companies worthy of more favorable credit support. The value of the credit support plans for the priority support group and the conditional support group was estimated at W 76.1 trillion up to the end of 1999. At the end of June 1999, the value of the credit extended to these companies amounted to W 65.7 trillion, or 86.5 percent of the planned amount for the year and 122.8 percent of the target that had been set for the end of June.

New entities to set accounting standards and guide corporate governance. At their second meeting, in October 1998, the government and the World Bank agreed on the establishment of an independent nongovernmental

Table 9.3 Summary of Progress with Workouts, End of June 1999
number of companies

Companies	*Selected*	*Rejected*	*Completion ahead of schedule*	*Under review*	*Finalized workout plans*		*Conclusion of workout agreement*
					Total	*Merged*	
6th–64th largest business groups							
A. End of 1998	43	4	0	8	31	2	0
B. End of June 1999	47	5	0	4[a]	38	9	38
Large independent (non-chaebol) companies							
A. End of 1998	34	0	0	14	20	0	0
B. End of June 1999	41	2	1	0	38	3	37[b]
Total							
End of 1998	77	4	0	22	51	2	0
End of June 1999	88	7	1	4	76	12	75

Source: Financial Supervisory Commission.

a. Four companies in the business group of Shindongbang.

b. Korea Industrial Co., which finalized a workout plan on June 24, 1999, could not conclude the workout agreement until the end of June 1999.

accounting standard-setting body by the end of June as part of the conditions for a Second Structural Adjustment Loan, of US$2 billion. Under the existing regulatory framework, the Securities and Futures Commission within the FSC had the authority to set standards, while the FSS was responsible for enforcement. This structure suffered from a lack of research relying on highly trained accounting specialists.

The Ministry of Finance and Economy (MOFE) used a World Bank Technical Assistance Loan to commission an independent in-depth study on the characteristics of a successful private accounting standard-setting body. The study eventually led to the creation of the Korea Accounting Institute with the key support of the FSS, the Korea Accounting Association, the Korea Chamber of Commerce and Industry, the Korea Federation of Banks, and the Korea Institute of Certified Public Accountants. The institute was to be staffed by around 20 professionals, though the number of accounting experts was to expand gradually.

Governance structure was the key determinant of transparency, accountability, and efficiency in corporate management and therefore played a crucial role in the sound development of capital markets and in establishing strong foundations for the economy. Establishing the proper governance structure was of paramount importance to policy makers. For this reason, the government sought to amend the Commercial Act and undertake regulatory changes to enforce tougher, more effective corporate governance. One key task in this endeavor was to foster voluntary private sector initiative and commitment to improve corporate governance. This was the background of the decision by the MOFE to create a committee charged with identifying a model for corporate governance based on global best practices, led by the private sector, and well tailored to the domestic environment.

The committee consisted of one chairman and 13 members. An advisory unit on technical research and analysis was set up within the committee. On September 22, the committee and the advisory unit held a joint session—the eighth meeting of the committee and the fifth meeting of the unit—and finalized the Korean Code of Best Practice for Corporate Governance. At the outset, the stated purpose of the new standards was to enhance corporate transparency and efficiency and thereby maximize corporate value. To achieve this goal, companies first had to earn the trust of shareholders and investors, and the prerequisite for this was transparent and responsible business management. Only then could a management structure conducive to creative entrepreneurship at a high level take hold. Moreover, it was recognized that harmonizing the competing interests within a company would lead to lower costs in doing business and enhance competitive strength. This had to be accomplished in a rational and fair fashion. For long-term business success, companies had to act ethically and responsibly.

The code contained a preamble and five main sections detailing the recommendations for shareholders, boards of directors, audit committees, and interested parties and for the monitoring of company management by market participants. Each section proposed specific rules and contained copious notes to ensure that the standards would be clear.

Government Reorganization

Private management consulting companies that had conducted an extensive review of government organization reported their findings at the end of February 1999 (see chapter 8). Based on the associated recommendations, a management evaluation coordinating committee drafted proposals for the reform of government organization and held a public hearing on March 8. The proposals led to legislation on government reorganization that took effect on May 24, 1999, following approval by the National Assembly.

Several important changes were brought about by this Government Organization Act. The key changes included the following: (1) the National Economy Advisory Council was to be formed and headed by the president; (2) the Economic Policy Coordinating Committee was to be created and headed by the minister of finance and economy; (3) the Planning and Budget Committee and the National Budget Administration were merged into the Ministry of Planning and Budget; (4) the Public Information Office and the government information office within the Ministry of Culture and Tourism were merged to create the Government Information Agency; (5) the Civil Service Commission was established directly under the president to ensure the fair and transparent appointment and promotion of the top three grades of the civil service; (6) 23 functions within seven government ministries and agencies, including the administration of primary and secondary schools by the Ministry of Education and the determination of the local tax base under the authority of the Ministry of Government Administration and Home Affairs, were transferred to local and regional government authorities; (7) 14 functions within eight government agencies were reshuffled, including the foreign capital promotion function of the MOFE (transferred to the Ministry of Commerce, Industry, and Energy) and the regulatory licensing authority of the MOFE (transferred to the FSC); and (8) 20 percent of the positions higher than director general in central government agencies were to be recruited through open competitive outsourcing.

As a result of the government-wide reorganization, the number of civil servants was to be reduced by 16,871 (11.9 percent of the total) by 2001, and five offices, 32 bureaus, and 83 divisions were eliminated. Including downsizing and other cuts in February 1998, the civil service was reduced by 16 percent (or 25,955 positions), and 16 offices, 74 bureaus, and 136 divisions were eliminated. Despite the significance of these numbers, there were criticisms that the reorganization had failed to achieve the recommendations resulting from the review by private consulting companies.

The Reform of Tax Administration

Public distrust and frustration over tax administration had been apparent when President Kim Dae-Jung took office. The government thus faced the urgent task of eliminating many questionable practices and revamping tax administration through the establishment of a new human and physical infrastructure and information system. This was the purpose behind the creation, in April, of the Tax Administration Reform Committee under the chairmanship of the deputy commissioner of the National Tax Service and consisting of representatives from academia and business and civic groups.

In early 1999, the MOFE sought advice on tax administration reform from the IMF. In its report, the IMF noted that tax administration reform was needed to secure additional tax revenues and restore, by 2006, balance to the government budge after the deficit caused by the expansive fiscal policies adopted by the government in the wake of the financial crisis (Casanegra et al. 1999). The IMF stressed that tax equity had to be reestablished by minimizing tax avoidance and evasion by self-employed business owners and others who were widely suspected of grossly underpaying taxes. Another important goal was to reduce the cost of tax compliance. The report argued that any meaningful change in the attitude and behavior of taxpayers required simplified tax codes, a straightforward tax payment system, consistent and effective enforcement, and rational penalties for noncompliance. The IMF emphasized that, to produce the desired outcome, all these efforts had to take place simultaneously rather than individually or piecemeal. The report noted that there were problems in the organizational structure by type of tax and in the excessively rigid personnel management practices of the tax administration authorities. It pointed out that the transparency of tax administration would improve through an unambiguous clarification of the rights and obligations of taxpayers and tax personnel and that this would contribute to the elimination of the corruption and graft that had historically plagued the tax authorities.

The implementation plan for tax administration reform that was announced at the meeting of the heads of the district offices of the National Tax Service on March 5, 1999 was largely based on the recommendations of the Tax Administration Reform Committee and the advice of the IMF. The plan covered an array of issues. First, the tax administration system was to be revamped to provide drastically improved taxpayer-friendly services. As part of this effort, the taxpayer guidance division at the headquarters of the National Tax Service was to be reorganized into a taxpayer service bureau to provide better tax services; the investigation function of the regional tax offices was to be reinforced; and the primary function of the district tax offices was shifted to providing taxpayer services. By 2000, 95 percent of all national tax payments were to be processed by mail, and new policies were instituted to administer taxpayer complaints and provide tax services by phone, mail, facsimile, and the Internet. An electronic program was developed to monitor taxpayer satisfaction with tax services more effectively. In addition, certification of the quality of services for taxpayers was sought through the International Organization for Standardization (ISO 9002).

Second, new measures were instituted to eliminate graft and corruption at the source. The assignment of tax collectors to specific individuals or businesses was replaced by computerized taxpayer management lists. The selection of individuals and businesses for tax investigation was computerized in an effort to prevent direct contact between tax collectors and taxpayers. The selection of cases for property tax investigations, the most common source of graft, was scaled back significantly to prevent tax collectors from unnecessary access to taxpayers.

Third, tax assessment was targeted for substantial changes. The enforcement of tax compliance among self-employed high-income individuals such as doctors, lawyers, and entertainers was to be stepped up. Integrated approaches to tax assessment—such as examination of overall taxable incomes and assets, living standards, and past tax payment compliance among taxpayers—were to be adopted in determining cases for tax investigation. A five-year plan (1998–2003) was drafted to expand, from 410,000 to 960,000, the number of self-employed business owners who were to be required to maintain accounting records. The government sought to increase the voluntary compliance of small business owners by publishing guides to maintaining accounting records for tax purposes, as well as simplified accounting books.

Fourth, the government had to foster a culture of compliance. In this endeavor, public information campaigns were launched in cooperation with various consumer and civic groups to promote the practice of providing customers with purchase and payment receipts and to encourage the payment of the associated taxes. Internet Web sites and toll-free telephone centers were to be set up to promote the reporting and prosecution of tax fraud and noncompliance and to improve the public surveillance function. Education on taxation among school children—future taxpayers—was emphasized.

Fifth, the organizational structure and personnel management of the tax administration were retooled. In May and July 1999, the organizational structure based on the type of tax was replaced by a function-oriented structure, and offices dedicated exclusively to assisting taxpayers were opened at the national headquarters of the tax authorities and at regional and district tax offices. An ombudsman directly under the head of the tax office was appointed to respond more effectively to taxpayer concerns. A performance- and integrity-based personnel evaluation system was created for use among the employees of the tax administration.

Sixth, unrealistic tax structures were targeted for reform. Several legal and regulatory provisions on value added taxes among small businesses were set for revision or repeal by 2000. Changes were also made to clarify and reinforce the legal basis for the requirement that public agencies submit tax-related documents. The administration of the capital gains tax—which was the responsibility of the tax authorities, was riddled with inefficiencies, and was distrusted by taxpayers—was altered to a taxpayer-reporting system. The new system took effect in January 2000.

The Investment Grade Rating and the Supply of Foreign Exchange to Markets

The Rating Upgrade and the Stabilization of Global Financial Markets

In early 1999, international financial markets were becoming skittish because of a looming financial crisis in Brazil. In January, Minas Gerais, Brazil's fourth-largest state by area, declared a 90-day moratorium on its US$13.4 billion debt to the federal government. This triggered a US$1 billion capital outflow from Brazil on January 12, and the stock market plummeted. A contagion quickly spread to Mexico and to Central American countries. Only after the Brazilian government announced its shift to a free-floating foreign exchange rate system and pledged fiscal reform did the situation begin to improve. By March, calm was returning to international financial markets, and the spread on the sovereign debt of emerging countries began to narrow (table 9.4).

Korea began 1999 with a spate of positive news. On January 5, Standard and Poor's announced that it had upgraded Korea's credit outlook from stable to positive. The upgrade was a follow-up to a possible rating upgrade by Moody's and Fitch announced in December 1998. At the time, Korea was the first country among the emerging countries in crisis to receive the positive outlook.

On January 19, Fitch raised Korea's sovereign credit rating from BB+ to BBB–, an investment grade, 13 months after it had downgraded Korea to below investment grade, on December 23, 1997. The January announcement by Fitch was followed by rating upgrades by Standard and Poor's, from BB+ to BBB–, on January 25, and by Moody's, from Ba1 to Baa3, on February 12. On June 24, Fitch raised Korea's sovereign credit rating one notch, from BBB– to BBB. Some of the key factors cited for the rating upgrades were the restoration of economic stability, the success with reform and restructuring, the rapidly growing foreign exchange reserves, the sharp drop in short-term external debt, and the improving economic outlook under the administration of President Kim Dae-Jung.

The rating upgrades came with the caveat that Korea needed to ensure continued progress in corporate and financial sector restructuring and the

Table 9.4 Trends in the Spreads on Treasury Bonds of Major Emerging Market Countries, First Half of 1999
basis points

Date	*Korea, Rep. 2003*	*Korea, Rep. 2008*	*Thailand 2007*	*China 2006*	*Philippines 2008*	*Mexico 2008*	*Malaysia 2006*	*Brazil 2008*	*Indonesia 2006*	*Russian Federation 2007*
Jan. 15	350	375	303	220	476	533	610	1,209	992	3,782
Jan. 30	250	303	279	222	414	525	500	1,211	1,130	3,109
Feb. 15	220	239	238	212	365	497	375	960	1,002	3,199
Feb. 28	240	257	200	213	382	510	380	1,003	883	3,791
Mar. 15	230	250	202	203	387	412	340	953	1,003	3,719
Mar. 31	225	260	194	190	376	430	320	867	851	3,547
Apr. 15	185	216	189	154	317	385	290	652	785	2,827
Apr. 30	190	213	177	154	317	351	275	668	714	2,413
May 15	175	210	173	160	312	370	260	649	620	2,394
May 31	180	233	211	152	329	439	310	786	738	2,081
June 15	175	219	208	140	338	413	287	754	575	1,865
June 30	155	208	198	134	329	369	270	741	570	1,819

Sources: J. P. Morgan; for Republic of Korea 2003 and Malaysia 2006: Salomon Smith Barney.
Note: The spreads refer to 10-year U.S. treasury bonds. The years under the countries in the column heads indicate redemption years.

injection of flexibility in the labor market. It was noted that Korea's credit ratings could be reversed if the reform of the chaebols stalled or if the government opted to rescue failing chaebols.

The Growing Dollar Supply and the Policy Response

The conditions and the sentiment in foreign exchange markets improved noticeably during the first half of 1999. The overall climate for the inflow of foreign capital brightened. Interest rates on overseas debt issues looked more favorable, and the credit situation at the six major domestic commercial banks became significantly better. As a result, the supply of U.S. dollars in the markets seemed set to increase. There was now sufficient room for policy makers to shift from a cautious stance because of excess demand to a more neutral stance because of the steady markets.

Confidence in the won grew, and the expectation was spreading in the markets that the won would gain ground against other currencies. When the Japanese yen reversed direction and started to weaken in February, the concern mounted that profits deriving from Korea's key exports, such as automobiles and ships, would suffer and that the fledgling economic recovery would be threatened. The focus now shifted to maintaining the fair value of exchange rates.

The government's response was to restrain the supply of dollars and cut interest rates. To restrain the dollar supply at home, the government decided to accelerate foreign debt payments. The decision was made to pay back the IMF Supplemental Reserve Facility loans as scheduled in early 1999, and the government delivered a payment of US$5.7 billion during the first half of the year. In addition, the government decided not to roll over, but to pay back US$3.76 billion (due April 7) of the US$21.7 billion short-term external debt of domestic financial companies that had been rolled over in early 1998. The Export-Import Bank of Korea paid back US$374 million from its outstanding debt before maturity. For the US$1.8 billion raised from the issuance of depositary receipts by the KT Corporation, the BOK directly acquired US$1.1 billion, and the rest was deposited in overseas accounts and used to pay off foreign debt. The Korea Asset Management Corporation also purchased US$900 million with its won holdings to acquire foreign-issued debt claims held by ailing domestic financial companies. Public enterprises and state-run banks such as Korea Electric Power Corporation (KEPCO) and the Korea Development Bank ceased borrowing from overseas and decided to meet their dollar needs at home. An early foreign debt payment of US$900 million was also made.

In the meantime, the government hoped to keep interest rates low and stimulate domestic demand, while encouraging early foreign debt payment and no new foreign borrowing. The cost of borrowing at home had to be at least as favorable as the cost of borrowing abroad to prod early foreign debt payments and check fresh overseas borrowing. In March, because of the low interest rates at home, KEPCO was able to pay off US$450 million of US$700 million in callable bonds with interest rates in the range of 10 to 15 percent.

Because of the free-floating foreign exchange system that had been adopted in the wake of the financial crisis, the government maintained its interventions in foreign exchange markets at a minimum. At nine meetings with the IMF, it kept to the position that the BOK should limit its interventions to achieving foreign exchange reserve targets and facilitating smoothing operations to minimize exchange rate volatility.

Daily foreign exchange trading averaged approximately US$1 billion. However, during the first quarter of 1999, seven or eight major infusions of foreign direct investment (FDI), including US$300 million from the sale of Anam Semiconductor, were expected. Repayments of IMF Supplemental Reserve Facility loans—US$600 million in May and US$3.1 billion in June—were also planned. Fearing sharp won/dollar swings, the BOK stepped up its dollar purchases in the markets during the quarter, and the government accelerated its IMF loan payments by paying US$1.3 billion in April, US$1.2 billion in May, and US$1.2 billion in June.

During the first half of 1999, the current account posted a US$12.2 billion surplus. Exports continued to decline until May, but turned around beginning in June. As domestic demand rebounded, imports began to surge in March. Overall, the capital account was in the negative by US$290 million. While FDI and portfolio investment jumped sharply, the repayment of the foreign debt was aggressive. During the first half of the year, usable foreign exchange reserves rose by US$11.92 billion, from the US$48.51 billion at the end of 1998. By the end of June, usable reserves exceeded US$60 billion.

The won began to appreciate in early January 1999 because an upgrade in the sovereign credit rating for Korea was expected. However, international financial markets were on edge over mounting fears of a crisis in Brazil and the downward spiral of the Japanese yen; the won therefore began to come under pressure and had depreciated to W 1,233.6 on the dollar by March 15. With signs of calm returning to financial markets in late March, the current account surplus continued, and inbound foreign capital and investment rose. As a result, the won gradually gained strength and had reached W 1,155 on the dollar by the end of June. The won broke through the W 1,000 mark per ¥100 in late April and had appreciated to W 945.97 per ¥100 by the end of June.

First Phase of the Liberalization of Foreign Exchange Transactions and the Expansion of FDI

The government began to implement the liberalization plan for foreign exchange transactions on April 1. With the implementation came the repeal of the bona fide (real demand) principle. The current account transactions of corporate companies were liberalized, as were most of the capital account transactions of corporate and financial companies. The licensing required of foreign exchange business institutions was replaced by a registration system. In a move designed to advance the first phase of the liberalization in foreign exchange transactions, the BOK computerized its monitoring of short-term foreign currency flows on April 1. The same day, the Korea Center for International Finance, which had been established to collect financial market information, provide analyses, and run early warning systems for foreign exchange markets, began its work.

Notwithstanding the supplementary measures taken to ensure a smooth liberalization, some market analysts were expressing concern that the rapid short-term ebb and flow in foreign currency values might increase the volatility of foreign exchange markets and that additional safeguards were needed as liberalization and deregulation moved forward. As a remedial measure, the government decided to prevent irresponsible foreign short-term borrowing by limiting short-term overseas financing to companies that had demonstrated strong financial positions. Thus, only companies with debt ratios below the industry average and with credit ratings above investment grade were allowed to undertake short-term overseas borrowing.

Out of concern that nonresident speculators might engage in significant forward foreign currency betting, the government capped won-based borrowing by foreign residents at W 100 million per borrower. Restrictions were placed on the issuance of won-denominated securities at maturities of less than one year. Derivatives trading, which, in effect, was equivalent to won borrowing, was restricted. Foreign investors had to pass through authorized local foreign exchange banks to execute foreign currency conversions before investing in locally issued securities.

The won/dollar exchange rates prevailing in nondeliverable forward markets after the liberalization of foreign exchange transactions had taken effect on April 1 corresponded closely to the exchange rates in home forward markets. This had not been the case prior to April because of the restrictions imposed on arbitrage trading between offshore nondeliverable forward markets and home markets and because nondeliverable forward exchange rates reflected the expectations of offshore traders and speculators. This changed when domestic residents were allowed to engage in nondeliverable forward trading, which accelerated the convergence between the exchange rates at the relevant offshore markets and the home forward markets.

During the first half of 1999, the number of industries open to foreign investors was significantly expanded. On February 26, biomedicine manufacturing was fully opened, and restrictions on foreign investment in the cable broadcasting industry were eased from 15 to 30 percent. On May 1, barriers on casino operation were lifted, and, on July 1, the cap on foreign investment in the wire and wireless communication sectors and other telecommunication sectors was raised from 33 to 49 percent. By the end of 1999, 1,127 industries out of 1,248 had become fully liberalized, 14 had become partially liberalized, and 7 were still closed to foreign investors; thus, 99.4 percent of local industries were now open to foreign investors.

The Debate over International Financial Architecture Reform

The debate on international financial architecture reform heated up during the first half of 1999. In February, the finance ministers of the G-7 countries met at Hotel Petersberg, near Bonn, and adopted the proposals presented by Hans Tietmeyer, president of Deutsche Bundesbank, on international cooperation in the supervision of financial markets. Included in the proposals was the creation of the Financial Stability Forum (FSF). In April, the FSF held its first meeting. The primary purpose of the FSF was to facilitate cooperation and coordination in financial market supervision and surveillance. Among the priority tasks set by the FSF was to address highly leveraged institutes, offshore financial centers, and short-term capital movements. The participation of emerging countries and international financial centers in the forum was encouraged.

In April, the Board of Directors of the IMF established a new contingent credit line (CCL) to prevent the spread of financial contagion to countries with sound economic policies and internationally accepted regulatory and market practices. The board abolished the two existing facilities: the Compensatory and Contingency Financing Facility and the Buffer Stock Financing Facility. The new CCL was initially proposed by U.S. President Bill Clinton and later embraced by IMF member countries (see chapter 8).

In March, the deputy finance ministers of the G-33, an expanded G-22, met in Bonn for discussions on international financial architecture reform. A follow-up meeting took place in April in Washington, DC. The meetings were not intended to produce concrete proposals on the participation of emerging economies in efforts to address multilateral issues, but were held for general discussions and an exchange of ideas on financial markets. At the Bonn meeting, the discussions centered on the foreign exchange system and macroeconomic policies, the involvement of the private sector in crisis prevention and resolution, and the best way to strengthen the role of the IMF and the World Bank. At the Washington meeting, the participants discussed ways to strengthen financial systems in developing countries, social welfare topics, and the regulation of short-term capital flows and highly leveraged institutes.

The Korea Report on International Financial Architecture Reform

In crisis-stricken Korea, the immediate task was to carry out meaningful reform and restructuring to renew the country's economic foundations and prevent future crises. However, a no less important task was to promote effective international cooperation and to contribute to the efforts under way to shore up the international financial architecture and reduce the chance that there would be new crises in the world's small, but open economies.

It was with the desire to tout Korea's success in dealing with the crisis and to contribute to the multilateral efforts to establish a new international financial order that the MOFE published the "Korea Report on International Financial Architecture Reform".

The Korea report was released on April 26 (MOFE 1999b). It contained several noteworthy proposals. First, in regard to transparency, the report expressed Korea's support for the work of the IMF to strengthen the special data dissemination standard in the areas of foreign exchange reserves, external debt, and indicators of financial sector soundness and to develop a new code of good practice in fiscal and monetary policy transparency. Korea expressed its support for the work of the Basel Committee on Banking Supervision and other financial supervisory-related bodies and the efforts under way by, among others, the International Accounting Standards Board, the OECD, and the World Bank to improve rules and regulations on corporate governance, accounting and audit, and bankruptcy and to encourage greater cross-border harmonization in such rules and regulations. Because many developing countries would not be able to adopt and integrate international standards quickly, the report emphasized that a grace period must be considered and that technical support had to be provided by international financial institutions to facilitate the process.

Second, the report noted that, in the task of reinforcing the integrity of the financial sector in emerging countries, a sound and efficient financial system was critical. It stressed the importance of restructuring the financial service sector, expanding the autonomy of financial markets, creating more effective prudential regulation and supervision, and developing human resources, including expertise in advanced financial management.

The report argued that, in restructuring the financial service sector, the first task was to carry out thorough due diligence and separate viable from nonviable institutions. Among viable institutions experiencing short-term difficulties, the report stressed that cleaning up nonperforming assets and recapitalization must be the priority. Public funds may be employed in this endeavor, provided that the injections of funding were swift and sufficient to prevent a protraction of the credit crunch and to restore market confidence and that there was fair and strict loss sharing to prevent moral hazard and minimize the amount of the funding injected by the government. Moreover, because restructuring inevitably has a short-term dampening effect on the economy and because nonperforming loans might grow and hamper the pace of restructuring, the report favored the adoption of countermeasures to keep economic growth on track.

To ensure financial market autonomy, the report argued that an environment favoring competition and deregulation had to be fostered, along with efforts to encourage capital markets so as to supplement bank-based financial systems. The report emphasized that the core principles of the Basel Committee on Banking Supervision should be firmly established as the basis for prudential regulation and supervision. To strengthen prudential supervision, the abolition of regulatory forbearance or implicit government guarantees had to be reviewed in light of the impact on the risk of market disruption.

In support of the development of highly trained human resources and the creation of expertise in advanced financial management, the report urged efforts to attract foreign capital and the latest management skills.

Third, to address the policy challenges in cross-border capital flows, the report supported the orderly and well-sequenced liberalization of the capital account in parallel with the adoption of initiatives to strengthen financial supervision and improve the efficiency of domestic financial markets. Temporary safeguards were needed to stem any sharp reversals in capital flows. The report expressed support for the proposals put forth by the Basel committee for a highly leveraged institute to enhance the transparency of financial transactions and minimize the downside risks of opaque financial activities. The report revealed the Korean government's belief that foreign exchange transactions had to be monitored, that soundness standards had to be established for financial companies to mitigate the risks associated with unimpeded cross-border capital flows, and that won-denominated borrowing by the highly leveraged institute must be selectively restricted to prevent speculative activities.

Fourth, given the government's experience in restoring market stability through concerted rollovers of short-term debt, the report proposed the following steps to encourage private sector involvement in crisis prevention and resolution:

- If a crisis country seeks emergency assistance from the IMF, a consultative committee on debt resolution should be created to seek the collective resolution of the liabilities of private sector financial companies. Membership in the committee must include government agencies and the central banks of the creditor countries, the IMF and other multilateral financial institutions, and the governments of the crisis countries. The committee was to recommend a three-month rollover of the debt liabilities of the crisis country so as to give creditor institutions time to evaluate the terms and conditions for participation in the debt resolution.
- A creditor committee should be formed to seek an agreement on debt relief and debt rescheduling by a majority or two-thirds vote of the members. The imposition of penalties or sanctions on nonparticipating creditor institutions should be considered within reasonable, internationally accepted bounds.

- Provisions in support of debt rescheduling should be included in the issuance of sovereign debt, and measures aimed at strengthening the role of the IMF in private sector debt relief and rescheduling should be explored.

Fifth, in reforming multilateral financial institutions, the report stressed that the issue of the establishment of a new institution to act as the lender of last resort should be studied as a mid- to long-term project and that it was more urgent to adopt the CCL under consideration by the IMF. Meanwhile, the World Bank and other multilateral institutions should expand their loan guarantees in support of developing countries that are struggling to return to international credit markets. Because of the IMF's active role in providing CCLs and other crisis management support, the financial resources of the IMF may come under pressure. Arrangements for additional contributions (higher member quotas) or new borrowing should therefore be explored. Regional financial cooperation should be stepped up to enhance the effectiveness of international financial institutions. The report put forth a number of proposals on the organizational structure of the IMF and the World Bank, such as the creation of a running council instead of an interim committee, but the focus was largely on improving the decision-making process. The report expressed the view that the existing quotas of member countries should be recalibrated and that the proportional representation of member countries should be reweighed. The report stated that the role and the support structures of multilateral financial institutions should be clearly established so as to ensure the effective and efficient implementation of crisis management programs.

Sixth, the report noted that the crisis among emerging economies and the launch of the euro compelled a review of existing foreign exchange systems. There was no consensus among policy makers and academics across countries on the optimal exchange rate system. Past experience clearly suggested that both fixed and floating exchange rate systems had inherently different strengths and weaknesses. It therefore made sense for each country to adopt an exchange rate system that was well suited to its overall economic situation, and economic policies consistent with the exchange rate system in place should be pursued. In particular, crucial factors such as macroeconomic policies, the stage of development of the financial system, the degree of openness of the economy, and integration and harmonization with the global economy had to be weighed in adopting the most appropriate exchange rate system.

Steady and predictable exchange rate movements of the dollar, the euro, the yen, and other key global currencies were critical to the stability of the international currency system and to crisis prevention. The report argued that such movements could be facilitated through enhanced policy coordination at the regional and international levels. The developed countries as a group should refrain from pursuing a benign neglect approach to exchange rate issues that tends to add to the burden on small open economies.

Seventh, the report argued that protecting economically disadvantaged or dislocated populations from economic hardship constituted a core policy challenge. Reinforcing social welfare systems to assist the growing number of the unemployed and households in poverty contributed to economic reform and reduced the share of the burden of reform these people and these households had to assume. In Korea, the negative effect of the financial crisis was especially acute because of the country's woefully inadequate social safety net. Nonetheless, Korea managed to build a broad national consensus on the need for a painful effort at restructuring, for the creation of a better social welfare system through an expansion in unemployment benefits early on, and for the establishment of the Korea Tripartite Commission, which consisted of representatives of the government, management, and labor, to foster cooperation and understanding in seeking ways to overcome the financial crisis.

Eighth, because of the limited resources available to the IMF and other multilateral institutions in providing assistance to crisis countries, the report favored more crisis initiatives based on mutual assistance at the regional level. Several proposals had been put forth to enhance regional cooperation. However, as practical short-term objectives, the report recommended the establishment of regional market surveillance mechanisms to preempt financial crisis, more vigorous efforts to expand regional trade and trade financing, and agreement on currency swap arrangements among central banks in a region to bring a quick end to market distress and prevent a contagion.

Finally, the report suggested that developing countries participate more widely in discussions on international financial reform, particularly at the IMF, the G-7, the G-22, and the G-33. The report argued that the emerging countries should have a place at the FSF, which was to be run mainly by the G-7. The report recommended that the representation of developing countries be expanded at the IMF and other multilateral institutions.

Restoring Calm to Financial Markets and Resuming Positive Growth

The Aggressive Response to Unemployment

In February 1999, the Korean Confederation of Trade Unions withdrew from the Korea Tripartite Commission and decided to stage protests and resist the government. The relations between business and labor were deteriorating rapidly.

In January 1999, the number of unemployed reached 1.76 million, and the unemployment rate climbed to 8.5 percent. In February, the unemployment figures jumped to 8.6 percent and 1.79 million, compared with 1.66 million at the end of 1998. Seasonal factors might account for the increases, but 1.8 million unemployed workers was clearly a heavy burden on the government. Relative to the 450,000 unemployed in October 1997 before the financial crisis erupted, the unemployment figures in early 1999 represented an increase of 1.34 million.

By region, unemployment was much worse in large metropolitan areas than in rural areas. Of the 1.79 million unemployed nationwide in February 1999, 1.39 million or 78 percent were in Seoul and six of the other largest metropolitan areas. Approximately 1 million of the 1.3 million people who had become unemployed since the onset of the financial crisis were either short-term temporary workers or workers who had been employed at SMEs. By age, people in their 20s made up 39.8 percent of the total. The number of workers who had job experience, but who had been unemployed longer than one year, totaled 140,000 in February 1998, but this figure had jumped to 240,000 a year later, signaling the long-term nature of the unemployment situation and the growing number of low-income households.

The policy response of the government to the mounting unemployment was to focus on the creation of new jobs, the increased provision of temporary jobs, the expansion of job training through effective programs, and the boost in the support for financially distressed households. First, to create new jobs, the government decided to offer additional support to venture start-ups among SMEs. It was unrealistic to expect more investment in start-ups by large companies because of the restructuring they were undergoing. The Small and Medium Business Corporation, a government agency, therefore decided to augment the funding for venture start-ups from W 150 billion to W 750 billion and assist more than 2,000 start-up companies. The government contributed W 10 billion to help the Kibo Technology Fund provide up to W 200 billion in credit guarantees to venture businesses and start-up companies. Income tax credits to individuals for investment in venture businesses or start-ups were raised from 20 to 30 percent of the investment. Business acquisition and registration taxes were fully exempted on investments by companies.

To boost job creation in the cultural and tourism industries, the government contributed W 50 billion to the Cultural Industry Promotion Fund and W 40 billion to the Tourism Industry Promotion Fund. To expand new housing construction, W 1.5 trillion was added to the National Housing Fund, and a raft of tax incentives were made available. Companies receiving government investment, such as Korea Telecom and KEPCO, were also to join hands to invest a total of W 2.4 trillion in job creation efforts through SMEs. The government expenditure for social overhead capital projects was boosted by W 800 billion.

Second, to provide temporary employment, the government decided to focus on urban job-seekers with advanced educational attainment through an allocation of W 1.05 trillion in the supplementary budget. Of this amount, W 255.2 billion was to be allocated for public works projects, such as information technology (IT) infrastructure, that were expected to create about 50,000 jobs for people with advanced education; W 94.8 billion was set aside for internship programs for about 35,000 high school graduates; and W 700 billion was to be provided to local government agencies for expanded public works projects.

Third, W 100 billion was allocated for job training programs in IT, cultural activities, tourism, and other emerging service industries, along with training programs to help traditional industries become more knowledge based. Foreign instructors were to be employed to ensure effective training for domestic instructors in emerging industries and for people seeking jobs overseas.

Fourth, allocations were aimed at increasing social welfare spending and providing minimum subsistence benefits among low-income households to cover medical, food, clothing, and educational expenses. The number of persons eligible to receive government welfare assistance in the form of minimum subsistence benefits was expanded from 570,000 to 760,000 through an additional budget outlay of W 104.7 billion. Spending on daily public works projects was raised by W 50 billion to provide extra support for individuals struggling to achieve self-sufficiency.

The value of government-supported loans to unemployed individuals in low-income groups was raised by W 500 billion. In the government budget, W 70 billion was set aside for tuition support for students in middle schools and high schools, and meal programs for students in low-income families were allocated an extra W 4.6 billion. The number of social welfare workers was raised by 1,200, and the number of consultants in job security programs was boosted by 650. The spending on meals and shelter for the homeless was raised. These programs overwhelmed the original government unemployment and social welfare budget of W 7.7 trillion; they required an additional W 2.55 trillion in a supplemental budget and W 5.76 trillion in special expenditures through various funds. As a result, the total unemployment expenditures for 1999, for example, came to W 16 trillion.

A Stimulus Package for the Macroeconomy

Heartened by the signs of economic recovery, the government set its sights on stimulating the economy for positive economic growth in 1999. As part of this effort, it aimed at a budget deficit of about 5 percent of gross domestic product (GDP) as it supplemented the expenditures for the social safety net and the stimulation of the real economy. It also accelerated the spending targeted on 580 major investment projects (W 43 trillion) by allocating 77 percent of the relevant budget in the first half of the year.

In April 1999, the government submitted to the National Assembly the first supplementary budget for additional unemployment expenditures. The supplementary budget totaled W 2.66 trillion and included W 2.56 trillion set for unemployment spending and W 100 billion for assistance to those affected by the recent fishery agreement with Japan. To finance the additional spending, the government, taking into account the decline in interest rates, decided to raise W 1.85 trillion by cutting the interest expenses on government bonds related to financial sector restructuring and make use of W 809.3 billion that had become available because of a surplus at the BOK. The National Assembly passed the first supplementary budget after adding W 100 billion in support for the fishery industry and reducing the interest payments on government debt by W 100 billion.

Mid-term plans for budget deficit reduction. In January 1999, the government announced its mid-term fiscal plans for 1999–2002. Because of spiraling fiscal expenditures for the reform and restructuring of the economy and the significantly expanded spending on social welfare and the social safety net since the onset of the financial crisis in late 1997, concern had been mounting about the growing budget deficits. So, the government was compelled to come up with a mid-term plan to bring the fiscal deficit under tighter control. Under the plan for 1999, the government was to strive for an early reversal of the fiscal deficit and provide the necessary expenditure support for higher potential growth. For fiscal prudence, the plan called for a narrower deficit beginning in 2000 and a balanced budget by 2006, when the government would be able to start the redemption of its debt. To reach this target, it was estimated that the rate of increase in gross fiscal expenditures would have to be kept 2 percentage points below the economic growth rate, while the ratio of taxes to GDP was to be raised from 19.8 percent in 1999 to 21 or 22 percent by 2002. To help boost the growth potential of the economy, the government identified mid- to long-term priority areas for investment: social overhead capital, culture and tourism industries, IT, science, training in knowledge-based industries, social welfare, health, the environment, SMEs, and export businesses.

Continued implementation of an accommodating monetary policy. Opinions varied on the best direction for monetary policy in 1999. The Research Department of the BOK took the position that foreign exchange rates should be stable and that procyclical fiscal spending by the government should support economic recovery, but that the reliance on loose monetary policies to fuel growth should be approached with caution. For the BOK, the interest rate cuts through market interventions since May 1998 and the incipient economic rebound called for patience because the effect of the rate cuts was likely only to be felt throughout the economy over time. Meanwhile, the IMF, in January 1999, argued that more aggressive interest rate cuts were needed to counter the appreciating won and that the overnight call rate could be pulled to below 5 percent.

Korea's effective interest rates were still high, and the likelihood that loose monetary policy would generate inflationary pressure was rather small. At a MOFE meeting with economists of leading private interdisciplinary research groups and research institutes, many argued that there was room for more interest rate cuts given the outlook for positive growth and low inflation.

As the debate on the optimal monetary policy continued, the Monetary Policy Committee of the BOK, the interest rate-setting body, decided, in February, to stick to an accommodating stance on interest rates in support of economic recovery, provided that the price stability target of 3 ± 1 percent would be maintained. Thus, the Monetary Policy Committee maintained the downward drift of call rates until April. However, as the economy showed clearer signs of rebound, the committee adopted a slightly more cautious stance and maintained the call rate at a steady level in May. It judged that conditions might favor the appearance of asset bubbles because the economy was gathering strength and stock markets were surging too quickly, while short- and long-term interest rates were still on a downward path. The shift in the economic outlook of the BOK was a noticeable departure from the low interest rate policy that had been in place since the second quarter of 1998.

Sector-specific stimulus measures. The estimated needs in export financing and in import financing had increased by US$2.3 billion and US$3.9 billion, respectively, since the end of 1998, for a total of US$6.2 billion for 1999. However, the situation was such that commercial banks would not be able to meet these financing needs on their own, particularly through overseas borrowing. It was felt that the banks would be able to finance only up to US$2 billion. A total of only US$2.7 billion was therefore available for 1999. Of the US$5.3 billion set aside for trade financing in 1998, US$800 million had not been used; US$1.9 billion in loans from the Export-Import Bank of the United States was also unused. So, an additional US$1.5 billion was needed to meet the expected demand. US$600 million of this was to come from funds passed through the capital increase of the Export-Import Bank of Korea from the BOK for export financing, and US$900 million was to come through overseas borrowing by the Export-Import Bank of Korea.

In light of shifts in export markets, such as liberalized foreign currency transactions and the diversifying patterns in exports, the BOK decided to revamp the trade financing system and implement the changes beginning on May 1. Under the new system, restrictions on the designated currency in local letters of credit were removed, and usance local letters of credit were introduced. The eligibility criteria among exporters for comprehensive trade financing were enlarged from companies with exports of US$20 million or less per year to companies with exports of US$50 million or less. Exporters who operated without manufacturing facilities were granted financing for export outsourcing, product development, and other, similar export-oriented activities. The limits and other requirements on imports of raw materials and on minimum foreign exchange earnings were also repealed in an effort to streamline trade financing.

The assistance for SMEs and venture capital companies continued to increase in 1999. In addition to the tax incentives and other support measures described elsewhere above, bank credit support was made available. The BOK encouraged the provision of credit for SMEs and venture capital companies by leveraging the Aggregate Credit Ceiling Facilities for commercial banks. In May 1999, the BOK set up a financing support section on its Internet home page to provide information on the financial assistance available to SMEs through the government and financial companies. In early 1999, commercial banks announced their own plans to help SMEs through business financing and initiated aggressive extensions of credit to businesses.

On March 12, the MOFE fine-tuned the full credit guarantee system so that only partial credit guarantees and, thus, only the partial assumption of losses could be provided through credit guarantee institutions. It was decided that the preparations for the partial guarantees would be carried out during the first half of the year and that about 30 percent of the total amount of guarantees would be used for partial credit guarantees during the second half of the year. The partial credit guarantee was to be fully instituted by the end of 2000.

Although full credit guarantees had clearly been effective in supporting the flow of bank credit even to somewhat shaky SMEs, they often led to the problem of moral hazard among banks because banks did not need to scrutinize guaranteed loans as closely as unguaranteed ones. This also meant that there were additional losses among the guarantee institutions. Payments by subrogation among credit guarantee institutions on behalf of guaranteed borrowers grew from W 788.3 billion in 1996 to W 1.17 trillion in 1997 and W 3.01 trillion in 1998. That these successive increases took place during an unprecedented financial crisis was a mitigating consideration. However, the ratio of payments by subrogation reached 9.2 percent in 1998. One reason the government opted to bring about partial credit guarantees gradually was the fear that banks would quickly tighten credit to SMEs if partial guarantees were suddenly implemented.

Restoring Stability to Financial Markets

By the first half of 1999, a sense of normalcy had returned to financial markets. The call rate hovered around 6 percent in January, but dropped to around 5 percent in February. It declined to the 4 percent range in March, stayed at 4.75 percent in April, and moved only slightly thereafter until the end of June. The yield on corporate bonds remained relatively stable.

Interest rates on bank loans dropped to a single digit by April and stayed at around 9 percent after May. The falling demand for credit among large companies was a factor. The interest rate on loans to prime SMEs fell to 8 percent in May as banks stepped up efforts to lend to low-risk borrowers. The borrowing rates on household loans also fell to the mid-10 percent range in June as banks expanded lending to relatively safe home mortgage borrowers. Deposit rates declined to 6 percent in May.

Stocks rallied in the first half of the year. Despite the brighter economic outlook, share prices continued to fall until February because of concerns over the crisis brewing in Brazil and the weak Japanese yen. However, they began to move up in March. On April 16, the Korea composite stock price index, the main stock index, reached 725.14, which was close to the 730.28 of August 27, 1997, before the financial crisis. Then, on June 29, the index broke through the 900 mark, at 903. The KOSDAQ index surged from 76.16 in January to 179.55 in June. The recovering real economy, the fact that companies were regaining their value after restructuring, and the ample liquidity resulting from falling interest rates all contributed to the stock market rally.

The climate for foreign investment in Korea improved because of rating upgrades by the major credit-rating providers. It helped that the Dow Jones Industrial Average climbed past the 10,000 mark on March 29 and buoyed markets in Hong Kong SAR, China, as well as markets elsewhere. For the first half of 1999, the value of net stock purchases by foreign investors totaled W 2.4 trillion, and capital inflows from overseas for stock investment reached US$3.3 billion.

Bank lending to SMEs and households surged during the first half of the year. The issuance of CP by companies jumped noticeably in the first quarter, but fell back in the following quarter. Net bond issues by financial and corporate companies fell gradually. Equity financing surged and exceeded W 7 trillion in June alone. As the KOSDAQ market rebounded, the proportion of equity issued through KOSDAQ climbed from 0.37 percent in the first quarter to 7.5 percent in the second quarter.

Because of the expansion in the patterns of portfolio shifts among financial companies, discrepancies appeared across the leading monetary aggregates (table 9.5). The growth rate of M3 (monetary aggregate for liquidity—see endnote 8 in chapter 5) during the first quarter jumped to 14.1 percent following the expansion in the money supply through the foreign sector because of the current account surplus and rising investor deposits in equity funds and short-term bond funds managed by investment trust companies. However, the growth rate slowed in April and fell to 12.7 percent in June. The growth of M2 (monetary aggregate for broad money—see endnote 8 in chapter 5) was 34.6 percent in April as the funds invested in certificates of deposit, repurchase agreements, and other short-term investments shifted to bank savings deposits. During May and June, growth moderated as the flow of money into time deposits from short-term marketable securities ceased.

Table 9.5 Trends in Basic Financial Indicators, First Half of 1999
won, billions

Indicator	*January*	*February*	*March*	*April*	*May*	*June*
Bank loans, month-on-month	–485.9	511.8	3,284.8	1,733.3	4,386.7	4,690.6
Issuance of corporate bonds[a]	4,383.5	3,975.2	2,826.6	3,894.0	2,665.9	3,132.4
Capital increases and initial public offerings[b]	272.9	3,629.8	2,390.4	2,879.2	2,289.4	7,138.9
Discounted CP, month-on-month	17,162.8	1,809.2	2,971.3	–8,976.9	–5,199.3	–12,841.4
M2 growth, year-on-year, %	26.3	29.9	33.7	34.6	30.6	27.1
M3 growth, year-on-year, %	13.1	13.8	14.1	13.9	13.3	12.7
Korea composite stock price index, monthly average	579.62	532.97	586.17	721.12	745.41	841.68

Sources: BOK 1999b; FSS 2000.
Note: M2 = monetary aggregate for broad money. M3 = monetary aggregate for liquidity.
a. Excludes bonds issued by leasing companies.
b. Includes offerings and sales of listed and unlisted companies.

An April survey by the BOK on lending behavior among financial companies indicated that credit demand was sluggish during the first quarter of the year and that banks were increasingly channeling loans to SMEs and households, signaling the dissipating credit crunch. However, as more lenders concentrated their lending on companies with low credit risk, the availability of credit varied widely depending on the level of credit risk individual borrowers represented for lending institutions.

A follow-up survey in July indicated that liquidity was abundant during the second quarter and that the overall credit risk had dropped. So, lending was becoming more relaxed, but credit demand was anemic and increased only modestly as companies found ample liquidity in the markets. An evaluation concluded that the competition among banks for low-risk loan customers, not a credit crunch, was now the main feature of the credit picture. As banks continued to focus on lending to SMEs and households, savings and finance companies began to encounter difficulty finding loan customers.

Financial markets were achieving a firm footing by June. Interest rates were returning to normal levels; share prices had rallied; bank lending to SMEs and households was on the rise; and large companies had little difficulty issuing debt and equity to raise capital. The credit crunch was disappearing rapidly, and the number of defaults on bills and other corporate debt was falling. Within the stabilized financial markets, there was intensifying competition among banks and other lending institutions for creditworthy loan customers, rather than a debilitating credit crunch.

Achieving Positive Economic Growth

The preliminary GDP growth rate the BOK announced in May for the first quarter of 1999 was 4.6 percent with respect to a year earlier. This was higher than most forecasts. It also marked a reversal in the falling GDP growth that characterized the year following the onset of the financial crisis. Growth continued to accelerate and spread throughout the economy in the second quarter.

During the first half of 1999, investment in the construction sector was still on a downward trend. However, the number of construction permits, a leading indicator on the health of the sector, rose in April. Analysis of the orders for domestically produced machinery suggested that the growth in the first quarter was led by automobiles, telecommunication equipment, and processed metals. In the second quarter, the demand for factory machinery jumped. The consumption of durable goods, including automobiles and mobile phones, surged during the period. Industrial production during the first quarter was marked by increasing momentum in the production of semiconductors, computers, automobiles, ships, and heavy chemical products. Most sectors were on an upswing by the second quarter, and both exports and imports showed clear upturns and were growing even more vigorously beginning in April.

Despite the pickup in production, inventories declined during the first half of the year because of surging domestic demand and exports. However, the pace of the decline slowed and, unlike in 1998, the changes in the level of inventories became a contributing factor in the overall increase in economic output. The manufacturing operation ratio continued to rise, jumping to 79.7 percent in June.

Consumer prices stabilized during the first half of the year and had increased only 0.6 percent in June with respect to a year earlier. The real estate market was rebounding, and housing prices started to move higher. Unemployment rose during the first two months of the year because of seasonal factors, mainly the weather and the addition of new high school and college graduates in the workforce. The jobless rate fell in March relative to February and continued to fall in April as the growth momentum picked up in the economy.

The ratio of dishonored bills reached 0.06 percent at the end of June, the lowest level since September 1991. The number of bankrupt companies stood at 528, another record low. In the seven largest metropolitan areas, newly established companies outnumbered defaulting companies by a factor of 13.5. Table 9.6 shows key economic indicators during the first half of 1999.

A Return to Normalcy after a Year and a Half of Financial Crisis

According to domestic and international assessments, the worst of the financial crisis was over by June 1999. The won and financial markets had returned to normal, and the real sector was experiencing a robust rebound. Foreign news media were quick to point out that Korea was the first economy in Asia to recover from the crisis and another miracle of Asia; it could thus be a model for other economies in overcoming financial crisis.

According to information pooled by the MOFE, the U.S. magazine *Time* reported, on March 15, that Korea was able to bounce back from the crisis much earlier than expected because it had embarked on ambitious economic reform under the leadership of President Kim Dae-Jung. Donald J. Johnston, the secretary-general of the OECD, noted, in an interview with the *Journal of Commerce* on March 18, that the extensive scope and rapid pace of the reform in which Korea had engaged for the previous 15 months were not found among OECD countries. On May 6, Reuters reported that, in a speech, Alan Greenspan, the chairman of the U.S. Federal Reserve Board, had cited Korea's unambiguous progress in economic recovery. On May 14, the *Wall Street Journal* quoted Larry Summers, at the time designee for the post of secretary of the U.S. Treasury Department, to the effect

Table 9.6 Trends in Key Economic Indicators, First Half of 1999, Year-on-Year
percent

Indicator	*January*	*February*	*March*	*April*	*May*	*June*
Domestic construction orders	–20.5	–52.0	–51.1	39.3	89.6	–6.2
Orders of domestically produced machinery	39.6	–1.0	15.8	23.6	40.5	51.1
Wholesale and retail sales	2.6	7.4	8.3	8.2	9.4	14.2
Industrial production	14.8	3.9	18.8	17.1	21.7	29.7
Average manufacturing operation ratio	69.6	69.7	74.7	74.1	76.5	79.7
Unemployment rate before seasonal adjustment	8.5	8.6	8.0	7.1	6.4	6.2
Nationwide ratio of dishonored bills	0.12	0.10	0.11	0.20	0.10	0.06

Sources: MOFE 1999c, 1999d, 1999e, 1999f, 1999g, 1999h.

that President Kim Dae-Jung was not a proponent of half-baked reform, that his strong leadership in carrying out reform and restructuring had contributed enormously to Korea's economic recovery, and that Korea's rigid labor market was loosening up under the effective government policies. At the Executives' Meeting of East Asia–Pacific Central Banks on May 20, Michel Camdessus, managing director of the IMF, declared that the Korean economy had left the crisis behind. When he met President Kim Dae-Jung, Camdessus also said that the success of Korea was the success of President Kim Dae-Jung.

However, along with the praise from overseas came advice. Donald J. Johnston, the OECD secretary-general, continued to express deep concern over the overinvestment and exceptionally high debt ratios of Korean companies and the rise in the rates of suicide, alcoholism, divorce, crime, child abandonment, and other social ills mainly because of the high level of unemployment that Korea's economic problems had helped aggravate. Larry Summers, the U.S. treasury secretary-designee, warned against unrestrained optimism in Korea given the lingering risks, including the overinvestment and avoidance of painful reform among chaebols, the nonperforming assets of banks, and the massive fiscal deficits. He cautioned that Korea could not afford to turn its back on needed reform or lose its resolve to change for the better.

Indeed, although the Korean economy had clearly turned the corner, it was premature to declare the financial crisis over. Korea still faced major challenges that required earnest and concerted effort. It could not afford to become complacent about the success that had been achieved; it had to forge ahead with the structural reform that was under way. The restructuring had thus far been more or less limited to cleaning up business failures and financial distress, recapitalizing., and resolving other pressing structural problems: what the government recognized as hardware reform. There now had to be software reform: a sea change in management and practices befitting the depth of the hardware reform. A wetware reform to enhance the ability and caliber of the workforce was also needed. These reforms were crucial if Korea was to compete on the global stage head-on with the world's best.

Moreover, Korea had to maintain social and political stability. Having turned the corner on the worst of the financial crisis, Korea could not afford to revert to narrow group interests or fractious regionalism.

Social welfare and the social safety net had to be drastically strengthened for the sake of the unemployed and people living in poverty. A series of aggressive actions had been taken—in March and August 1998 and in March 1999—to cushion the impact of unemployment and significantly augment the social safety net. Going forward, the challenge was to make the social welfare infrastructure more effective and more accessible to those in need.

Korea had to keep pace with the evolving global economy and learn to adapt quickly to the changing world. The global economic outlook was not bright. The Japanese economy was facing difficulties, and the growth outlook in Europe and Latin America was not positive. Even as international financial markets were slowly returning to normal, risks and uncertainties abounded. There were signs that protectionism was reemerging in the industrialized countries.

Could Korea genuinely claim that it had tamed the financial crisis and walk away from the umbrella of the IMF? If graduating from the IMF mandate meant overcoming the liquidity crisis and producing positive economic growth, Korea had received the diploma by the first half of 1999. On the other hand, if graduating from the IMF meant embracing global standards and practices, improving global competitiveness, and competing and cooperating with the rest of the world, the diploma would require at least another three to five years of earnest reform and restructuring. If graduating from the IMF meant a return to the precrisis years of disorder, irresponsibility, and excess, Korea was never going to see the light at the end of the tunnel.

10

The Settlement of the Daewoo Shock and the Expanded Economic Recovery, July–December 1999

Policy Challenges and Responses during the Second Half of 1999

Economic Outlook and Policy Direction in the Second Half of 1999

The economic outlook improved markedly in the Republic of Korea in the second half of 1999. Growth was expected to be widespread and peak in the 5 to 6 percent range. Private consumption was forecast to pick up by about 6 percent relative to the same period during the previous year. The construction sector was not likely to experience a full turnaround, but investment in plant and equipment appeared set to rise by at least 20 percent on the back of healthy growth in information technology and logistics, including telecommunications and transportation. Consumer prices were expected to rise by 2 percent.

The current account posted a US$12 billion surplus during the first half of 1999 and was expected to gain an additional US$8 billion in the second half of the year. In terms of amounts, exports and imports were projected to jump 8 and 30 percent, respectively, during the period. Total external liabilities were likely to drop by between US$10 billion and US$14 billion for the year. Because of increases in external financial claims, there was optimism that Korea would make the switch to a net creditor position in 1999. The unemployment rate was projected to stay in the 5 percent range and the number of unemployed in the 1.2 million range during September and October. Household incomes in urban areas, which had fallen 6.7 percent in 1998, were expected to rise by about 7 percent in 1999 and return to the levels of 1997. The budget deficit for the year was also expected to fall, from 5 to 4 percent of gross domestic product (GDP). In domestic financial markets, interest rates were likely to remain tamed and impose a smaller burden on businesses. In equity markets, surging share prices were expected to provide firm support for healthy financial conditions among many companies.

As the overall economic situation improved, the government set its sights on promoting the development of a market-oriented economy through restructuring, job creation through economic recovery, the laying of a stronger foundation for productive social welfare, and facilitation of the establishment of knowledge-based industries for the 21st century.

In the restructuring of ailing financial companies, the government resolved to push aggressively for the sale of Korea First Bank, Seoul Bank, and seven distressed life insurance companies. It also vowed to forge ahead with software reform, which was aimed at ridding the financial industry of outdated customs, practices, and attitudes. In the restructuring of troubled companies, the government reaffirmed its resolve that the top five *chaebols*—the large family-controlled and family-run groups that dominate business in Korea—should faithfully carry out the financial soundness improvement plans to which they had agreed. It also decided to revamp the tax system with an eye to facilitating ongoing business restructuring. To prevent the chaebols from acquiring excessive control of the nonbank financial service sector, the government set about restricting investment in chaebol-affiliated financial service firms such as investment trust companies. It also stepped up enforcement against the unlawful financial assistance being given by the chaebols to companies they controlled. Companies carrying out workouts and judged to be competitive, but facing temporary liquidity shortages, were to be provided with debt-for-equity swaps and other assistance so that they could achieve turnarounds. Nonviable firms were to be swiftly shuttered.

To foster sustained economic recovery, the government believed that inflation and interest rates had to be held down. Because the supply of the U.S. dollar was outpacing the demand, fresh measures had to be implemented to maintain a balance in foreign exchange supply and demand. Small and medium enterprises (SMEs) and venture companies were to be promoted, and incentives were to be beefed up to encourage companies to move from the Seoul metropolitan area into regional areas as a way to stimulate regional economic growth. To stabilize living conditions among the middle class, the tax burden on salaried workers and other wage earners was to be reduced by W 1.4 trillion. An additional W 1.1 trillion of budget expenditure was to be allocated for assistance to low-income households. The interest rate on loans for management in the agriculture and fishery sectors was to be lowered from 6.5 to 5.0 percent.

The government recognized that the productive welfare system had to be expanded and improved on an ongoing basis, but wanted the basic design of the system to be completed by August and concrete implementation plans for specific areas to be ready by year's end. Work on the transition to a knowledge-based economy for the 21st century got under way early in 1999.

The 10th Meeting with the International Monetary Fund

The International Monetary Fund (IMF) and the government discussed economic policy programs at their 10th program review and policy consultation meeting, on November 24, 1999. At the meeting, the IMF presented an outlook for the Korean economy in 1999 and 2000 that was more upbeat than the one it had shared early in January.

Table 10.1 summarizes the specifics of the agreements between the government and the IMF. For the second half of 1999, it was agreed as follows: (1) steps should be taken to sustain the burgeoning economic recovery, (2) the pace of the restructuring of ailing corporate and financial companies should pick up to ensure continued economic recovery and job growth, and (3) the social safety net should be augmented to provide effective assistance to the unemployed and other people in need.

Table 10.1 IMF Predictions on the Economy of the Republic of Korea

Meeting	*Forecast year*	*Economic growth, %*	*Prices, %*	*Current account*
10th meeting, November 1999	1999	8–9	Below 1	Surplus of 6% of GDP
	2000	5–6	About 3	Lower surplus than 1999
Meeting, July 1999	1999	6–7	Below 2	Surplus of US$20 billion
	2000	5–6	Below 3	Lower surplus than 1999
Meeting, January 1999	1999	2	About 3	A large surplus

Source: MOFE 1999i.

Strategies for the Transition to a Knowledge-Based Economy

The Need for New Strategies

The way for the Korean economy to slip out of the nutcracker—the dilemma of lagging behind developed countries while being chased closely by emerging countries (see chapter 2)—was to make the leap to an advanced, knowledge-based economy as quickly as possible. In this perspective, Korea's future economic growth had to arise from knowledge and cutting-edge technologies. The transition to a knowledge-based economy involved a paradigm shift, and few appreciated the need; in fact, many wondered if it truly represented a new framework for Korea's economic future or merely a momentary fix.

The dearth in understanding and appreciation of the importance of the shift to a knowledge-based economy was characteristic not only of Korea, but also of the developing world. In *World Development Report 1998–99: Knowledge for Development*, the World Bank (1998) highlighted knowledge as a driver of development and urged that, to reduce the income gap, the information and knowledge gap be narrowed between the rich countries and the poor countries. It argued that the income gap could widen without bold action.

As a way to facilitate a smooth transition to a knowledge-based economy, the government decided to draft a comprehensive plan some time in the first half of 1999. Ten major research institutes, including the Korea Development Institute and the Korea Educational Development Institute, took part in producing the comprehensive plan. In September, public hearings and seminars were held to gain feedback on the findings and recommendations of the research institutes.

Prerequisite for a Knowledge-Based Economy

The debates led the government to introduce a new strategy, the Paradigm for the New Millennium: The Development Strategies for the Knowledge-Based Economy. The new strategy identified knowledge as the key determinant of the competitiveness and performance of the economy and defined a knowledge-based economy as an economy in which the core strength is derived from knowledge creation, diffusion, assimilation, and use.

The strategy described Korea's prospects for a knowledge-based economy as follows. First, the strategy analysis found that Korea's knowledge-based competitiveness lagged behind that of the developed countries (table 10.2).

Second, Korea had to address an array of weaknesses and shortcomings. Thus, there were weaknesses in the process of knowledge formation in Korea. This is because knowledge outputs are determined both by the

Table 10.2 Relative Knowledge Index, Republic of Korea, 1997
average among five advanced countries = 100

	Flow index			*Stock index*		
Input index	*Investment in research and development*	*Education expenditure*[a]	*In-house training*	*Researcher ratio*[b]	*College graduate ratio*	*Average*
	117.2	101.6	83.5	65.4	83.3	90.2
	Product index		*Spillover index*			
Output index	*Patent applications*[c]	*Article publications*	*Contribution to growth*[d]	*High-technology industry share*[e]	*Receipts of royalties*	*Average*
	68.3	3.4	23.9	57.0	11.1	32.7

Source: MOFE and KDI 1999.

a. 1995 basis.

b. United States: 1993. Germany: 1995. Japan, France, and United Kingdom: 1996. Republic of Korea: 1997.

c. 1996 basis.

d. 1970–93.

e. 1995.

quantity of knowledge input and by the efficiency of the process of knowledge formation. As shown in table 10.2, the knowledge input indexes of Korea held up well against those of the advanced economies, but the output indexes fell well short of those of advanced economies.

According to the National Knowledge Assessment model introduced by the U.S. National Research Council and the World Bank, knowledge formation can be analyzed in terms of motivation, creation, access, assimilation, diffusion, and use (MOFE and KDI 1999). In the strategy analysis, the process of knowledge formation in Korea was contrasted with the experiences of other countries, and Korea stood out because of weaknesses in motivation, diffusion, and use. The motivation for knowledge activities could be said to be determined by the economic and social compensations offered. In this respect, Korea lagged behind countries such as Canada, Singapore, and the United States in terms of legal system, institutional transparency, and the protection of intellectual property.

With respect to the diffusion of knowledge, surveys of the research and development (R&D) flowing into business enterprises from universities and public institutions for commercialization and knowledge sharing among companies indicated once more that Korea was behind. Korea was also being outpaced by other countries in the use of knowledge and, especially, in the support systems needed for effective knowledge utilization. Surveys found that Korean managers badly trailed their competitors elsewhere in the ability to apply information technology effectively.

In addition, there were problems in basic industrial and technological structures in Korea. Industries form the foundation of commerce and represent the product of individual and corporate knowledge. It is unrealistic to envision advanced industrialization without a strong knowledge base, and it is equally difficult to expect a high level of knowledge specialization and development without advanced industrialization. In developed countries, a large portion of the industries generating high value added are more knowledge intensive and more specialized in R&D relative to industries engaging in simple manufacturing. In the intensiveness of R&D, Korea's high-technology industries fell behind the corresponding industries in many of the other countries of the Organisation for Economic Co-operation and Development.

Korea's lagging knowledge intensiveness showed up in lower labor productivity relative to the developed countries (table 10.3). Whereas most of the industrial activities of the developed countries were concentrated in knowledge-intensive endeavors that produce high value added, such as product design or applied research, Korea excelled only in the processing of products that had been designed and created in the developed countries and in improving manufacturing production skills.

Third, notwithstanding the wide-ranging problems outlined above, the strategy analysis concluded that Korea possessed sufficient potential to make the transition to a knowledge-based economy. This conclusion

Table 10.3 International Comparison of Labor Productivity in Major Industries, 1994
labor productivity of the U.S. manufacturing sector = 100

Industry	*United States*	*Japan*	*Germany*	*France*	*United Kingdom*	*Italy*	*Korea, Rep.*	*Korea, Rep./ highest country*
Manufacturing	100.0	104.9	91.1	100.6	55.5	66.9	49.7	0.47
Top six industries	109.4	104.6	93.8	105.6	55.7	64.5	44.4	0.41
Textiles and wearing apparel	52.5	31.4	56.0	67.2	33.5	46.8	19.8	0.29
Chemicals and chemical products	151.6	148.7	134.9	156.2	91.0	91.0	60.8	0.42
Machinery	106.7	94.2	76.2	94.2	47.5	71.2	44.3	0.34
Electrical and electronic products	149.2	133.1	92.0	107.2	49.2	77.8	51.2	0.34
Transport equipment	94.3	120.7	94.5	87.2	54.0	62.6	57.1	0.61
Optical instruments and apparatus	86.9	100.7	63.6	102.1	42.6	79.8	31.1	0.30

Sources: STAN Structural Analysis Database, Organisation for Economic Co-operation and Development, http://www.oecd.org/sti/stan/ (data of 1997); MOFE and KDI 1999.

Note: Productivity = the ratio of real value added to the number of workers based on W/US$; for ¥, based on ¥123/US$ (the appropriate exchange rate is assumed for Japan).

was based on the can-do attitude that had enabled the country to achieve such an impressive track record in economic development and industrialization and entertain big dreams about the goals it could reach. Recent proof was available in the fact that the people of Korea had been able to unite so quickly to overcome a devastating financial crisis. Moreover, Korea possessed a deep pool of highly educated youth in a workforce that was literate, intelligent, skilled, and extremely competent. Indeed, the general population possessed a world-class educational foundation that they could use to acquire new skills to solve problems and add value to the economy.

In many ways, Korea was ideally situated to attract inflows of knowledge. Asia had consistently posted the world's highest economic growth rates, and there was a general expectation that the region would emerge as a key pillar of the global economy in the not-too-distant future. It was also widely believed that companies in Europe and North America would continue to establish themselves and expand their presence in the region. Korea could exploit this trend because of its highly educated workforce and mastery of advanced technologies.

A Key Strategy for Knowledge-Based Development

The main thrust of the new growth strategy was based on the conviction that Korea had to leverage its advantages and its potential to make up for its weaknesses so as to create the proper environment for knowledge generation, utilization, and diffusion. This approach had to be undertaken in a consistent and systematic fashion. Korea's weaknesses revolved around two broad gaps: a resource gap caused by shortfalls in the quantity and the quality of knowledge, technology, and capital and an institutional gap caused by inadequate market institutions and mechanisms to support and enforce orderly and dynamic economic activities.

Korea possessed geographical advantages that could enable it to exploit the knowledge-intensive business activities of multinational companies in northeast Asia. It held the learning potential to absorb advanced knowledge and technologies easily from the developed countries. The economy-wide restructuring in the wake of the financial crisis was cited as a unique advantage that could spur an economic renaissance in Korea.

The core of the government's development strategy, which took account of these advantages and weaknesses, involved (1) establishing an orderly market economy through restructuring, (2) attracting tangible and intangible world-class knowledge resources through market opening, and (3) creating an environment for innovative and knowledge-intensive economic activities by fine-tuning microeconomic policies.

An orderly market economy was an indispensable systemic asset that could pave the way to a knowledge-based economy. The transition to a knowledge-based economy could not be achieved through the promotion of a single industry: there was no single solution. The socioeconomic transition had to be all-encompassing. This required a rethinking and reordering of the policies, traditional approaches, and socioeconomic institutions and relationships that had been established during Korea's rapid industrialization.

Korea could not narrow the gap in knowledge resources with the developed countries on its own in the short run. Therefore, the way forward would consist of boldly opening up the economy so as to absorb knowledge from the outside. This could be effectively accomplished by inducing multinational companies to do business in Korea. Knowledge-based activities such as marketing, R&D, and innovative business management could be acquired and expanded through joint endeavors and other hands-on exchanges with outside practitioners and enterprises.

Supporting innovative and knowledge-generating activities required the reestablishment and reorientation of the microeconomic policy framework. The key challenges were (1) creating of a flexible and efficient system for human resource development that contributed to the country's talent pool, (2) shoring up science and technology infrastructure and installing productive R&D mechanisms to boost the nation's ability to innovate, (3) expanding the information infrastructure to pave the nation's information highway, (4) promoting knowledge-intensive industries and supporting the access of the entire industrial complex to globally competitive knowledge and expertise, and (5) improving the legal and regulatory framework with the goal of reinvigorating knowledge markets.

Such a development strategy had to be systemic and involve the design and implementation of measures that were consistent across traditionally disparate areas of policy making (Dahlman and Andersson 2000). It had to be comprehensive rather than a short-term patchwork of responses, and it had to be realized with consistency and harmony throughout the economy and among private and public sector institutions. Horizontal and mutually reinforcing networks and relationships among key economic institutions and policy makers were crucial in building a genuine knowledge-based economy.

As could be seen in the experiences of countries such as Canada, Finland, Ireland, and the United Kingdom, the formulation and implementation of a knowledge-based economic development strategy had to proceed with the full understanding and backing of the private sector and civil society. Korea had made significant strides in this respect through consensus building and other cooperative endeavors with the private sector. Yet, there was clearly room for improvement in many other areas as well, particularly in building broad commitment and support among the general public. Moreover, because the knowledge and information revolution, coupled with globalization, was a dynamic process, it was critical that meaningful evaluation be part of the implementation process. The process had to be judged and directed according to the outcome. However, that the entire nation had to take the lead in embracing the desired changes outweighed all other considerations.

The Collapse of the Daewoo Group and Restoring Calm to Financial Markets

Troubles at the Daewoo Group

The Daewoo Group increasingly faced a loss in the confidence of the market and, by June 1999, was running into a severe credit squeeze (see elsewhere above). As the situation deteriorated day by day, Daewoo managed to avoid default on debt coming due through money raised on overnight call markets by three affiliated financial companies: Daewoo Capital, Daewoo Securities, and Diners Club of Korea. However, when the business swap between Daewoo Electronics and Samsung Motors that was part of the Big Deal scheme (see chapters 7–9) failed to materialize on June 30, Daewoo was pushed out of the overnight call markets, and the group came perilously close to defaulting.

The underlying cause of the technical default of Daewoo was the group's reckless and unsustainable business expansion at a time when the overriding concern should have been bold restructuring and improvement in the group's financial soundness. Thus, for example, the business group assumed control of Ssangyong Motor Company in April 1998 and overtook Samsung Group as the second largest chaebol in terms of assets. For a while, sales grew at a hectic pace. Daewoo Corporation, the mainstay of the group, saw its sales jump to W 13 trillion in 1998, which was 54 percent over the sales the previous year, but about 75 percent of this amount (W 9 trillion) was in the form of uncollected receivables from overseas business units. The group's overly expansive business management strategy quickly led to high interest expenses, narrower cash flows, and mounting credit shortages.

In a move aimed at discouraging its domestic and foreign creditors from demanding immediate debt payments, Daewoo announced, on July 19, 1999, that it was undertaking accelerated business restructuring and detailed implementation plans. Under the announced plans, the group was to be reorganized around Daewoo Corporation and Daewoo Motor Company. Other companies under the group's control were to be merged or dissolved through share dispositions. As a sign of the group's commitment to fulfilling its promises, Kim Woo-Choong, chairman of the group, together with the affiliated companies, pledged to provide creditors with stocks and real estate valued at approximately W 10.1 trillion as collateral.

Daewoo's 69 domestic creditor institutions—22 banks, 24 investment trusts, 14 insurance companies, and 9 merchant banks—formed the Council of Creditor Financial Companies and decided, at the council's first meeting on July 19, to assist the group in the restructuring. As a first step, the creditors opted to provide W 4 trillion through the purchase of the group's commercial paper (CP), but with strings attached, including the repayment of short-term debt. The creditors also decided to extend the maturity of the W 12.4 trillion in medium- and long-term debt when it comes due in the future.

In contrast to the generous support of creditor institutions for Daewoo, the markets did not react favorably to Daewoo's announcement, judging it unrealistic and lacking in concreteness. As a result, the July 19 announcement turned out to be merely an unofficial declaration to the markets that the group was experiencing mounting troubles. Indeed, the group's distress began to disrupt the markets severely. On bond markets, trading in Daewoo debt paper was halted, and investment funds that had put money into the group's CP and other debt securities faced a run from nervous investors. This triggered debilitating funding problems among investment trusts. Share prices tumbled quickly, and interest rates climbed.

Despite W 4 trillion in fresh funds from creditor institutions, Daewoo's funding situation deteriorated during August, and the group was unable to pay off trade bills coming due. Recognizing the urgent need to restore market confidence in Daewoo's restructuring plans, the main creditors reached a special agreement with Daewoo on August 16 to undertake efforts to improve the financial soundness of the group. Under previous agreements, the main creditor banks were essentially passive observers in the restructuring process; their role was limited to monitoring the group's progress with restructuring. This time, however, the creditors belonging to the council, in consultation with Daewoo management, drafted a new execution plan for restructuring. Under the plan of the creditors, only six of the Daewoo Group's companies—Daewoo Capital, Daewoo Corporation, the machinery business of Daewoo Heavy Industries & Machinery (the shipbuilding business was to be detached), Daewoo Motor, Daewoo Motor Sales, and Daewoo Telecom—were to remain in the restructured business group.

The head of the Financial Supervisory Commission (FSC) expressed the hope that the new round of restructuring at Daewoo would be more favorably received by the markets. However, once again, the market reception was not warm. Doubts began to mount about the long-term viability of Daewoo, and new sales and orders began to dry up among the group's companies. The situation became dire: it was no longer realistic for Daewoo to proceed with restructuring on the assumption that the group would become viable.

As the situation became more difficult, Daewoo applied to the creditors on August 26 for a workout. On the same day, the council selected 12 companies in the Daewoo Group for workouts. The start of the workouts meant that Daewoo's debt obligations to financial companies would be suspended and that the Daewoo Group would be given a chance to carry out restructuring in a less hostile environment. The workout agreement also enabled creditors to remain closely engaged in the restructuring effort.

There were several reasons for Daewoo's decision on the workouts, legally still a shaky process, rather than court receivership. One reason was that the Daewoo restructuring was likely to have a huge impact on financial markets, while court-supervised receivership would be too time-consuming. Daewoo could not afford protracted court proceedings; after all, it had taken nearly a year for the Kia Group to draft a reorganization plan after it had filed for court receivership. Another reason was that Daewoo's problems were not well suited to court receivership. A receivership would have required court proceedings on each company in the Daewoo Group but the group had not made its affiliates into independent companies. There was also a serious concern that court receivership, which would have involved freezing all of Daewoo's commercial liabilities, would have inflicted a heavy blow on Daewoo's suppliers and subcontractors.

The government hoped that the new round of restructuring would be successful. In particular, it hoped that, because the debt obligations to creditors would be suspended, sufficient liquidity would become available to the Daewoo Group so that the subsidiaries could continue operations even as they pressed ahead with restructuring. The expectation was that the competing creditors and other stakeholders would be able to agree on equitable ways to share losses and develop rescue plans that would enable Daewoo companies to turn around or become prepared for dissolution after successful turnarounds. Because the executives of the affiliated companies would be given clear objectives, it was expected that the value of the affiliated companies as independent business units would be preserved.

On August 31, the six banks that had been assigned by the council to undertake the workouts decided to conduct due diligence on the assets and liabilities of the 12 Daewoo companies selected for workouts. The results of the due diligence indicated that the assets were valued at W 59.8 trillion, while the liabilities were worth W 89.0 trillion, representing a W 29.2 trillion inroad on the capital of the companies. Relative to the book value of the companies at the end of June 1999, assets had shrunk by W 32.1 trillion, and liabilities had increased by W 11.2 trillion, for a net asset loss of W 43.3 trillion. The workout plans for the 12 companies were drafted and finalized during October and December, while the workout agreements were concluded from December 1999 to March 2000. The agreements primarily covered debt restructuring with creditors and the self-help efforts of Daewoo companies. The debt adjustments and rescheduling by the creditors included suspension of debt obligations, interest rate reductions, debt-equity swaps, the assumption of convertible bonds, fresh credit facilities, and the netting of bank deposits and liabilities.

Under the debt suspension agreement, the creditors suspended debt payments to a total of W 54.5 trillion (as of March 2000) for from one to five years for the 12 companies. W 53.5 trillion represented reduced interest payments, while the remaining W 1.2 trillion was normal interest payments. Daewoo Corporation was given debt relief of W 25.8 trillion; Daewoo Heavy Industries & Machinery, W 7.0 trillion; and Daewoo Motor, W 6.4 trillion.

Debt-equity swaps and the assumption of convertible bonds represented a total of W 8.6 trillion for 8 of the 12 workout companies; the eight companies were Daewoo Capital, Daewoo Corporation, Daewoo Electronic, Daewoo Heavy Industries & Machinery, Daewoo Motor, Daewoo Telecom, Keangnam Enterprises, and Ssangyong Motor; and the four excluded companies were Daewoo Electronic Components, Daewoo Motor Sales, Diners Club of Korea, and Orion Electric. The debt-equity swaps represented W 4.7 trillion, while the convertible bonds represented W 3.9 trillion. Of the eight companies given debt-equity swaps, seven (Daewoo Heavy Industries & Machinery being excluded) showed share prices below face value or net asset values below the minimum legal capital requirement. The creditors therefore decided to write off the equity of the existing shareholders.

Except for Daewoo Corporation, which had not yet concluded a workout agreement with creditors, the Daewoo-affiliated companies pressed ahead with their self-help plans, which were valued at W 2.8 trillion (February 2000), representing W 1.9 trillion in asset sales, W 700 billion in business improvements, and W 200 billion in other turnaround activities. The amounts deriving from the self-help restructuring were small relative to the size of the assets involved, mostly because negotiations were still under way to find buyers for Daewoo Motor Company and other large business units even as normal business operations were being maintained at these companies.

Restoring Calm to Financial Markets in the Aftermath of the Daewoo Shock

When the heavily indebted Daewoo Group came perilously close to collapse, Korea's financial markets went into a tailspin. The liabilities of Daewoo, the country's second largest business group, totaled approximately W 60 trillion at the end of 1998, not far from the W 69 trillion total liabilities of the 6th to 30th largest (chaebol) business groups. Of Daewoo's debt, about W 43.9 trillion was owed to domestic financial companies.

Following the onset of the Daewoo shock, the yield on (three-year) corporate bonds jumped from 7.85 percent on July 7 to 9.01 percent on July 19 and then to 9.50 percent on July 23. The stock market (the Korea composite stock price index, or KOSPI) slumped sharply as well, from 1,005.98 on July 7 to 904.96 on July 23. The market lost nearly 72 points on July 23 alone.

On July 25, the government announced a set of measures aimed at restoring calm to financial markets in the wake of the Daewoo shock. Under the measures, the government pledged to provide ample liquidity to financial companies, keep interest rates low, and step up market monitoring through the creation of a special response team headed by the vice-chairman of the FSC. Despite the government response, however, fears mounted on the markets over the possible level of the losses among Daewoo creditors as the financial condition of the group deteriorated. Investors who had put their money into the group through investment trusts demanded that their funds be withdrawn as the uncertainties associated with Daewoo continued to thicken.

The yield on corporate bonds climbed to 9.87 percent on August 11, edging closer to double digits. The rising interest rates led to the withdrawal of more investors from exposure in the Daewoo Group and triggered a slide in share prices.

On August 12, the government announced that, if investors demanded the redemption of their investments in funds managed by investment trusts, cash could be dispensed on the portion of debt securities unrelated to Daewoo, but that the redemption would be delayed on the portion in Daewoo debt securities. Delayed redemptions on Daewoo debt securities were to be applied under different sets of rules for financial companies and for individuals and corporate investors. For financial companies, all Daewoo debt investments were to be suspended and settled at mark-to-market values after July 1, 2000. For individual and corporate investors, redemptions for the portions of Daewoo debt securities in funds were to be delayed, but some fixed amount of cash, differentiated according to the timing of the redemption demands, was to be dispensed. Final settlements were to take place after July 1, 2000. For the coverage of redemption requests, the priority was as follows: 50 percent of redemption requests made within 90 days (November 10, 1999), 80 percent of the requests made within 180 days (February 8, 2000), and 95 percent of the requests made after 180 days. As of August 4, 1999, the assets under the management of investment trusts were valued at W 253.5 trillion, among which bond-type funds accounted for W 207.7 trillion (81.9 percent), and stock-type funds accounted for W 42.5 trillion (16.8 percent). Of the assets under the management of investment trusts, Daewoo securities represented W 27.5 trillion or 10.9 percent.

On August 26, the government announced additional measures to restore financial market stability in a bid to offset the risks arising from the workouts among Daewoo companies and ensure steady credit flows to Daewoo suppliers and subcontractors. To make the yield go down on corporate bonds on which the yield had risen in double digits since late August, the government decided to implement liquidity-boosting measures on credit markets. Meanwhile, the Bank of Korea (BOK), the central bank, examined ways to provide a liquidity facility for banks that were assisting investment trusts struggling to meet Daewoo redemption demands. In addition, the government sought to stimulate bond markets by encouraging investment in mutual funds and creating new government bond funds. The government decided to act swiftly if additional public funds were needed to support financial companies during the restructuring of the Daewoo Group. A special market-monitoring unit was set up at the FSC to help facilitate credit assistance to Daewoo suppliers.

Notwithstanding these efforts, the redemption crisis among investment trusts persisted, pushing interest rates on corporate bonds to 10.8 percent on September 17, a record high for the year. As the date for the switch in the priority among redemptions from 50 to 80 percent approached (November 10), speculation began to be heard that there would be a new round in the financial crisis in November. In response, the government, on September 18, undertook additional measures to deal with the market turmoil. Thus, it reaffirmed the need for gradual redemptions of Daewoo-related investments and pledged more aggressive liquidity support for investment trusts. To expand the deposit base of investment trusts, it decided to allow private equity funds to be exempted from the 10 percent cap on any single securities investment in public and corporate bonds and to permit the introduction of money market funds subject to redemption restrictions.

In a bid to encourage more stable long-term market interest rates and boost bond markets, the government announced, on September 21, the creation of a special one-year Bond Market Stabilization Fund involving the participation of 18 banks and 22 insurance companies having a relatively strong funding capability. The size of the new fund was to be set at approximately W 20 trillion, and the first batch of W 10.5 trillion was to be funded by October 15. When the new fund was first used to purchase bonds, on September 27, the corporate bond yield began to drop; it fell to around 9 percent in October.

On November 4, the government followed up by issuing a comprehensive plan to achieve financial market stability in the face of the Daewoo workouts. The plan was prompted by the need to ensure continued financial market stability as the specific details of the loss-sharing arrangements in the Daewoo workouts began to emerge. It included an effort to take stock of the likely impact of the loss-sharing arrangements on financial companies. This stocktaking produced estimates of the debt adjustments among financial companies resulting from the Daewoo workouts. Steps to achieve stabilization were set out for each financial sector. The total amount of debt to be restructured was estimated at W 31.2 trillion (table 10.4).

Under a plan agreed upon by the chief executive officers of related financial companies to normalize ailing investment trusts, the losses resulting from Daewoo-related redemptions were to be shared out among investment trusts (asset managers) and securities companies (sales brokers)

Table 10.4 Daewoo Debt Adjustments, by Financial Industry
won, trillions

	Credit		
Indicator	*Amount*	*Ratio, %*	*Debt under adjustment*
Bank	22.0	38.6	12.5
Investment trust	18.6	32.6	10.4
Seoul guarantee insurance	7.2	12.6	3.4
Merchant bank	2.9	5.1	1.8
Insurance company	1.1	1.9	0.6
Securities company	1.1	1.9	0.7
Other	4.1	7.3	1.8
Total	57.0	100	31.2

Source: MOFE, FSC, and BOK 1999.
Note: The data exclude Daewoo Capital and the Diners Club of Korea.

according to the proportions in the distribution of fund sale fees. Normalization among distressed investment trusts was also proposed. (Most, but not all investment trusts could absorb their Daewoo-related losses without resorting to any drastic measures.)

Investment trusts with controlling shareholders, such as Hyundai Investment & Securities, were to push for recapitalization under the discretion of the controlling shareholders. However, Daehan Investment & Securities and Korea Investment & Securities—two large trusts without controlling shareholders—were to receive public funds to facilitate business normalization. The Korea Development Bank injected W 1.3 trillion into Korea Investment & Securities; the government, W 600 billion; and existing shareholders, W 100 billion, for a total of W 2 trillion. In the case of Daehan Investment & Securities, the Industrial Bank of Korea injected W 600 billion; the government, W 300 billion; and existing shareholders, W 100 billion, for a total of W 1 trillion. The Korea Development Bank and the Industrial Bank of Korea were to lead the business turnaround endeavor by both companies. The Korea Securities Finance Corporation decided to provide liquidity support totaling approximately W 2 trillion to the companies.

Banks with exposure in Daewoo were required to use forward-looking criteria to determine loan-loss provisions as of late 1999. Because the capital ratio set by the Bank for International Settlements (BIS) for banks was expected to average 10.5 percent even with full provision for the Daewoo losses, no serious problems were anticipated for the banking sector as a result of the losses.

Seoul Guarantee Insurance decided to provide insurance coverage only for restructured debt under the Daewoo workouts, and it was believed that the company had more than sufficient funds to provide the coverage. Merchant banks and insurance companies with exposure in Daewoo were expected to absorb the losses from the Daewoo workouts.

Financial Market Trends during the Second Half of 1999

The BOK pursued an accommodating stance on interest rates, and the overnight call rate stayed in the low 4 percent range during the second half of 1999. Corporate bond yields surged in mid-July as a result of the rush of investors to withdraw from Daewoo debt instruments. They reached 10.8 percent on September 17, the record high for the year. They dropped to the 9 percent range in October when the Bond Market Stabilization Fund started acquiring corporate bonds, but swung up in November as the pace of economic recovery quickened.

Interest rates on bank loans headed lower in the second half of 1999 amid intensifying competition among banks for creditworthy loan customers. They were averaging 8.6 percent by year's end. The rates on bank deposits dropped to 5.9 percent in July, but reversed direction and headed up in August, reaching 6.2 percent in December. Rising market interest rates in the wake of the Daewoo shock and the slightly higher time deposit rates banks were offering in a bid to attract steady long-term deposit flows were two key factors in the rise in deposit interest rates.

Share prices advanced in early July, but soon slumped as the concerns about Daewoo mounted and as corporate bond yields and other long-term interest rates rose. In mid-September, stocks tumbled, mostly because of developments outside Korea, such as interest rate increases and falling share prices in the United States. In November, share prices began to surge again after stock markets rallied abroad, the drafting of the Daewoo workout plans reached the final stages, and Standard and Poor's raised Korea's sovereign credit rating to BBB+. By year's end, the KOSPI capped at 1,028.1, the highest level for the year.

With respect to corporate funding, bank lending picked up sharply during the second half of the year. As investors shifted money from investment trusts to banks on a massive scale, bank deposits soared, enabling banks to increase corporate lending. Lending to SMEs showing low credit risk jumped. Household lending surged as the cash demand for publicly placed stock buyings, recapitalization, and mortgage loans all increased.

In the second half of the year, the discounted purchase of CP continued to decline sharply relative to the second quarter. This was mostly because investment trusts, which were the primary investors in CP, were dumping CP on the market to raise funds and meet the surging redemption demand among investors. To reduce their debt ratios as the end of the year approached, corporations began to buy back the debt paper they had issued.

Corporate bond issues began to shrink sharply in August and fell to W 9.8 trillion during the second half of 1999. The two key reasons for the drop were (1) the diminishing ability of investment funds and other institutional investors to buy up corporate bonds in the wake of the Daewoo shock and (2) payments by large companies—using funds generated through new equity issues—on bonds issued at high interest rates immediately after the onset of the financial crisis.

The value of equity issues reached approximately W 40 trillion in 1999 as stock markets rallied, large companies sought to reduce debt ratios, and many technology companies went public by listing shares in the market of Korea Securities Dealers Automated Quotations (KOSDAQ). During the third quarter, stock markets tumbled in parallel with the drops on world markets, pushing down new equity issues. However, equity issues soared again as markets began to rebound in November.

Key monetary indicators showed discrepancies during the second half of 1999 (table 10.5). M1 (monetary aggregate for narrow money—see endnote 8 in chapter 5) grew by 23.7 percent as the monetary authorities pumped up liquidity to keep the overnight call rate steady. M2 (monetary aggregate for broad money—see endnote 8 in chapter 5) and MCT (see endnote 2 in chapter 4) swung up as investors shifted their deposits from investment trusts to banks. M3 (monetary aggregate for liquidity—see endnote 8 in chapter 5) grew moderately, at 8.3 percent, as money flowed out of investment trusts and companies redeemed their CP and other debt obligations, while increasing their equity issues to reduce their debt ratios.

Pressing Ahead with Structural Reform

The Implementation of Corporate Restructuring

The most important task in corporate restructuring during the second half of 1999 was the workout of the Daewoo Group. However, the reform of the four other top chaebols and the workouts of the 6th to 64th largest business groups and other large independent (non-chaebol) companies could not be overlooked.

The continuing reform of the chaebols. Follow-up measures in chaebol reform were discussed at an August 25 meeting of representatives of the government, the chaebols, and banks. The government proposed five tasks, as follows: (1) strengthen the governance of chaebol-controlled financial companies, (2) improve the governance of chaebol companies, (3) prevent unlawful wealth inheritance and other transfers among chaebol families, (4) minimize intragroup investment, and (5) eliminate other unlawful intragroup transactions.

The governance problems of chaebol-controlled nonbank financial companies essentially stemmed from the fact that chaebol-controlled insurance

Table 10.5 Trends in Key Indicators of Financial Markets, Second Half of 1999
won, billions

Indicator	*July*	*August*	*September*	*October*	*November*	*December*
Total bank loans, month-on-month	4,187.2	7,054.6	7,134.4	6,005.8	4,407.5	–659.3
Issuance of corporate bonds	2,831.7	1,736.2	449	1,035.8	1,162.8	2,681.3
Capital increases and initial public offerings	3,817.4	2,418.7	2,226.4	1,151.7	3,953.5	8,983.3
Discounted CP, month-on-month	4,513.8	–4,240.0	–5,372.6	–227.8	–1,931.6	–11,879.8
M2 growth, year-on-year, %	24.2	25.0	26.2	24.0	26.0	28.5
M3 growth, year-on-year, %	11.5	10.4	9.6	8.3	8.1	8.3
KOSPI, monthly average	971.43	933.07	926.88	828.88	950.12	984.48

Sources: Bank of Korea and Financial Supervisory Service.
Note: M2 = monetary aggregate for broad money. M3 = monetary aggregate for liquidity.

and investment trusts were privately held and lacked essential governance standards even as their market power increased (table 10.6). Moreover, investor protections and the efficient allocation of financial resources were at risk because of inadequate firewalls among chaebol-affiliated companies, which enabled them to prop up each other improperly.

As a remedy, several measures were proposed. For more effective and meaningful governance, the government suggested the nomination of independent outside directors, the establishment of audit committees, the appointment of compliance officers, and enhanced protection for minority shareholders in chaebol-controlled nonbank financial companies. To reinforce the separation between the chaebol families and the affiliated companies they controlled, the government proposed scaling back investment and lending limits on chaebol-controlled insurance and investment trust companies. It also proposed the creation of a new monitoring unit at the Financial Supervisory Service to monitor the investment funds managed by the chaebols.

To promote greater transparency in the management of chaebol-controlled financial companies, the government proposed more transparent management of money and the flow of funds among chaebol-affiliated companies in accordance with the new financial reporting requirements—known as combined financial statements—that took effect with the 1999 accounting year. To enhance transparency in business management, the government proposed that quarterly financial reporting by unlisted financial companies begin on January 1, 2001 and that the disclosures for the benefit of investors in investment trust companies be expanded.

The legal framework to facilitate more stringent corporate governance was significantly fine-tuned and improved following the passage of legislation in 1998. However, the framework was not embraced or

Table 10.6 Market Shares of the Top Five Chaebol-Controlled Nonbank Financial Companies, March 1996–March 1999
percent

Indicator	*March 1996*	*March 1997*	*March 1998*	*March 1999*
Beneficiary certificates of investment trusts[a]	5.8	6.2	23.7	31.6
Premiums on life insurance	30.0	30.5	33.4	36.4
Deposits of nonbank financial companies	17.6	18.6	29.6	34.0

Source: MOFE, FTC, FSC, and MCIE 1999.

a. Assets under the management of the top five chaebol-controlled investment trust companies as of the end of July 1999: Hyundai (W 31.7 trillion), Samsung (W 22.3 trillion), Daewoo (W 12.6 trillion), LG (W 10 trillion), and SK (W 5.1 trillion).

aggressively implemented by companies. The Korean Code of Best Practice for Corporate Governance was therefore proposed. The expansion of the proportion of independent outside directors from one-quarter to one-half of company board members and enabling institutional investors to benefit from more effective checks and balances on management were likewise proposed. Resolutions communicated in writing, video participation in board meetings, the formation of subcommittees under boards of directors, and other measures designed to make corporate boards more meaningful were suggested.

The problem of unlawful inheritance and other transfers of wealth among chaebol families had persisted because of loopholes in inheritance tax law and the gift tax system and rules and regulations that were lenient relative to the corresponding rules and regulations in developed countries. The inheritance and gift tax system was criticized for failing to keep pace with the growing array of sophisticated financial techniques that chaebol families and other rich individuals were employing to transfer wealth without paying adequate taxes. As a remedy, the government pledged to enhance the inheritance and gift tax system significantly. It lowered the threshold of the top taxable income bracket from W 5 billion to W 3 billion and raised the top tax rate from 45 to 50 percent. It proposed to step up the scrutiny of individuals who enjoyed high net worth and to scrap the 15-year limitation on claims for back taxes on gifts and inheritance bequests. To prevent the use of complex financial techniques to make illegal bequests and gifts, the government proposed a more punitive capital gains tax for stock transactions undertaken by controlling shareholders. To prevent tax evasion through the stratagem of bequeathing or making gifts of unlisted shares that later appreciated when the relevant company became listed, the value of the stock after the company went public and became listed was to become the basis for taxation. A rise in the amount of taxable income was proposed if controlling shareholders transferred stocks as gifts or bequests to their families. Stringent measures were suggested to control the channeling of wealth and other tax abuses associated with nonprofit entities.

The chaebol families typically succeeded in exercising control over companies in their business groups, though they owned only a relatively small fraction of the controlling shares, by encouraging affiliated companies to acquire shares among each other. This meant that, through capital increases without cash infusions from affiliated companies (that is, cross-shareholdings), debt ratios were held artificially low and failing chaebol companies were improperly propped up.

The value of cross-shareholdings among the largest 30 business groups had jumped from W 17.7 trillion at the end of 1998 to W 29.9 trillion on April 1, 1999, an increase of W 12.2 trillion. Of this total, actual investments in the affiliated companies represented W 10.9 trillion or 89 percent. The internal cross-shareholdings of the 30 largest business groups had therefore climbed from 44.5 to 50.5 percent. To address this perverse ownership structure, the government proposed amending the Monopoly Regulation and Fair Trade Act to introduce new ceilings on cross-shareholdings in a business group beginning in April 2001. Specific measures such as the precise ceiling to be imposed, the time to be allowed for the resolution of existing cross-shareholdings, any exceptions to be provided, and other details were to be worked out among the relevant government ministries.

Improper intragroup transactions were widely used by chaebols to facilitate reckless business diversification and convoy-like business structure and management (see chapter 7). A frequent outcome was that poorly performing companies dragged down strong companies and, eventually, entire business groups. As a preventive step, the government proposed amending the Monopoly Regulation and Fair Trade Act to require voting by boards of directors before large intragroup transactions could be carried out among the 10 largest chaebols and strengthening public disclosure requirements to enable minority shareholders, creditors, and other stakeholders to monitor and impose discipline on management.

On the basis of the discussions at the August 25 meeting, the government reached an understanding with the chaebols on measures to deal with three issues: the governance of chaebol-controlled nonbank financial companies, the reduction of cross-shareholdings, and the end of improper intragroup transactions. The chaebols were therefore to proceed with reform on the basis of the five principles of corporate restructuring that they had agreed to previously and these three new supplemental measures in what came to be known as the 5 + 3 principles. The five principles of corporate restructuring were (1) improvement in business transparency; (2) elimination of cross-debt guarantees; (3) strengthening of the underlying financial structure of companies, including chaebol-affiliated companies; (4) a focus on the core competence of businesses; and (5) accountability among controlling shareholders and management (see chapter 5).

The restructuring of the top four chaebols (excluding Daewoo) was well under way and making progress in the second half of 1999. These chaebols made some headway in selling off assets, raising fresh capital, attracting foreign investment, scaling back cross-debt guarantees, downsizing or shutting down affiliated companies, and improving corporate governance. As a result, these chaebols were able to attain a debt ratio below 200 percent by the end of 1999.

The Hyundai Group faced the risk of a worsening debt situation after its takeover of Kia Motors, but had managed, since the end of 1998, to raise W 18.3 trillion on its own to boost its capital holdings and reduce its debt (by W 8.9 trillion). This left the group's debt-equity ratio at 181 percent at the end of 1999. During the year, Hyundai also managed to raise US$2.67 billion from foreign investors and reduce its cross-debt guarantees by W 1.7 trillion.

The Samsung Group, meanwhile, boosted its capital holdings by raising W 7.4 trillion during 1999; it had also lowered its debt by W 6.3

trillion since the end of 1998. It thereby achieved a debt-equity ratio of 163.3 percent by the end of 1999. The group managed to bring in US$1.75 billion from foreign investors and dissolve cross-debt guarantees totaling W 830 billion.

The LG Group sold off its stake in LG Semicon and raised W 8.5 trillion, which enabled the group to recapitalize and cut its debt by W 10.1 trillion with respect to the situation at the end of 1998. This left the group with a debt-equity ratio of 184.2 percent at the end of 1999. The relatively large drop in the debt of the LG Group occurred because of the sale of the group's stake in the heavily indebted LG Semicon. LG succeeded in raising US$2.78 billion from foreign investors and removing W 380 billion from its cross-debt guarantees.

The SK Group raised W 3.6 trillion, which enabled the group to boost its capital base and reduce its debt by W 200 billion. Its debt-equity ratio had dropped sharply, to 161 percent, by year's end.

The workouts of the 6th–64th largest groups and large independent companies. A total of 90 companies belonging to the 6th to 64th largest business groups (chaebols) and large independent (non-chaebol) companies had been selected for workouts by the end of 1999. Of these, eight were rejected, one managed to complete its workout earlier than scheduled, and 15 were merged, leaving 66 companies involved in workouts at the end of 1999. The workout plans of all but one company had been finalized by the relevant creditor institutions. During the second half of 1999, 12 companies belonging to the Daewoo Group (one of the top five chaebols) also began workouts. If the Daewoo Group companies are included, the number of companies subject to workouts was 102. The workouts in the Daewoo Group were finalized in two stages, on November 25 and December 1. Including these companies, the total number of companies set for workouts was 77.

Among the 65 companies belonging to the 6th to 64th largest business groups and large independent companies that had firm workout plans at the end of 1999, W 33.7 trillion in debt was to be restructured. Of this amount, (1) reduced and immunized interest payments represented W 19.4 trillion or 90.7 percent of the total (W 21.4 trillion) in the workout plan; (2) debt-to-equity swaps totaled W 2.2 trillion, which represented 40.0 percent of the total (W 5.5 trillion) in the plan; and (3) other debt amounted to W 6.3 trillion or 92.2 percent of the total (W 6.8 trillion) in the plan. Apart from the restructuring, creditor banks provided the 65 companies with fresh loans as operating funds, and trade financing totaled W 1.7 trillion, which accounted for about 94.4 percent of the total (W 1.8 trillion) in the workout plan. Among the 64 companies that had concluded memorandums of understanding on the implementation of workout plans with creditors by the end of 1999, (1) asset sales totaled W 1.35 trillion; (2) induced foreign investment amounted to W 958.8 billion; (3) the shutting down of affiliated companies brought in W 103.1 billion; (4) capital increases represented W 301.8 billion; and (5) other amounts came to W 531.6 billion. The total was thus W 3.25 trillion or about 34.3 percent of the implementation plan (W 9.48 trillion) for workouts.

By the end of 1999, 17 groups, including 16 among the 6th to 64th largest business groups (chaebols) and the Daewoo Group, had been selected for workouts. Of the 303 affiliated companies belonging to the 17 groups, 237 companies, excluding the 54 companies (encompassing also 12 set for mergers) with workouts under way and the 12 companies set to continue as going concerns, were to be dissolved by year's end. In fact, 128 companies had completed the dissolution process by the end of the year. Of the 237 companies, 68 of 112 companies had been sold off, 28 of 52 companies had completed liquidation, 32 of 51 companies had completed mergers, and 22 companies were under court receivership or were involved in the process of composition with creditors.

Among the large independent companies that had been selected for workouts, 109 affiliated companies belonged to the 18 large independent companies with at least two affiliated companies as of the end of 1999. Of these affiliated companies, 52 companies, excluding 39 companies (encompassing 3 set for mergers) with workouts under way and 18 companies set to continue business operations as going concerns, were to be dissolved by year's end. Of the 52 companies, 14 of 27 companies had been sold off, 9 of 19 companies had completed liquidation, 2 companies were yet to merge, and 4 companies were in the process of court receivership.

During the second half of 1999, companies in the 6th to 64th largest groups that had not been targeted for workouts forged ahead with the financial soundness improvement plans they had agreed to with the creditors between February and April 1998. SME restructuring, which was divided into the priority support group, the conditional support group, and an others group, also proceeded on schedule.

As a result of the painful restructuring after the onset of the financial crisis, there was a noticeable improvement in the health of the manufacturing sector. Financial soundness was markedly strengthened. Debt ratios averaged 214.7 percent at the end of 1999, which is in stark contrast to the 396.3 percent at the end of 1997 (table 10.7). The strength of stockholder equity relative to total assets also improved. Total borrowing and the value of payable bonds relative to total assets was reduced. Profitability improved; in terms of operating incomes and net incomes relative to sales, two years of income losses in 1997 and 1998 had finally turned into gains in 1999. Finally, growth picked up momentum; in particular, sales driven by domestic demand shifted from negative to positive growth in 1999.

Restructuring Financial Companies

Restructuring in the financial sector accelerated in the second half of 1999. The focus was on completing the turnaround of distressed financial

Table 10.7 Major Financial Ratios in the Manufacturing Sector, 1997–99
percent

Indicator	*Ratio*	*1997*	*1998*	*1999*
Financial structure	Debt ratio (total liabilities/ equity capital)	396.3	303.0	214.7
	Equity capital ratio (equity capital/total assets)	20.2	24.8	31.8
	Borrowing ratio ([borrowings + bonds]/ total assets)	54.2	50.8	42.8
Profitability	Operating income ratio (operating income/sales)	–0.3	–1.9	1.7
	Net income ratio (net income/sales)	–1.0	–4.4	0.0
Growth	Sales	11.0	0.7	8.0
	Exports	19.2	29.6	1.8
	Domestic sales	7.2	–14.9	12.6

Source: BOK (various years), *Financial Statement Analysis.*

companies, improving efficiency in financial supervision, and enhancing capital markets.

The turnaround of distressed financial companies. After exchanging a memorandum of understanding on the sale of Korea First Bank on December 31, 1998, the FSC and Newbridge Capital engaged in negotiations to finalize the details of the deal (see chapters 8–9). On September 17, 1999, they finally signed off on the terms of investment.

Under the agreement, Newbridge Capital was to invest W 500 billion to take over 50.99 percent of the government-owned common stock in Korea First Bank. It was also to take steps to raise the capital of the bank to 3 percent of total assets and satisfy the 10 percent BIS capital ratio requirement. The government was to be given newly issued warrants entitling it to acquire, over three years, common stock representing up to 5 percent of the total as a premium for giving Newbridge outright management control over the bank. In addition, the government was to buy back any loans that soured within two years after the takeover (or within three years for workout loans) and to compensate the bank for any credit provision that might become necessary as a result of loan defaults. For its part, Newbridge was to purchase all loans other than those classified as substandard or worse by the Financial Supervisory Service as of the date of the sale of the bank.

After finalizing all the details, the two sides signed the agreement on the sale of Korea First Bank on December 23, 1999.

Discussions on the sale of Seoul Bank continued after the government and HSBC signed a memorandum of understanding on February 22, 1999. However, the two sides were unable to narrow their differences over the terms of the sale and terminated the negotiations in August. The FSC then decided to attempt a turnaround of Seoul Bank and announced its plan on August 31. The government announced that public funds would be injected into the bank because of the sizable amount of nonperforming assets owned by the bank. Under the FSC plan, an expert management team consisting of professional bankers or a qualified domestic or foreign bank was to lead Seoul Bank. However, no suitable qualified bank in developed countries was found, and the focus therefore turned to bringing in a widely recognized chief executive officer to lead the bank. In September, Seoul Bank sold off additional distressed loans to the Korea Asset Management Corporation (KAMCO), and the Korea Deposit Insurance Corporation (KDIC) invested W 3.3 trillion in the bank. Thus, the government took the first major step to help Seoul Bank turn around.

Among merchant banks, LG Merchant Bank was merged into LG Securities on September 18. SangEun Lease was merged into Hanvit Finance in November. Samsung Investment Trust was taken over by Samsung Life Insurance on December 29.

During the year, two banks merged, and the total number of banks was therefore 23 (table 10.8). One merchant bank lost its business license, and, counting the three merchant banks that had merged, there was a total of 10 merchant banks. The business licenses of three securities companies were revoked, and one securities company was opened. The business licenses of two investment trust companies were revoked, and one investment trust company merged with a life insurance company. One leasing company also merged with a finance company. A sizable number of savings and finance companies and credit unions merged, while the business licenses of others were revoked.

As a result of the large-scale restructuring of financial companies, a significant share of the financial sector workforce was eliminated (table 10.9). The number of bank employees fell by 47,800, from 145,530 at the end of 1997 to 97,738 at the end of 1999. At merchant banks, the number of employees fell even more drastically, from 3,646 at the end of 1997 to 943 at the end of 1999.

The amount of public funds allocated for the restructuring of financial companies escalated between November 1997 and the end of 1999 (table 10.10). In 1999, the KDIC used W 23.4 trillion for financial restructuring, while KAMCO used W 2.9 trillion. The government took W 2.45 trillion from the budget and the funds for the recapitalization of the state-run banks and other supports, while the BOK invested W 700 billion in the Export-Import Bank of Korea, which redirected part of the funds to

Table 10.8 Restructuring of Financial Companies, 1997–99
number

Entity	*End of 1997*[a]	*End of 1998*	*Restructuring and newly established in 1999*	*End of 1999*
Bank	33	25	Merger:[b] 2 (Kangwon + Chohung, Chungbuk + Chohung)	23
Merchant bank	30	14	License revocation: 1 (Daehan); merger: 3 (Korea International + Korea Exchange Bank, Hyundai + Kangwon Bank, LG + LG Securities)	10
Securities company	36	34	License revocation: 3 (Hannam, KLB, Dongbang-Peregreen); newly established: 1 (Jeil)	32
Investment trust company	31	27	License revocation: 2 (Hannam, Coryo); merger: 1 (Samsung + Samsung Life Insurance)	24
Insurance company[c]	50	45		45
Leasing company	25	21	Merger: 1 (Sangeun Lease + Hanvit Finance)	20
Savings and finance company	231	211	License revocation: 21; merger: 10; newly established: 6	186
Credit union	1,666	1,592	License revocation: 103; merger: 45	1,444
Total	2,102	1,969	License revocation: 130; merger: 62; newly established: 7	1,784

Source: Financial Supervisory Commission.

a. Excluding bridge companies and branches of foreign financial companies.

b. Number of companies closed because of merger.

c. Excluding postal insurance.

Table 10.9 Number of Workers by Financial Industry, End 1997–End 1999
number of persons

Entity	*A. Year-end 1997*	*Year-end 1998*	*B. Year-end 1999*	*B/A, %*
Banks	145,530	102,519	97,738	67.2
Commercial banks	113,994	75,677	74,744	65.6
Securities firms	26,771	22,355	32,005	119.6
Investment trusts	4,217	3,668	3,352	79.5
Life insurance companies	51,693	38,947	36,903	71.4
Other insurance companies	31,191	25,605	24,705	79.2
Nonbank financial companies	58,221	47,947	44,452	76.4
Merchant banks	3,646	1,289	943	(25.9)
Savings and finance companies	9,975	7,971	6,610	(66.3)
Credit unions	30,122	27,775	26,313	(87.4)
Specialized credit companies	14,478	10,915	10,586	(73.1)
Total	317,623	241,041	239,155	75.3

Source: FSS 2002.

the Korea Exchange Bank. From November 1997 to the end of 1999, the KDIC used W 51.3 trillion, while KAMCO used W 22.8 trillion. The government and the BOK used W 18.8 trillion and W 700 billion, respectively. Initially, the government took W 32.5 trillion by issuing Non-Performing Asset Management Fund (NPA Fund) bonds and W 31.5 trillion by issuing Deposit Insurance Fund bonds, for a total of W 64 trillion (see chapter 6). However, as the demand for Deposit Insurance Fund bonds outpaced the amount of money initially set aside, the government added another W 12 trillion to the fund, but decided to reduce the NPA Fund bonds by the same amount. The relevant amendment was approved by the National Assembly in August 1999.

By the end of 1999, the KDIC had used up the W 43.5 trillion raised through the Deposit Insurance Fund bonds. With the additional W 3.4 trillion recovered during the restructuring process, the total spending from Deposit Insurance Fund bonds came to W 46.9 trillion. The KDIC also injected W 4.4 trillion of its own funds. KAMCO used up the W 20.5

Table 10.10 Use of Public Funds for Financial Restructuring, 1999
won, billions

	KDIC						Government				
Entity	*Subtotal*	*Capital increase*	*Compensation for loss*	*Purchase of assets*	*Substitute payment of deposits*	KAMCO	*Subtotal*	*Capital increase*	*Purchase of subordinated bonds*	BOK	*Total*
Banks	18,018.9	10,466.6	3,865.9	3,686.4	n.a.	2,764.0	1,550	1,000	550	700	23,032.9
Commercial	18,018.9	10,466.6	3,865.9	3,686.4	n.a.	2,443.6	100	n.a.	100	n.a.	20,562.5
Regional	n.a.	n.a.	n.a.	n.a.	n.a.	298.9	450	n.a.	450	n.a.	748.9
Specialized	n.a.	n.a.	n.a.	n.a.	n.a.	21.5	1,000	1,000	n.a.	700	1,721.5
Merchant banks	n.a.	n.a.	n.a.	n.a.	n.a.	n.a.	n.a.	n.a.	n.a.	n.a.	n.a.
Securities	0.3	n.a.	n.a.	n.a.	0.3	n.a.	n.a.	n.a.	n.a.	n.a.	0.3
Insurance	5,392.1	5,144.7	247.4	n.a.	n.a.	0.3	n.a.	n.a.	n.a.	n.a.	5,392.1
Investment trusts	0.1	n.a.	n.a.	n.a.	0.1	n.a.	900	900	n.a.	n.a.	900.1
Savings and finance companies, credit unions	n.a.	n.a.	n.a.	n.a.	n.a.	105.1	n.a.	n.a.	n.a.	n.a.	105.1
Other[a]	0.1	0.1	n.a.	n.a.	n.a.	n.a.	n.a.	n.a.	n.a.	n.a.	0.1
Total	23,411.5	15,611.4	4,113.3	3,686.4	0.4	2,869.1	2,450	1,900	550	700	29,430.6
Nov. 97–Dec. 99	51,265.4	21,927.4	11,045.8	3,686.4	14,605.8	22,776.4	18,777.9	12,406.9	6,371	700	93,519.7

Source: MOFE and FSC 2000.
Note: n.a. = not applicable.
a. Contribution to the Resolution and Finance Corporation, a subsidiary of the KDIC.

trillion raised through the NPA Fund bonds. Of the W 2.7 trillion recovered, W 2.1 trillion was reallocated to purchase the nonperforming assets, bringing the total spending from the bonds to W 22.6 trillion. KAMCO also used W 164.3 billion of its own funds.

On December 31, 1999, the government made several changes to the legal provisions pertaining to KAMCO (which had been known as the Management Corporation since April 1962) to alter the legal Korean name of the company, as well as its mandate. The changes enabled KAMCO to buy a wider range of distressed assets and provide broader loan guarantees in support of corporate restructuring. The level of payment guarantees was boosted to five times the sum of paid-in capital, retained earnings, and business expansion reserves.

Measures for financial supervision and capital markets. As a result of a major government reorganization in May, the licensing authority under the Ministry of Finance and Economy (MOFE) for the incorporation of financial service firms and new financial services was transferred to the FSC. This enabled the FSC to produce less restrictive licensing guidelines for financial service firms in July. The FSC also streamlined and reclassified financial service businesses into 10 broad groups in the licensing guidelines: banking, securities (brokerage, investment trusts, and futures), insurance, savings and finance companies, merchant banks, consumer finance companies, credit unions, trust companies, special-purpose vehicles for mortgage-backed securities, and credit bureaus.

In December 1999, the FSC amended the licensing guidelines so that controlling shareholders of mismanaged financial companies or other financial services firms controlled by them could not expand into new financial service businesses. The restrictions were to be relaxed if the controlling shareholders assumed management responsibility and shared economic losses. In September 1999, forward-looking criteria for bank asset classification and provisioning requirements were introduced, and the effective date was set for the end of the year.

For capital market revitalization and advancement, the government, on July 22, designated 24 financial companies as primary government bond dealers, including Kookmin Bank and 11 other banks, Kyobo and 10 other securities firms, and Tong Yang Merchant Bank.

In December, convinced that market integrity and investor protection were crucial to the success of KOSDAQ as a market support for technology start-up companies, the government drew up a plan for KOSDAQ market development. However, KOSDAQ's listing and delisting standards had to improve drastically so that sound and promising companies could be differentiated from others on KOSDAQ and become effective at attracting investors. As an important step toward strengthening the listing requirements, the ownership diffusion among minority shareholders was raised from a minimum of 100 shareholders and 20 percent of the outstanding number of shares to a minimum of 500 shareholders and 30 percent of the outstanding number of shares.

In addition, venture capital companies that invested in a start-up company were required to hold 10 percent of the outstanding shares of the company until at least six months after the company had become listed on the KOSDAQ market. Securities firms that managed the listings for new companies were required to conduct an examination of the financial soundness of the companies and provide comprehensive assessments at the time of listing. The new rules were to take effect on April 1, 2000, after a grace period to exempt companies that had already started the listing process and enable them to complete their listing under the old rules.

The new rules toughened the reviews of companies applying for KOSDAQ listing. A new position, full-time director of the KOSDAQ Committee, who would be responsible for reviewing listing applicants, was to be created, and the composition of the committee was changed to increase the representation of experts (fewer representatives of the securities industry, a new director representing institutional investors, and increased representation of venture technology and accounting experts).

Delisting was made more stringent. Investor alerts on stocks were divided into two types: investor warnings and a watch list. Companies that met the delisting criteria were to be delisted promptly. Companies that failed to comply with disclosure rules twice in one year were to be put under the investor warning alert. New rules were instituted to prevent the practice of backdoor listing. The revised delisting rules were set to take effect in January 2000.

New measures such as stiff enforcement actions against unfair share trading and stepped-up market monitoring were proposed to improve market transparency and fairness. As part of this effort, the government amended the Securities and Exchange Act to strengthen ongoing disclosure and expanded the scope of material information subject to mandatory disclosure.

Stiffer enforcement measures against noncompliance were instituted. A new electronic market-monitoring system was set to be launched at the beginning of 2000 to stamp out unfair stock trading. To ensure rationally priced public offerings at the time of listing, the FSC was to introduce a standard pricing model in January 2000.

The administration and operational activities of KOSDAQ-related institutions were targeted for improvement as well. As part of this initiative, responsibility for registration (listing and delisting) and disclosure, which had been jointly handled by the KOSDAQ Committee and the KOSDAQ Securities Company, was reorganized. The KOSDAQ Committee would now handle registration, and the KOSDAQ Securities Company would administer disclosure. Electronic systems and other market infrastructure for the KOSDAQ market were to be enhanced.

The aggressive restructuring led to significantly improved health in the financial services industry (table 10.11). The BIS capital ratios of banks averaged 11.8 percent in 1999, a drastic improvement over the situation in 1997. Aggregate net bank income was still in the negative in 1999, but the losses were becoming smaller as the pace of the clean-up of nonperforming assets picked up. The number of bank loans classified as substandard or worse surged in 1999, mostly because of the mounting bad loans associated with the collapse of the Daewoo Group.

The Implementation of Labor Reform

Since the pivotal pact that the government, businesses, and labor unions had reached in February 1998, labor reform had taken on a more definitive shape. The main thrust of labor reform can be summed up as guaranteeing basic labor rights and boosting labor market flexibility, while promoting new labor relations. A key objective was to establish the Korea Tripartite Commission (KTC) and build a consensus in four major areas of reform: businesses, the financial sector, the public sector, and labor markets.

Among the agreements sought on basic labor rights, the key demands of labor unions were the formation of a union for government employees, the legal authorization for a teachers union and the Korean Confederation of Trade Unions, and the right of labor unions to engage in political activities. According to the Act on the Establishment and Operation of Public Officials' Councils, which became law on February 17, 1998, the

Table 10.11 Trends in Key Financial Indicators among Banks, 1997–2001

Indicator	*1997*	*1998*	*1999*	*2000*	*2001*
BIS capital ratio, %	7.0[a]	8.2[a]	11.8	10.6	11.7
Net income, W, billions	-3,901.2	-19,029.7	-5,484.5	-4,195.9	4,686.2
Return on assets, %	-0.50	-2.43	-0.83	-0.59	0.66
Return on equity, %	-11.45	-51.72	-14.38	-11.02	12.76
Per capita net income, W, millions	-27	-187	-46	-43	58
Substandard or below-loan ratio, %	6.0	7.6	12.9	8.0	3.4

Source: Financial Supervisory Service.

a. Excluding specialized banks.

formation of a government employee union was to take effect in January 1999. On October 31, 1998, the KTC reached an agreement on the issue of the legal basis for the formation of a teachers union. This was followed, on January 29, 1999, by the passage of the Act on the Establishment and Operation of Teachers' Unions that recognized the right of teachers to organize and engage in collective bargaining, but not the right of teachers to strike. The new law took effect on July 1, 1999. The Korean Confederation of Trade Unions was legally recognized on November 22 the same year. The long and often bitter and divisive debate on the legality of labor unions thus came to an end. The right of labor unions to engage in political activities was recognized on April 30, 1998, when new legal provisions recognized the right of labor unions to participate in election campaigns. The constitutional court declared several legal provisions on political contributions unconstitutional in early 2000, thereby paving the way for labor unions to make political contributions and support political parties.

To improve labor market flexibility, a legal framework was established in February 1998 that introduced an employment adjustment system and a system for the protection of temporary agency workers. The aim of the push for a new relationship between labor and management was to foster a culture of cooperation and partnership between labor and management based on mutual trust and respect. However, the effort was soon focused on the issues of the organization of work and personnel management at individual firms. In the end, it therefore did not differ much from past efforts to foster cooperation between labor and management. The broad collective partnership originally envisioned between labor and management failed to materialize.

Following its creation in January 1998, the first KTC became instrumental in building public consensus on a social pact to cope with the financial crisis. The second KTC, which began work in June the same year, focused on facilitating restructuring and enhancing basic labor rights through proposals on public sector restructuring, the union membership of laid-off workers, protections for the political activities of labor unions, and the legal standing of a teachers union.

Labor unions vehemently demanded that the KTC be given the statutory recognition that they had proposed to President-elect Kim Dae-Jung in February 1998. They supported their demand with the threat that they would withdraw from the KTC. This situation was resolved when the Act on the Establishment and Operation of the Tripartite Commission became law on May 24 and the legal standing of the KTC was thereby recognized. The third KTC was thus launched on September 1 on the basis of the statutory recognition coveted by the labor unions.

The KTC achieved some measure of success in forging harmony and consensus as the country dealt with a wide array of difficult issues that had arisen because of the financial crisis. However, it had to deal also with the frequent threats and refusal of the representatives of labor unions and business to take part unless their demands were met. For instance, the Korean

Confederation of Trade Unions, citing the delay in legalizing the teachers union, refused to take part in the KTC on December 31, 1998. The KTC had to suspend its activities after the Federation of Korean Trade Unions declared, on April 9, 1999, that it would not participate until the legislation on the statutory recognition of the KTC was enacted. As the KTC faltered, business representatives complained that it was not operating in accordance with rules and principles and that its activities were being sidetracked by political considerations. The labor unions, meanwhile, contended that the KTC was not a true consensus-building entity, but only a politically expedient means to justify layoffs and restructuring.

Economic Hardship among Low- and Middle-Income Households and the Government Response

The Implementation of Unemployment Measures and the Drop in Unemployment

In March, the government allocated W 16 trillion to boost expenditures on job creation through new start-ups, public works programs, job training, and social welfare. These efforts continued in the second half of 1999. In anticipation of the seasonal slowdown in construction and agriculture during the winter, the government expanded job training programs and public works projects for the approximately 300,000 new high school and college graduates who were about to enter the labor force.

Throughout the second half of the year, as the economic recovery gained strength, more laid-off workers were finding employment. The unemployment rate began to drop quickly in August, and, by November, it had fallen to 4.4 percent, the lowest level since the onset of the financial crisis (table 10.12). The number of unemployed fell below 1 million, to 971,000. Wages climbed relative to the first half of the year and rose by 12 percent during 1999. Because of improving business profits and increases in overtime work, special bonuses and overtime pay were most likely responsible for the sharp wage growth in 1999.

Economic Hardship among the Low- and Middle-Income Classes Arising from the Crisis

The number of unemployed workers was 450,000 as the financial crisis loomed in October 1997 and peaked at approximately 1.78 million in February 1999. The surge in unemployment affected especially unskilled workers and low-income households.

The number of companies that dishonored their bills totaled 17,168 in 1997, but quickly jumped to 22,828 in 1998 at the height of the crisis and then fell to 6,718 in 1999. The spike in business debt defaults led to a near collapse of independent middle-class business owners.

Table 10.12 Trends in Unemployment and Wages, Second Half of 1999
individuals, 1,000s

Indicator	*July*	*August*	*September*	*October*	*November*	*December*	*Annual*
Economically active population	21,907	21,767	22,069	22,176	22,087	21,654	21,634
Economic activity participation rate, %	61.2	60.8	61.6	61.8	61.5	60.3	60.5
Employed	20,558	20,527	21,000	21,155	21,116	20,614	20,281
Unemployed	1,349	1,241	1,069	1,021	971	1,040	1,353
Unemployment rate, %[a]	6.2	5.7	4.8	4.6	4.4	4.8	6.3
Job offer ratio, new job offers/new job-seekers[b]	0.39	0.53	0.29	0.52	0.53	0.26	0.31
Nominal wage growth rate, %[c]	12.0	11.4	22.8	9.4	13.2	23.1	12.1

Sources: MOFE 1999j, 1999k, 1999l, 1999m, 2000a, 2000b.

a. Before seasonal adjustment.

b. Data of the Korea Employment Information Service.

c. Annual change in the wages of full-time workers at workplaces with 10 or more workers in nonagriculture and fisheries.

The government's response to the growing unemployment brought some measure of relief to workers who had been laid off and to low-income families in need of government assistance. However, it was not sufficient to stem the contraction of the middle class and the inequitable redistribution in incomes.

Estimated using methodologies of the Organisation for Economic Co-operation and Development, the share of the middle class in Korea's population was 69.8 percent in 1991 and varied slightly from 68 to 70 percent until 1996, shortly before the onset of the financial crisis. During the crisis, between 1997 and 1999, this share shrank, falling to 66.4 percent by the second quarter of 1999. The inequality in income distribution also increased during the crisis years. Korea's Gini coefficient was 0.283 in 1997, but had worsened to 0.320 by 1999. A comparison of the top and bottom 20 percent income groups shows that the multiplier jumped from 4.49 in 1997 to 5.49 in 1999. As a direct result of massive layoffs, a large number of low-skilled workers and low-income households, along with other vulnerable segments of the population, fell into poverty. However, the high-income group was, for the most part, able to expand their wealth by leveraging their assets and exploiting high interest rates.

The financial crisis took an enormously heavy toll on low- and middle-income households. Letters describing economic pain and hardship that were broadcast by a popular local radio station during the crisis years captured the anxieties, financial difficulties, and uncertainties with which many families had to contend. One obvious change the crisis imposed on families was in consumption. The homemaker whose spouse had not been paid by his employer for three months could no longer afford even pizza or chicken for their two sons; she could only afford a small bag of cheap snack food. A mother who earned money from handicrafts feuded with her daughter after offering to subscribe to a newspaper rather than signing the daughter up for extracurricular essay writing classes that the mother could not afford so that her highly motivated daughter might prepare for the rigors of the college admission process. Sales of treasured household assets became commonplace. One author of a letter wrote of the pain of having to sell an apartment that took years of sacrifice to acquire, while another recalled lingering with her daughter before an apple tree she had planted in the front yard of the house she now had to sell.

Housewives began to take a more active role. Among the letters was the story of a wealthy family. The father's business had failed, and the family had been obliged to move to a smaller house. After a financial struggle, the mother ended up working as a cleaning lady in the same house in which she had lived before the family's troubles. There was also the story of a mother who, at the age of 47, after much hardship in Korea, decided to take her daughter to Buenos Aires, where she had found work as a seamstress.

The crisis was a heavy blow to the personal relationships and friendships of many Koreans. There were stories of people stealing the paychecks of their friends, an act thought to be impossible until then: people breaking the law and betraying friends to make ends meet. There was the story of a thief who stole food from a refrigerator and left a note of apology, but did not touch the valuables in the home.

Watching the country's economic and political elites continuing to act out of narrow self-interest and not holding themselves accountable, a 46-year-old unemployed worker wondered what to make of public ad slogans urging people to make sacrifices. Many fell into despair, and the number of suicides by people jumping from tall buildings increased. However, there were also many moving stories of families renewing their lives. One family, in tatters after the financial crisis, moved to Jeju Island off the southern coast, sent their two children to a local school with fewer than 200 students, rented a small house for W 600,000 a year, and lived happily growing tangerines. One head of household, out of work running a sewing factory, became a taxi driver. He struggled on the first day of work, but received encouragement from people around him, some of whom considered him fortunate to be a taxi driver because they had no driver's licenses themselves.

Numerous socioeconomic indicators showed clearly that low- and middle-income households bore a disproportionately high share of the burden of the crisis (table 10.13). The rates of crime, divorce, child abandonment, illicit drug use, and suicide all climbed during the crisis years.

The Social Welfare of Low- and Middle-Income Households

Tax revenues were expected to increase by the middle of 1999 because of the unmistakable economic recovery and the vigorous enforcement of laws against tax evasion. The government therefore decided, on June 18, to channel some of the increased tax revenue to low- and middle-income

Table 10.13 Trends in Socioeconomic Indicators, 1996–99

Indicator	*1996*	*1997*	*1998*	*1999*
Divorce, number of cases	79,895	91,159	116,727	118,014
Divorce, per 1,000 people	1.7	2.0	2.5	2.5
Suicide, number	5,856	6,022	8,569	7,075
Crime, number of cases	1,419,811	1,536,652	1,712,233	1,651,064
Crime, per 100,000 people	3,117	3,341	3,688	3,530

Sources: Data on divorce and suicide: Statistics Korea; crime: Korean National Police Agency.

households. The core of the government plan was to reduce the tax burden on wage earners and set aside additional fiscal spending for low- and middle-income households. In August, the tax laws were amended to provide expanded deductions on the taxable incomes of salaried workers, including higher deductible limits on wage incomes from W 9 million to W 12 million and higher special deductions for educational and medical expenses. Support for venture start-ups was expanded, and tax credits for business investment were temporarily extended.

The second supplementary budget formulated in August 1999 totaled W 2.7 trillion. Of this amount, W 279 billion was targeted at helping low-income families start up small businesses, W 515.5 billion was aimed at supporting child education and housing expenses, and W 95.4 billion was allocated for families in low-income farming and fishing communities, the elderly, and the physically disabled. In addition, W 357.9 billion was to be disbursed as direct subsidies to help local governments improve the efficiency of information networks for commodity distribution so as to enhance stability in household prices. The government also allocated W 1.49 trillion for natural disaster recovery and harbor upkeep.

Government receipts increased by W 3.3 trillion: W 400 billion from tax revenues and W 2.9 trillion from nontax receipts. The government cut its debt issues by W 600 billion, to W 2.7 trillion.

In August, the National Basic Living Security Act was enacted; the effective date when the law would be in force was set for October 1, 2000. One justification for the new law was that the existing Protection of Minimum Living Standards Act had been grossly inadequate in supporting low-income households and families in poverty and that no support had been provided for people struggling to escape poverty on their own. The government assistance scheme for the poor provided that minimum living expenses, including expenditures for food, housing, education, and medical services, should be met by the government if people were unable to pay on their own. The scheme also provided that people who were able to work would be linked to welfare programs that supported their self-help, such as welfare payments in return for job training and participation in public works programs.

Accelerating Economic Recovery and the Transition to Net Creditor Status

Expansive Fiscal and Monetary Policies and the Quickening Pace of Economic Recovery

Throughout the second half of 1999, the government and the BOK pushed forward with market stabilization measures to contain the adverse impact of the collapse of the Daewoo Group on investment trust companies and bond markets. To support the ongoing economic recovery and prevent another credit crunch, the government placed a high priority on economic policies, especially maintaining low interest rates and keeping credit flowing. Expansive fiscal policies were retained. When the second supplementary budget was being drafted, the fiscal deficit was estimated at W 24.4 trillion (4 percent of GDP). However, tax revenues surged as the economy improved, and the fiscal deficit had fallen sharply, to W 13.1 trillion (2.7 percent of GDP), by year's end.

During the second half of 1999, the economy gathered strength on the back of the government's aggressive macroeconomic policies. Investment in the construction sector continued to slump, but construction orders and permits—both leading indicators in the sector—were rising. Orders for domestically produced machinery, an indicator of investment in plant and equipment, grew significantly as orders for office and transportation equipment and equipment for other industrial purposes increased (table 10.14). Private retail and wholesale consumption perked up. Purchases of durable goods, including automobiles, mobile phones, and office equipment, rose sharply in the second half of the year. With the exception of the construction sector, industrial production improved throughout the economy, but particularly in office equipment, automobiles, heavy industrial goods, and audio, video, and telecommunication equipment. The production of light industrial goods such as rubber, plastics, and leather products improved drastically. Outbound shipments were increasing, and growth was apparent across office equipment, semiconductors, automobiles, and audio, video, and telecommunication equipment. Inventories continued to fall as domestic consumption and exports outpaced industrial production, but the rate of decline moderated in the second half of 1999. In December, inventories grew as automobiles awaited shipment

Table 10.14 Economic Trends, Second Half of 1999, Year-on-Year
percent

Indicator	*July*	*Aug.*	*Sept.*	*Oct.*	*Nov.*	*Dec.*
Domestic construction orders	0.1	1.0	36.5	33.9	17.5	8.9
Orders for domestically produced machines	29.4	29.1	9.2	24.2	3.8	14.2
Wholesale and retail sales	18.6	18.3	3.9	15.5	15.4	14.9
Industrial production	33.2	29.8	18.3	30.8	26.8	24.6
Average manufacturing operation ratio	80.8	78.6	79.0	78.6	80.6	80.6
Consumer price increase	0.3	0.9	0.8	−0.2	−0.2	−0.2
Nationwide ratio of dishonored bills	0.09	1.12	1.12	0.57	0.39	0.14

Sources: MOFE 1999j, 1999k, 1999l, 1999m, 2000a, 2000b, 2000c.

overseas. The average manufacturing operation ratio had reached 80.6 percent by December.

Prices stabilized in the second half of the year. Consumer prices had risen only 1.4 percent by December relative to a year earlier. Housing prices picked up modestly in July, but turned downward in November. The ratio of dishonored bills in December was down to 0.14 percent; it had been as high as 1.12 percent in August, when the Daewoo companies were declared in default and placed under creditor-led workouts. The number of companies that had defaulted on their debt totaled 6,718, and the ratio of newly established to bankrupt companies in the seven largest cities reached 12.6 in December.

The Transition to Net Creditor Status

External financial markets were favorable to Korea in the second half of 1999 as the conditions for borrowing improved, the supply of foreign exchange liquidity exceeded demand, the won strengthened against the dollar, and Korea was becoming a net creditor nation.

With respect to external borrowing conditions, the market distress triggered by a looming financial crisis in Brazil in early 1999 had subsided drastically by March, and markets were calm throughout the second half of the year. Interest rates rose as the global economy picked up steam, and inflationary concerns grew. International credit-rating companies boosted Korea's sovereign credit ratings. Standard and Poor's raised Korea's BBB– rating (below investment grade), which it had assigned on January 25, one notch up, to BBB, on November 11. Moody's took a similar step, raising Korea's rating from Baa3 (February 12) to Baa2 (December 16). The ratings were upgraded despite the distress on financial markets prompted by the Daewoo Group situation; this helped Korea earn greater respect in international financial markets.

The improved borrowing climate was also evident in the shrinking spread on Korea's 10-year Foreign Exchange Stabilization Fund bonds, the improved roll-over ratio on short-term bank borrowing, and the low risk premium paid by Korean banks in international credit markets. The spread on the sovereign Foreign Exchange Stabilization Fund bond due to mature in 2008 jumped in mid-July in the wake of the Daewoo collapse, but began to drop in August. By the end of the year, the spread had fallen to 157 basis points. The roll-over ratios of the six largest commercial banks were above 100 percent during the second half of 1999. In November, they had fallen to 87.1 percent, but only because domestic banks were aggressively repaying their loans, not because their credit risk had worsened. The spread on Korean banks fell below 100 basis points during July and August even as interest rates on international credit markets moved up. By December, the spread had increased to around 140 basis points.

The supply of foreign exchange liquidity was more than sufficient to meet demand in the second half of the year, and the government took a number of steps to keep the supply and the demand within a more preferable range. Exports picked up, and the likelihood of a current account surplus for the year grew. Because of expanded foreign direct and indirect investments, the capital account looked favorable. Thus, the expectation was that the won would appreciate sharply against the dollar. The government established a plan, on July 7, to replenish the Foreign Exchange Stabilization Fund by W 5 trillion by issuing fresh debt, and the National Assembly approved the plan on August 12. By year's end, the government had issued debt totaling W 2.8 trillion to purchase foreign exchange.

The government rushed to repay the external debt. In September, it paid off the outstanding balance on its IMF Supplemental Reserve Facility loan, which meant the entire US$13.4 billion Supplemental Reserve Facility that Korea had borrowed since the onset of the financial crisis had been paid off. In October, approximately US$8.8 billion of the US$21.7 billion debt of domestic financial companies that had been changed from short- to long-term debt and that was due in 2000 and 2001 was paid off ahead of schedule. After about US$4.2 billion was repaid in April, the outstanding debt balance stood at US$9 billion. In December, the government decided not to take on an additional borrowing of US$500 million from the IMF and US$300 million from the Asian Development Bank.

On December 7, the government put into effect several measures aimed at boosting the Overseas Securities Investment Fund, set to be launched in January 2000, including tax exemptions on the gains by individual investors who participated in the fund. In an effort to augment foreign exchange reserves, the authorities absorbed part of the massive current account surplus and recovered foreign exchange that it had lent to domestic financial companies in the wake of the onset of the financial crisis. As a result, Korea's usable foreign exchange reserves had reached US$74.0 billion by the end of 1999, a drastic improvement over the US$48.5 billion only a year earlier.

The current account surplus came to US$12.28 billion for the second half of the year and to US$24.48 billion for the whole year. The size of the surplus was smaller in 1999 than the US$40.56 billion in 1998, mostly because of surging imports as the economy recovered and a change of balance in the service sector from surplus to deficit because of rapidly growing overseas travel and loyalty payments. Automobiles, semiconductors, and heavy chemical products led the export growth in the second half of the year. Imports also picked up because of rising oil prices and increasing domestic demand. The capital account posted a US$2.04 billion surplus for the year through increased foreign direct and indirect investments.

The won began to lose ground against the dollar in July as the Daewoo crisis unfolded and stayed at around W 1,200 until November, when it began to strengthen against the dollar. The resolution of the Daewoo crisis through the creditor-led workouts, the continued current account surplus, and a surge in inbound foreign investment all helped to buoy the won against the dollar. By the end of December, the won/dollar exchange

Table 10.15 Trends in External Debt and External Credit Claims, Second Half of 1999
US$, billions

Indicator	*July*	*Aug.*	*Sept.*	*Oct.*	*Nov.*	*Dec.*
A. External debt	142.7	141.9	139.9	136.4	136.1	137.1
Long term	108.4	106.5	105.3	98.0	97.2	97.8
Short term	34.3	35.4	34.6	38.4	38.9	39.2
Public sector	31.4	29.9	28.3	28.5	28.9	29.5
Financial sector	67.3	67.1	66.6	61.3	60.0	61.0
Private sector	44.1	44.8	45.0	46.6	47.2	46.6
B. External credit claims	140.8	141.9	141.6	140.3	144.3	145.4
Net external credit claims, B–A	–1.9	0.0	1.7	4.0	8.2	8.3

Source: Foreign Exchange Regulations and External Debt Division, Ministry of Finance and Economy.

rate had reached W 1,138 per dollar, a 5.8 percent appreciation over the rate a year earlier. The yen reversed direction and began to gain ground as the outlook for the Japanese economy improved. The won ended the year at W 1,121.84 per ¥100, a 6.1 percent depreciation relative to the end of 1998.

Korea's external liabilities totaled US$137.1 billion at the end of 1999 (table 10.15). Of this total, long-term debt accounted for US$97.8 billion (71.4 percent), while short-term debt accounted for US$39.2 billion (28.6 percent). The total external debt in 1999 represented a drop of US$11.61 billion from the US$148.7 billion at the end of 1998. The drop in the external debt of the public sector was US$7.05 billion, while the decline in the financial sector was US$9.98 billion. However, external private sector debt increased by US$5.42 billion, accounting for the total drop of US$11.61 billion. At year's end, Korea's external credit claims totaled US$145.4 billion, US$8.3 billion more than Korea's external debt. Korea's shift from a net debtor to a net creditor occurred in September 1999, when the external claims net of the external debt totaled US$1.7 billion.

11

Korea's Economic Renewal: Challenges and Solutions for the Transition to the Next Level

Questions about the Korean Economy

The diagnosis of the economy of the Republic of Korea was not bright in 2004. Some believed that the 4 to 5 percent growth in the economy was mostly fueled by exports and noted that domestic demand was severely depressed. Others felt that the entire economy was anemic. In July 2004, Standard and Poor's announced it would maintain the A– sovereign credit rating on Korea that it had assigned in July 2002. Standard and Poor's cited the potential for military confrontation with the Democratic People's Republic of Korea and the government's frequent intervention in markets, among other reasons, as justification for sticking with the two-year-old credit rating. In its survey of national competitiveness among 60 economies, the International Institute for Management Development (IMD) ranked the Republic of Korea near the bottom, especially with respect to labor and management relations, political instability, and university-level education (table 11.1).

Numerous assessments of the Korean economy from various angles and different perspectives have been undertaken. However, for a meaningful future strategy agenda to ensure stable long-term economic growth, more systematic diagnoses and an evaluation of the remedies already attempted are needed.

In this chapter, the Korean economy is diagnosed from three distinct perspectives: (1) short-term economic stability in terms of growth, unemployment, and inflation; (2) long-term growth potential; and (3) necessary adaptations to the evolving global economy in the face of transitional

Table 11.1 Comparison of National Competitiveness, 2004
ranking

Indicator	*Korea, Rep.*	*United States*	*Japan*	*Singapore*	*Taiwan, China*	*China*
Labor relations	60	21	5	1	14	39
Bureaucracy	26	15	28	4	11	55
Political instability	55	20	27	13	54	47
Investment incentives	41	16	44	1	23	13
College education	59	10	58	3	28	46
Knowledge transfer	42	4	23	3	13	46

Sources: IMD 2004; SERI 2004.
Note: The table shows a ranking whereby 1 is the most competitive.

change. Through the diagnosis, emerging challenges and the measures needed to achieve the transition to a higher level of economic development are identified (Lee 2004).

Diagnosis of the Korean Economy

Diagnosis from the Perspective of Short-Term Economic Stability

The problems that the Korean economy faced may be summarized in three points from the perspective of short-term economic stability. First, in early 2004, many experts predicted that the economy and the employment situation would improve in the latter half of the year. Unexpectedly, however, the pace of economic recovery was slowing. Second, as uncertainties in the economy mounted, the level of confidence among the Korean people about the future was slipping. Third, rather than focusing on how to meet the challenges for the future through cooperation and competition, Korea was deeply mired in conflicts and confrontations.

The slowdown in economic recovery and employment. The Bank of Korea (BOK), the central bank, reported that, during the first half of 2004, the economy had grown by 5.4 percent with respect to the growth rate during the same period of the previous year and compared with 3.1 percent in all of 2003. Meanwhile, on a quarter-to-quarter basis, the economy had expanded 0.7 percent during the first quarter and 0.6 percent during the second quarter of 2004. So, the pace of economic growth was fairly slow.

Employment growth was also anemic, particularly in the service sector, which accounted for a substantial share of employment. During May 2004, the number of the employed increased to 22.7 million, which was 1.6 percent higher than the number a year earlier, but the number of workers laboring more than 36 hours a week had hardly changed. The unemployment rate reached 3.3 percent in May, but it was 10.6 percent among eligible workers under 20 years of age and 7.6 percent among workers in their 20s.

The growth outlook for the latter half of 2004 and for 2005 was not becoming brighter. The BOK revised its growth estimates downward for the latter half of 2004 from 5.6 to 5.0 percent. Sluggish consumer spending was cited as the major risk factor. The problem of heavily indebted households was not going to be resolved quickly, and the prospect for sharply improving employment was becoming cloudy. Externally, the rise in oil prices posed a threat to the economy. Geopolitical unrest in the Middle East, increasing demand by China for oil, and speculative oil trading by hedge funds were contributing to continuously volatile oil prices.

Falling confidence in the future amid growing uncertainty. Amid the mounting economic uncertainty, the confidence of consumers and businesses in the future was falling. Many households were heavily indebted, and the number of individual borrowers who had defaulted on loans was rising, which was dampening consumption. Moreover, the availability of lifetime jobs was shrinking because seniority was being replaced by individual ability and performance as the criteria for advancement in the new workplace culture. Many were worried about job security and the loss in incomes, which was also hurting consumption and fanning uncertainty about the future.

The proportion of the elderly in the population was rapidly increasing, and postretirement welfare was becoming a major social issue. According to Statistics Korea, the Korea National Statistical Office, people aged 65 or older represented 7.2 percent of the population in 2000. The corresponding share of the elderly was expected to exceed 14.4 percent by 2019 and 20.1 percent by 2026.

The gap between the rich and the poor had significantly widened since the onset of the financial crisis. The Gini coefficient, a measure of income inequality, worsened from 0.284 in 1995 to 0.306 in 2003. An expanding segment of low-income households was unable to make a living.

Many companies were bracing for more difficult times. The BOK business survey index for August 2004 clearly indicated that the share of companies expressing a positive outlook for the future was overwhelmed by the share expressing a negative outlook . Many entrepreneurs were losing the will to start up businesses. The number of new businesses that were incorporated fell by 19.2 percent, from 41,460 to 33,497, between 2000 and 2003. The number of venture companies recognized by the Small and Medium Business Administration declined from 11,392 to 7,607 between 2001 and April 2004.

There were several reasons that the appetite of entrepreneurs for new businesses had diminished. Many companies were unable to find a fresh source of growth. While China and other developing countries were rapidly industrializing, and the developed countries were becoming knowledge-based economies, Korea was hesitating: it lacked confidence in the future. Business restructuring in the wake of the financial crisis, which rendered many companies passive and defensive about their businesses, was also a factor.

Moreover, unlike in the past, when the government had underwritten much of the risk faced by companies in raising capital, companies now had to assume all the risk themselves. In weighing investment decisions on cutting-edge technologies, a company usually faces four types of risks: uncertainty over future success, information asymmetry between the entrepreneur and the financial company providing credit, the difficulty of appraising the value of the technology, and financial market conditions (Gompers and Lerner 2001). In any case, survival was never a sure proposition even among companies that started well. Every company had to pass through a valley of death at some point. Indeed, according to statistics of the Organisation for Economic Co-operation and Development (OECD), about one-third of newly created companies perished within two years (OECD 2003a).

The antibusiness sentiment that prevailed across the country, labor conflict, and heavy-handed government regulations on business investment were each playing a part in dampening the investment climate and raising the costs of investment. A survey conducted by the Korea Chamber of Commerce and Industry in December 2003 showed that Koreans, on average, rated their pro-business sentiment at only 38.2 on a scale of 100. In terms of government regulation, lifting the brakes on the limitation on the amount of the total investments of the *chaebols*—the large family-controlled and family-run groups that dominate business in Korea—emerged as a crucial test for policy makers (see chapter 10).

As risk factors in the Republic of Korea, foreign investors and international credit-rating agencies frequently cited the nuclear problem of the Democratic People's Republic of Korea, the extreme clashes between labor and management, and opaque corporate governance. Indeed, there was no question about the damage the Republic of Korea suffered from these risks. "Korea discount" was the term coined for the extra cost Korea had to pay because of the negative effect of these risk factors on foreign investors.

Political and social instability. The Korean people and Korean society were more accustomed to confrontation than to cooperation and competition, and signs of discord abounded across society. There were clashes over the political and economic order. The divisions over the issue of globalization are a good example. The antiglobalists argued strongly against the process of globalization now under way, such as the liberalization of agricultural markets and the spread of neoliberalism. The antiglobalists were challenged by those who saw globalization as an irreversible trend. The debate over whether economic growth or income redistribution should be the priority caused sharp divisions.

There were many conflicting views on the relationship with the Democratic People's Republic of Korea. Some favored abolishing the National Security Act, considered an efficient tool for deterring espionage by the Democratic People's Republic of Korea, as a way to usher in a new era of harmony. Others cited the support for the Democratic People's Republic of Korea as more than sufficient justification for retaining the National Security Act.

Conflicts arose over significant development projects. Thus, proponents of efforts to keep the supply of clean drinking water safe upstream from the Han River for the millions of residents in the Seoul metropolitan area were pitted against advocates of the economic freedom and rights of upstream residents; there were confrontations among various factions over the issue of the proper storage site for nuclear waste; and, similarly, though all readily acknowledged the need, no one wanted crematories or cemeteries to be located near their homes.

Korea's competitiveness in terms of labor relations was at the bottom among countries (see table 11.1). Not only the frequency of the confrontations between labor and management, but also the intensity and the degree of violence of the conflicts set Korea apart.

Though earnest efforts had been undertaken to reframe and reorient labor relations, labor regulations and labor laws were often ignored or dismissed by both management and labor on the factory floor as each sought to protect their own narrow self-interest. The institutional mechanisms and other procedures in place for mediation were inadequate to settle labor disputes and did not encourage the two sides to work out the differences on their own.

The bitter hostility between labor and management was hurting production and exports and dampening the climate for investment by domestic and foreign businesses. Data of the Korea Labor Institute indicate that the number of workdays per 1,000 workers lost because of labor strikes in 2000 was 0.3 in Germany, 0.7 in Japan, 20.3 in the United Kingdom, and 144.1 in Korea. In the summer of 2004, the unions of the Seoul metropolitan subway system and the unions at LG-Caltex and KorAm Bank were able to settle their differences with management and end their disputes, while the government waited on the sideline. This was a welcome outcome, but it was impossible to predict whether it represented a true break from the past or was merely an exception.

Besides the confrontational attitude that prevailed throughout Korean society, there was also a culture of irresponsibility and indiscipline. In his criticism of Korea, Ikehara Mamoru (1999), a well-known Japanese author, scolded Koreans for their dearth of order and loyalty and their self-serving disregard for the rule of law and advised Koreans to make a start at change by at least complying with traffic laws.

The shortage of these kinds of basic social assets in Korea engendered a culture of mutual distrust. The distrust was amplified by rooted behaviors, such as the back-room politics, the unseemly, improper ties between government officials and businessmen, widespread corruption, and cronyism. Koreans did not generally meet easily and calmly in the marketplace of ideas. No matter the words used, who spoke the loudest controlled the debate. The result of these shortcomings was a society that stifled respect and trust among its members and became mired in bitter division and chaos.

Diagnosis from the Perspective of the Long-Term Potential for Growth

Per capita income broke through the US$10,000 mark in Korea in 1995 and then stagnated for the next nine years. The sharp contraction brought about by the financial crisis was certainly a major contributing factor. Nonetheless, the sluggishness endured sufficiently to prompt worries that Korea might become forever stuck in the second-tier group of countries behind the developed countries.

According to a study by the Korea Development Institute (KDI), Korea's potential growth averaged 7.8 percent between 1981 and 1990, 6.6 percent between 1991 and 1995, and 6.0 percent between 1996 and 2000, for a total of 6.3 percent between 1991 and 2000 (Han et al. 2004). The lower total factor productivity and factor input were widely suspected as the culprits behind the smaller growth potential. A breakdown of the 7.8 percent average potential growth between 1981 and 1990 suggests that factor input accounted for 6.1 percent, while productivity accounted for 1.7 percent. Similarly, the 6.3 percent average potential growth between 1991 and 2000 could be broken down into 5.3 percent for factor input and 1.0 percent for productivity gain. These figures unmistakably demonstrate that Korea's growth was driven not by productivity gains, but by higher doses of labor, savings, and capital investment.

The KDI estimated that Korea's growth potential would average 5.2 percent over the 10 years from 2003 to 2012 provided that Korea maintained the reform agenda and continued to liberalize the economy. If the levels of commitment to reform and liberalization were to stay about where they were in 2004, the KDI projected growth at 4.6 percent (Han et al. 2004). The Institute for Monetary and Economic Research at the BOK forecast the growth rate at between 4.6 and 4.9 percent. Samsung Economic Research Institute predicted a lower potential growth rate of 4 percent.

A breakdown of these figures indicates that labor input would account for between 0.6 and 1.2 percent, that capital input would account for between 1.4 and 2.2 percent, and that total factor productivity gains would account for between 1.5 and 2.0 percent. These forecasts have in common that the pace of employment was expected to slow sharply as the overall birthrate fell and the population aged. Another common observation is that the rapid increases in capital inputs were expected to decelerate. Domestic savings were expected to stay at around 27 percent. More important, it was noted that Korea would have to make the transition from an economy in which growth derives merely from growth in factors of production to an economy fueled by overall productivity growth.

Diagnosis from the Perspective of the Great Transition of the Global Economy

The world has been making four broad transitions (Stevens, Miller, and Michalski 2000). The first is the transition to knowledge-based economies among the leading OECD countries. This is the shift to a society in which the production and consumption of knowledge dominate the daily lives of citizens. The second is the transition to industrialization among emerging countries such as Brazil, Peru, and Thailand. This transition is accompanied by a large government presence in the economy, along with mass production and consumption. Third is the transition to a market-based economy by the centrally planned economies of China, India, and the former Soviet Union. The fourth transition is convergence and integration with the global economy. In addition to these transitions, the world must make the transition from economic growth strategies centered on environmental destruction to growth strategies centered on environmental conservation. Without this last transition, the natural system of the globe cannot recycle and regenerate itself.

These transitions are not ordinary, everyday events, but transformative developments that fundamentally alter the way we produce, work, and consume. Each of these transitions has the potential to reshape the familiar landscape substantially. The impact of these transformative transitions is therefore enormous, though still difficult to ascertain. Moreover, the pace of these transitions has been so rapid and the intensity of the change so great that the associated uncertainties and complexities multiply quickly. To take advantage of the transformative changes unfolding in the global economy, Korea had first to understand fully the globally evolving landscape and adapt to it in the most effective fashion.

The path to a knowledge-based economy. The race toward knowledge-based economies being led by the developed countries is founded on technological breakthroughs and a wave of innovations. Rapid advances have occurred in information and communication technologies (ICTs), new materials technologies, biotechnology, new fuels, and nanotechnology (Lipsey 1999). In particular, ICTs have been improving at breakneck speed and generating wide applications in all economic activities. The computing power of microprocessors has been doubling every 18 months almost in lockstep with Moore's Law.

New materials began to become important following key developments in the chemical industry at the end of the 19th century. However, the role of new materials has recently become crucial in wide-ranging industrial activities such as electronics, transportation, construction, automobiles, and energy.

The field of biotechnology started with the discovery of the model of the structure of DNA in 1953. It is one of the most promising and critical technologies of the 21st century. There are already significant applications such as the use of stem cells for cell regeneration, the genetic engineering of disease-resistant grains, and the production of genetically modified bacteria for use in mining.

Among the new fuels, fuel cell technologies and the use of solar and other natural sources of energy have begun to emerge as realistic alternatives to the production of energy through fossil fuels.

Nanotechnology involves the production of goods through the rearrangement of individual atoms and molecules into desired aggregates. It is radically different from existing bulk manufacturing technologies whereby goods are produced by paring away the useless portion of the raw materials. Although still at the infant stage, nanotechnology is considered particularly promising for its potential to bring about a revolution in manufacturing, as well as advances and applications in biotechnology, information technology (IT), new materials technology, and other areas. In addition, it has opened up new possibilities for hitherto unimagined medical technologies, smaller and low-cost computers, and polymer nanomaterials with unparalleled strength and adhesive power.

There were several common characteristics among the emerging technological innovations. These technologies were general purpose, that is, they had broad applications in various fields. As in the past, the latest advances in IT were making possible new products, new work processes, and new business models. Another characteristic was that, because technological advance was an inherently uncertain process, it was nearly impossible to predict the potential applications or the speed of the technological evolution. IT, for instance, was now widely embedded in the economy, but the applications were still expanding at a lightning pace. Because of the infancy of biotechnology, new materials technologies, and nanotechnology, the potential was difficult to gauge. Thus, the best estimate of the size of the market for the computers with 18,000 vacuum tubes that appeared after World War II was fewer than 10.

The unique characteristics of knowledge. Knowledge has a unique characteristic: it is not bounded by the principle of scarcity as is the resource-intensive economy with which we are familiar (Schwartz, Kelly, and Boyer 1999). At the early stages of knowledge creation, fixed costs such as the cost of research and development (R&D) are high, but the marginal costs are nearly negligible. In a market environment in which the principle of increasing returns applies, rather than the principles of scarcity and diminishing returns, a natural monopoly is highly likely to occur. This has been seen in the case of Cisco, Microsoft, and Oracle in the United States. The costs of R&D for network business were high. However, as sales increased, the unit cost fell drastically, enabling the product provider to secure a significantly competitive market position. In addition to their low marginal cost of production, knowledge products are also easy to replicate. For this reason, once they are produced, it is difficult to control their availability. Not surprisingly, the market sometimes fails to compensate businesses adequately for the costs of R&D and for other costs; such is the situation in, say, new drugs or software.

Another characteristic of knowledge is that it is not homogeneous, and a competitive market price does not always emerge. As a result, consumers are often able to dictate the market value. Much as the quality of a lecture is not known to an audience member until the lecture is over, the value of knowledge is often only appreciated after the user has used it. Thus, reputation or brand name matters enormously in the marketplace for knowledge products.

People accumulate knowledge. Knowledge pertaining to know-what or know-why is stored in books or in digital format, but knowledge pertaining to know-how or know-whom is accumulated in brains. In a sense, therefore, knowledge workers who have the wetware in their heads can be said to possess the proprietary production method, which they can take with them wherever they go.

A scientific discovery becomes an addition to the inventory of scientific knowledge and thereby facilitates other discoveries. The invention of Morse code eventually led to the invention of the telephone by Alexander Graham Bell. The self-reinforcing cycle of knowledge inventory and technological innovation thus makes possible a new source of increasing returns in a technologically advanced economy.

In similar fashion, the IT network that forms the backbone of the knowledge economy is enabling the convergence of the creation of value in business, communication, and the distribution of services based on integrated digital platforms. In this new environment, consumer feedback is reflected in the products they purchase. It may therefore be more appropriate to call consumers "prosumers".

Economic evolution and social evolution. Knowledge has come to constitute the core of the modern economy, causing the basic industrial framework that has been developed over the past two centuries to be in flux (Stevens, Miller, and Michalski 2000). Producers and consumers, along with the products that reach markets, are becoming increasingly more individualized and specialized, thus triggering waves of socioeconomic diversification. From the perspective of qualitative improvement, socioeconomic change has become more complex.

A laborer is thus no longer a cog in a giant system for mass production in factories established according to the principles of scientific management characteristic of Taylorism (Taylor 1911), but a source of fresh ideas and value creation. Consumers no longer readily accept the same mass-produced goods, but prefer goods fitted to their individual tastes. Investors are no longer putting their savings blindly into pension funds, but are taking an active part in managing their investments. The methods of product development and production and the business models of the industrial era are becoming outdated and less relevant, and business managers are therefore struggling to design new business strategies. Governments have begun to offer tailored services that people actually desire and prefer.

The governance structure in industrial societies has begun to reflect the evolution in socioeconomic structures and adapt to the new landscape. Common in the older industrial societies, mass production and mass consumption accompanied by a large government presence were distinctly characterized by the rigid planning, control, and hierarchies built into organizational structures: top managers drafted the plans to execute, and mid-level managers passed these plans down to the production level and exercised management and internal supervision to ensure that the desired product or service was produced.

In a knowledge-based economy, decision-making authority is shared with the knowledge-equipped line workers. There is less need for mid-level communication and management, and the role of mid-level managers is diminished or these managers are replaced by smaller work teams that can be more easily adapted so as to add to and transmit knowledge. Outsourcing for specialized functions is becoming more commonplace. Individuals with highly specialized skills can now perform their tasks at home without coming to centralized locations. The work site and the site of final production are no longer necessarily identical.

It was inevitable that there would be changes in the way valid contracts were established. The knowledge acquired or transferred from a party could be resold, but the sellers might also retain what they had sold, thus raising tricky ownership issues following legally valid commercial transactions. Conventional contracts used for, say, the supply of produce to groceries could not be readily applied to transactions involving knowledge transfers. Buyer-seller contracts had to be modified to allow for the sale or transfer of knowledge.

The need for change extended to employer-employee contracts. In a society in which knowledge workers engage in businesses through networks, it is important to recognize the quality of the skills of workers and provide the corresponding compensation accordingly. However, the quality of the skills is often difficult to gauge until they are applied and tested. Moreover, intellectual endeavors are exceedingly difficult to supervise. For these reasons, the standard labor contract widely used in the industrial economy that assigns responsibilities according to a worker's seniority in the hierarchy is not well suited to a knowledge-based economy. Thus, the position-based assignment of responsibilities is being replaced by the self-motivation of workers, and strict performance oversight is being replaced by an appropriate sense of responsibility and ethical accountability among workers.

The compensation provided through the market for the creation or development of knowledge has often been inadequate. Strong protection for intellectual property rights represents one way to supply additional rewards. However, excessive protection can lead to limits on the distribution of knowledge. Therefore, a new system that strikes the correct balance between the creation and the distribution of intellectual property is needed. Natural monopolies often appear in a knowledge-based economy (see elsewhere above). This has to be countered by tougher rules and regulations on market competition.

The shift toward a knowledge-based economy requires reform in the educational system. The transition is a creative process through innovations in general-purpose technologies. People become acclimated to diverse and complex products and work processes. The educational system must therefore provide quality education that spurs creativity and adaptability and prepares the members of society for an increasingly diverse and complex economic and social environment.

It is widely recognized that early childhood education has an enormously positive impact on individual development. In a knowledge-based economy, early childhood education acquires even greater importance. People who join the workforce after completing the established educational requirements are often poorly equipped to cope with the rapidly expanding and diversifying technological and economic environment. Today's workers thus need continuing education and training that raises their productive potential. Clearly, the educational system must ensure uninterrupted education and training from preschool to professional career.

The march toward a knowledge-based economy has sparked concern over the widening inequality in income distribution partly caused by the digital divide. A backlash against the gap in educational opportunities is likely if the divide persists. Social tensions would rise, and the long-term potential for economic growth would suffer. Irrespective of their socioeconomic backgrounds, all members of society must therefore have equitable access to educational opportunities.

Korea's transition to a knowledge-based economy. Korea possesses human capital capable of identifying its own competitive intellectual capacities and exploiting these capacities to economic advantage. At present, however, Korea's overall competitiveness as a knowledge-based economy has fared poorly against that of the developed countries, particularly in the area of knowledge performance.

The evolution of industrial structures highlights the dichotomies in the Korean economy. According to the BOK, heavy industry and the chemical sector grew steadily beginning in 2002 (table 11.2). However, the growth in light industry was flat in 2002 and declined in 2003. The dependence of Korea's exports on the heavy and chemical industries such as semiconductors, wireless communication equipment, automobiles, computers, and ships, continued to deepen. The value added by the IT sector easily outstripped the value added by the non-IT sector. The pace of the growth in value added by the manufacturing sector was robust, while the corresponding pace in the service sector stagnated beginning in 2003.

There was a wide gap in business structure between large companies and small and medium enterprises (SMEs) in terms of profit, financial soundness, growth momentum, and funding capabilities. In 2003, the operating income ratios and debt ratios of large companies averaged 8.2 and 113.5 percent, respectively. In contrast, the corresponding ratios for SMEs were 4.6 and 147.6 percent, respectively.

The acceleration of globalization. Globalization is not a recent development. Thus, European countries sought to extend their sphere of influence in East Asia in the late 19th century. Nonetheless, modern globalization is vastly different in terms of the sheer scale and the reach across the globe. It has been accompanied not only by the free cross-border flow of goods, but also by trade in previously nontradable services such as education and medical care. The unimpeded cross-border flow and transfer of technologies have also become commonplace. The liberalization of capital across countries has led to the creation of a truly global market for capital and finance.

Table 11.2 Trends in the Growth of Value Added, by Industry, 2001 to Q1 2004
percent

Industry	*2001*	*2002*	*2003*	*2004, Q1*
Manufacturing	2.2	7.6	4.8	12.1
Light industry	–0.6	0.1	–3.4	–0.4
Heavy industry and chemical industry	2.9	9.7	6.9	15.1
Services	4.8	7.8	1.8	1.6
IT industry	—	17.6	11.5	25.1
Non-IT industry	—	5.9	2.1	3.0

Source: BOK (various years), *Quarterly National Accounts in Korea.*
Note: The table is based on prices in 2000. — = not available.

A global network of manufacturers led by multinational giants is being formed, and companies across countries are rushing to establish strategic ties with foreign business partners. In this evolving environment, inbound foreign investment is seen as a new way to facilitate job creation and technology transfers, thus triggering fierce competition for foreign investment around the globe. Other than workers who are bounded by their national borders, globalization has paved the way for the creation of a truly single marketplace for all nations.

The deep integration across space that has been made possible by globalization has been facilitated by technological advances in transportation and communication. Another major contributing factor has been the political will and commitment to globalization. Thus, the system of free trade that is now readily accepted is a result of a collective global effort that dates back to the negotiation of the General Agreement on Tariffs and Trade after World War II and to the Uruguay Round, which involved eight sets of arduous negotiations on reducing or eliminating tariff and nontariff barriers to trade. Intraregional cooperation has also been crucial to the success of free trade. From the European Union (EU) and the North American Free Trade Agreement to Asia-Pacific Economic Cooperation, a variety of cooperative endeavors have been launched over the years (some within a homogeneous and harmonious context, others less so). In particular, the number of free trade agreements has expanded significantly: a total of 208 agreements were in effect as of May 2004.

The characteristics of globalization. Several general trends in globalization may be observed. First, there was a deepening interdependence among countries. The world was being transformed into a single, interconnected network. Trade, investment, and the transfer of technology expanded and accelerated. Interest rate changes in the United States had a direct impact on the macroeconomic conditions of countries around the world. In matters of defense, the old paradigm of the preservation of sovereignty independently by each individual national actor was giving way to collective security schemes based on military cooperation among nations.

Second, there was a wider array of global issues of collective interest. With respect to preserving and protecting the environment, sustainable growth emerged as a genuinely global issue. The recognition of universal human values became more widespread. Promoting human rights and freedom was no longer a matter reserved to the domain of a single country, but had become the mandate of the entire world. Interest in the international financial architecture and in agreements on free trade, which inevitably affect people all over the world, grew rapidly.

Third, even as the world converged and became more uniform, there was much diversity. The activities of peoples around the world were increasingly prescribed by global standards, and the flow of information and knowledge across borders quickened. As a result, television programs transmitted in any country could now be watched in any living room, in any hotel, and in any other place in the global village, sometimes tempting us to lose sight of the fact that we live in a world that is still divided according to language, religion, culture, and race.

Friction and conflict in a globalizing world. In the course of globalization, frictions and conflicts are inevitable. One reason is that the fruits of globalization are not being shared equally or fairly. While countries that are the home of globally competitive companies tend to enjoy significant economic growth, other countries are experiencing anemic growth and falling incomes. In individual countries, many globally competitive exporters may be thriving, while uncompetitive sectors (such as agriculture in Korea, for example) are suffering greatly. The same is true among workers. While highly skilled workers may see their incomes and earnings potential rise sharply, workers with few or no marketable skills are experiencing the opposite. As the winners have emerged in the course of globalization, the demands by the losers for help have intensified. This has tended to raise the political resistance to globalization.

Notwithstanding the resistance, globalization is expanding because the major developed countries and most other countries are net beneficiaries. While countries are striving to provide compensation to those population segments that are being hurt by the forces of globalization, they are also pressing for restructuring and other needed internal changes. From this perspective, embracing globalization and enhancing social welfare among those people who are struggling to become competitive may be said to be two sides of the same coin (Rodrik 1997).

It must also be said that today's global financial order is associated with a host of difficult challenges because of numerous uncertainties and risks. Thus, for example, extreme volatility in exchange rates and interest rates has often been observed in global financial markets. Under the fully liberalized system of short- and long-term capital flows, there have been repeated booms and busts in the boom-bust cycle for some time. To an extent, the origin of Korea's 1997 financial crisis may be traced to the inherent instability in the global financial system.

Korea's globalization. Korea's import-export system has been liberalized. So have the country's short- and long-term capital flows. Except for imports of certain agricultural products and certain service sectors such as education and medical care that have been restricted under special laws, most sectors have been opened to foreign investment. The number of Korean students studying abroad has continued to increase each year, but foreign educational service providers have been effectively denied market entry in Korea. Similarly, while many Koreans have received medical care overseas, foreign medical service providers have been banned from doing business in Korea. There has, in fact, been a gradual shift among Koreans in their attitude toward foreign investment in the wake of the 1997 financial crisis. However, there has been only a beginning, and many foreign businesses continue to point to the difficulties of doing business in Korea.

Securing a sustainable environment. Following the industrial revolution, the emerging economic powers relied on energy-intensive industrialization and were able to achieve economic prosperity through mass production and consumption. However, the prosperity came at the cost of severe environmental degradation, which impaired the self-regenerating capacity of water, soil, and atmosphere. In recent years, there has been a growing recognition that the world economy can no longer count on energy-intensive, environment-degrading production and consumption to drive growth and prosperity.

Environmental degradation. Air pollution is one of the most pressing environmental problems. Acid rain caused by pollutants from industrial and chemical manufacturing facilities, power plants, and automobiles are not only degrading the structural integrity of buildings, but are also contributing to water pollution and the destruction of the ecosystems upon which fish, forest, and farm depend. Chemicals such as chlorofluorocarbons, haloalkanes (halons), and methyl bromide are causing ozone depletion, which exposes all of humanity to the threats of skin cancer and the weakening of the natural immune system and damages plant chloroplasts.

Even more serious than acid rain and ozone depletion is the global warming caused by human activities that release greenhouse gases into the atmosphere. Among the greenhouse gases, carbon dioxide accounts for the largest share. The primary source of carbon dioxide is the burning of fossil fuels. It is estimated that the accumulation of carbon dioxide has risen drastically, from 280 parts per million (PPM) in 1790, before the industrial revolution, to 360 PPM in 1998, and it is projected to increase to between 540 PPM and 970 PPM in the next 100 years. The average temperature is expected to increase by 0.8°C to 2.6°C between 1990 and 2050 and by 1.4°C to 5.8°C by 2100 (IPCC 2001). Rising temperature disrupts rainfall patterns and causes severe drought and flooding, threatening the global agricultural system. Sea levels are also likely to rise and overwhelm lowland areas, estuaries, and islands. Mass migrations of people and mass relocations of industrial facilities will likely ensue.

Two other major problems connected with the global environment is the exhaustion of clean water and ocean pollution. Already, a third of the world's population is said to suffer from water shortages, and, unless steps are taken to improve water supplies throughout the world, nearly half the world's population is expected to face water shortages within the next 30 years (World Bank 2003). Severe water shortages will threaten the survival of humanity, cause unprecedented calamities, and spark international friction and conflicts.

The oceans make up 75 percent of the world's surface and hold 90 percent of the world's water resources. They are the largest habitat and affect the world's climate by interacting with the atmosphere. Human dependence on the oceans for resources and maritime activities has been growing. This has led to increasing pressures on ocean biodiversity, eutrophication, and the ecosystem. According to a study by the World Bank (2003), 58 percent of the world's coral reefs and 34 percent of the world's fish stocks are already endangered.

The destruction of the ecosystem has emerged as a serious threat. The number of forms of life on earth has been estimated at between 10 million and 30 million, and roughly 1.75 million life forms have been identified. Tropical areas are said to account for about 74 to 84 percent of biological entities, and the rain forests are said to contain about half of all life forms even though they account for only about 7 percent of the earth's surface.

Because most developing countries are concentrated in tropical areas, the pro-growth policies of these countries are continually exerting destructive pressure on rain forests. Biologists warn that approximately 0.5 percent of the world's biological entities are becoming extinct each year. The diminishing biodiversity not only reduces the potential sources of food and medicines, but also leads to damage to the food chain.

Forests contribute to the stability of the ecosystem by preventing soil erosion and reducing the accumulation of carbon dioxide in the atmosphere. Forests covered 6.2 billion hectares of the earth's surface about 100,000 years ago, well before the agricultural revolution. Now, they cover roughly only 3.9 billion hectares, a loss of about a third. In recent years, the area covered by forests has increased modestly in some developed countries. In many developing countries, however, it is shrinking at a rapid pace, and this is raising concerns about soil erosion and the deterioration of air quality.

The need for sustainable growth. The gravity of the problems posed by the degradation of our natural environment points more to the diminishing ability of the natural system to recycle and regenerate itself than to the limits to growth, as argued by the Club of Rome in 1972 (Meadows et al. 1972). The world managed to maintain a steady supply of energy through the regular discovery of oil fields and alternative energy development. However, carbon dioxide emissions, a byproduct of the burning of fossil fuels, have exceeded the carrying capacity of the ecosystem and challenged the assumption of uninterrupted economic growth and prosperity. For sustained economic growth, there must be a transition from traditional resource- and energy-intensive industrial and economic structures to resource- and energy-saving structures. In this endeavor, the core of energy development must be based on energy generated by wind, water, the sun, and other renewable noncarbon sources. Efficient energy systems must be built into urban area infrastructure, housing, transportation, and factories. Energy-saving technologies must be pursued vigorously, and there must be a fundamental shift in social beliefs and attitudes toward energy and natural resource use and consumption so as to do more with less. If these goals are to be met in the next several decades, the direction of technological progress must be reset. This cannot be accomplished by simply fine-tuning old habits.

The unique characteristics of environmental challenges and responses. Despite the urgent need for a fundamental shift in our economic activities to protect and preserve the environment, most business activities and most enterprises continue to exert serious stress on the environment. This is basically caused by externalities associated with environmental problems. In a free market, businesses that employ cheap coal to produce energy pay no additional cost for releasing carbon dioxide into the air. For this reason, businesses have little or no incentive to limit voluntarily their release of carbon dioxide, and this, in essence, leads to carbon releases in excess of the limit that would be optimal for society as a whole. Such externalities then lead to market failures and tragedy for the global community.

Direct regulation or the levying of a fee for carbon releases are considered effective remedies that could significantly reduce the negative externalities arising from the underpricing of the environment. Direct regulation may vary from an outright ban to minimum benchmarks for the use of the environment. Through such schemes, activities that seriously harm the environment would be strictly banned, while those that could be tolerated are permitted at a controlled level. Enforcement, such as stiff penalties for noncompliance, needs to be embedded in these schemes.

Incorporating the cost of the use of the environment could be accomplished by internalizing negative externalities. In this endeavor, environmental taxes imposed on businesses and individuals who now bear no cost for releasing carbon dioxide into the air could be introduced. Cost sharing in the form of environmental charges could also be used to repair the damage caused by polluters.

Another unique characteristic of environmental problems is that they span wide geographical areas. An example is the periodic yellow dust containing harmful pollutants that is borne by winds across the sea from China to Korea. Deforestation from environmental distress may be locally isolated, but it also diminishes the ability of the environment to absorb carbon dioxide across countries and contributes to the problem of global warming. Concerted global action must therefore be taken.

As in the case of global warming, environmental degradation often takes place over a long period of time, which means that it is especially difficult to deal with the problem because of the propensity of some to be shortsighted. However, delays will only aggravate the problem: to restore the environment, once it has been gravely harmed, takes a long time. There may also be instances in which the environment is irreversibly damaged.

Therefore, strong and effective organizations and institutions must be established to address environmental problems in a timely way and to advocate for the necessary measures on a global scale.

The world's response to environmental problems. The Stockholm Declaration was adopted at the 1972 United Nations Conference on the Human Environment, held in Stockholm. This was a watershed development that sparked a long series of debates and discussions on the protection of the environment. The global environmental movement took more concrete shape at the United Nations Conference on Environment and Development, which was held in Rio de Janeiro in 1992. The conference adopted the Rio Declaration, which outlined Agenda 21, the program for environmentally sound and sustainable development. In 2002, the World Summit on Sustainable Development met in Johannesburg and adopted implementation plans based on the recognition that addressing poverty must be a necessary condition for sustainable development and growth.

Countries are addressing environmental concerns through some 800 bilateral, regional, and multilateral agreements and treaties. Multilateral environmental agreements accounted for 221 of these agreements as of April 2003 (table 11.3). Korea is a party or signatory to 45 international treaties.

One shortcoming in tackling the world's environmental concerns is that no comprehensive or authoritative entity capable of resolving cross-border disputes has emerged in the case of many environmental agreements and treaties. This is a noteworthy contrast to international organizations such as the World Trade Organization (WTO), which oversees and promotes international trade and maintains an independent administrative structure.

Nonetheless, many international environmental treaties share core principles. The first is the precautionary principle, which calls for safeguard steps to prevent actions that may cause harm to the environment in the absence of firm scientific evidence that the actions do cause environmental harm. Under this principle, precaution should be taken against genetically modified agricultural products if scientific evidence leaves open the possibility, however small, of potential risks to consumers.

The second is the polluter-pays principle, under which polluters should cover the costs of removing any harm they have done to the environment. Although this is a rather intuitively fair conceptual guide, it is too vague to be readily applied in international environmental treaty negotiations. An appropriate example may be the Kyoto Protocol, which was finalized only following prolonged negotiations among countries. To reach agreement on the protocol, a number of compromises had to be made on burden sharing between the EU and the United States, as well as among the developed countries and between the developed and the developing countries. Compromises also had to be made on the implementation of

Table 11.3 International Environmental Agreements, April 2003
number

Agreements	*Total*	*Atmosphere climate*	*Freshwater protection*	*Marine fishery*	*Wildlife preservation*	*Nuclear safeguard*	*Noxious substances*	*Other*
Multilateral agreements[a]	221	14	15	86	50	13	13	30
Agreements signed by Korea, Rep.	45	7	0	17	7	6	1	7

Source: Ministry of Environment.
a. Based on adoption.

steps to achieve greenhouse gas reductions. Once the first commitment period (2008–12) of the Kyoto Protocol expires in 2012, more disagreements and compromises are likely on burden sharing between the rich and the poor countries and on anti–global warming measures between the EU and the United States.

Korea's environmental policies. Most developed countries have already begun to shift their technological focus to environmental sustainability. Their economic structures are being changed from more resource-intensive manufacturing to less energy-intensive services, and innovative ICTs that drastically improve energy efficiency in such areas as transportation and construction are continually coming to the market.

Knowledge, information, and technology in Korea are driving a transition to an energy-saving knowledge-based economy. However, relative to the developed countries, energy consumption in Korea remains exceptionally high. Between 1990 and 2002, energy use in the developed countries grew by an annual average of 1.4 percent. In contrast, the annual average in Korea was 6.8 percent. According to 2002 data of the International Energy Agency, Korea ranked 10th in energy consumption in the world, and it ranked seventh in petroleum consumption. Energy consumption for industrial and transportation purposes accounted for the bulk of the increasing rate of energy use.

Korea's energy intensity, measured as the ratio of energy consumption to gross domestic product (GDP), was relatively higher than that of the developed countries. Changes in energy-intensity patterns indicated that Korea's total energy consumption grew at a rate of 9.0 percent between 1981 and 1997, higher than the country's GDP growth (8.1 percent) during the same period. Between 1997 and 2003, however, Korea's GDP growth (4.2 percent) was higher than Korea's growth in energy consumption (3.0 percent). Overall, Korea's energy intensity showed an upward trend until 1997, but a downward trend thereafter. However, it is unclear if these were, in fact, long-term trends.

Many Korean businesses rated domestic environmental rules and regulations as less strict than those of the developed countries. This reinforces the need for an accelerated transition to a less energy-intensive industrial structure. As the living standards of Koreans improved, so did their environmental awareness. Yet, the level of information and knowledge needed for accurate assessment and decision making on environmental degradation, the real costs associated with environmental degradation, the costs of prevention, and the benefits of related development projects is still unsatisfactory. As a result, the number of conflicts and confrontations on environmental issues has been rising. For effective environmental regulation, a proper balance between economic means—such as the imposition of taxes and charges—and regulation will need to be struck. Preparations for well-functioning emission trading should be undertaken.

Concerted actions are needed. At the regional level, close coordination and cooperation with China on the prevention of acid rain and the yellow dust storms originating in the deserts of northern China, Kazakhstan, and Mongolia are a priority in Korea. This is because both acid rain and yellow dust are likely to worsen for some time to come as China's economic development accelerates. At the multilateral level, reducing greenhouse gas emissions is a serious concern. During the first commitment period of the Kyoto Protocol, Korea was not obliged to reduce greenhouse gases. However, it is noteworthy that Korea's emissions of greenhouse gases jumped 86 percent between 1990 and 2001. As a member of the OECD and the world's ninth-largest greenhouse gas producer, Korea cannot afford to neglect its disproportionately large carbon dioxide emissions for long.

The Challenges Ahead in Korea's Economic Revival

The Korean Economy at the Crossroads of Opportunity and Threat

The transformation of the global economy can provide long-term growth opportunities for Korea. This optimism is, however, accompanied by the concern whether Korea will, in fact, be able to exploit the opportunities available to surge ahead of the developing countries and reduce the income gap with the developed countries. Korea must surmount major hurdles to catch up with the developed countries in the expansion of the foundations of knowledge and technology.

This is especially pressing in light of the relative ease with which the developing countries can catch up with Korea's processing skills and technologies. The fear is that Korea will experience an industrial hollowing-out because of lagging high-technology industries and the transfer of existing technologies to China and other emerging economies. Korea may face the real risk of becoming caught in a nutcracker, that is, lagging behind developed countries, while being chased closely by emerging countries (see chapter 2). Another concern is that Korean agriculture, a traditionally uncompetitive industry, has been damaged severely in the process of globalization, and Korea as a small open economy could be vulnerable to new crises should the international financial system become destabilized again. The slowing growth of the size of the country's labor force could lead to reduced potential growth.

These are all daunting challenges for Korea. Yet, the historical opportunity for Korea to take a leap forward could be lost if the country loses its way through indecision and hesitation. Although Korea trails the advanced countries in technological prowess, it can exploit its advantages of backwardness—an economic terminology used by Alexander Gerschenkron (1904–78)—and continue to narrow the gap. At the same time, it can leverage its superior industrial technologies and manufacturing capabilities to stay ahead of the developing countries.

Korea now possesses the wherewithal to compensate industries and income groups that suffer from market liberalization. As it provides the appropriate relief and pushes for the restructuring of the affected industries, it must seize the opportunity to leverage market liberalization for economic revival and growth. Korea must take steps to reinforce the financial system so that it is capable of absorbing and withstanding external shocks. As the growth of the labor force slows, human capital must be constantly developed to ensure sustained productivity gains.

As the global economy experiences an overwhelming transformation, Korea stands at the crossroads. The choice should not be to achieve yet more quantitative growth (can do), but to achieve qualitative growth (do better), and not to hesitate, but to utilize boldly the opportunities available simply because the opportunities will not wait for Korea.

The Tasks Ahead for a New Economic Revival

The new revival Korea should strive for is (1) a prosperous economy that enhances the quality of the lives of all; (2) a democratic society that, within a context of diversity, provides a level playing field and peaceful and harmonious social cohesion; and (3) a noble culture that is firmly founded on the country's traditional strength and breeds an innovative mindset. To this end, Korea must accomplish several key tasks.

Stable macroeconomy. An unstable macroeconomy reduces living standards. Sharp economic contraction increases unemployment and hurts wage growth, while an overheated economy triggers inflation. Under these conditions, low-income groups bear the brunt of the hardships. Not only do they face threats to their living standards, but they also face the prospect of becoming mired in poverty and passing their poverty on to the next generation.

An unstable macroeconomy discourages investment. Volatile inflation makes the future less predictable and investment decisions more uncertain, while a prolonged economic downturn dampens investment sentiment. As the failure of the financial reform efforts of the countries of Latin America at a time of inflationary pressures in the 1970s clearly demonstrates, an unstable macroeconomy makes a poor backdrop for policy reform.

A stable macroeconomy requires well-honed macroeconomic policies so that the desirable levels of growth, inflation, and the current account balance can be maintained. It also means that interest rates, exchange rates, and fiscal balance should all reflect the economic reality. In an economic downturn, lower interest rates and fiscal stimulus should be favorably considered. At a time of rising current account deficits, depreciation in the exchange rate should be an option.

Reponses to the aging population and falling birthrates. The Korean population is aging; the size of the population is projected to peak at 50.7 million in 2023 and fall thereafter. Whereas it took France 156 years, the United Kingdom 92 years, the United States 86 years, Italy and Germany 80 years, and Japan 36 years before the share of the elderly (aged 65 and over) in the population grew from 7 to 20 percent, Korea is expected to do the same in 26 years. Korea reached the world's lowest birthrate, 1.2, in 2002, a development that is expected to turn into a structural long-term phenomenon, not a short-term aberration.

In an aging society, the size of the productive labor force is shrinking, and the potential growth of the economy suffers. This is in contrast to a population bonus phase, when people born during a baby boom join the labor force in large numbers and fuel high economic growth.

The cost of supporting senior citizens surges as a population ages. In Korea, the ratio of workers (between 25 and 64 years of age) to the aged was 12 to 1 in the 1970s. It fell to 7.6 in 2000 and is expected to fall to 2.4 by 2030. The financial burden on households because of the support of senior family members will increase as well. Because no systemic support structure is yet in place, the aging population is emerging as a major social issue.

To prevent what is often described as an agequake, the birthrate must pick up and the size of the young population must expand.[1] In this endeavor, the quality of child care is crucial and deserves priority support and investment. For sustained economic growth in the face of a long-term trend toward low birthrates, labor productivity must improve, and the participation of women and senior citizens in labor markets must be actively expanded. Meanwhile, because the tradition of family support for retired senior citizens who are normally not well off is on the ebb in recent Korean society, support systems for the elderly should be established and augmented. Postretirement pension systems must be reformed into a three-tier system: a basic national pension, an employee retirement pension, and personal pensions.

The transition from a resource-intensive to a knowledge-based economy. The global economy cannot continue to depend on resource-intensive, energy-consuming structures for growth. Likewise, the Korean economy cannot rely on growth driven by the intensive use of labor and by significant capital inputs. A knowledge-based economy saves energy and other resources and yet fosters high productivity. This is thus where Korea should look for stable long-term growth.

The successful transition to a knowledge-based economy requires the vigorous creation, distribution, and application of knowledge. In parallel, the technological foundations of the economy must be reinforced. This requires sound human resource development to reinforce creative and adaptive capabilities and the development of the information infrastructure necessary for knowledge expansion. The first priority must be encouragement for human capital development through genuine educational reform with a view to the emergence of a creative learning society.

In terms of industrial applications, new opportunities and new frontiers capable of driving future growth must be pursued. In the promotion of next-generation technologies, it will not be sufficient to move from the current level of technology to the next level; the jump must be three or four levels ahead. As the developed countries have already demonstrated, Korea must reinvigorate the social services, including education and medical care, and the service industry, including business support services and the component and materials industries. Industries that lack a competitive edge in the marketplace must be restructured and rationalized. This is the only way to prevent the industrial dichotomy—that is, the divergence between the competitive and the uncompetitive—and to find new sources of competitiveness.

The transition to a knowledge-based economy is inherently a complex and uncertain process requiring creation and adaptation. It is a long-term process. Overcoming uncertainty will require constant experimentation. Our historical experience tells us that private business enterprises must be given a free hand in utilizing human and physical resources and testing their ideas in the marketplace. If their ideas succeed, the enterprises must be duly rewarded. Moreover, competition encourages experimentation to achieve innovation. In essence, this means that private property rights and a market-directed pricing system must be firmly established. Market freedom and competition must be guaranteed.

Expanding market openings. From resources to climate, the natural environment of the world is diverse. So is the social environment, from technology to culture and religion. Such diversity is the source of market opportunities for producers and consumers alike. On the global economic stage, liberalization is expanding, and competition is intensifying. The free competitive environment promotes technological innovation and business productivity.

In an era of globalization, expanding market liberalization and tapping into the opportunities available in the global marketplace will be crucial to Korea's economic success. This is the rationale behind the effort to turn Korea into the main economic pillar of northeast Asia.

To benefit from globalization, Korea must take several steps. First, it must strive to become an active member of the global community and contribute to the world economic order. To a significant degree, the world trade system is shaped by the WTO, which sets the foundations for free trade and rational trade rules. Korea may reap many benefits as free and open trade expands and trade rules become firmly established. Korea must therefore become an active player in the global trade initiatives of the WTO.

Meanwhile, the global financial system is guided by the International Monetary Fund (IMF), which supports the principle of the free movement of capital and the prevention of financial crisis. The free movement of capital enables businesses to access capital efficiently. It also gives investors wider choices in allocating their savings. The downside is that it can amplify the boom-bust cycle and propagate the contagion of a financial crisis from one country to another. Therefore, taking an active part in the agenda the IMF sets for the global economy and for financial markets is in Korea's interest.

Second, Korea must revamp its institutions and practices in line with global standards, which are being reshaped on various fronts. Thus, for example, efforts have been undertaken to harmonize technical and safety standards across countries to facilitate world trade. International standards in accounting and auditing and core principles in banking supervision and corporate governance are being developed to reinforce market mechanisms and promote financial market stability.

Third, Korea must aggressively seek out foreign direct investment (FDI). The general perception among Koreans that foreign businesses drain national wealth is outdated and harmful to Korea's interests. FDI brings in cutting-edge industrial technologies and contributes to job creation at home. To make Korea an attractive investment destination, Korea must create a positive, inviting business climate that helps domestic companies thrive and encourages foreign companies to do business in Korea. A positive investment climate cannot be formed without improvements in labor market conditions, the foreign exchange system, the tax system, and the general quality of the lives of foreign nationals in Korea.

Fourth, Korea must expand its free trade agreements with the world's major economies, beginning with East Asian economies. Korea is looking to expand bilateral free trade agreements, in addition to multilateral agreements under the auspices of the WTO, so that it can deepen and accelerate free trade with other countries with an eye to attracting investment and technology transfers and leveraging free trade to build comprehensive and cooperative relations with other countries.

Many Asian countries are competing with each other to accumulate free trade agreements. Korea must move aggressively to reach trade deals with as many Asian countries as possible. A free trade agreement must be promoted with the United States, a key trading partner. Because agriculture and other traditionally protected sectors are likely to suffer under free trade agreements, compensation and restructuring schemes will have to be undertaken to mitigate the losses in these sectors.

Rallying the support of the public for open trade will be crucial. The failure of Korea to respond to the Western powers in the 19th century is a useful reminder in this endeavor. A virulently antiforeign local doctrine of Confucianism prevailed in those days, but, today, openness and engagement with the outside should be the focus of the national discourse on free trade.

A sound microfoundation against external shocks. Korea must be prepared for uncertainties arising from global financial markets. It must be an active participant in discussions among countries on the reform of the international financial architecture and must work to resolve the weaknesses at home. In this effort, beefing up the microeconomic structures of domestic corporate and financial companies must be a priority. Financial soundness is a necessary condition for achieving this. Uncontrolled debt and channeling of short-term borrowing to long-term investment can leave the economy vulnerable to outside shocks and even a crisis. The confidence of foreign investors must be secured through the utmost transparency in corporate governance. Business structures must be revamped around high-profit, high-growth areas of business activity.

Given the reality that short-term hot money is moving around among global financial markets, Korea must expand its foreign exchange reserves. If the reserves fall short, the entire economy may be exposed to external shocks, and this may trigger a crisis at home. Any benefit deriving from not having significant foreign exchange reserves will be overwhelmed by the enormous economic and social costs in the event of a financial crisis. Liquid assets should make up a large portion of the foreign exchange reserves. To the extent that emergency credit lines of foreign exchange can be secured through currency swaps with foreign central banks and an increase in the IMF quota, there will be less pressure on the government to build up huge foreign exchange reserves. This is one of the reasons Korea stresses the need for currency swap facilities among Asian countries.

From confrontation and conflict to cooperation and competition. Korean society is becoming increasingly complex and diversified. Typical household structures, traditionally represented by large extended families, now include a substantial share of one-person households. Women's labor force participation has risen significantly. As the income gap has widened, the quality of family life across income groups has begun to diverge. Standardized mass production and consumption are giving way to more individualized and lean production and consumption. Differing views and perspectives on economic efficiency versus equitable income distribution, relations with the Democratic People's Republic of Korea and with the United States, labor issues, rural development, and environmental concerns are now aired openly in the Republic of Korea.

As the world becomes more interconnected and interdependent, people throughout the world are tending to conduct their lives within a truly global network. The world is converging toward global standards and becoming integrated in a homogeneous community. A closer look reveals, however, a world still vastly separated by race, culture, religion, and value systems. In terms of economic prosperity, wide discrepancies may be easily observed across countries and regions.

Diversity unleashes creative power and fuels long-term dynamism. Diversified market demand opens up new market opportunities, and fresh ideas and dreams lead to new products and drive advances in technology. Diversity in social structure, social values, and social behavior stimulate learning. At the same time, diversity is often the source of social conflict. As groups with divergent identities compete and adapt to a changing environment, conflicts of interest are inevitable. As a new balance is worked out, a consensus must be forged. However, conflicting attitudes on whether the changes taking place are desirable or how quickly they should proceed are bound to arise during the transformation of social structures, behavior, and values and the resulting disruption among established authorities and in the sense of security. In the words of Mark Twain, "I am all for progress; it's change I don't like."

The increasing complexity of change necessarily requires a large information set, and failure to acquire this in a timely fashion can lead to misunderstanding. This contributes to more vocal conflict and confrontation among competing groups and leads to social unrest. The outcome may be passivity, the dissipation of economic dynamism, the emergence of a wait-and-see attitude, and a flight to quality. The competing goals of divergent groups must therefore be channeled constructively to foster a new social order in which the constituents strive for harmony within diversity.

Unfortunately, Koreans have not yet established an orderly society in which competition and cooperation can thrive. Rather than resolving conflicts in a competitive, yet cooperative spirit, Koreans are often more likely to fight to the end, through whatever means necessary—legal or illegal—to achieve their objectives. It is often said that brinkmanship is one of the most common negotiating tactics in Korea.

A culture of disorder, irresponsibility, and indiscipline, as well as the tendency to blame others for one's failure, prevails in parts of Korean society. There is an old saying in Korea that a well-mannered individual treats himself with a fall frost and treats others with a spring breeze. In modern Korea, however, the reverse has become the norm, and discipline at the societal level has not yet been firmly established.

It is difficult to expect a society undergoing a major transition amid uncertainty and a shifting environment to carry out creative and adaptive processes smoothly and in an orderly fashion. Inevitably, there will be frictions as competing interests clash. However, when friction amid chaos becomes the norm and disorder settles in, failure is inevitable. There is a line that should not be crossed at all times.

What should we do given this context?

First, the security of people must be firmly assured. In this regard, industries hurt because of market liberalization not only must be restructured as soon as possible, but they also must be compensated properly for the losses they incurred during the liberalization process. In a broader sense, this means that social welfare and the safety net must be expanded and reinforced for the benefit of the most vulnerable members of society. Support must be provided to low-income families so they may maintain a minimum measure of dignity. Educational support must be actively provided so that poor families have a chance to gain a competitive edge in the marketplace in the future. Educational support for children is especially crucial in eliminating the cycle of poverty that passes from one generation to the next.

Second, a system of social governance that is sufficiently effective to absorb and respond to complex and divergent viewpoints is needed. This entails the efficient processing of the voices of all members of society. Views on matters of significant political importance should be routinely conveyed to policy makers so that they have a chance to be reflected in the decision-making process. However, because of the difficulty of building consensus in the National Assembly, the legislative branch, Korean society as a whole suffers from extreme political frustration and friction. A more effective way must be found to facilitate communication and consensus building through the elected representatives of the National Assembly.

The participation of citizens in decisions on matters of significant public interest must be drastically expanded. For instance, it makes sense for the government to survey the poor about what they desire from public assistance before arbitrarily designing or implementing this assistance. In parallel, the general public, civic groups, and nongovernmental organizations should improve their judgment and their capacity to manage social affairs. Otherwise, waste and an approach based on trial and error are likely.

For efficient conflict resolution among competing interest groups, the rule of law must be respected. The rule of law requires objectivity, predictability, a level playing field, and respect for a normative hierarchy that puts the constitution above ordinary legislation and requires politicians to respect established rules of procedure (Tarschys 2001). The time has come to resolve differences within the framework of the rule of law. Established rules must be honored and enforced equally with respect to every member of society without exception.

The political will of the people must be expressed on the basis of the rule of law for the resolution of conflicts. In particular, groups in superior bargaining positions must not abuse their power. Nor should disadvantaged groups be allowed to exploit their positions merely for the sake of their anger and to engage in brinkmanship so as to achieve maximum advantage.

Efforts must be expended to strengthen mutual trust and respect among the members of society. As society increasingly functions through networks and as outsourcing becomes the norm, trust becomes an enormously vital social glue. Trust is built on transparency, accountability, and integrity. Transparency and accountability are never perfect in the real world. Yet, there is no question that sane investors do not put their money in companies that practice accounting fraud and that leaders who set the bar high for others, but insist on setting it low for themselves, cannot earn the trust of the people.

The Reform of Korea's Economic System

The Basic Framework of a New Economic System

Economic systems may be defined in various ways. It therefore pays to frame a broad definition that encompasses the policies, institutions, social norms, and social values upon which economic activities are based. For a country striving for effective responses to challenges, the economic system must also evolve. Otherwise, there is a risk of crisis.

The 1997 financial crisis may well be a classic example of the failure of an economic system to evolve and adapt. There is a strong case to be made that the crisis was fatally linked to the continuation of an economic system deeply flawed because of cronyism, protectionism, and government regulation at a time when the world was converging and demanding free markets, democracy, and the rule of law.

So, what should be the basic framework of Korea's economic system? First, market flexibility and openness must be secured. Only then can responses be produced efficiently to the challenges posed by the complex and rapid transformative changes unfolding in the global economy. A simple analogy may be the driver who applies the steering wheel, the brakes, the lights, and the windshield wipers in a timely fashion to respond to the shifting driving environment, including road conditions, weather, and traffic flows.

Second, the social safety net must be enlarged. Those who are harmed in the process of market liberalization must be assisted through appropriate compensation and a helping hand in restructuring, and those who are exposed to economic hardship must be aided by a well-functioning social welfare system. Otherwise, instability will reign, and investment will dry up. The government must stand ready to give aid to the most vulnerable and disadvantaged members of society to enable them to enjoy the dignity to which every member of society has a right.

Third, sound social governance based on the principle of the rule of law and democracy must take hold. The expanding diversity of society is a double-edged sword. It may be a source of new alternatives and opportunities for learning about other people, but it may also be a source of conflict and fuel social polarization. There will be efficiency gains and a more diversified division of labor as the complexity of social structures and organizations increases, but there is also the downside risk that misunderstandings will become more frequent because of a dearth of timely information. Social misunderstandings, confrontations, and discord must be replaced by mutual cooperation and fair competition in the exploitation of the advantages diversity and sophistication may offer. To foster this change, efforts must be expended to establish a new structure of social governance.

Fourth, the collective resilience of Korean society must be strengthened. The transition currently under way is a process of revival driven by fresh ideas, new aspirations, and accumulated knowledge. It is also a process of wrenching change and restructuring that alters existing institutions, technologies, and the social order. If we do not enhance the creative and adaptive capacity of society, society will stagnate during this process. Especially in Korea, the creative capacity to spark scientific advances must be harnessed, along with the capacities of people to absorb and adapt to emerging technologies such as ICT and the capacities of society to implement good governance.

Fifth, a new, noble culture befitting the kinds of broadbased transformations Korea seeks must take root. As Max Weber argued, Western capitalism was founded on the Protestant work ethic, and a society's values and norms are the foundations of that society's economic vibrancy. Undertaking the transition to a higher level of development is akin to striving among the members of society to achieve a balance between flexibility (the burden of risks involved in change) and security and between competition and cooperation. In this process, a culture of respect for individual freedom and responsibility must take hold. Korea has drifted because of a lack of discipline. Amid a diminishing sense of order, responsibility, and temperance, a culture of mutual distrust has been settling in. Korea cannot make the leap to a higher level under such circumstances. Nor should the pendulum be allowed to remain stuck in one position, either individual freedom or responsibility. There should be a simultaneous respect for and balance between individual freedom and responsibility.

Sixth, the transition to a higher level should represent an opportunity to establish a new vision and instill confidence for the future. (The broad technological, economic, and social goals and the accompanying tasks are discussed at length in chapter 3.) Another key ingredient of success in Korea's future is a broadbased consensus among the people on the direction in which the country should be headed. All the competing visions and priorities should be openly shared and debated in a spirit of community and collective good and in line with the *Zeitgeist*, the spirit of the times. If people are able willingly to pursue their economic goals with confidence, there is a good chance their shared collective vision will be realized.

The core values for which Korea should strive are creativeness to achieve technological innovation, adaptability to the evolving global landscape and new technologies, fairness for the resolution of deepening conflicts and inequalities, and soundness to absorb and recover from economic dislocations and shocks. In the effort to reach broad social consensus and work toward shared goals, strong political leadership that instills confidence among the people and nourishes the collective dynamism of society is a must.

The Evaluation of the Postcrisis Reform of the Economic System

As the economic environment shifts and evolves, the economic system must adapt and respond to the changing circumstances and the new reality. Sluggish adaptation can lead to a crisis. A costly overhaul of the system then becomes necessary. This overhaul and the adjustments needed because of the evolving situation after the overhaul are not straightforward tasks.

Several major systemic surgeries were performed in the wake of the financial crisis in Korea. First, the underlying economic system was overhauled and restructured. The extensive restructuring of corporate and financial companies enhanced their soundness, efficiency, and future earnings potential (table 11.4).

The government managed to accumulate US$199 billion in foreign exchange reserves by the end of 2004; this provided an added measure of protection against economic emergencies. The government established the Korea Center for International Finance, which it made responsible for early warning on financial market risks. The risk awareness of the public improved so much that, before putting their savings in financial companies, it became routine for people to check whether the companies offered deposit insurance protection. The widely held belief before the crisis that some companies were simply too big to fail or that banks never fail disappeared after the crisis. The risk management capabilities of financial service companies improved markedly. Regulatory forbearance ceased, and tight financial oversight was instituted. These efforts produced benefits when large companies such as Hyundai Engineering & Construction and Hynix Semiconductor got into financial trouble or when massive credit card problems and high household debt created severe distress in the financial system.

Second, the government-led economic planning and development model gave way to a private-sector-driven and self-disciplined open market economic model. Much of the unseemly relationship and collusion between officialdom and the business community were ended, and rent-seeking behavior and moral hazard were sharply curtailed. Trade barriers such as tariffs and nontariff barriers were lowered, and markets were liberalized in line with the principles of a competitive market economy. The regulations on foreign investment were liberalized. In financial markets, the BOK was given greater independence, and restrictions on foreign exchange and capital flows were lifted. Regulations on the entry into new businesses were significantly relaxed, and fair trade organizations were strengthened to promote a level playing field and fair market conduct. For greater flexibility on the labor market, the temporary agency worker system—an employment system in which workers at subsidiary companies are dispatched to the parent companies as temporary agency workers—and the employment adjustment system were introduced.

Table 11.4 Trends in Key Financial Indicators in Manufacturing and Banking, 1997–2003
percent

	Korea, Rep.							*United States*	*Japan*
Indicator	*1997*	*1998*	*1999*	*2000*	*2001*	*2002*	*2003*	*2003*	*2003*
Manufacturing industry									
Financial structure									
Debt ratio[a]	396.3	303.0	214.7	210.6	182.2	135.4	123.4	154.8	156.2[b]
Equity capital ratio[c]	20.2	24.8	31.8	32.2	35.4	42.5	44.8	39.3	39.0[b]
Borrowing ratio[d]	54.2	50.8	42.8	41.2	39.8	31.7	28.3	26.0	30.9[b]
Profitability									
Ordinary income ratio[e]	–0.3	–1.9	1.7	1.3	0.4	4.7	4.7	7.0	3.2[b]
Return on assets	–1.0	–4.4	0.0	–2.0	0.0	6.3	3.8	3.5	0.1[b]
Growth									
Growth in sales	11.0	0.7	8.0	15.2	1.7	8.3	6.1	—	—

Banking industry									
Financial structure									
Bank for International Settlements capital ratio	7.0[f]	8.2[f]	11.8	10.6	11.7	11.3	11.2	12.7	11.3
Productivity									
Per capita net earnings, W, millions	–2.7	–18.7	–4.6	–4.3	5.8	5.8	2.2	—	—
Asset soundness									
Substandard and below-loan ratio	6.0	7.6	12.9	8.0	3.4	2.3	2.6	1.2	4.6

Sources: BOK 2004; FSS 2000.

Note: Some numbers are rounded. — = not available.

a. The ratio of total liabilities to stockholder equity.

b. Figures for 2002.

c. The ratio of stockholder equity to total capital.

d. The ratio of borrowing, plus bonds, to total capital.

e. The ratio of ordinary income to sales.

f. Excluding specialized banks.

Third, new foundations were laid for ongoing efforts at democratization and transparent governance structures. Government organizations, functions, and regulations were revamped to reorient the role of government from rowing to steering and from directing to enabling. Corporate governance standards incorporating OECD principles were established.

Fourth, a new welfare system was introduced to expand the social safety net and protect the most vulnerable members of society more effectively. The relief available for people laid off in the wake of the financial crisis was augmented. A system was instituted to provide protection for low-income groups and ensure a minimum standard of living.

Despite the massive surgeries following the financial crisis, the Korean economy remains in a state of anemia (see elsewhere above). One reason Korea has not been able to recover fully is the poor execution of the surgeries. An example is the Movement for Rebuilding Korea, an initiative the government started to encourage the public to adopt a fresh attitude and more positive behavior. The initiative failed to reach its goal. Another reason is the postsurgery response. The sharp division within the workforce and in the labor market among regular and temporary workers is a result of an inadequate effort at fostering flexibility in the labor market.

During the postcrisis years, Korea has managed to carry out the necessary hardware reform successfully throughout the economy. However, the software reform that is needed to exploit the hardware reform has never truly materialized. Korea must implement a systemic reform of the software to prepare for a better, brighter future.

Urgent Tasks in the Economy

Let us now survey the tasks that must be completed to implement the urgent software reform and push for a fresh launch of the Korean economy.

Recognition of the need for consensus building on future goals. Korea suffers from endless conflict and chaos, and Korean society is fractured by small, competing, and unyielding special interest groups. It must be impressed on the public as clearly as possible that the actions of these groups reduce the efficiency and aggregate incomes in society and cause political life to become more divisive (Olson 1982). It must be made equally clear to the public that it is the most vulnerable and economically disadvantaged segment of the population that will suffer the most if the economy falters as a result of continued conflict and chaos. Therefore, a sense of solidarity must be fostered among the people, and small, narrowly focused interest groups must yield way for the good of the collective well-being that all Koreans cherish. The people must also do their part. The country's political establishment and the elites of society must contribute through a sense of responsibility and leadership. If society comes together as a community with a shared vision and a commitment to collective endeavor so as to tackle the tasks ahead, Korea will have found a new source of dynamism within a well-rooted Zeitgeist. Otherwise, confrontations and disputes among small competing groups will sap the economic vitality of the nation, and this might cause a new round of economic calamity. Such a possibility should not be casually dismissed; extra attention should be paid to preventing fractioning and bipolarization within Korean society.

The frontier beyond traditional boundaries in thought and action. If Korea does not strive for new business opportunities as globalization progresses and if it stays behind protected markets at home, the country's growth potential will surely decline. Korea must find new dynamism and vitality through a frontier spirit by developing an open mindset and going beyond traditional boundaries.

For example, Korea must seek to take part in the construction of power plants in China and East Asia's development projects. It has been said that China experienced power shortages of between 25 million and 30 million kilowatts during the summer of 2004 and thus had to curtail the power supply to 24 cities. This is a striking development given the proven design, construction, and operational capabilities and funding ability of Korea in the construction of power plants. Korea's entry into the power plant construction sector in China could become a win-win situation for both China and Korea. However, reportedly, it has not been smooth sailing for Korea. Korea should therefore focus on establishing a foothold in the market in China for power plant construction and in East Asia's infrastructure and other development projects. Korean firms must cultivate close cooperation among the companies that would undertake the projects in related areas and strengthen their ability to take part in the projects.

In financial, educational, and medical services, Korea must expand its playing field to the world marketplace. In the past, services were treated more or less as nontradable goods. In today's rapidly converging markets, more services are becoming tradable. Services tend to grow and become more diversified and sophisticated as the economy advances. For this reason, services account for a big share of the workforce and the creation of value at home.

Korea's air travel, shipping, and construction services have matured into globally competitive industries, but the country continues to lag behind in high-end service industries such as financial, educational, and medical services. In contrast, Singapore has undertaken a concerted effort to position itself as the hub of logistics, financial, educational, and medical services in Asia.

Korea's financial companies are accustomed to borrowing from foreign lenders, but are not known for lending to others. Yet, Korea's balance of payments shows that the current account continues to be in surplus, and even the capital account is turning positive. This raises questions: Is Korea needlessly holding on to excess foreign exchange reserves? Should the continuing surplus in Korea's balance of payments simply be added to the growing foreign exchange reserves? These are legitimate questions because the maintenance of high levels of foreign exchange reserves has a cost. For the sake of price stability, the BOK absorbs increases in the money reserve being accumulated through its purchases of foreign exchange by issuing monetary stabilization bonds, which adds to the cost of interest and pushes up market interest rates.

Korea's financial companies must expand their businesses within a global perspective and seek business opportunities by raising and providing credit on a global basis in overseas markets. Steps must be taken to attract countries and companies in foreign countries, including East Asia, to issue and trade securities in Korea. The financing by Korean companies of large projects in these countries must grow, along with the short-term capital supply to foreign financial companies.

If Seoul is to become the financial hub of East Asia, companies in the region must be able to raise funds cheaply and efficiently in Seoul, and foreign investors must be able to find ample, safe, and attractive investment opportunities in local markets. Korea's financial companies have a key role to play in this endeavor. To achieve success in this area, they must drastically improve their ability and their capacity to compete.

In educational services, Korea must seek to set its sights on the Asian market. Recently, many Korean universities have begun attracting students from abroad to make up for the dwindling pool of local students who are eligible. The result has not yet been positive. Meanwhile, among the Korean students studying abroad in 2003, 159,903 were seeking degrees from colleges or other higher educational establishments, and 10,132 were seeking high school or lower educational certificates. This compares with 9,456 foreign students who were studying in Korea that year. Among these students, there were 5,400 Chinese, 870 Japanese, and 737 Americans. Among the OECD countries, the number of foreign college students grew at an average rate of 9 percent between 1995 and 1999, compared with 5 percent among nonforeign students (OECD 2003b). A breakdown of the almost 1.7 million foreign students who were studying in the OECD countries in 2001 shows that the United States accounted for 28 percent; the United Kingdom, 14 percent; Germany, 12 percent; France, 9 percent; Australia, 7 percent; and Japan, 4 percent. Together, these six countries accounted for nearly three-quarters of the total.

The pool of students in East Asia looking for overseas study is reportedly substantial. For example, in China, there were 1,020 colleges and universities, but only 4 million of some 7.5 million students were being admitted because of the inability of the schools to absorb more students. Because of the lack of financial means among the students who are not admitted, it will likely be some years before the pool of students willing and able to study abroad reaches a significant size. Nonetheless, Korea already enjoys some comparative advantages over the OECD countries. Its tuitions tend to be lower, and there are many scholarship opportunities for students from East Asia because of the large number of Korean companies investing in the region. For instance, one scholarship supported by each of the 50,000 Korean companies investing in East Asia would translate into 50,000 scholarships for students wishing to study in Korea. This and other educational service advantages should be pondered carefully by Korean companies and institutions.

Korea's medical services must expand so as to become a growth-driving, job-creating industry. Acute shortages of doctors and other high-skilled medical service practitioners often force countries such as Japan and the United States to seek out foreign specialists. In China and East Asia, medical services are underdeveloped and unevenly distributed. Korea can exploit its strength in advanced medical technology and service quality to serve these markets. The aggressive efforts of countries such as Singapore and Thailand to supply foreign medical service markets should be a useful lesson and guide for Korea. If educational and medical services in Korea are to be revitalized as competitive service industries, domestic markets must first be open, and for-profit medical and educational service providers must be permitted.

Strengthening market infrastructure. Investment has recently been rather sluggish in Korea, and some wonder whether the focus during the postcrisis years on sound and conservative business management came at the expense of bold risk-taking and the can-do attitude that many Korean businesses used to possess. The paucity of investment can also be attributed to the increasing difficulty of securing profitable business opportunities, the heightened risk of failure associated with starting a new business, the hostility between labor and management, and antibusiness sentiment. Often overlooked is the failure to reinforce market infrastructure in the transition to a market economy led by the private sector.

There are several relevant issues. First, a mutually reinforcing cooperative system is absent from the economy. In the old days when the government took the lead, a development project in East Asia, for instance, would have been managed and coordinated by the Ministry of Commerce, Industry, and Energy, which would have set the timetable for the project and the level of assistance to be provided by the government. Though sometimes overworked, a functional, collegial coordinating structure would have been in place to complete the project successfully. A private sector version of such a structure or system may be needed to help companies communicate and coordinate more effectively. Some measure of synergy should be expected from this structure. The scope of activities in which companies are able to cooperate at home and abroad might be expanded.

Second, a risk-sharing system befitting an economy led by the private sector has not yet been fully established. In the wake of the financial crisis, a risk-averse corporate culture took hold because many companies had experienced insolvency and bankruptcy. However, avoiding risk inevitably invites anemia in the economy. Shareholders and management must voluntarily assume a measure of business risk. Moreover, corporate risk must be allocated among market participants through methods such as loans and venture initiatives so that companies are able to continue to search for success. In this process, the importance of the role of the financial system cannot be overemphasized. Because the financial system acts as a clearing house for information by, for example, analyzing and evaluating corporate disclosures and vetting the soundness of companies and business ideas, it is instrumental in cushioning the adverse impact of uncertainty and risk in the marketplace. Experience has consistently demonstrated that countries with a strong financial system show more vigorous growth, while countries with sagging financial systems are more susceptible to financial crisis.

A strong financial system necessarily entails efficient financial markets, competitive financial service companies, sound financial market infrastructure, and well-functioning and effective financial regulation and supervision. Korea's financial hardware, that is, the legal and regulatory framework, appears to be firmly in place, but the software to run the hardware is not adequate. For this reason, Korea's financial markets have been badly shaken by, for instance, debt delinquencies and the massive credit card bubble. Likewise, many SMEs continue to rely heavily on government credit guarantees for survival, and foreign investors exert a strong influence on local capital markets. Few venture start-up companies thrive, and the downside risks to investing in new technologies are too large for many companies. Korea must therefore accelerate the software reform so as to upgrade the risk management system and help companies access financial markets more effectively.

Third, many markets are rigid. Only when markets operate flexibly can prices send the appropriate market signals based on fundamentals, and only then can rational investments occur. Markets must be sufficiently flexible to cope with the rapidly changing conditions that accompany a major transition. Korea engaged in reform initiatives to improve market flexibility following the financial crisis, but the evidence indicates that the effort has not produced the basic changes that were envisioned. This is particularly true in the agricultural and fishery sectors and other protected industries in which high tariff and nontariff barriers have been used to keep out foreign competition. Many also point to the stubborn rigidity of labor markets.

Problems of protection and the entry barriers associated with politically sensitive sectors such as agriculture are not limited to Korea. However, during this era of deepening globalization, the way to move forward is not to turn a blind eye to rent seeking in the marketplace, but to reinvigorate the economy through technological development by opening up protected industries and removing the entry barriers to competition. This can be facilitated through effective industry restructuring and appropriate compensation for those market actors who may be adversely affected.

Labor market rigidity is an especially serious problem. Despite the joint efforts undertaken by the government, businesses, and labor unions to reform labor markets in the wake of the financial crisis, labor and management relations in Korea ranked at the bottom of 60 countries surveyed by the IMD in 2004 (see table 11.1). To protect their self-interest, workers who felt threatened by the prospect of massive layoffs in the course of business restructuring during the crisis rallied around labor unions and vehemently resisted, sometimes unlawfully, the reforms initiated by the government.

Rather than dealing head-on with such thorny issues as layoffs and wage concessions, businesses increasingly turned to temporary workers and outsourcing so as to take advantage of the flexibility and cost-savings the businesses desired. As a result, temporary workers, who are given no long-term job security, now make up about half the total workforce. Their wages are also about half the wages of permanent workers. Such a dichotomy cannot continue in labor markets. The long-term job security that permanent workers desire can emerge only if the skills of these workers become inseparable assets of employers, not a costly wage headache. In an environment in which job security is guaranteed and the wages of permanent workers are an established component of cost, labor conflict usually intensifies. Moreover, if permanent workers are assured of job security and generous working conditions, the conflict between permanent and temporary workers worsens. If such conflicts intensify between labor and management and among various labor groups, the economy becomes vulnerable to crisis.

The generous job security guarantees given to permanent workers must be reduced, but the job protection enjoyed by temporary workers must be drastically improved. Should temporary workers gain greater job benefits and job security guarantees without any concessions from permanent workers, employers will become overburdened and shift their business overseas. The result will be reduced employment for permanent and temporary workers alike.

This is yet another argument in favor of an effective and reliable social welfare system that enables both employers and workers to adjust to downsizing during economic downturns. Retraining among workers with outdated skill sets to help them acquire marketable skills is crucial to labor market flexibility. Job stabilization programs that help the unemployed obtain access to information on job opportunities must be expanded.

Reforming the educational system for the knowledge-based era. For Korea's economic revitalization, a transition to a learning-intensive society is crucial. If this transition is to succeed, the country's educational system must provide quality education through numerous channels. Opportunities for lifelong learning, from kindergarten to adult training and retraining, must be made available to all without regard to socioeconomic circumstances.

According to *Education at a Glance 2003*, a study by the OECD (2003b), 24 percent of Koreans between the ages of 25 and 64 had received at least a two-year college education, slightly higher than the 23 percent average in the OECD countries, but lower than the average in Japan, the United Kingdom, and the United States. By age group, people between 25 and 34 made up 40 percent of the population, which was higher than the 37 percent average among the OECD countries, while people between 45 and 54 accounted for 13 percent, much lower than the 21 percent average in the OECD. That the proportion of adults with some advanced education is greater in Korea than in the OECD suggests that Korea has a relative advantage in the educational attainment of its workforce.

Moreover, an assessment of learning outcomes among 15-year-old students by the OECD Program for International Student Assessment 2000 indicated that Korea ranked sixth among the OECD members in reading literacy (after Australia, Canada, Finland, Ireland, and New Zealand), second in mathematical literacy (after Japan), and first in scientific literacy, which put Korea significantly above the OECD average (OECD 2003b). In addition, the performance of Korean students was mostly distributed in the high level of proficiency, and there was relatively little variance among the students. In reading literacy, however, the share of Korean students at the top proficiency level was below the OECD average. The OECD 2000 assessment clearly shows Korea's strong potential to achieve a smooth transition to a knowledge-based economy. However, Korea's poor showing in reading literacy suggests that Korea will encounter difficulties in building a deep reservoir of highly creative people in the workforce.

IMD's assessment of Korea's educational advantages was not so encouraging. In 2004, Korea was ranked 35th among 60 countries in the overall national competitiveness category; its rank in education was 40th (IMD 2004). Korea fared well in literacy and in economic knowledge, but received the bottom ranking in finance literacy and the availability of well-qualified engineers. Despite the obvious need, the country has not been able to carry out meaningful systemic educational reform to promote a learning-intensive society.

Korea needs to undertake important broadbased educational reform so that the country is prepared for the era of knowledge-based globalization. First, the primary objective of educational policy should be to deliver quality education on an equitable basis. Both quality and equability are required because there is a dichotomy in Korea between the proponents of quality who wish to rely on competition in education and the proponents of uniform and standardized education who wish to ensure fairness.

If Korea's educational system fails to foster creativity, an essential condition for a knowledge-based economy, and meet the expanding demands of market competition, the country may face serious consequences. Korea's education system will be inadequate if college graduates continue to be the subject of complaints because the quality and content of their education fail to satisfy the needs of the market and if the country continues to show poorly in the top proficiency level of the OECD Program for International Student Assessment. Moreover, if the educational system does not satisfy the high expectations of parents in the provision of high-quality foreign language classes in elementary schools, parents will begin to favor private education and early overseas education. This will also occur if the current system is maintained that promotes one-size-fits-all education without differentiation between those who excel and those who underachieve.

The lack of educational opportunities for students eager to learn, but unable to do so because of economic hardship or other difficulties, will lead to a diminishing pool of human capital and lower growth potential. Korea therefore needs to take steps to retain or reduce the relatively small gap in academic performance among students that the OECD program assessment 2000 report identified (OECD 2003b).

Irrespective of whether one supports competition to improve the quality of education or favors uniform educational standards in the interest of fairness, it must be recognized that efforts should be undertaken to achieve both goals. No one-sided effort will succeed; a win-win compromise should therefore be sought. To improve educational quality, the proponents of uniform education must acknowledge the need for better education and engage with the proponents of educational competition. Similarly, the proponents of competition in education must acknowledge the considerable beneficial effects of socioeconomic advantage on academic performance and engage with the proponents of fairness to find a more level playing field for all students.

One of the most salient socioeconomic boundaries in Korea's education system is the boundary between the Seoul metropolitan area and the rest of the country. Because socioeconomically advantaged families tend to cluster in and around Seoul, the capital, elementary, middle, and high school students from economically disadvantaged families are less common in Seoul and the surrounding areas, raising the specter of a permanent class distinction across regions. Likewise, the difference between the Seoul metropolitan area and elsewhere in terms of private educational spending is striking. The financial and psychological burdens can be quite heavy on parents who do not live in the Seoul metropolitan area but send their children to schools there. In attempting to address the performance gap between schools in the Seoul metropolitan area and elsewhere, it is more efficient to help underperforming schools raise their educational standards than to suppress the gap by regulating well-performing schools.

Meanwhile, the number of specialized high schools, private independent high schools, and alternative high schools must be significantly expanded to give students more choice in the selection of schools so that they may pursue their aspirations more effectively.

Government rules and regulations on college admission should be eliminated so that colleges can determine on their own the type of students they wish to admit. High school students nearing graduation will soon be eligible to vote. So, they should be considered sufficiently mature to decide for themselves which college they wish to attend. Competition by foreign educational institutions should be encouraged.

Second, lifelong learning must be a realistic option. This will require significantly expanded investment in early childhood education, the high cost of which directly contributes to low birthrates and keeps mothers out of the workforce. The number of hours in the classroom in primary and middle schools is lower in Korea than in most OECD countries. It should be extended. This would have the advantage of reducing the need for private educational activities after school. Job training and adult education should be expanded to help older workers learn new marketable skills and adapt to the shifting economic landscape. Job training programs and the system of special professional certification must be adjusted in a timely fashion as economic circumstances change. Outdated training programs and certification requirements should be terminated so that the skills demanded by a knowledge-based economy can be properly acquired and exploited. The cross-border recognition of professional certification systems should be pursued so that, for instance, a doctor licensed in Korea can practice in Japan.

Third, the school system must be made more efficient. In this regard, the analysis offered by the OECD Program for International Student Assessment 2000 raises many important issues (OECD 2002). Thus, investment in schools is crucial to raising the quality of education, but it is no guarantee of academic achievement or excellence. This is because some countries achieve academic excellence with relatively few resources, while other countries require many resources to achieve the same result. Encouraging students to read and to concentrate on schoolwork has a broadly positive effect on academic achievement and helps reduce gaps created by various socioeconomic factors. Indeed, in terms of academic achievement, the benefits of intensive or avid reading have been found to be greater than the benefits of the presence of highly educated parents in the household. It has been said that the development of the habit of reading forms the foundation for lifelong learning. Likewise, the study environment in schools appears to exert a strong influence on student academic performance. It has been shown that students in schools that set high standards, provide a pleasant, yet disciplined, study environment, and maintain good relations between teachers and students outperform their peers in other schools. Students in countries that allow school administrators more latitude and independence in teaching, but stress academic performance, tend to show better academic performance. However, expanded school independence alone is not necessarily related to achievement gaps among schools.

The wide range of analyses mentioned above provides the basis for proposals aimed at improving the efficiency of Korea's school system. Thus, the pupil-teacher ratio and the number of students per class should be lowered to provide education that is more well suited to students with different interests and learning abilities. Because the desire of students to read, learn, and devote attention to schoolwork tends to exert a greater influence on academic performance than does family background, a positive school environment is a must.

In school administration, independence cannot be separated from accountability. Educational content, educational standards, and enforcement of standards must be enhanced to meet the needs of a knowledge-based economy. Schools that fail to satisfy performance standards should be targeted for improvement. Efforts should be undertaken to raise the quality of teachers. The quality of an educational system is limited by the quality of the teachers in the system. If carried out faithfully, these steps should help restore confidence in public education.

Improving the efficiency of government services. Public sector restructuring in the aftermath of the financial crisis has led to fewer regulations, but better services and a more participatory democracy in which citizens play a more active role in the government decision-making process. Despite these positive results, however, much remains to be done.

The government needs to shift from the current arbitrary one-size-fits-all approach to management to a new system that provides services more well suited to the wide-ranging demands of the public. During the 1970s, the government made bulk purchases of winter overalls and handed them out to all women bus fare collectors. The handout was widely perceived as an act of caring; there was no criticism because of a lack of sufficient attention to the color, fabric, or style of the clothing. The government now provides free school meals to needy students. However, rather than widespread appreciation from the general public, the service is criticized because of the quality of the food and the way it is provided through schools. Most likely, the different reception in these two cases has arisen because times have changed. People were not necessarily more gracious in the 1970s, but, as living standards have improved, the public's main interest has shifted to focus more on the quality of government services. Moreover, the advances in the knowledge-based economy and the government's aggressive efforts to deliver public services through electronic means have paved the way for more individually tailored public services.

This highlights that the provision of public services must reflect current socioeconomic conditions and the views of the actual consumers of the services. In this perspective, the government has made real strides in the implementation of projects. For example, the creation of industrial cities, the construction of industrial clusters, and the establishment of delivery systems for welfare services have been executed so as to reflect the needs and opinions of the inhabitants of the relevant regions. Nonetheless, more needs to be done to improve, for instance, the delivery of public services that are actually beneficial to users and can more readily incorporate feedback from the public.

For the past decade, the government has channeled some W 70 trillion to farming communities, but the agricultural sector as a whole has experienced little real improvement. Over the next decade, the government expects to invest up to W 120 trillion to enhance the economic vitality and living standards of farming communities. One may express skepticism about the returns the government may generate from this huge investment.

Government policy in the agricultural sector is aimed at bringing about structural improvements, while protecting the land and conserving environmental resources. It is also conditioned by the aging population in agricultural communities and the need to invest in the redevelopment of poor regions. The issue is complex and multidimensional. The only way to realize genuinely positive change is to take account of the diverse interests and the unique characteristics of each individual region and respect the aspirations of the inhabitants. So, it makes sense to allow local governments to set their own agendas for development and revitalization, while the central government limits its role to evaluating those agendas and providing appropriate support. In many ways, it is akin to the approach of the World Bank, which reviews development projects proposed by developing countries and lends a helping hand.

An effective and efficient system for the implementation of policy must be established. In this endeavor, choice and focus are important. For instance, the government's response to issues raised because of low birthrates and the aging of the population resembles a patchwork and has not been particularly successful. The bewildering array of cash support payment schemes to promote childbirth, all of which purport to encourage families to have more children, is a case in point. A more logical first step might have involved investment in affordable high-quality daycare centers for small children—the lack of which is the roadblock most frequently cited by working women—so that the system of daycare centers can be at least brought up to the average quality level in the OECD as quickly as possible. Promptly addressing the problem of the rapidly aging population through the reform of the national pension fund, a ticking time bomb, is essential. Most countries have already switched to a three-tiered retirement plan—national pension, employee pension, and personal pension—and taken steps to ensure continuing solvency. The issue is unpopular, and compromise is difficult, but pension reform is an urgent challenge that, in Korea, cannot be delayed. The government must execute its policies strictly and fairly. For instance, it must cease the practice of compensating individuals who purchase land, undertake bogus construction projects, or merely plant trees in areas designated for redevelopment as if these people were legitimate long-time residents.

In carrying out needed reforms, who has ownership matters enormously. A bewildering number of reform initiatives are being drawn up by an equally bewildering number of presidential commissions. The roadmap for reform is not being executed properly mainly because of ambiguity over who is in charge or who is accountable. A more effective approach might be to hand over responsibility for reform initiatives to the appropriate ministries and assign ownership to the ministers. Otherwise, it may be unrealistic to expect any marked improvement in execution.

It is time for a transition to a higher level. This is a time of epoch-making change that could set the course for the future. It is a time of great transition, a rare historic opportunity for world leaders to take center stage and apply their creative power. Whether a political leader charting a new course for the nation, a scientist on the verge of a great technological breakthrough, an artist in the vanguard, a pioneering entrepreneur, a labor leader struggling for a fundamental solution in the relationship between labor and management, or an office worker utilizing the latest advances in technology, now is the time for the stars of Korean society to take advantage of the fresh opportunities that have suddenly appeared because of the transition and help drive the economic advancement and long-term prosperity of Korea. At such a historic time of transition, it is important that you, the stars of Korean society, rise up to support each other and help each other thrive. Should we fail to exploit the opportunities available to all of us, stagnation may ensue. Koreans must recognize that, right now, the world—particularly the countries in East Asia—is bustling to seize the opportunity of the moment to make the leap to a higher level and ensure future prosperity.

Note

1. Paul Wallace (1999) argues that rising longevity and lower fertility are causing a seismic shift in the profile of populations worldwide.

References and Other Sources

BAI (Board of Audit and Inspection). 1998. "Analysis and Assessment of the 1997 Financial Crisis." April, BAI, Seoul.

BOK (Bank of Korea). 1997a. "Conditions and Measures for Foreign Currency Liquidity." November, BOK, Seoul.

———. 1997b. "Recent Movement of Foreign Currency Market and Response." December, BOK, Seoul.

———. 1997c. *Foreign Exchange System in Korea*. February. Seoul: BOK.

———. 1998a. "Relief Measures for the Credit Crunch." June 2, BOK, Seoul.

———. 1998b. *Money and Credit Policy Report*. March. Seoul: BOK.

———. 1999a. *Economic Statistics Yearbook*. Seoul: BOK.

———. 1999b. "Economic and Financial Market Trends in June 1999." Press release, July 6, BOK, Seoul.

———. 2001. *Monetary Policy Report*. March. Seoul: BOK.

———. 2002. *Foreign Exchange System in Korea*. May. Seoul: BOK.

———. 2004. *Monthly Statistics*. June. Seoul: BOK.

———. 2008. *Monetary Policy in Korea*. August. Seoul: BOK.

———. Various years. *Balance of Payments*. Seoul: BOK.

———. Various years. *Financial Statement Analysis*. Seoul: BOK.

———. Various years. *Quarterly National Accounts in Korea*. Seoul: BOK.

Booz Allen Hamilton. 1997. *Revitalizing the Korean Economy toward the 21st Century: Vision Korea Report*. October. Seoul: Maeil Business Newspaper.

Casanegra de Jantscher, M., K. Baer, R. Adair, and G. Seymour. 1999. "Korea: Priorities for Tax Administration Reform." April, International Monetary Fund, Washington, DC.

Cho, Namju. 1997. "Heard in Seoul: Professionals Post 'No Fishing' Signs for Korean Market." *Wall Street Journal Europe*, December 11.

Cho, Yoon Je. 1998. "The Financial Crisis in Korea: Causes and Challenges." Unpublished draft, September, Asian Development Bank, Manila.

Choi, Bong. 1998. "Explanation and Counter Measures for Eroding Industrial Base." *CEO Information*, September, Samsung Economic Research Institute, Seoul.

Dahlman, Carl J., and Thomas Andersson, eds. 2000. *Korea and the Knowledge-Based Economy: Making the Transition.* Washington, DC: World Bank Institute; Paris: Organisation for Economic Co-operation and Development.

Federal Reserve Bank of Atlanta. 1999. *Economic Review.* 2nd quarter, Federal Reserve Bank of Atlanta, Atlanta.

FSC (Financial Supervisory Commission). 1998a. "Plans to Restructure Financial Sector." June 19, FSC, Seoul.

———. 1998b. "Announcement by the Chairman on Failing Banks." Press release, June 29, FSC, Seoul.

———. 1998c. "Status of Financial Sector Restructuring and Planning." July 15, FSC Structural Reform Unit, FSC, Seoul.

———. 1998d. "Announcement by the Chairman on Corporate Distress Evaluation." Press release, June 17, FSC, Seoul.

———. 1998e. "Announcement by the Chairman on Advancement of Financial Supervisory Policies." Press release, December 15, FSC, Seoul.

———. 1999a. "Report on Challenges to National Policy Reforms." March 29, FSC, Seoul.

———. 1999b. "Government's Position toward Daewoo Group Workouts." Press release, August 26, FSC, Seoul.

———. 2000. "Financial and Corporate Restructuring in Korea." April 1, FSC, Seoul.

FSC (Financial Supervisory Commission) and FSS (Financial Supervisory Service). 2001. *Banking Regulations.* Vol. 2 of *The Financial Supervisory Regulations of the Republic of Korea.* October. Seoul: FSC.

FSS (Financial Supervisory Service). 2000. *Monthly Financial Statistics Bulletin.* January. Seoul: FSS.

———. 2002. "Characteristics and Progress in Financial Industries." March, FSS, Seoul.

Gerschenkron, Alexander. 1962. *Economic Backwardness in Historical Perspective: A Book of Essays.* Cambridge, MA: Belknap Press.

Ghosh, Swati R., and Atish R. Ghosh. 1999. "East Asia in the Aftermath: Was There a Crunch?" IMF Working Paper WP/99/38 (March), International Monetary Fund, Washington, DC.

Gompers, Paul A., and Josh Lerner. 2001. *The Money of Invention: How Venture Capital Creates New Wealth.* Cambridge MA: Harvard Business Press.

Ham, Jun-Ho. 1999. "Macro Evaluations of External Debt Servicing Ability and Efficient Management Plans for External Liabilities." Unpublished report, March, Korea Development Institute, Seoul.

Han, Jin-Hee, Kyung-Soo Choi, Dong-Seok Kim, and Kyung-Mook Lim. 2004. *Prospects for Potential Growth of Korean Economy for 2003–2012.* Seoul: Korea Development Institute.

IIF (Institute of International Finance). 1998. "Capital Flows to Emerging Market Economies." IIF Research Note, September 29, IIF, Washington, DC.

———. 1999. "Capital Flows to Emerging Market Economies." IIF Research Note, January 27, IIF, Washington, DC.

Ikehara, Mamoru. 1999. *Criticism of Korea and Its People: A Book Written at the Risk of Being Bitten to Death.* January 1. Seoul: Joongang M & B.

IMD (International Institute for Management Development). 2004. *World Competitiveness Yearbook 2004*. Lausanne: IMD.

IPCC (Intergovernmental Panel on Climate Change). 2001. *IPCC Third Assessment Report: Climate Change, 2001*. Cambridge U.K.: Cambridge University Press.

Jang, Tae-Pyung. 1999. *Corporate Restructuring and Tax Support Measures*. January 1. Seoul: Kwangkyo Academy Publishing Co.

Kim, June-Dong. 1999. "Inward Direct Investment Regime and Evidence of Spillover Effects in Korea." KIEP Working Paper 99–09, Korea Institute for International Economic Policy, Seoul.

Kim, Kyeong-Won. 1998. *One Year after the IMF Bailout: A Review of Economic and Social Changes in Korea*. Seoul: Samsung Economic Research Institute.

Kindleberger, Charles P. 1984. *A Financial History of Western Europe*. London: George Allen & Unwin.

Krugman, Paul. 1994. "The Myth of Asia's Miracle." *Foreign Affairs* 73 (6): 62–78.

Lane, Timothy, Atish Ghosh, Javier Hamann, Steven Phillips, Marianne Schulze-Ghattas, and Tsidi Tsikata. 1999. "IMF-Supported Programs in Indonesia, Korea, and Thailand: A Preliminary Assessment." Occasional Paper 178, International Monetary Fund, Washington, DC.

Lee, Kyu-Sung. 1996. "The Establishment of the Institutional Backbone for the New Leap Forward in the 21st Century." Paper presented at Hyundai Research Institute, Seoul, December 13.

———. 1998. "Korean Financial Crisis." Paper presented at Graduate School of Management, Korea Advanced Institute of Science and Technology, Seoul, February.

———. 2004. "Solutions to Address the Economic Challenges that Korea Faces." Paper presented at the KAIST CEO Forum, Korea Advanced Institute of Science and Technology, Jeju, Republic of Korea, September 16.

Lipsey, Richard G. 1999. "Sources of Continued Long-Run Economic Dynamism in the 21st Century." In *The Future of the Global Economy: Towards a Long Boom?*, ed. Organisation for Economic Co-operation and Development, 33–76. Paris: Organisation for Economic Co-operation and Development.

Meadows, Donella H., Dennis L. Meadows, Jørgen Randers, and William W. Behrens III. 1972. *The Limits to Growth: Report for the Club of Rome's Project on the Predicament of Mankind*. Washington, DC: Potomac Associates.

MOFE (Ministry of Finance and Economy). 1996. *Economic White Paper*. Gwacheon, Republic of Korea: MOFE.

———. 1997a. *Monthly Economic Bulletin*. March, MOFE, Gwacheon, Republic of Korea.

———. 1997b. "Is There Any Difference between the Baht and Kia?" Report, July, MOFE, Gwacheon, Republic of Korea.

———. 1997c. "Letter of Intent." December 3, MOFE, Gwacheon, Republic of Korea.

———. 1998a. *Open Tomorrow with Peoples*. Gwacheon, Republic of Korea: MOFE.

———. 1998b. *Economic White Paper*. Gwacheon, Republic of Korea: MOFE.

———. 1998c. "Report to the President," March 16, MOFE, Gwacheon, Republic of Korea.

———. 1998d. "Letter of Intent." January 7, MOFE, Gwacheon, Republic of Korea.

———. 1998e. "Letter of Intent." February 7, MOFE, Gwacheon, Republic of Korea.

———. 1998f. "Letter of Intent." May 2, MOFE, Gwacheon, Republic of Korea.

———. 1998g. "Korea's Key Economic Policy Issues." June 2, MOFE, Gwacheon, Republic of Korea.

———. 1998h. "Korea's Key Economic Policy Issues." June 17, MOFE, Gwacheon, Republic of Korea.

———. 1998i. *Monthly Economic Bulletin.* June, MOFE, Gwacheon, Republic of Korea.

———. 1998j. *Monthly Economic Bulletin.* July, MOFE, Gwacheon, Republic of Korea.

———. 1998k. *Monthly Economic Bulletin.* August, MOFE, Gwacheon, Republic of Korea.

———. 1998l. *Monthly Economic Bulletin.* April, MOFE, Gwacheon, Republic of Korea.

———. 1998m. *Monthly Economic Bulletin.* May, MOFE, Gwacheon, Republic of Korea.

———. 1998n. "1998 Macroeconomic Forecasts by Economic Research Institutions." July 15, MOFE, Gwacheon, Republic of Korea.

———. 1998o. "Cause and Policy Measures to Ease the Credit Crunch." August 23, Financial Policy Division, MOFE, Gwacheon, Republic of Korea.

———. 1998p. *Monthly Economic Bulletin.* September, MOFE, Gwacheon, Republic of Korea.

———. 1998q. *Monthly Economic Bulletin.* October, MOFE, Gwacheon, Republic of Korea.

———. 1998r. *Monthly Economic Bulletin.* November, MOFE, Gwacheon, Republic of Korea.

———. 1998s. "Measures to Increase Consumer Financing." Press release, September 26, MOFE, Gwacheon, Republic of Korea.

———. 1998t. "Comprehensive Analysis for Recent Economic Trends and Policy Direction." September 2, MOFE, Gwacheon, Republic of Korea.

———. 1998u. "Policies for Economic Revival." Report presented at the 11th meeting of the Economic Policy Coordination Committee, October 20, MOFE, Gwacheon, Republic of Korea.

———. 1998v. "Economic Policy Direction for 1999." Report presented at the cabinet meeting, December 29, MOFE, Gwacheon, Republic of Korea.

———. 1998w. "Korea's Key Challenges." June 2, MOFE, Gwacheon, Republic of Korea.

———. 1998x. "Korea's Key Challenges." June 17, MOFE, Gwacheon, Republic of Korea.

———. 1999a. "Progress of Corporate Restructuring." April 24, Banking System Division, MOFE, Gwacheon, Republic of Korea.

———. 1999b. "Korea Report on International Financial Architecture Reform." April, MOFE, Gwacheon, Republic of Korea.

———. 1999c. *Monthly Economic Bulletin.* March, MOFE, Gwacheon, Republic of Korea.

———. 1999d. *Monthly Economic Bulletin.* April, MOFE, Gwacheon, Republic of Korea.

———. 1999e. *Monthly Economic Bulletin.* May, MOFE, Gwacheon, Republic of Korea.

———. 1999f. *Monthly Economic Bulletin.* June, MOFE, Gwacheon, Republic of Korea.

———. 1999g. *Monthly Economic Bulletin.* July, MOFE, Gwacheon, Republic of Korea.

———. 1999h. *Monthly Economic Bulletin.* August, MOFE, Gwacheon, Republic of Korea.

———. 1999i. "Final Results of the Second Consultation with IMF in 1999." Press release, November 30, MOFE, Gwacheon, Republic of Korea.

———. 1999j. *Monthly Economic Bulletin.* September, MOFE, Gwacheon, Republic of Korea.

———. 1999k. *Monthly Economic Bulletin.* October, MOFE, Gwacheon, Republic of Korea.

———. 1999l. *Monthly Economic Bulletin.* November, MOFE, Gwacheon, Republic of Korea.

———. 1999m. *Monthly Economic Bulletin.* December, MOFE, Gwacheon, Republic of Korea.

———. 2000a. *Monthly Economic Bulletin.* January, MOFE, Gwacheon, Republic of Korea.

———. 2000b. *Monthly Economic Bulletin.* February, MOFE, Gwacheon, Republic of Korea.

———. 2000c. *Monthly Economic Bulletin.* March, MOFE, Gwacheon, Republic of Korea.

MOFE (Ministry of Finance and Economy) and FSC (Financial Supervisory Commission). 2000. "Public Fund White Paper." September, MOFE, Gwacheon, Republic of Korea.

MOFE (Ministry of Finance and Economy), FSC (Financial Supervisory Commission), and BOK (Bank of Korea). 1999. "A Plan for Financial Market Stability in Connection with Daewoo Workouts." November 4, MOFE, Gwacheon, Republic of Korea.

MOFE (Ministry of Finance and Economy), FTC (Fair Trade Commission), FSC (Financial Supervisory Commission), and MCIE (Ministry of Commerce, Industry, and Energy). 1999. "Checking on Implementation of Top Five Chaebol Restructuring and Follow-Up Measures for Chaebol Reform." August 25, MOFE, Gwacheon, Republic of Korea.

MOFE (Ministry of Finance and Economy) and KDI (Korea Development Institute). 1999. *A New Paradigm for the Knowledge-Based Economy: Vision and Strategy for the 21st Century.* December 1. Gwacheon, Republic of Korea: MOFE.

Nam, Duck-Woo. 1998. "Korean Economy in Crisis: Causes and Responses." [In Korean.] In *Causes and Lessons of the IMF Bailout*, ed. Samsung Economic Research Institute, 9–56. Seoul: Samsung Economic Research Institute.

OECD (Organisation for Economic Co-operation and Development). 1998. *OECD Economic Survey: Korea.* Paris: Economic Policy Bureau, OECD.

———. 2002. *Education Policy Analysis 2002*. Paris: OECD.

———. 2003a. *The Sources of Economic Growth in OECD Countries*. Paris: OECD.

———. 2003b. *Education at a Glance 2003: OECD Indicators*. Paris: OECD.

Olson, Mancur. 1982. *The Rise and Decline of Nations: Economic Growth, Stagflation, and Social Rigidities*. New Haven, CT: Yale University Press.

Rodrik, Dani. 1997. *Has Globalization Gone Too Far?* Washington, DC: Institute for International Economics.

Rosenberg, Nathan, and L. E. Birdzell Jr. 1986. *How the West Grew Rich: The Economic Transformation of the Industrial World*. New York: Basic Books.

Schwartz, Peter, Eamonn Kelly, and Nicole Boyer. 1999. "The Emerging Global Knowledge Economy." In *The Future of the Global Economy: Towards a Long Boom?*, ed. Organisation for Economic Co-operation and Development, 77–114. Paris: Organisation for Economic Co-operation and Development.

SERI (Samsung Economic Research Institute). 2004. *CEO Information*, 459 (July 14), SERI, Seoul.

Stevens, Barrie, Riel Miller, and Wolfgang Michalski. 2000. "Social Diversity and the Creative Society of the 21st Century." In *The Creative Society of the 21st Century*, ed. Organisation for Economic Co-operation and Development, 7–24. Paris: Organisation for Economic Co-operation and Development.

Stiglitz, Joseph E. 1999. "Lessons from East Asia." *Journal of Policy Modeling* 21 (3): 311–30.

Tarschys, Daniel. 2001. "Wealth, Values, Institutions: Trends in Government and Governance." In *Governance in the 21st Century*, ed. Organisation for Economic Co-operation and Development, 27–43. Paris: Organisation for Economic Co-operation and Development.

Taylor, Frederick Winslow. 1911. *The Principles of Scientific Management*. New York: Harper & Brothers.

UNCTAD (United Nations Conference on Trade and Development). 1999. *World Investment Report 1999: Foreign Direct Investment and the Challenge of Development*. Geneva: United Nations.

Wallace, Paul. 1999. *Agequake: Riding the Demographic Rollercoaster Shaking Business Finance, and Our World*. London: Nicholas Brealey.

World Bank. 1998. *World Development Report 1998–99: Knowledge for Development*. Washington, DC: World Bank; New York: Oxford University Press.

———. 2003. *World Development Report, 2003: Sustainable Development in a Dynamic World; Transforming Institutions, Growth, and Quality of Life*. Washington, DC: World Bank; New York: Oxford University Press.

Yoshitomi, Masaru, and Kenichi Ohno. 1999. "Capital-Account Crisis and Credit Contraction: The New Nature of Crisis Requires New Policy Responses." ADBI Working Paper 2 (May), Asian Development Bank Institute, Tokyo.

Index

Figures, notes, and tables are indicated by f, n, and t, respectively.

E

ECO-AUDIT

Environmental Benefits Statement

The World Bank is committed to preserving endangered forests and natural resources. The Office of the Publisher has chosen to print ***The Korean Financial Crisis of 1997*** on recycled paper with 50 percent post-consumer fiber in accordance with the recommended standards for paper usage set by the Green Press Initiative, a nonprofit program supporting publishers in using fiber that is not sourced from endangered forests. For more information, visit www.greenpressinitiative.org.

Saved:

- 17 trees
- 15 million British thermal units of total energy
- 1,614 pounds of net greenhouse gases
- 7,775 gallons of waste water
- 472 pounds of solid waste

www.ingramcontent.com/pod-product-compliance
Lightning Source LLC
Chambersburg PA
CBHW060515220326
41599CB00022B/3334

9780821382394

www.ingramcontent.com/pod-product-compliance
Lightning Source LLC
Chambersburg PA
CBHW060515220326
41599CB00022B/3334